Current and Future Developments in Law

(Volume 2)

(The Rights of Minorities: Cultural Groups, Migrants, Displaced Persons and Sexual Identity)

Edited by

J. Alberto del Real Alcala

Department of Criminal Law, Legal Philosophy, Moral Philosophy & Philosophy,
Faculty of Law and Social Science,
'Gregorio Peces-Barba' Observatory for Human Rights and Democracy,
University of Jaén, 23071 Jaén, Spain

Bentham Science Publishers Ltd.
Executive Suite Y - 2
PO Box 7917, Saif Zone
Sharjah, U.A.E.
Email: subscriptions@benthamscience.org

BENTHAM SCIENCE

CONTENTS

DEDICATION

To the victims of intolerance

PREFACE I

The history of human rights in the 20th century can be described as an open process towards non-discrimination, a feature that has been present in what we have so far seen of the 21st century and that will probably remain so for the rest of it. In this respect, and regardless of the presence of other milestones, two key ideas, which correspond to a number of other historical rights processes, have been present and continue to be so. On the one hand is the process of generalisation; and on the other hand, specification. The first of these aims to extend the enjoyment of rights to people and collectives whose rights are not respected; the second aims to justify the granting of specific rights to people and groups.

In effect, the historical process of generalisation, at its most basic, meant extending the respecting of rights to individuals and collectives who did not hold them and, in doing so, taking into account the specific circumstances surrounding individuals.

As we all know, the historical origin of rights is associated with a social class, the bourgeoisie, and the respect of rights is not, at this time, universal. Rights are fully recognised for individuals who possess a series of characteristics relating to their economic status, gender, etc. Although in the process of positivisation, the first great historical rights process, equality is talked about, it is not about universal equality.

On the other hand, this process, the process of generalisation, is characterised by the abandoning of constructions in which the philosophical tone takes precedence, with others being carried out that seek to ensure that rights and liberties are upheld in law in a concrete, not abstract, manner. The attention to the specific situation, the context in which the needs and demands of human beings are situated, is another characteristic of this process, from which the appearance of economic, social and cultural rights can be understood.

Ultimately, the generalisation process is thus an attempt to link the discussion on rights with reality. A discussion that considers rights to be natural, that is to say that they belong to all human beings, and a reality that limits the enjoyment of rights to a particular social class, the bourgeoisie. A discussion that constructed a generic, abstract and timeless formula of rights and a reality in which certain categories of human beings do not enjoy these rights and in which needs arise, demanding to be incorporated into the catalogue of rights. A discussion based on defending the natural equality of human beings and a reality susceptible to being described in terms of inequality.

As for the process of specification, this entails the recognition of the rights of specific collectives, who find themselves in special situations, thus implying an idea of material equality. N. Bobbio refers to this as “the increasingly marked move towards a subsequent determination of the owners of rights”. Specification has indeed occurred with regards to gender (recognition of women's specific differences compared with men), age (children's rights, rights for the elderly), and certain states of human existence (rights for sick and disabled people, etc.).

Both phenomena stem from the principle of equality in its two main dimensions: on the one hand, that which sees equality as non-discrimination, and on the other hand that which lets us talk about equality as a requirement for differentiation (positive differentiation).

Equality as non-discrimination means equal treatment of different circumstances or situations which, however, it is believed should be considered irrelevant when it comes to the enjoyment or exercise of certain rights or the application of rules. In relation to rights, it implies non-differentiation in terms of entitlement, exercise and guarantees. In any event, this perspective cannot be understood without the other. Equality as a requirement for differentiation (such as positive differentiation), involves the giving different treatment to circumstances and situations that are considered relevant.

Within the process of generalisation, it is possible to encounter the use of both of these views of equality. In effect, although it is common to affirm that it is a process in which the idea of formal equality is replaced, or even combined, with that of material equality, we should not overlook the fact that one of the main characteristics of this process is the extension of entitlement to rights to certain individuals or collectives which, in terms of equality, amounts to negative differentiation (non-discrimination). But equally, this process also captures an idea of equality as positive differentiation (requirement for differentiation) through the appearance of social rights and, nowadays, through paying attention to specific situations that people and groups find themselves in.

Within the process of specification, the idea of equality is positive differentiation. It involves protecting certain individuals and collectives who are in special situations, by recognising specific rights.

Both dimensions of equality appear in the discussion on rights, linked to the idea of universality. In effect, equality and universality are two closely related principles that appear both in the ethical and legal dimension of rights. Within the ethical dimension, the concept of universality shows the existence of a series of characteristics that are present in every human being and so must be considered in an egalitarian manner. In the legal dimension, attaining this idea requires an equal treatment that is not incompatible with the consideration of difference and, therefore, different treatment. In this respect, the theory of rights, in its legal conception yet still conditioned by the moral dimension, opens up the possibility of justified positive differentiation. And with this, it can reject the universality of rights as long as that does not mean rejecting the universality of ethics. In other words, the theory of rights, in its legal dimension, does not demand universality of rights, as long as the universal value of the legal rights they protect continues to be upheld. Although positive differentiation entails leaving universality aside, it demands that the reasons justifying this be coherent with the universality of ethics.

So, the issue of assisting vulnerable groups is clearly inscribed within the scope of the phenomena of generalisation and specification, and stems from these two perspectives of equality through the lens of universality.

This book refers precisely to human rights and vulnerable groups. Before briefly commenting on its content, it is necessary to clarify that the term vulnerable group is relative. What I mean by the term is that vulnerability often occurs because of situations and contexts and this means, on the one hand, people and groups may be vulnerable at certain moments but not others and, one the other hand, it is very difficult to talk about natural vulnerability. So for example, I have sometimes heard disabled people be referred to as a naturally vulnerable group. However, as defenders of the social model of disability have demonstrated, these people's vulnerability is largely social.

Indeed, *Rights and Vulnerable Groups (Vol. 1)*, edited by J. Alberto Real, deals with the issue of the rights of vulnerable groups in a new and comprehensive way, focusing on the main problems faced by the groups that are generically considered vulnerable.

On the one hand, we have works that mention the rights of women, one of the main historical exponents of the process of generalisation which, at the time, served to demonstrate the lack of justification for using gender as a criterion for differentiation in the enjoyment of rights. From this idea, the use of measures that unfold from both the principle of equality and non-discrimination and that of positive differentiation gain meaning in the present day.

From a theoretical point of view, and as part of a theory of rights, it is possible to defend three key principles in the field of differentiation:

1. A comprehensive theory of rights justifies differentiation that aims to satisfy the basic needs of individuals.
2. A comprehensive theory of rights justifies differentiation that aims to place individuals in identical conditions in the field of moral and political discussion.
3. The enjoyment of rights should be open to all even though differences may be established that, by virtue of the different types of inequality, dealing with the context in which these arise, and taking into account their different distribution criteria, are accepted by the majority of the rational individuals involved.

The theory of rights provides a series of parameters from which the social reality can be analyzed. If we focus our attention on the situation of women, I do not think it is too much to say that this is a collective for which, in general, both the requirement for the satisfaction of basic needs and, to a much greater extent, the requirement for equal value or power in public discussion, present undeniable problems. These are two issues that are very closely related and are a consequence of a historical allocation of social roles associated with sex-based differentiation.

This historical allocation of roles has been supported by a sexist approach characterised by the consideration of women as inferior beings, as beings who are not capable of performing certain tasks yet are “naturally” gifted in others.

The theory of rights must react to this situation and, in this respect, there are three possible paths: prohibiting negative differentiation; justifying positive differentiation; and designing an education system based precisely on its own hypotheses.

The prohibition of negative differentiation entails restricting any action that could directly or indirectly result in the non-respect of human rights due to being a woman. It is a path which allows the current reality to be addressed but does not serve to fully tackle this phenomenon. One of its manifestations is criminal punishment, from the understanding of criminal law as an instrument to repress those attitudes whose extreme extent is the non-respect of the legal right to life. In any case, although it is a well-travelled path, it is not a safe one, in the sense that it does not guarantee the disappearance of discrimination.

Justifying positive differentiation means allowing measures directed at women that aim to both satisfy their needs (sometimes needs specific to women and sometimes those shared with men but not satisfied for women), as well as include them in fields of political and legal power. In this case, these are policies that tackle the phenomenon in the medium term. It can also involve the use of criminal law, now considered as a preventative instrument, through the specification of criminal acts. In any event, it is a less travelled path than the previous one, yet safer (though not entirely).

The design of an education system based precisely on human rights involves raising awareness of the importance of human dignity and the equal value of human rights regardless of their sex, whether at school, in the family, or in the media. Obviously this is a long path, whose fruits are not immediate. In any case it is the safest path. The Convention on the

Elimination of all forms of Discrimination against Women of 1979 indicated the "need to change attitudes, through educating men and women to accept equal rights". This human rights education will allow us to do away with this differentiation of power and any type of sexism.

The book also looks at immigration and the rights of immigrants. Although immigration is not a recent phenomenon, it is possible to observe how nowadays there are factors affecting how it is dealt with. Immigration has become an important issue for certain developed countries that, on the other hand, have helped to construct the idea of human rights as instruments that limit power. This has started the search for a political approach that deals with this phenomenon and that does not betray a social model dominated by human rights.

In this respect, it is important to observe how the term immigrant has become an emotive term. In language we tend to differentiate, controversially to say the least, between foreigner and immigrant. This is a value-based differentiation (there are several studies showing that the perception of foreigners is better than that of immigrants). While the term foreigner marks a difference from nationals, this is even more the case for the term immigrant.

Normally, we tend to use this term to refer to a specific group of non-nationals present in our country. We neither normally do this to talk about home-owners and pensioners from northern Europe; nor the people with qualifications who have come here following the flow of capital and are working for large companies, or who have moved to Spain because it benefits them more (language teachers, shop owners, doctors, etc.), rather, we use it to refer to those who flee degrading living conditions. We even use it more to refer to unqualified people within this group.

All of this means that in the debate on immigration it is taken as read from the start that immigrants should not have the same rights. Or we even discuss how they should enjoy such rights, taking for granted the idea that not being a national (and being in a certain situation) is a reason with moral weight.

The theory of rights, when it appears in the topic of the rights of non-nationals, and therefore immigrants, reveals how it is rooted in two fundamental poles that form the basis of the construction of modern law but that can clash with the purpose of rights: political power and nationality.

These are two poles that must be questioned. I believe that the fact of being born in a country, or having acquired its nationality, is not in itself a relevant argument for differentiating negatively (not treating people the same) in terms of enjoyment of human rights, although it could perhaps be so (whilst still respecting such rights) for differentiating positively (recognising other rights). In any case, and with regards to the previous point it seems to me to be a secondary issue, and it is extremely difficult for me to defend actions of positive differentiation based on arguments related to nationality or culture. Regarding power, rights must present real limits on power. For this it is important to increase the power of the international courts (which should recognise the participation of all) with the aim that they contribute to the strengthening of rights, albeit through strengthening the power of the states at the same time. However, this refers to states that are committed to rights, and whose migration policy is underpinned by rights.

On this subject I think that the first step is to design policy that recognises rights whilst excluding the national or cultural aspect as far as possible. With this in mind, and from the perspective of recognising rights, it is necessary to start to discuss the recognition of this aspect, not in a negative sense (restriction of rights), but in a positive sense whilst respecting the idea of human dignity. All of this requires that the value of solidarity be recovered and its role in the discussion on rights be recalculated.

Another of the groups traditionally included when talking about vulnerability is children. The issue of childhood has been a key issue in the field of human rights since the second half of the 20th century. The emergence of international regulations in this regard, supported by doctrinal approaches, and the attention given to the real situations in which children live in certain countries, has made this a current issue, with greater or lesser success, not just in the academic and scientific field but also in the political agenda. Furthermore, it is a question that affects fundamental political and social issues and, ultimately, the social model that we want.

There is a certain tendency to include this phenomenon within the process of specification. However, the treatment of the rights of children cannot remain solely within the process of specification; it must also be considered within the process of generalisation.

Some will think that this observation is merely an academic detail. However, I do not believe that it is just that. The process of generalisation constitutes the attempt to extend human rights to collectives that do not enjoy them, and this idea may have its place when we are dealing with the issue of children's rights. In effect, the recognition of specific rights is one thing and the generalisation of rights is another. Although we can find some common elements in both phenomena, there is no doubt that the justification for each may be different. And in this sense, by characterising the recognition of children's rights as belonging to the specification process we are saved from having to make a series of reflections on which a theoretical handling of these rights cannot be avoided.

Certainly, for many, dealing with the question of childhood in terms of rights from a theoretical point of view is an unnecessary task, given that the important point on this subject (as with anything to do with rights) is the question of guarantee. The problems regarding the concept and foundation of rights tend to be left aside. It is sometimes stated that these issues are impossible to resolve, but there are also those who believe that they have already been resolved (especially when we have a Universal Declaration of Rights). And in any case, there is a certain tendency, particularly in the field of legal doctrine, to ignore these subjects by claiming that they are irrelevant. In this regard, it is common to come across pronouncements stating that the important issue nowadays when dealing with rights is protecting them. However, the process of determining a concept and basis for rights is given great importance, obviously in terms of the manner in which it is interpreted, but also in the solution of problems relating to their effective guarantee, both legal and social, and including in terms of the aspects relating to the catalogue of rights itself.

And this importance is very evident when it comes to the rights of children. Not without reason, Neil MacCormick wrote, a while ago now ("Children's Rights: A Test-Case for Theories of Right") that the question of children's rights is one of those issues that puts the theory of human rights to the test. Indeed, for those of us who work on issues relating to the theory of human rights, the treatment of children's rights presents us with questions that are difficult to resolve, which basically affect the coherent development of the theory itself.

The previous reflections on children's rights can also be applied to the analysis of the rights of people with disabilities (the topic of some of the articles in this book). This is a collective which, like children, currently receives special attention (an example of this is the recent passing of the United Nations Convention on the Rights of Persons with Disabilities). On the other hand, the focus on their recognition from a perspective of generalisation, and not so much from one specification, is also significant. Beyond this, it is worth highlighting how a rigorous and serious handling of this issue requires us to adopt a human rights perspective.

Human Rights Issues and Vulnerable Groups (Vol. 1), also looks into the rights of indigenous peoples. This is surely the topic that is most closely related to the dimension of equality as positive differentiation, and which tackles one of the most important problems regarding the grounds for rights: the moral value of groups or collectives. Like in the previous cases, this is an issue that is receiving a lot of attention in the area of rights declarations, and which equally affects another of their key principles: universality. All of this justifies the attention received.

But as well as this, this work contains pieces on other issues that are equally important when looking at the fight against discrimination, such as poverty, and the rights of victims, sexual minorities, linguistic minorities and refugees. In many cases, but especially in the case of refugees, studies and reality confirm how the system of human rights (and in particular their application by states), continues to be contradictory with much room for improvement.

I would like to end by thanking and congratulating Professor J. Alberto del Real for his hard work and effort in ensuring this work went ahead.

Rafael de Asís Roig
'Bartolomé de las Casas' Human Rights Institute,
Carlos III University of Madrid, Madrid
Spain
E-mail: rafael.asis@uc3m.es

PREFACE II

Current and Future Developments in Law, Volume 1 (Human Rights Issues and Vulnerable Groups) and *Volume 2 (The Suffering of Minorities and Human Rights)* deal with rights and vulnerable people. It covers a wide range of topics, but all center on people who, upon finding themselves –for different reasons– in a *hostile* situation that overwhelms them, fall into a position of *vulnerability*. Vulnerability arises as a consequence of a person's inability to overcome a risk or danger by themselves, due to a *disadvantage*, *deprivation* or *harm*, whether physical, moral, social, economic, political, or family-related. The situations of vulnerability discussed in this book are related to those caused by the moral, family, social, economic or political conditions in which the people, and the groups they belong to, live.

Vulnerable people display *weakness*, *fragility* and *inability* to recover from unexpected problems (real or potential). This means that vulnerability is linked to "human suffering". Because of this, vulnerable people are people who *suffer*: a) from the potential risk of *enduring* harm, deprivation or disadvantage that overwhelms them and that the person does not have the capacity to confront on their own; b) from the fact of *having already endured* such a harm; and c) from the potential risk of *continuing to endure it* if they do not escape the position of vulnerability in which they find themselves. In fact, *human suffering* is behind each of the chapters in this book. Suffering is, without a doubt, synonymous with a person's "poor living conditions" and is the opposite of "living well" or well-being.

While the human suffering of vulnerable people is a theme that runs throughout the whole book, there is also another thread running through every page: *rights*, as an instrument through which civil society and the Rule of Law try to compensate for, curb or even eliminate the suffering of these people through the aim of restoring them to a situation of normality. The "rights mechanism" is a useful instrument because it aims to satisfy needs and claims (relating to freedom, equality and human dignity) which, when not satisfied, generate harm, deprivation and disadvantages that prevent people from living in conditions of minimum personal and collective well-being.

Both volumes establish a clear relationship between "living well" (well-being) and rights. And, on the other hand, societies that deny basic rights are societies in which the people suffer from "poor living conditions". Societies that recognize a set of basic rights for the general population and ensure that they are upheld achieve a higher level of well-being ("living well") and the people enjoy better living conditions in general.

Volume 1 and *Volume 2* are organized into different types of vulnerable people. In this respect, *Volume 1* (*Human Rights Issues and Vulnerable Groups*) contains 8 groups of vulnerable people, which contain 16 chapters. Part I (Chapter 1) highlights the relationship between rights and human dignity, and is the starting point for all the other chapters. Part II (Chapters 2, 3, 4 and 5) brings together a group of chapters on people with disabilities, to discuss the relationship between this vulnerable position and rights, the universalization of these rights, the Constitution and the social inclusion that these rights are capable of achieving. Part III (Chapter 6) summarizes the examination of cultural rights with regards to the situation of the Bolivian indigenous peoples, as specific examples of groups of highly vulnerable people in Latin America. Part IV (Chapters 7 and 8) takes into account women, who make up more or less half of the world's population and who continue to be subject to serious discrimination, deprivation and disadvantage. Women's rights, equality and gender discrimination make up the content of this Part.cvcvcccvvvvz

Part V (Chapters 9, 10 and 11) includes people who have been victims of terrorist attacks as a vulnerable group. The huge amount of human suffering present among this group of people, the harm they continue to suffer after the terrorist acts (such as post- traumatic stress) and the need to find out the truth about the acts during trials for this type of crime all appear in these chapters. Part VI (Chapters 12, 13 and 14) deals with the difficult situation of poor people. Specifically, it deals with the problem of poor workers, the position within the European Treaties of social rights that deal with situations of poverty, and the issue of the right to housing as an effective and fundamental right for escaping poverty. Part VII (Chapter 15) contains another group of very vulnerable and forgotten people: people in prison. This part focuses on which rights are affected when a person is deprived of his liberty. Finally, Part VIII (Chapter 16) takes into account one of the most defenseless groups: children, and the context of the consumer society in which they form their personal identity.

Volume 2 (*The Rights of Minorities: Cultural Groups, Migrants, Displaced Persons and Sexual Identity*) contains 5 groups of vulnerable people (vulnerable minorities), which contain 13 chapters. Part I (Chapters 1, 2 and 3) deals with the petitions and claims for cultural freedom of people and the groups they belong to. It does this by examining the rights (cultural rights) which seek to satisfy these demands for cultural freedom, but also by looking at case-law instruments which may contribute to making this possible. Part II (Chapters 4, 5 and 6) on the other hand looks at the very serious problem of vulnerability faced by migrants in much of the world, from a human rights perspective. Part III (Chapters 7 and 8) includes a group of vulnerable people whose suffering accompanies huge humanitarian disasters and is often forgotten about: internally displaced people and migrant people. These are very vulnerable people in need of protection, who are the subject of very serious human rights violations, especially when their fragile situation is a consequence of armed conflict. Part IV (Chapter 9) deals with the extremely difficult issue of people who we can group together under the banner of "sexual minorities", when confronted with the intolerance they sometimes face from the heterosexual majority. The position of vulnerability in which these people often find themselves frequently starts within the family itself, which makes this a high factor of discrimination and breach of basic rights. This situation arises when sexual identities that differ from the heterosexual identity are not accepted. This type of discrimination is very serious when aimed against non-heterosexual adults, but it is even more so when aimed against girls and boys of a young age. Suicide (an indication that a person was no longer able to cope with their suffering) occurs in this type of situation where a person's most private identity is not respected and is attacked at its very core. Finally, Part V (Chapters 10, 11, 12 y 13) analyses the situation of minorities in general, exploring the situation of disadvantage in which they often find themselves, the factors surrounding their political integration, and the more specific issue of national minorities and secession within the Constitutional State today.

Of course, the list of groups of vulnerable people included in both volumes is not a definitive list, but an incomplete one. Wherever there is human suffering in the face of hostile situations that overwhelm people, we can find human beings in a vulnerable situation and, as such, in need of help and protection. This is the idea presented on every page of both books.

J. Alberto del Real Alcalá
Department of Criminal Law, Legal Philosophy, Moral Philosophy & Philosophy,
Faculty of Law and Social Science,
'Gregorio Peces-Barba' Observatory for Human Rights and Democracy,
University of Jaén,
23071 Jaén,
Spain
E-mail: adelreal@ujaen.es

List of Contributors

Ana María Jara Gómez	Derecho Penal, Criminología, Derechos Humanos y Democracia, University of Jaén, Spain
Ángeles Solanes Corella	Department of Philosophy of Law and Political Philosophy, University of Valencia, Valencia, Spain
Catalina Ruiz-Rico Ruiz	Faculty of Law, University of Jaén, Jaén, Spain
Cristina Churruca Muguruza	Pedro Arrupe Human Rights Institute, University of Deusto, Bilbao, Spain
Cristina Monereo Atienza	Department of Legal Philosophy, University of Málaga, Málaga, Spain
Eva Pons-Parera	Faculty of Law, Department of Constitutional Law and Political Science, University of Barcelona, Barcelona, Spain
Iñigo Urrutia-Libarona	Faculty of Economics and Business Studies, Department of Administrative Law, University of the Basque Country (UPV/EHU), Bilbao, Spain
J. Alberto del Real Alcalá	Department of Criminal Law, Philosophy of Law, Moral Philosophy and Philosophy, University of Jaén, Jaén, Spain
Joan Ridao Martin	Department of Constitutional Law, University of Barcelona, Catalonia, Spain
José Antonio López García	Department of Legal Philosophy, University of Jaén, Jaén, Spain
Juan Antonio Gómez García	Department of Legal Philosophy, Faculty of Law, UNED, Madrid, Spain
Luis Francisco Sánchez Cáceres	Faculty of Law, University of Jaén, Jaén, Spain
María Elósegui Itxaso	Faculty of Law, University of Zaragoza, Zaragoza, Spain
Maria Isabel Garrido Gómez	University of Alcalá, Alcalá de Henares (Madrid), Madrid, Spain
Patricia García Amado	Pedro Arrupe Human Rights Institute, University of Deusto, Bilbao, Spain

Current and Future Developments in Law, 2017, *Vol. 2*, 1-33

CHAPTER 1

Cultural Rights and Vulnerable People in a Multicultural World

J. Alberto del Real Alcalá*

Department of Criminal Law, Legal Philosophy, Moral Philosophy & Philosophy, Faculty of Law and Social Science, 'Gregorio Peces-Barba' Observatory for Human Rights and Democracy, University of Jaén, 23071 Jaén, Spain

Abstract: In this chapter, we address the rights of the persons and groups to cultural freedom. This issue is particularly important in the context of our current diverse, multicultural society. The cultural diversity that makes our modern societies unique has reconsidered some of the relevant notions on the Constitutional State and the theory of rights, leaving room for questions of identity and belonging. The starting point of the right that concerns us here is the unquestionable fact that cultural uniformity and religious unity have disappeared as the essential elements of identity on which the birth of the modern State was based. This occurrence has led to a *recognition* of the "cultural differences" among the Constitutional State's population. The fact has been reflected in constitutional theory, and thus Peter Häberle goes so far as to refer to "culture" as the fourth element in the Constitutional State, as opposed to the conventional notion that limits the elements that make up the State to the traditional ones of territory, population and power. This chapter addresses the subject of people's freedom to *belong* to a culture and to identify themselves through it as a *significant* fact in the area of rights. This applies to individuals' "freedom rights" in particular, but it is also part of each person's *right to a cultural identity*. A right to cultural freedom as part of a person's right to cultural identity is permanently disassociated from the type of *uniform equality* that was protected by the abstract universality that used to be proclaimed. On the contrary, such a right is associated with each individual's *specific* life, evaluating cultural belonging in the context of diversity and as part of people's essential development. Cultural self-identification is incorporated into the category of subjective rights, with the intention of overcoming any situation of discrimination that may arise in this regard.

Keywords: Belonging, Constitutional State, Cultural equality, Cultural freedom, Cultural identity, Cultural rights, Diversity, Non-discrimination, Vulnerable groups, Vulnerable persons.

* **Corresponding author J. Alberto del Real Alcalá:** Department of Criminal Law, Legal Philosophy, Moral Philosophy & Philosophy, Faculty of Law and Social Science, 'Gregorio Peces-Barba' Observatory for Human Rights and Democracy, University of Jaén, 23071 Jaén, Spain; Tel: 0034 953 212707; Fax: 0034 953 211905; E-mail: adelreal@ujaen.es

1. THE INTERNATIONAL LEGAL CONTEXT: RECOGNITION OF A MULTICULTURAL WORLD

In the theory of rights, there can be no doubt that cultural rights are internationally recognized in the universal human rights system. However, when we consider the "consolidated" content that should be assigned to rights of this nature and the relationship with the individual making these rights meaningful "relevant rights", the question is less clear. On the contrary, they raise doubts and uncertainties to the point of making cultural rights "insecure rights". And it is this insecurity that cultural rights manifest in today's world, despite their extraordinary role in people's development. Within the broad group of ESCR (Economic, Social and Cultural Rights), they are the most misunderstood subset of rights, set aside and even marginalized.

Insofar as they are universal human rights from the point of view of the most important international documents, contemplating an analysis of cultural rights from a legal point of view should start with the *Universal Declaration of Human Rights* (UDHR), adopted and proclaimed by UN General Assembly Resolution 217A (III) of 10 December 1948; and also the *International Covenant on Economic, Social and Cultural Rights* (ICESCR), adopted by Resolution 2200 A (XXI) of 16 December 1966 and entered into force on 3 January 1976. In turn, the cultural rights proclaimed in the UDHR and the ICESCR, which make up the universal human rights system, have been developed in several directions by another set of international instruments, including *Convention No 169 Concerning Indigenous and Tribal Peoples in Independent Countries* of 1989, of the International Labor Organization (ILO); *Declaration on the Rights of Persons Belonging to National or Ethnic, Religious and Linguistic Minorities*, approved by the General Assembly in Resolution 47/135, of 18 December 1992; the UNESCO *Universal Declaration on Cultural Diversity* 2001; the UNESCO *Convention on the Protection and Promotion of the Diversity of Cultural Expressions* 2005, meeting in Paris; and, more recently, the Fribourg *Declaration on Cultural Rights* 2007.

Although they are not a question of agreement in the doctrines on rights, the cultural rights that make up the universal human rights system are closely linked to *human dignity* and the *free development of one's personality* in international documents, and even to sustainable development in their *subsequent implementation*. Thus, Article 22 of the UDHR stipulates that "Everyone, as a member of society, has the right to realization… of the economic, social and cultural rights indispensable for his dignity and the free development of his personality". Moreover, the ICESCR recognizes in its *Preamble* that cultural rights "derive from the inherent dignity of the human person". The cultural rights enshrined in the UDHR and ICESCR (which limits the previous rights in the UDHR to narrower fields) start off as rights of the "dignity of the person". Therefore, that is where their main *raison d'être* will reside. Similarly, the ICCPR recognizes in its *Preamble* that cultural rights are one of the inalienable elements required to attain the "ideal of free human beings", because "the ideal of free human beings enjoying freedom from fear and want can only be achieved if conditions are created whereby everyone may enjoy his economic, social and cultural rights, as well as his civil and political rights".

The direct and extremely close link between culture, cultural rights and the dignity of human beings permits the assertion that cultural rights are "unalienable rights". The "unalienable" nature of cultural rights would be confirmed in Article 3 of the ICESCR, which recognizes the "generality" of human beings (and not peoples) as the holders of cultural rights, without distinguishing holder from gender: "The States Parties to the present Covenant undertake to ensure the equal right of men and women to the enjoyment of all economic, social and cultural rights set forth in the present Covenant ". If cultural rights are linked to the fulfilment of essential aspects of human dignity and we affirm the "equal dignity" of all people, then they are the rights of anyone and not restricted exclusively to minorities. They are rights that make up the "rights of persons" in general (*unalienable rights*), barring exceptions, among which we could cite the recognition of the rightful possession and enjoyment of some forms of collective ownership of land, according to ILO Convention No 169.

Of course, attributing ownership of cultural rights to *everyone* has two main consequences. *One*, the "unalienable" nature of cultural rights leads us to dismiss the idea that they are essentially based on the *collective dignity* of peoples. Cultural rights can only uphold the development of the collective dignity of peoples if the members of the peoples exercise said rights, but not as a collective (essentially *collectivist*) right that is above the rights of individuals. *Two*, the ownership of cultural rights as unalienable rights must necessarily *result* in individual and collective respect for the cultural diversity of civil society.

One of the most important international documents that establish cultural rights based on the universal human rights system is the aforementioned ILO's *Convention No 169 Concerning Indigenous and Tribal Peoples in Independent Countries* of 1989, which entered into force on 6 September 1991. The Convention, which assumes the relationship between culture, human dignity and the free development of the person has marked a milestone in the defense of the dignity of cultural minorities marginalized in their own States. The Convention's provisions were drafted in collaboration with the United Nations, the United Nations Educational, Scientific and Cultural Organization, the World Health

Organization and the Inter-American Institute of Indigenous People. They mark the change from the assimilation of the indigenous and tribal peoples (explicitly or implicitly) consented by the international community to the defense of their cultural heritage in a context of *positive* recognition of their cultural diversity and in view of the *erosion* of their laws, values, customs, perspectives, culture, way of life and institutions.

The UNESCO *Universal Declaration on Cultural Diversity* 2001, which is based on the cultural rights proclaimed in the United Nations' UDHR and the ICESCR, is another significant international document on cultural rights that aims to implement the human dignity of everyone. It also seeks to achieve the free development of the person according to each individual's habitual cultural parameters and not those imposed by groups or the State. Its main objective is to give "universal cover" to a set of basic principles – which the States are prompted to respect – that are summarized in the preservation of cultural diversity as the common heritage of mankind and the idea that cultural rights are the best instrument for fulfilling said aim. To that end, the *Universal Declaration* 2001 is structured on four basic principles that create cultural rights: a) " Identity, diversity and pluralism"; b) "Cultural diversity and human rights"; c) "Cultural diversity and creativity"; and d) Cultural diversity and international solidarity".

In the same sense, the Preamble of UNESCO *Convention on the Protection and Promotion of the Diversity of Cultural Expressions* (CPPDCE) 2005 emphasizes "the importance of culture for social cohesion in general" and the possibilities for improvement and social welfare, as well as "the need to incorporate culture as a strategic element in national and international development policies, as well as in international development cooperation, taking into account also the United Nations Millennium Declaration (2000) with its special emphasis on poverty eradication". Article 13 of the Convention advocates the "*integration of culture in sustainable development*", in the "development policies at all levels for the creation of conditions conducive to sustainable development and, within this framework, foster aspects relating to the protection and promotion of the diversity of cultural expressions". More recently, the 2007 Fribourg *Declaration on Cultural Rights*, in *Recital "(2)"* of the *Preamble*, has reaffirmed the idea that "human rights are universal, indivisible and interdependent and that cultural rights, as much as other human rights, are an expression of and a prerequisite for human dignity"

2. CULTURAL RIGHTS: AN INSTRUMENT FOR HUMAN DIGNITY

The universal human rights system clearly links cultural rights to human dignity, the free development of personality and, more recently, sustainable development.

Despite this, the implementation of this particular group of rights is vague and meaningless, and lacking in content as a result.

The content of cultural rights of the person recognized in the UDHR corresponds to the right to be free to participate in the cultural life of the community, in accordance with Article 27 (1) of the UDHR: "Everyone has the right freely to participate in the cultural life of the community, to enjoy the arts and to share in scientific advancement and its benefits". Article 27 of the ICESCR declares the right of the person – together with all other members of the group – to have their own cultural life and use their own language for that purpose (*linguistic human rights*): "In those States in which ethnic, religious or linguistic minorities exist, persons belonging to such minorities shall not be denied the right, in community with the other members of their group, to enjoy their own culture, to profess and practice their own religion, or to use their own language".

It can be inferred from the preceding Article that if cultural rights are unalienable and, therefore, they are not collective rights that should not prevent recognition of the "collective dimension" of cultural rights. Their collective aspect is obvious, considering that they are *exercised in common* (collectively) by the members of a community. Moreover, Article 1 (1) of the ICCPR and the ICESCR establish a link between the cultural development of peoples and the content of "the right to free self-determination" of peoples, based on the fact that "All peoples have the right of self-determination. [And that] By virtue of that right they freely determine their political status and freely pursue their… cultural development".

In addition to Article 27 (1) UDHR, Article 15 (1) of the ICESCR configures the *core content* of the recognition of cultural rights, and also reaffirms that they are the rights of persons and not collective rights. It establishes that "The States Parties to the present Covenant recognize the right of *everyone*: a) To take part in cultural life; b) To enjoy the benefits of scientific progress and its applications; c) To benefit from the protection of the moral and material interests resulting from any scientific, literary or artistic production of which he is the author". In the same vein, Article 15 (3) establishes the duty of the States Parties to "respect the freedom indispensable for scientific research and creative activity", and (Article 15 (4)) to recognize "the benefits to be derived from the encouragement and development of international contacts and cooperation in the scientific and cultural fields". Moreover, the ICESCR also assumes that cultural rights are linked to the conservation, development and dissemination of culture, as outlined in Article 15.2 of the ICESCR.

Finally, Article 27 (2) of the UDHR establishes that the copyright on intellectual, cultural and artistic production also come under cultural rights, when it outlines that "Everyone has the right to the protection of the moral and material interests resulting from any scientific, literary or artistic production of which he is the author". The UNESCO *Paris Convention on the Protection and Promotion of the Diversity of Cultural Expressions* (CPPDCE) 2005 has recognized "the importance of intellectual property rights in sustaining those involved in cultural creativity".

The ILO's *Convention No 169 Concerning Indigenous and Tribal Peoples in Independent Countries* of 1989 has attempted to limit the cultural rights of the universal human rights system to specific groups: indigenous and tribal peoples. The overall aim of ILO Convention No 169 is for indigenous and tribal peoples to enjoy fundamental rights to the same extent as the rest of the population of the States where they live. Thus, Article 3 (1) of the Convention stipulates that "Indigenous and tribal peoples shall enjoy the full measure of human rights and fundamental freedoms without hindrance or discrimination". To that end, the Convention outlines a set of rights intended to enable said peoples to exercise control over their own ways of life and institutions; maintain and develop their identities, languages and religions within the framework of the States in which they live; and carry out their culture, education, and economic and social development according to their habitual cultural parameters (Articles 7, 10 and 11). These are measures that the States in which the indigenous and tribal peoples are integrated should protect and respect (Article 5).

ILO Convention No 169 recognizes indigenous and tribal peoples as peoples with their own identity and organization (not "mere populations"). The criterion for recognition is based on the "awareness of their indigenous or tribal identity" (*the right to self-identification*, Article 1 (2)). Therefore, no State or group should deny the "cultural identity" freely chosen by the members of the indigenous and tribal peoples. Moreover, the Convention assumes the indigenous and tribal peoples' rights of collective property and possession over the lands and territories that they traditionally occupy and the right to live on them (Articles 14, 15 and 16). It also establishes the highly important "right to consultation" (Article 6) as a mechanism for integrating the opinion of indigenous and tribal peoples in the collective decision-making of the countries where they live. In this respect, the right to consultation operates "whenever consideration is given to legislative or administrative measures which may affect them directly" (Article 6 (1) (a)) Article 24 is extremely important, in that it urges the States to extend the right to social security, public health and medical care to indigenous and tribal peoples, in a way that is compatible with their respective cultures: "Social security regimes shall be extended progressively to cover the peoples concerned, and applied without discrimination against them". Moreover, when a State extends health services, it shall do so by organizing and planning them at community level and in cooperation with the indigenous and tribal peoples (Article 25). Articles 26-31, on extending the right to education to indigenous and tribal peoples, and including their culture and cultural criteria in their education are also worth highlighting.

Another important instrument on cultural rights is the *Declaration on the Rights of Persons Belonging to National or Ethnic, Religious and Linguistic Minorities*, approved by the General Assembly in Resolution 47/135 of 18 December 1992, which outlines in Article 1 (1) that "States shall protect the existence and the national or ethnic, cultural, religious and linguistic identity of minorities within their respective territories and shall encourage conditions for the promotion of that identity". In Article 2.1, the Declaration sets outs that "Persons belonging to national or ethnic, religious and linguistic minorities... have the right to enjoy their own culture... and to use their own language, in private or in public, freely and without interference or any form of discrimination". Article 2 (2) establishes "the right to participate effectively in cultural... and public life". Article 3 (1) declares that "Persons belonging to minorities may exercise their rights, including those set forth in the present Declaration, individually as well as in community with other members of their group, without any discrimination". Corresponding with said rights, Article 4 (2) states that "States shall take measures to create favorable conditions to enable persons belonging to minorities to express their characteristics and to develop their culture, language,... traditions and customs, except where specific practices are in violation of national law and contrary to international standards". Moreover, the States are requested to carry out the foregoing (Article 4 (4)) "in the field of education", where the States Parties undertake to "encourage knowledge of the history, traditions, language and culture of the minorities existing within their territory".

The *Universal Declaration on Cultural Diversity* (UDCD) 2001 is an extremely important instrument (probably the one that provides the best guidelines and the most criteria) for translating the vagueness that is prevalent in the group of cultural rights to a more detailed description of the content of rights. The *Preamble* of the UDCD ratifies the UNESCO's aim "that the wide diffusion of culture and the education of humanity for justice and liberty and peace are indispensable to the dignity of man and constitute a sacred duty which all the nations must fulfil in a spirit of mutual assistance and concern". Said Universal Declaration provides continuity to the provisions on cultural diversity and the exercise of cultural rights outlined in other international instruments promulgated by the UNESCO, such as the Florence Agreement of 1950 and its Nairobi Protocol of 1976; the Universal Copyright Convention of 1952; the Declaration of Principles of International Cultural Cooperation of 1966; the Convention on the Means of Prohibiting and Preventing the Illicit Import, Export and Transfer of Ownership of Cultural Property of 1970; the Convention concerning the

Protection of the World Cultural and Natural Heritage of 1972; The Declaration on Race and Racial Prejudice, approved by the General Conference of the UNESCO in 1978; and the Recommendation on the Safeguarding of Traditional Culture and Folklore of 1989.

The *Universal Declaration on Cultural Diversity* 2001 is structured on four basic principles:

a) "Identity, diversity and pluralism": which declares "cultural diversity" as the common heritage of humankind (Article 1) and a "factor in development" (Article 3); and "cultural pluralism" as the democratic political response to the empirical fact of diversity (Article 2).

b) "Cultural diversity and human rights": which declares that human rights ensure cultural diversity. The Declaration deems that cultural diversity is *inseparable* from human dignity (Article 4), and therefore cultural rights are unalienable, not collective rights. It also configures cultural rights (in accordance with Articles 27 UDHR, and Articles 13 and 15 ICCPR) as *universal, indivisible and interdependent* rights that constitute an appropriate framework for cultural diversity (Article 5).

The Universal Declaration on Cultural Diversity limits the content of cultural rights in the following groups of more specific rights (Article 6): (i) everyone's *right* to express themselves, create and disseminate their works in the language they prefer and in their mother tongue in particular (*linguistic human rights*); (ii) everyone's *right* to *education* and good quality training that fully respects their *cultural identity*; (iii) everyone's *right* to *participate in the cultural life* of their choice and conduct their own cultural practices, subject to respect for human rights and fundamental freedoms (Article 5); and (iv) the *right* to cultural diversity accessible to *everyone*. This last right establishes a guarantee of cultural diversity that enables all cultures to be included in the methods for expression and dissemination. It also specifies everyone's right to the free movement of cultural ideas *via* words and images, so every culture can find expression and become known. Other rights, such as the right to freedom of cultural expression, cultural pluralism of the media, multilingualism, equal access to artistic expressions, and scientific and technological knowledge (including computer technology) are some of the more specific rights that are referred to here.

c) "Cultural diversity and creativity": which declares that "cultural heritage" is a source of creativity (Article 7), supporting the right to the preservation of cultural heritage and handing it down to future generations. In the same vein, (Article 8) cultural assets and services, insofar as they are the vectors of identity, values and meaning, also merit special consideration and must not be considered ordinary goods and commodities like any others. The same is true of the copyright of authors and artists on their intellectual, cultural and artistic production. The Declaration also advocates cultural policies as catalysts of creativity and cultural diversity (Article 9).

d) "Cultural diversity and international solidarity": the Universal Declaration advocates strengthening the capacity for creation and dissemination worldwide, as well as international cooperation and solidarity so that all countries (especially developing countries and countries in transition) can establish viable and competitive cultural industries at national and international levels (Article 10). In the same sense, the Universal Declaration (Article 11) also promotes building partnerships between the public sector, private sector and civil society because market forces alone cannot guarantee the preservation and promotion of cultural diversity, which is the key to *sustainable human development.* It recommends reaffirming the pre-eminence of public policy, in partnership with the private sector and civil society.

The UNESCO *Paris Convention on the Protection and Promotion of the Diversity of Cultural Expressions* (CPPDCE) 2005, completes the *Universal Declaration on Cultural Diversity* 2001, which was forged in the same international organization. In this respect, the basic premise that lends strength to the entire international document, as established convincingly in its *Preamble*, is the general principle that "cultural diversity is a defining characteristic of humanity", "culture takes diverse forms across time and space and that this diversity is embodied in the uniqueness and plurality of the identities and cultural expressions of the peoples and societies making up humanity". Cultural diversity "forms a common heritage of humanity and should be cherished and preserved for the benefit of all". The reason is that "cultural diversity creates a rich and varied world, which increases the range of choices and nurtures human capacities and values, and therefore is a mainspring for sustainable development for communities, peoples and nations". All this only highlights "the importance of cultural diversity for the full realization of human rights and fundamental freedoms proclaimed in the Universal Declaration of Human Rights and other universally recognized instruments".

According to Article 1 (a) adopted in this Convention, the purpose of this UNESCO Convention is to "protect and promote the diversity of cultural expressions". To that end, it adopts the following eight guiding principles (Article 2): 1) Principle of respect for human rights and fundamental freedoms; 2) principle of sovereignty; 3) principle of equal dignity of and respect for all cultures; 4) principle of international solidarity and cooperation; 5) principle of the complementarity of economic and cultural aspects of development; 6), principle of sustainable development; 7) principle of equitable access; 8) principle of openness and balance. Moreover, Article 4 (1) defines cultural diversity as "the manifold ways in which the cultures of groups and societies find expression" and that "these expressions are passed on within and among groups and societies". This Article expresses the idea that cultural diversity "is made manifest not only through the varied ways in which the cultural heritage of humanity is expressed, augmented and transmitted through the variety of cultural expressions, but also through diverse modes of artistic creation, production, dissemination, distribution and enjoyment, whatever the means and technologies used".

In addition to the aforementioned documents of a universal scope, other international instruments of a *regional* nature have also undertaken the task of protecting and safeguarding cultural diversity. Such is the case in the European *Framework Convention for the Protection of National Minorities* (FCPNM) 1995 within the scope of the Council of Europe. Similarly, the *Charter of Fundamental Rights of the European Union* is no stranger to acting as a guarantee for cultural diversity. In Article 22, it stipulates that "The Union shall respect cultural, religious and linguistic diversity". This can only be achieved *via* the recognition and enjoyment of cultural rights. The *European Social Charter* (which falls under the sphere of the Council of Europe) has also assumed similar content. As outlined in the *Preamble*, it is based on the "indivisibility" of human rights of the person, insofar as they are all intended for a single recipient: human beings, whose needs and dignity cannot be divided. In this sense, "the Ministerial Conference on human rights, held in Rome on 5 November 1990, underlined the need... to secure the indivisibility of all human rights, whether they are civil, political, economic, social or cultural".

The FCPNM has outlined the most important cultural rights more specifically and in a European context. Such is the case of the "right to cultural identity". To a large extent, *respect* for cultural diversity is the result of the recognition of said right. The right to cultural identity, however, is not recognized clearly and explicitly in the universal human rights system (UDHR and ICESCR), although it is present with one or the other in the international documents that implement the universal system. For example, Article 1 (2) of the ILO's *Convention No 169 Concerning Indigenous and Tribal Peoples in Independent Countries* of 1989 recognizes the "right to cultural self-identification", which is based on the indigenous and tribal peoples' "awareness of their identity". The Convention determines that the "cultural identity" freely chosen by the members of instance must not be denied by any State or group. The *Declaration on the Rights of Persons Belonging to National or Ethnic, Religious and Linguistic Minorities* of 1992 assumes the right to cultural identity in Article 1 (1), when it establishes that "States shall protect the existence and... cultural... identity of minorities within their respective territories and shall encourage conditions for the promotion of that identity". In Article 6, the UNESCO *Universal Declaration on Cultural Diversity* 2001 proclaims everyone's *right* to education and good quality training that fully respects their *cultural identity*. Article 8 assumes special attention for cultural goods and services as vectors of identity, values and meaning. And the UNESCO *Convention on the Protection and Promotion of the Diversity of Cultural Expressions* 2005 also recognizes "that cultural activities, goods and services that are at the same time economic and cultural, because they are vectors of identities, values and meaning".

Possibly one of the most *complete* configurations of the right to cultural identity is outlined in the *Framework Convention for the Protection of National Minorities* of 1995, which estimates that "a pluralist and genuinely democratic society should not only respect the ethnic, cultural, linguistic and religious identity of each person belonging to a national minority, but also create appropriate conditions enabling them to express, preserve and develop this identity". It is assumed "that the creation of a climate of tolerance and dialogue is necessary to enable cultural diversity to be a source and a factor, not of division, but of enrichment for each society". Article 5 of the FCPNM recognizes everyone's right to cultural identity. The Parties to the Framework Convention undertake "to promote the conditions necessary for persons belonging to national minorities to maintain and develop their culture, and to preserve the essential elements of their identity, namely their religion, language, traditions and cultural heritage".

In the same sense, Article 6 (2) of the FCPNM encourages the Parties to protect the cultural identity of persons from hostile acts: "The Parties undertake to take appropriate measures to protect persons who may be subject to threats or acts of discrimination, hostility or violence as a result of their ethnic, cultural, linguistic or religious identity". Article 9 (4) of the FCPNM urges the Parties to the Convention, "in the framework of their legal systems" to adopt "adequate measures in order to facilitate access to the media for persons belonging to national minorities and in order to promote tolerance and permit cultural pluralism". Similarly, in the fields of education and research, Article 12 (1) FCPNM proposes to "foster knowledge of the culture, history, language and religion of their national minorities and of the majority". The Preamble of the *Paris Convention on the Protection and Promotion of the Diversity of Cultural Expressions* 2005 also takes into account "the need to take measures to protect the diversity of cultural expressions, including their contents, especially in situations where cultural expressions may be threatened by the possibility of extinction or serious impairment".

It is obvious that, although the FCPNM, is a framework convention for the protection of national minorities, rights (including cultural rights) are still attributed to persons. Once again, I stress that that fact does not prevent considering the collective dimension of cultural rights, but always as a *result* of the *common exercise* of said unalienable rights by community members. In fact, as established in Article 1 of the FCPNM, the "collective" protection of national minorities is outlined in this convention by assigning "rights and freedoms" (including those of a *cultural* nature) of persons belonging to national minorities. Said rights are classified as rights that form an integral part of "the international protection of human rights".

Everything said until now may give the idea that international recognition of cultural rights has been *configured* within the scope of the universal human rights system, on the basis of the UDHR of almost 66 years ago and the ICESCR of almost 50 years ago [1], and the subsequent implementation in other international instruments. In general, it is characterized by:

a) A certain "vagueness" of *content* and *meaning*, because cultural rights are *sensed* but there is no clearly defined outline of what cultural rights are and what they consist of;

b) "Dispersion" in the way they are formulated in the declarations and regulations of the international instruments that attempt to implement them.

Currently, the development of the content of cultural rights is an *unfinished* task [2]. Said development is a necessary preliminary step to subsequent implementation [3]. We have seen that cultural rights include highly significant aspects of people's lives: *i)* their *dignity*; *ii)* their *personal identity* and also *collective* identity in relation to their relations with others [4]; and *iii)* the *free development of their personality* by having access to cultural goods and participating in them; the capacity to configure them in their own way, preserve and transmit them; and (in civil society) to enjoy their use individually and collectively, all in conditions of freedom and equality (*non-discrimination*) [5]. These are aspects that undoubtedly link the exercise of cultural rights *iv)* to *collective development* and *human progress and well-being*. Of course, due to everything they invoke, *v)* these are rights that have a highly relevant effect on the content of other fundamental human rights. The result of exercising cultural rights is the guarantee of cultural diversity, which requires a concordant relationship between rights and diversity [6].

Due to the vital fields generally included in the cultural rights of persons, this group of rights is generally concretized in the right to cultural identity (including the right to free cultural self-identification) [7]; linguistic human rights; the rights of *free* access, participation, configuration, enjoyment, preservation and handing down to future generations of one's own culture and cultural heritage; and the copyright of intellectual, cultural and artistic production. However, despite the aforementioned transcendence of cultural rights in people's lives, compared to civil and political rights, and economic and social rights, cultural rights have not yet acquired *sufficient importance* as "full rights" in the doctrine of the general theory of rights or in the inclusion and protection of legal instruments in international and state regulations.

Taking into consideration the distinction between generations of rights often used by the general theory of rights, which depends on the historic period in which each group of rights emerged, the group of cultural rights are included in the general group of "second generation rights". Historically, first generation rights, identified with the group of "liberty rights", opened the field of rights in the late 18th century and more forcefully since the 19th century, when they even served as the foundation for a particular model of a State of Law: the *liberal* State of Law, which is characteristic of the 19th century [8]. The emergence of those "first generation rights" corresponded to a large extent with the appearance of the historical-legal process of state recognition (regulation) of rights, although the process is permanently open to new social demands.

However, regulating the freedom rights was not sufficient to extend the rights to *everyone* in a formal and material manner. Later, the task of *generalization* gave rise to another group of rights (social, economic and cultural rights) linked to equality (*rights for all and not only a few*). This second group of rights, considered "equal rights" and classified as "second generation rights", has also laid the foundation for a particular model of the State of Law. They have been the main instrument that fuelled the transition from a liberal to a *social* State of Law, for which they have provided core identifying features [9].

The social State of Law is also known as the "Welfare State". It was imposed gradually after World War II, at least in Western Europe, at the same time as the framework for a Constitutional State was built. In other latitudes, such as Latin America, abandoning the liberal State (identified with the 19th century) and a decisive commitment to a social State of Law has only taken place since the late 20th century. Such is the case of the latest constitutional reforms in several Latin American countries and new constitutions, like those of Ecuador in 2008 and Bolivia in 2009 [10]. Currently, however, owing to the economic crisis, some sectors are questioning the population's social and economic rights and their satisfaction with the social State. In any case, the emergence of the second generation of rights (ESCR) is mostly due to the historic-legal process of *extending* rights, which has also remained constantly active. Cultural rights, therefore, would come under the second generation of rights and would be subject to the same problems experienced by this group of rights today.

Later, the regulation and generalization of rights led to the "internationalization" of rights after World War II, which generated a universal human rights system *via* the UDHR, and the ICCPR and ICESCR Covenants. However, from an analytical point of view, it may not be appropriate to contemplate the broad group of social, economic and cultural rights as such a *compact* group as it may seem to be at first. Basically, there are three reasons for this, related to the issue of the vagueness that still plagues cultural rights:

Firstly, the "asymmetric" consideration of the broad group of ESCR.

Paradoxically, the minor relevance of cultural rights is not in line with the important transcendence of this group of rights in the course of people's lives and its impact on huge humanitarian conflicts. In fact, that leads to denying their interdependence and indivisibility, proclaimed in human rights [11]. The *Preamble* of the UNESCO *Universal Declaration on Cultural Diversity* 2001 has provided good reasons for pointing out said relevance, such as the idea that "culture is at the heart of contemporary debates about identity, social cohesion, and the development of a knowledge-based economy", that "respect for the diversity of cultures, tolerance, dialogue and cooperation, in a climate of mutual trust and understanding are among the best guarantees of international peace and security", aspiring to "greater solidarity on the basis of recognition of cultural diversity, of awareness of the unity of humankind, and of the development of intercultural exchanges". The Preamble also declares a set of principles, to which it gives universal validity, "to ensure the preservation and promotion of the fruitful diversity of cultures".

However, although most of the analyses on ESCR show that vital transcendence, they are conducted in relation to social and economic rights with very few references to cultural rights. Thus, they are relegated to the status of *minor rights* or even ignored because they are deemed to be addressed, whereas in fact sometimes they are not even mentioned. The secondary position of cultural rights within the broad group of ESCR is evidenced by *minor* development they have experienced within the universal human rights system, and something similar has occurred at State level. Even where a State has recognized cultural rights, it has usually been in a *dispersed and sectoral* manner [12]. It any case, they have been limited to the *rights of minorities* but not the "broad consideration" urged by the universal human rights system as the "rights of persons" and, therefore, *universal* human rights.

Secondly, open cultural rights to the rights of persons.

The analyses' asymmetrical consideration of the rights belonging to the broad group of ESCR corresponds to a rather *partial* recognition of cultural rights that is almost exclusively *sectoral* and *reduced* to the rights of national minorities [13] and culturally marginalized indigenous and tribal peoples [14]. Although said recognition is positive, if cultural rights remain enclosed and constricted there, it undermines the consideration of *universal rights* attributed to them in the universal human rights system and relegates them to the position of *minor rights*. In a sense, breaking down the reductionism of the rights of minorities and opening their configuration and justification up as the rights of *all persons* could be a positive factor in specifying and clarifying the meaning and content of cultural rights. Moreover, it may be a mistake to reduce cultural rights almost *exclusively* to equal rights because, with regard to their content, it would be difficult to deny *also* that they are the rights of cultural freedom (*civil and political rights*). In other words, cultural rights are "the rights of egalitarian freedom", to use the terminology of Professor Peces-Barba [15].

Thirdly, the group of cultural rights lacks "specific grounds".

From the point of view of providing *grounds*, *meaning* and *content*, and the resulting *legitimation* of cultural rights as "essential rights of persons", perhaps it is not appropriate to approach an analysis of the three groups of human rights as a *compact set* of rights when referring to ESCR. That is because the justification for the group of cultural rights as the rights of persons does not share the same *grounds* as other rights within the broad group of ESCR, although they share some of the same structures. Whereas the grounds for social and economic rights are much more elaborate and outlined, those of the group of cultural rights are scarce and rather thin. Therefore, cultural rights have ended up absorbing the justification for other rights *of the same group* (ESCR). However, in doing so, the justification has become unclear and not sufficiently framed, making the rights somewhat *blurred* and *unclear*.

Of course, in the words of R. de Asís, "attributing meaning to rights will obviously depend on the position held on their concept and grounds" [16]. Consequently, the grounds strongly outline the "meaning" (content) of the rights as well as their "legitimacy" (justification) and relevance as unalienable rights. And here it should be noted that, in view of the above, the *lack* of *sufficiently specific grounds* is probably one of the main reasons that explain why cultural rights are relegated to a *secondary* position in the broad group of ESCR. In this respect, in some Latin American scenarios, late 20th century post-colonial thought may have a positive effect in providing more support for cultural rights or a different justification for the implementation of culture, like the Republican State had been doing [17].

Thus, whereas the grounds for first generation rights are clearly identified with the group of *freedom rights* (the broad group of Civil and Political Rights, or CPR) and second generation rights with the group of *equal rights* (the broad group of ESCR), the cultural rights of persons share the content of both groups. However, they have their *own idiosyncrasy* to which the general theory of rights has not yet provided a very satisfactory response. By this I mean that if the intention is to provide a satisfactory explanation of cultural rights as universal human rights based on human dignity, they must approach the relationship between the CPR group and the ESCR group as a relationship of "complementarity" rather than one of *opposition* [18].

This is not a trivial fact, because "poor grounds" for the rights can only give rise to "vague meaning" and content. It is very difficult to establish a *clear* legitimacy of the content and transcendence of core human rights on the basis of vague content or meaning. Rather, it would be quite "incomplete". Poor grounds, lack (vague) meaning and incomplete legitimacy constitute a *trilogy* that explains why, when referring to the group of cultural rights, we are still faced with a group of rights that have "insufficient conceptual importance" in the world of rights.

3. PROTECTION ON CULTURAL IDENTITY: A NECESSARY AND POSSIBLE RIGHT

Actually, in the 20th century, the cultural rights have been assumed – throughout the second half of the century – very gradually and mainly in partial or sectoral aspects, and only with respect of some content. The 21st century is following the same path. This is mainly the case in Western Europe, Canada and some of the Latin American countries. The recognition of cultural rights as transcendental rights is related to the fact that the notion of *cultural diversity* that makes our contemporary societies unique was accepted (and integrated) in the 20th century, particularly in the last decades. Here we can include the cases of Western Europe, Canada and some of the Latin American countries. This fact has implied the need to *rethink* some relevant notions of the Constitutional State [19] and the general theory of rights [20], to provide room for matters related to cultural identity [21].

These are rights that flourished after the conquest of a "culturalist" view of the Constitutional State, as opposed to a strictly "formal" view [22]. At least, this has what has occurred in Western Europe where, since the last decades of the 20th century, the Constitutional State has drifted, with greater or lesser intensity, towards a Constitutional State with a markedly cultural bent [23]. P. Häberle even refers to "culture" as the fourth element of the Constitutional State [24]. It is a fourth element of the State that is not included in the theory of State based on the *Staatsnation*, but restricts the elements that configure the State to the classical ones of *territory*, *population* and *power*. The rights that concern us here start with the fact that it is "unquestionable that cultural uniformity or religious unity has ceased to be the essential component of identity on which the birth of the modern State was based". This fact has led to the *recognition* of the existing "cultural differences" among the population of the Constitutional State [25] and promoted its treatment by the theory of rights. The cultural rights *increase the value* to culture in the field of rights. One could say that its overall aim is to preserve the cultural context that normally accompanies people's life.

Truly this is a topic of great current relevance and construed as such by Habërle "at the national, European and global level". According to Habërle, *globalisation*, the global *market* with no limits or barriers and the internal *decentralisation* of Constitutional States have given rise to "a new awareness of culture as a builder of identity [and, therefore,] on cultural freedom as a freedom directly related to human dignity"; intended to protect "cultural difference (from plurality to the protection of minorities)", in contrast, for instance, with "economic freedom, of solely instrumental significance" [26].

I should like to approach me the cultural rights by providing a group of general justificatory *legal* criteria in the Constitutional State. In my opinion, this would encourage its legal recognition. I do not approach the criteria strictly from the point of view of an international or a single national regulatory framework, but from the broader, from the perspective of the general theory of rights. To a large extent, the legal justification will necessarily condition the configuration and structure of the cultural rights and, ultimately, its legal significance because "the attribution of meaning to the rights will depend on the position taken towards the concept and its fundament" [27].

Therefore, I will follow clear, general criteria that will provide coherent guidelines for the moral grounds and the legal justification that I intend to develop. In my view, the most adequate parameters for conveying this aim are in On Liberty, by John Stuart Mill, specifically in the part on the relationship between *liberty* and *diversity*. Very briefly, Mill considers that diversity is an asset to be preserved and not an evil to avoid [28], just as it is useful for more than one way of life to exist, providing it is not detrimental to others (*principle of harm*) [29], based on the idea that "the free development of each person's individuality" is one of the fundamental pillars of well-being of individuals and society [30]. I would argue that this would be the leading criterion-guideline (tolerant and liberal) under which a person's cultural right becomes one of the main mechanisms for integrating the cultural plurality of civil society into the theory of rights.

Undoubtedly, one of the most controversial issues posed by these rights is how to determine what is protected and what is secured *via* the legal classification of "subjective rights". Perhaps it would help to be able to "delimit the notion of culture as a preliminary step towards establishing a future catalogue or declaration of subjective rights and fundamental social rights linked to cultural identity" [31]. In this respect, seeking to crystallize the above terms, Habërle arrived at the conclusion that "identity is only possible *via* culture" and not *via* the economy, for example. Identity is *grounded* on "culture" and *connected* to tangible actions; to the real life of people, whose the resulting general context outlines a mosaic of "pluralism" [32]. Habërle deduces the opinion – which we share – that the foundation for the notion of cultural identity can only be an open and pluralistic conception of culture that includes the following three "mutually permeable categories". Firstly, "high culture", which includes all that is authentic, good and beautiful. Secondly, "popular culture", for example, which is particularly alive in Latin America among the indigenous peoples. Thirdly, the "underground culture" or *alternative* culture, "from the Beatles to football". All of these are ways of expressing the people's cultural identity [33].

Naturally, an *open* foundation for cultural rights includes the idea that the "singular elements" that provide the grounds for cultural identity "are actually open" and "linked to historical changes", as a result of which "identity is also transformed", esteemed, and therefore subjective, not objective. The singular elements must also remain "open to the circles of participants and formal and informal procedures" that create them [34]. A significant, yet not essential difference between Habërle and Habermas emerges from this issue. Whereas Habermas advocates reintegrating the collective identity into the Constitution as a (formal/procedural) value in itself [35], Habërle, while maintaining the same non-substantialist tradition, adds that the Constitution is a *cultural* as well as a *formal* matter. He speaks of the "Constitutional culture" and "[material] culture of human rights" in the constitution.

4. THE LINGUISTIC CULTURAL RIGHTS OF INDIVIDUALS AND GROUPS

Linguistic rights are among the most relevant of cultural rights. It may prove interesting to mention them as an example of a cultural right that has a more specific content. In this respect, the first approach to establishing the notion of linguistic rights would be to identify them with human rights pertaining to *linguistics*. *Linguistic human rights* rest on the (individual or collective) free choice of a specific language (generally the mother tongue) to communicate (privately or publicly) with other people and the institutions that represent the public authorities of the State that has jurisdiction over him.

Linguistic human rights fall within the *more general right of freedom of expression* and the *cultural rights* of persons and *peoples*. Insofar as they are the rights of *persons*, linguistic rights are a specific class or group of "civil rights" and unalienable rights, which become individual "freedom rights" as well as "equal rights". As individual unalienable rights, the content of linguistic rights entails the corresponding duty (in relation to other community members but also with regard to the State) of "non-discrimination" against individuals and groups who are within the jurisdiction of a state but belong to community that is a linguistic minority (prohibition of "non-discrimination").

As the rights of *peoples*, linguistic rights are one of the main elements of the content of the "collective right" to the cultural identity of a differentiated community, which in turn is part of the right to self-determination of indigenous peoples. Unlike the previous concept, in this case linguistic rights are presented as a collective right. As such, linguistic rights correspond to the *right of preference* for one language as opposed to others that have social presence in a territory. This idea of linguistic rights as a collective right is problematic, because the configuration of the sort of rights that belong to a differentiated cultural community are liable to infringe the (individual, as civil rights) linguistic rights of individuals.

Linguistic rights enjoy international recognition in the universal human rights system. Here, for their legal analysis, they must be contemplated as outlined in the Universal Declaration of Human Rights (UDHR), adopted and proclaimed by UN General Assembly Resolution 217A (III) on 10 December 1948. They must also be contemplated as what is mainly outlined in the International Covenant on Civil and Political Rights (ICCPR), adopted by Resolution 2200 A (XXI) of 16 December 1966, which entered into force on 23 March 1976.

The international recognition of linguistic rights in the universal human rights system was carried out in Article 2 (1) of the Universal Declaration of Human Rights, which affirms that "Everyone is entitled to all the rights and freedoms set forth in this Declaration, without distinction of any kind, such as… language", and this regardless of their "national or social origin, property, birth or other status". Moreover, this was also recognised in Article 27 of the Covenant on Civil and Political Rights, according to which "In those States in which… linguistic minorities exist, persons belonging to such minorities shall not be denied the right, in community with the other members of their group,… to use their own language.

Other documents pertaining to the international recognition of linguistic rights are also worthy of mention. Some are normative and others are merely statements of principles. In this sense, it is worth mentioning the *European Convention for the Protection of Human Rights and Fundamental Freedoms* within the framework of the Council of Europe; the *European Union Charter of Fundamental Rights*; the Council of Europe's *Framework Convention for the Protection of National Minorities* and the *Universal Declaration of Linguistic Rights of Barcelona* (1996) in the World Conference on Linguistic Rights in favour of the defence of linguistic minorities and against forced cultural homogenisation. It also recognises *individual linguistic rights* and *collective linguistic rights*.

From the point of view of their *legal content* and from a *systematic* perspective, linguistic human rights enshrined in Article 2 (1) of the UDHR and Article 27 of the ICCPR present the following characteristics:

A) Essential content and recipients. The linguistic rights proclaimed in Articles 2 (1) UDHR and 27 ICCPR outline the idiomatic "freedom of persons". Linguistic freedom ensures to all individuals the right of "freedom of choice" to use the language of his cultural and life context to communicate privately or publicly with other people and the public institutions that represent the public authorities of the State that has jurisdiction over him. Respect for linguistic freedom is imposes on the States the "duty" of "non-discrimination" in the choice of language. *Linguistic freedom* is a specific freedom that falls under the broader scope of the right to freedom of expression within the individual's cultural identity. It therefore carries the concomitant prohibition of any State interference that involves a discriminatory act or legislation against any person on *linguistic grounds*.

To summarise, it could be said that the proclaimed linguistic rights contain an affirmation of the *individual freedom* of *persons* (*freedom to choose a language*). Linguistic rights also *protect* said freedom *via* the imposition of a *duty* on the States to prohibit any act or legislation that violates the freedom to choose one's language, with the concomitant prohibition to discriminate on *linguistic grounds*.

In view of the above, linguistic rights fulfil four important functions as universal human rights: *i)* they enable highly relevant aspects of human dignity to be fulfilled that are necessary for people's normal development within their community; *ii)* they facilitate the "free development of a person's personality"; *iii)* they constitute a vital instrument for implementing other highly important fundamental human rights; and *iv)* they create a mechanism for the *preservation* of minority languages within the State. Such is the significant case of the indigenous peoples of Latin America [36] and of minority languages in Europe.

The linguistic rights recognised in the universal human rights system target two types of recipients, depending on their content:

Firstly, the recipients of linguistic rights are the "individual persons" to whom the aforementioned international instruments assign these *rights* in the universal human rights system, not peoples (Article 2 (1) UDHR and Article 27 ICCPR). Therefore, it could be said that the international recognition of linguistic rights involves an "individualistic conception" of said rights that, in my opinion, is the only one capable of providing a clear support of said rights in their status of "universal human rights".

Secondly, linguistic rights also target the member States of the United Nations (Article 2 (1) UDHR) and the States Parties to the International Covenant on Civil and Political Rights (Article 27 ICCPR). These States are the recipients of the *duty* imposed on the State to not carry out any acts or enact legislation against anyone within their jurisdiction on linguistic grounds.

Said duty imposed on the States should also be viewed systematically, in accordance with Article 2 (1) ICCPR, when it affirms that "Each State Party to the present Covenant undertakes to respect and to ensure to all individuals within its territory and subject to its jurisdiction the rights recognized in the present Covenant, without distinction of any kind, such as race, colour, sex, language, religion, political or other opinion, national or social origin, property, birth or other status".

In this respect, the ICCPR provides special protection for childhood against potential discrimination by the States on idiomatic grounds, when it establishes in Article 24 (1) that "Every child shall have, without any discrimination as to... language,... the right to such measures of protection as are required by his status as a minor, on the part of his family, society and the State".

Moreover, the States' duty of non-discrimination may not contemplate exceptions that clear the way for discriminatory acts or legislation on idiomatic grounds, as outlined in Article 4 (1) of the ICCPR: "In time of public emergency which threatens the life of the nation and the existence of which is officially proclaimed, the States Parties to the present Covenant may take measures derogating from their obligations under the present Covenant to the extent strictly required by the exigencies of the situation, provided that such measures are not inconsistent with their other obligations under international law and do not involve discrimination solely on the ground of...language...".

Other instruments – such as the Council of Europe's *European Convention for the Protection of Human Rights and Fundamental Freedoms* – that aim to develop a universal human rights system in Europe, also outline the "prohibition of discrimination" on idiomatic grounds in Article 14, which establishes that "The enjoyment of the rights and freedoms set forth in this Convention shall be secured without discrimination on any ground such as…language…". Moreover, Part V, Article E (Non-discrimination) of the European Social Charter, when it affirms that "The enjoyment of the rights set forth in this Charter shall be secured without discrimination on any ground such as… language…"

Article 22 (Cultural, religious and linguistic diversity) of the *Charter of Fundamental Rights of the European Union* recognises that "the Union shall respect… linguistic diversity". It also outlines the prohibition of discrimination on linguistic grounds in content on equality, in Article 21 (Non-discrimination), which affirms that: "1. any discrimination based on any ground such as… language… shall be prohibited".

B) Connection with the legal content of other fundamental human rights. As mentioned previously, linguistic rights are a part of the *general right to freedom of expression* and *cultural rights*. However, they are also included in the content of other rights that are highly important in people's lives. For that reason, linguistic rights are referred to "in plural", in accordance with the multiple manifestations that linguistic or idiomatic freedom (which constitute the essential content of such rights) has in other fundamental rights and the *specific* nature that linguistic freedom adopts in each of said rights.

Take into consideration that linguistic rights include the individual's right to choose the language in which he wants to express his feelings and articulate his reasoning in the social, cultural and institutional contexts to which he belongs and in which he participates as a member of a community. It is in this aspect that linguistic rights are necessarily included in other fundamental rights that are essential in a person's life, such as: (b1) the *right to freedom of expression* and *cultural rights*; (b2) the *right to an education*; (b3) the *right to medical care*; (b4) *fundamental procedural rights*; and (b5) the *rights to political participation*.

Thus, (b1) it should be stressed that linguistic freedom, which constitutes the essence of linguistic rights, is a *specific freedom* in the more general right to freedom of expression in the specific sphere of an individual's cultural identity. As such, it is another "cultural freedom" of the individual and a part of the *right to cultural identity* as a universal human right predicable to everyone [37]. In any case, the content of linguistic rights includes the right to freedom of expression and the right to a cultural identity as highly fundamental human rights. Therefore, linguistic rights are not only included in the *general right to freedom of expression* but also in the content of *cultural rights*.

In this respect, linguistic rights are the "right to choose" the language in which one wishes to communicate with other people and public institutions. It is also the language one wants to use to understand the world, one's own life and the life of others, regardless of national or social provenance, economic position, birth or any other personal status. Therefore, linguistic rights seek to protect individuals from acts and legislation of the State that aim to impose on them a language that is foreign or outside of their normal everyday context.

Although the aforementioned content is implicit in the universal human rights system, it is more clearly stated in more specific international instruments such as the *Framework Convention for the Protection of National Minorities*. Article 9 (1) therein outlines that "The Parties undertake to recognise that the right to freedom of expression of every person belonging to a national minority includes freedom to hold opinions and to receive and impart information and ideas in the minority language, without interference by public authorities and regardless of frontiers. The Parties shall ensure, within the framework of their legal systems that persons belonging to a national minority are not discriminated against in their access to the media". Article 5 (1) sets out that "The Parties undertake to promote the conditions necessary for persons belonging to national minorities to maintain and develop their culture, and to preserve the essential elements of their… language". Moreover, Article 10 (1) stipulates that "The Parties undertake to recognise that every person belonging to a national minority has the right to use freely and without interference his or her minority language, in private and in public, orally and in writing".

Linguistic rights also include (b2) the right to receive *formal education* in a freely chosen language that belongs to their normal everyday context. In most cases, the language chosen is the individual's "mother tongue", which is probably the educational instrument that proves most comfortable and enables individuals to feel free to develop their personality.

In this respect, Article 14 (1) of the *Framework Convention for the Protection of National Minorities* does specify an individual's right to learn their minority language. Therefore, it should be preserved in the context of their education: "The Parties undertake to recognise that every person belonging to a national minority has the right to learn his or her minority language".

Linguistic rights also contemplate (b3) the importance of ensuring that the linguistic freedom of the individual is not absent from (and is extended to) State actions related to basic services and provisions of an essential nature, such as medical care. One can easily imagine the severe consequences to health that can be caused by an individual's inability to communicate with medical staff due to language. Thus, the right to medical care must consider the situation of linguistic diversity in the population of the State when meeting the fundamental right to health of the individuals who live in that State. This also implies the right of an individual who needs medical care to be *understood* in the language normally used in his everyday context.

Moreover, (b4) the linguistic right of *persons* and the *State's* corresponding duty of non-discrimination on idiomatic grounds proclaimed in linguistic rights include the right for legal, administrative and judicial proceedings to be conducted in a language that is "understood" by the individual in question. It is here, undoubtedly, that linguistic rights assume a highly important role where *procedural rights* are concerned, if the administrative or state act is a serious violation of an individual's *fundamental procedural rights*, by including discrimination on linguistic grounds. This respect for linguistic rights includes the right to be informed in a language that is *understood* by the individual and the right to make a statement and act before the judicial authorities in a language that corresponds to the individual's normal everyday context. If necessary, it also involves the right to carry out such acts free of charge *via* a translator of the language chosen and understood by the individual concerned.

The connection between linguistic rights and fundamental procedural rights, and the corresponding procedural guarantees, are so relevant to personal freedom that the ICCPR provides for it in Article 14 (3) (a): "3. In the determination of any criminal charge against him, everyone shall be entitled to the following minimum guarantees, in full equality: (a) To be informed promptly and in detail in a language which he understands of the nature and cause of the charge against him… (f) To have the free assistance of an interpreter if he cannot understand or speak the language used in court".

Other international instruments, such as the *European Convention for the Protection of Human Rights and Fundamental Freedoms*, have attempted to make linguistic rights effective in the area of procedural guarantees. The European Convention outlines in Article 5 (Right to liberty and security) that "2."Everyone who is arrested shall be informed promptly, in a language which he understands, of the reasons for his arrest and of any charge against him". And in Article 6 (Right to a fair trial), according to which "3. Everyone charged with a criminal offence has the following minimum rights: to be informed promptly, in a language which he understands and in detail, of the nature and cause of the accusation against him", as well as (Article 6 (3) (e)) "to have the free assistance of an interpreter if he cannot understand or speak the language used in court".

In the same sense, the *Framework Convention for the Protection of National Minorities* outlines in Article 10 (3) that "The Parties undertake to guarantee the right of every person belonging to a national minority to be informed promptly, in a language which he or she understands, of the reasons for his or her arrest, and of the nature and cause of any accusation against him or her, and to defend himself or herself in this language, if necessary with the free assistance of an interpreter".

Finally, (b5) linguistic rights have an important effect on the *rights to political participation*, in their *active* aspect (right to be elected) and *passive* aspect (right to elect public representatives). In this respect, linguistic rights are not of minor relevance because they affect the forming of the "collective will" of the community and democratic collective decision-making. Discrimination based on the language of linguistic minorities within a State, with regard to their active or passive political participation has the negative effect of making them *invisible* "politically" but also "institutionally". They are left out of community decisions and, consequently, it is highly probable that they will be absent from State institutions and legislation will not take them into consideration. These consequences can have a serious effect on the rights that ensure a community's democratic collective decision-making and the principle of *generality* and *equality* before the law. They are liable to distort the democratic system of the State in question, change the *quality* of democracy and even the elementary rules of the State.

C) The content: linguistic freedom and linguistic equality. In accordance with the analysis made from the point of view of their legal content, it could be affirmed that linguistic rights are internationally recognised in the universal human rights system as the individual "freedom rights" of persons. However, the *linguistic freedom* of everyone, for everyone, is also recognised as "equal rights", based on the "equal dignity" that international recognition declares predicable for everyone. In this sense, Article 26 of the ICCPR outlines that "All persons are equal before the law and are entitled without any discrimination to the equal protection of the law. In this respect, the law shall prohibit any discrimination and guarantee to all people's equal and effective protection against discrimination on any ground such as… language…".

5. FINAL OBSERVATION: CULTURAL FREEDOMS AS CO-FREEDOMS FOR ALL

In cultural rights, the right to cultural identity is in the first position. The position one assumes with respect to *providing the grounds* for a person's right to cultural identity not only determines the attribution of *meaning* to the right, but also the manner of *guaranteeing* it, which is no less than its "legal configuration". By this we refer to the legal justification of the cultural rights that concerns us here, and which I approach from the perspective *building* a legal configuration for it based on a theory of general rights. Not from the point of view of regulations and jurisprudence, however, because the scope of the matter in question would far exceed the purpose of this paper and its limited length.

The justification of the cultural rights, and in particularly of the right to cultural identity, has to do with its *regulatory* configuration. This datum is absolutely essential for a right to be effective. Merely considering a right as a *moral right* [38], with no legal potentiality whatsoever (to use the terminology of Eusebio Fernández [39]), or as a "universal moral right", as it is defined by A. Gewirth [40], irremediably restricts the right to a mere *moral ambition*, but nothing more. It would lack the necessary guarantees that define subjective rights as a "legal category" and, therefore, lack the potential for being a legal "requirement" in court for the holders of the right [41]. Beyond doubt, that is one of the main conditions for verifying whether we are before a "full recognition" of a *legal* right.

Given the impossibility of covering all the legal implications of the right in a paper, I have selected some issues that have the most influence on the overall regulatory configuration of the right in the theory on rights in general, such as its legal *nature*, the issues posed by *entitlement* to it, and with what *content* it is configured as a *subjective right*.

When referring to the legal configuration of cultural identity as a right, we should specify that "cultural identity" is what is protected and ensured as a "legal asset" [42]. However, that does not say much, because the notion is controversial, with no single meaning and, moreover, it should be reinterpreted from the contemporary viewpoint of acceptance of cultural diversity. Cultural identity as a *protected legal asset* [43] would include the series of "cultural assets" that individuals *assume* and consider *as their own*. As such, they presume to have free access to those assets and be able to develop through them, with *no barriers* raised by state authorities, groups or other individuals. In this respect, the cultural assets that protect the right to cultural identity would be defined by a *series* of "cultural freedoms" directly linked to the fulfilment of the universal moral value of *human dignity*, and to the aspect of the equal dignity of all people, which makes cultural freedom an "egalitarian freedom" and, therefore, with no restrictions on entitlement to that freedom (*generalisation*).

The legal configuration of a fundamental right is a task that usually presents the "highest degree of indetermination", according to R. Alexy [44]. In addition to the task of legislating, it also means integrating court decisions in order to determine their meaning as legal precepts [45]. This is particularly true in the case of the Constitutional Court. In any event, the regulatory configuration of cultural identity as a right would have to do with:

a) The "subjective right" category: the right to cultural identity is presented as a *subjective right* "when a person identified with a legal obligation arising from the right (the passive party) appears as opposed to the holder of the right (the active party)". A is said to be the holder of a subjective right to cultural identity when A can require X of B, or when B has an obligation X towards A. As can be seen, "the correlation of the right is a [specific] duty or obligation" towards B [46].

b) The "legal freedom" category: the right to cultural identity is a freedom "if its holder A is free to do or not to do X with respect to B. In other words… no none has a right to interfere with us. In this case, the other party (B) is not a specific and identifiable [passive] holder, but a generic holder", given that the freedoms are rights *erga omnes* [47].

The difference between one legal configuration and the other of the right to cultural identity resides in the passive party to the legal obligation that the right creates: *individuals* or *groups* (the right to cultural identity as a subjective right in the strict sense) or a *generic* party (the right to cultural identity as a legal freedom *erga omnes*).

In view of the above, it could be inferred from a *legal-regulatory* point of view, that a right to cultural identity constitutes a *mechanism* intended to secure and implement a series of significant *cultural freedoms* and make them effective for *everyone*, thereby specifying the requirements for the legal values of freedom and equality. The outcome of this is that the effective implementation of said right should lead to a context of "cultural tolerance" [48] and, therefore, of "cultural peace" [49], as a sort of social and institutional value that is implemented *via* laws, and even more so if it is *via* constitutional laws [50]. If this occurred, we would be in the best disposition to avoid the *cultural conflict* between institutionalism and civil society or a collision within civil society. Apart from its connection with the fulfilment of specific aspects of human dignity, the right to cultural identity is a very *useful* right, as the motor for important social "benefits", such as a vehicle for collective tolerance and peace.

However, there is no choice but to accept that the recognition and development of the right to cultural identity is meagre, although it has improved in recent years. Nonetheless, it is true that, in general, the regulatory configuration of the right to cultural identity is mostly absent in constitutional texts. It is also true that *partial or implicit* recognition of a "right to cultural difference" has existed, and that, as G. Ruiz-Rico asserted, the partial recognition has occurred mostly *via* "sectoral regulations" on "sensitive matters in which it is preferable to offer unequal treatment to individuals and collective social groups with marked cultural differences compared to the majority of society: laws on language and teaching, civil rights, laws on religious freedom and so forth". In this partial or sectoral recognition; "any *regularisation* of cultural diversity of this sort is due to a series of constitutional mandates, without which the recognition of certain exemptions, privileges, interpretive modulations of rights or specific rights granted to collective groups targeted for territorial, national, ethnic or religious reasons that are granted to a minority of citizens". It was "after these legal areas of expertise [when] a new category of the *right to cultural difference* was configured", which was "a right not generally positivized as an autonomous right, but which arose and was derived from the implementation of the parameter of cultural or religious pluralism above other fundamental rights", whose "ultimate support for the fundamental right to be different would be found in the value of dignity, as such" [51]. In any event, the foregoing description demonstrates the "loopholes and gaps in national constitutional texts" regarding the express recognition of the right [52].

Precisely, mostly *sectoral* recognition of the right to cultural identity only allows us to refer to the regulatory configuration of the right in a "partial" sense, as a "specific right" for minorities (a *right to cultural difference*) and, therefore, armed as a right restricted to *sectoral legislation* on minorities. From this standpoint, the logic of such laws is to deprive the members of the cultural majority of the right. This manner of addressing the right is not useful as a criterion for managing multicultural societies in the broadest sense of the word, but only societies made up by a central/majority culture and two, three or four territorially well-defined minority cultures, at the most (*restricted multiculturalism*). Here we would find a more primitive or initial conception in the genesis of the right, which would imbue entitlement to the right with its more *collective* meaning, configuring the right to cultural identity as a *peoples*' right (and not the right of an individual *person*). In this sense, the right would only target a limited number of cultural groups.

Therefore, against the preference of restricted entitlement, we can distinguish the notion of the right as a "generic" right (a *right to cultural identity*). Unlike the *collectivist notion*, we currently refer to a *full* right with respect to the entitlement to exercise it. In other words, the entitlement is extended to *everyone*, whether they belong to minorities or now belong to majorities, claiming *each person's* right to their cultural identity, which is based on the *equal dignity* attributable to everyone. This last concept could be considered more sophisticated or elaborated. In any case, it is an "individualistic" notion of *cultural freedoms*, whose protection for *everyone* is guaranteed *via* the "equality" content included in the right [53]. Precisely, that equality consists in not denying anyone the right to their cultural (self-identification).

Anchoring the right to cultural identity in human dignity would determine, in its legal configuration, whether the right was included in the group of "rights that belong to people, as such". Said entitlement could not be restricted to the citizenship of one country, as opposed to immigrants, for instance, or to cultural minorities, for example, as opposed to the members of the majority, because then all those to whom the right is not attributed would be legally *acultural*. That would *not make any sense*. Consider that, as a right that belongs to the group of *rights of the person*, that basis "would force it to be recognised to anyone" in the Constitutional State [54]. The result would be (and integrate) the notion of "complex citizenship", in line with our times. The contrary would imply acceptance of the existence of *acultural* people who are regarded as having no cultural freedoms and, therefore, it would make no sense for them to be entitled to the right to cultural identity. This not only leads to a *legal, social and political absurdity*, but also to an *anthropological absurdity*, which is much more serious.

Based on the fact that constitutional doctrine presupposes that "dignity is recognised for all people, in general" [55], Spain's Constitutional Court has gradually established a framework of rights related to human dignity, considering them to be an "inherent spiritual and moral value of the individual, which is manifested in the conscious and responsible self-determination of one's life and carries with it a propensity for the respect of other people" [56]. It is a framework of rights of the person "that do not constitute a full, closed list" [57]. For example, it includes part of the right to cultural identity, such as "the right not to be discriminated against for any personal or social condition or circumstance" [58]. With respect to other new rights, the Constitutional Court has generally given the democratic legislator freedom to decide the regulatory configuration of such rights of the person, although it establishes the condition that entitlement to the right must not be restricted [59].

It could be asserted categorically that the right to cultural identity pertains to the field of rights related to the personality [60] and that it comes under the "*cultural* rights of the personality", because it affects relevant and significant aspects of the moral person in their dignity as human beings. Therefore, we must arrive at the conclusion that the legitimate holders of the rights are individual people, *every* individual person, because the *equal dignity* of all people would make no sense if the right were recognised for some people and not for others. However, this data on *individuality* and *generality* are fought by the more *collectivist* conceptions of cultural identity, which are more rooted in the praxis and legal grounds of the 19th century than the turn of the 21st century, conceiving it as a "peoples' right" as opposed to an individual right [61].

Individuality and generality in the entitlement to a right that we examine in accordance with its legal nature as a right of the personality means that, in general, there are *two* ways to exercise the right. *One*, in an "autonomous manner", when the person does not encounter barriers to fulfilling his or her cultural freedoms and, therefore, can satisfy the human needs affected by the right. *Two*, in an "assisted manner", when, to the contrary, the person *does* encounter barriers to fulfilling one (or all) of his or her cultural freedoms on his or her own, creating a situation of "negative discrimination" as a sort of "cultural discrimination" that puts the person in question in a "position of inequality" with respect to all the other holders of the right, which, as I.M. Young explains, "leads to exclusion" [62]. In the two aforementioned cases, one (or all) of the human needs affected by the right are unsatisfied, the legal system must provide *assistance* to the person by delivering the proper mechanisms and guarantees to remove the negative discrimination and eliminate the actual inequality. In short, it must supply the instruments that will make it possible to *give back* to the person the *enjoyment* of the cultural freedoms to which he or she has a fundamental right.

CONFLICT OF INTEREST

The author declares no conflict of interest, financial or otherwise.

ACKNOWLEDGEMENTS

Declared none.

REFERENCES

[1] Márquez Carrasco E. Logros y desafíos en el 600 aniversario de la declaración universal de derechos humanos. Bilbao: Universidad de Deusto 2008; pp. 21-45.

[2] del Real Alcalá JA. Plenitud e incompletitud de las reglas y principios del derecho y su incidencia en la interpretación jurídica. In: Jiménez Liébanas D, Ed. Estudios en homenaje al Profesor José González García. Pamplona: Thomson Reuters-Aranzadi 2012; pp. 41-52.

[3] del Real Alcalá JA. El legislador en la implementación de los derechos sociales. In: Garrido Gómez I. La eficacia de los derechos sociales hoy. Madrid: Dykinson 2013; pp. 3-5.

[4] Peces-Barba G. La dignidad de la persona desde la filosofía del derecho. Madrid: Dykinson 2002.

[5] del Real Alcalá JA. El derecho a la identidad cultural: criterios de fundamentación. Derechos y Libertades 2013; 29: 149-182.

[6] Ansuátegui Roig FJ. Derechos Humanos: entre la universalidad y la diversidad. In: Ruiz Vieytez EJ, Urrutia Asua G, Eds. Derechos humanos en contextos multiculturales: ¿acomodo de derechos o derechos de acomodo? Bilbao: Padre Arrupe Institute of Human Rights/Deusto University-Provincial Council of Gipuzkoa 2010.

[7] del Real Alcalá JA. El derecho a la identidad cultural: criterios de fundamentación. Derechos y Libertades 2013; 29: 149 ff.

[8] Pérez-Luño AE. Derechos humanos, Estado de derecho y Constitución. Madrid: Tecnos 1984.

[9] Peces-Barba G. Curso de derechos fundamentales: Teoría general. Madrid: BOE-Carlos III University of Madrid 1995.

[10] del Real Alcalá JA. Neoconstitucionalismo con descentralización como mecanismo de generalización de los derechos. El caso Bolivia. In: Storini C, Alenza García FJ, Eds. Materiales sobre

neconstitucionalismo y nuevo constitucionalismo latinoamericano. Pamplona: Thomson Reuters-Aranzadi 2012; pp. 361-79.

[11] Gómez Isa F. El derecho al desarrollo: entre la justicia y la solidaridad. Bilbao: University of Deusto 2003; pp. 10-3.

[12] Ruiz-Rico Ruiz G. Derechos de la personalidad como elementos de articulación de la constitución política y la constitución civil. In: Ruiz-Rico G, Moreno-Torres ML, Pérez Sola N. Principios y derechos constitucionales de la personalidad. Valencia: Tirant lo Blanch 2010.

[13] del Real Alcalá JA. Nacionalismo e identidades colectivas: la disputa de los intelectuales. Madrid: Dykinson 2007.

[14] del Real Alcalá JA. The Value of National Plurality in the Design of the Constitutional State. European Scientific Journal 2013 June; pp. 641-7.

[15] Peces-Barba G. Lecciones de derechos fundamentales. Madrid: Dykinson 2005.

[16] De Asís Roig R. Sobre el concepto y el fundamento de los derechos: una aproximación dualista. Madrid: Dykinson 2001; pp. 5-10.

[17] Martínez de Bringas A. La cultura como derecho en América Latina: ensayo sobre la realidad postcolonial en la globalización. Bilbao: University of Deusto 2005; pp. 40-8.

[18] Chacón Mata AM. Derechos económicos, sociales y culturales: indicadores y justiciabilidad. Bilbao: University of Deusto 2007; pp. 54-9.

[19] Habërle P. El Estado Constitucional, México DF: UNAM 2003; pp. 21 ff.

[20] Kymlicka W. La política vernácula: nacionalismo, multiculturalismo y ciudadanía. Barcelona: Paidós 2003; pp. 99-128.

[21] García Inda A. Identidades y derechos colectivos. In: Susín Beltrán R, *et al.* Sobe identidades. Reconocimiento y diferencia en la modernidad líquida, Valencia: Tirant lo Blanch 2008.

[22] del Real Alcalá JA. Nacionalismo e identidades colectivas: la disputa de los intelectuales. Madrid: Dykinson 2007; pp. 422-24.

[23] del Real Alcalá JA. Teoría del Estado de F. Meinecke: los modelos de Estado moderno según las doctrinas Staatsnation y Kulturnation. Revista de Estudios Políticos 2011; 154: 177-210.

[24] Habërle P. El Estado Constitucional, México DF: UNAM 2003; pp. 21-8.

[25] Ruiz-Rico Ruiz G. Identidad cultural y derechos constitucionales de la personalidad. El problema de la integración jurídica de la multiculturalidad. In: Ruiz-Rico Ruiz G, Ed. Principios y derechos constitucionales de la personalidad. Valencia: Tirant lo Blanch 2010; p. 385.

[26] Habërle P. Aspectos constitucionales de la identidad cultural. Derechos y libertades 2006; 14: 89-90.

[27] De Asís Roig R. Sobre el concepto y el fundamento de los derechos: una aproximación dualista. Madrid: Dykinson 2001; pp. 5-10.

[28] Mill JS. Sobre la libertad. Madrid: Alianza Editorial 1997; p. 164.

[29] Mill JS. Sobre la libertad. Madrid: Alianza Editorial 1997; p. 164.

[30] Mill JS. Sobre la libertad. Madrid: Alianza Editorial 1997; p. 165.

[31] Ruiz-Rico G. Identidad cultural y derechos constitucionales de la personalidad. El problema de la integración jurídica de la multiculturalidad. In: Ruiz-Rico Ruiz, G, Ed. Principios y derechos constitucionales de la personalidad. Valencia: Tirant lo Blanch 2010; p. 386.

[32] Habërle P. Aspectos constitucionales de la identidad cultural. Derechos y libertades 2006; 14: 98.

[33] Habërle P. Aspectos constitucionales de la identidad cultural. Derechos y libertades 2006; 14: 95.

[34] Habërle P. Aspectos constitucionales de la identidad cultural. Derechos y libertades 2006; 14: 99.

[35] Habermas J. Más allá del Estado Nacional. Madrid: Trotta 2001.

[36] del Real Alcalá JA. Constitución de 2009 y nuevo modelo de Estado de Derecho en Bolivia: el Estado de Derecho Plurinacional. Cuadernos de la Fundación Manuel Giménez Abad 2011; 1: 115-126.

[37] del Real Alcalá JA. El derecho a la identidad cultural: criterios de fundamentación. Derechos y Libertades 2013; 29: 149-182.

[38] García Inda A. Identidades y derechos colectivos. In: Susín Beltrán R, *et al.* Sobe identidades. Reconocimiento y diferencia en la modernidad líquida. Valencia: Tirant lo Blanch 2008; p. 92.

[39] Fernández García E. Dignidad humana y ciudadanía cosmopolita. Madrid: Dykinson 2001; pp.95-6.

[40] Gewirth A. The basis and Content of Human Rights. In: VVAA, Eds. Derecho y moral. Ensayos analíticos. Barcelona: Ariel 1990; pp. 125-146.

[41] Kelsen H. Teoría pura del Derecho. México DF: Porrúa 1993; p. 147.

[42] Nino CS. Consideraciones sobre la dogmática jurídica. México DF: UNAM 1974; pp. 55-77.

[43] Nino CS. Consideraciones sobre la dogmática jurídica, México DF: UNAM 1974; p. 66.

[44] Alexy R. Los derechos fundamentales en el Estado Constitucional democrático. In: Carbonell M, Ed. Neoconstitutionalism(s). Madrid: Trotta 2003; pp. 32-7.

[45] del Real Alcalá JA. Interpretación jurídica y neoconstitucionalismo. Bogotá: Autónoma University of Occidente-Cali 2011; pp. 26-43 y 74-93.

[46] Peces-Barba G. Derechos sociales y positivismo jurídico. Madrid: Dykinson 1999; p. 144.

[47] Peces-Barba G. Derechos sociales y positivismo jurídico. Madrid: Dykinson 1999; p. 144.

[48] Walzer M. La política de la diferencia. La estatalidad y la tolerancia en un mundo multicultural. In: McKim R, McMahan J, Eds. La moral del nacionalismo. Vol. II. Barcelona: Gedisa 2003; pp. 84-5.

[49] del Real Alcalá JA. Derecho a la paz frente a la nación obligatoria. In: Garrido Gómez I, Ed. El derecho a la paz como derecho emergente. Barcelona: Atelier 2011; pp. 87-104.

[50] Díaz E. Legitimidad y justicia: la constitución como zona de mediación. Doxa 1987; 4: 350.

[51] Ruiz-Rico Ruiz G. Derechos de la personalidad como elementos de articulación de la constitución política y la sociedad civil. In: Ruiz-Rico Ruiz G, *et al.*, Eds. Principios y derechos constitucionales de la personalidad. Su proyección en la legislación civil. Valencia: Tirant lo Blanch 2010; pp. 22-3.

[52] Ruiz-Rico G. Identidad cultural y derechos constitucionales de la personalidad. El problema de la integración jurídica de la multiculturalidad. In: Ruiz-Rico Ruiz G, *et al.*, Eds. Principios y derechos constitucionales de la personalidad. Valencia: Tirant lo Blanch 2010; p. 395.

[53] Pérez Luño AE. Dimensiones de la Igualdad, Madrid: Dykinson 2007, particularly Chapters I and II.

[54] This legal position on the entitlement to rights rooted in the dignity of the person is doctrine of Spain's Constitutional Tribunal. See, for example, sentence of the constitutional tribunal (STC) 236/2007, of 7 November, Legal Ground 3; and STC 95/2000, of 10 April, Legal Ground 3.

[55] STC 53/1985, of 11 April, Ground 3.

[56] STC 53/1985, of 11 April, Ground 3.

[57] STC 236/2007, of 7 November, Legal Ground 3.

[58] STC 137/2000, of 29 May, Legal Ground 1.

[59] For example, STC 236/2007, of 7 November, Legal Ground 17.

[60] Soriano R. Compendio de teoría general del Derecho. Barcelona: Ariel 1993; p. 172.

[61] The question of its nature as a right of the personality and individual entitlement could frequently and quite possibly create "hard cases" in practice and in court. For a distinction between difficult cases and

tragic cases, see Atienza M. Interpretación Constitucional. Bogotá: Autónoma University of Occidente-Cali 2010; pp. 126-53; also, del Real Alcalá JA. Deber judicial de resolución y casos difíciles. Panóptica-Revista Acadêmica de Direito 2010; 18: 40-60.

[62] Young IM. La justicia y la política de la diferencia. Madrid: Cátedra 2000; p. 285.

CHAPTER 2

The Case-Law Concept of Reasonable Accommodation: The European Court of Human Rights Facing the Governance of Cultural and Religious Diversity in the Public Space

María Elósegui Itxaso*

Faculty of Law, University of Zaragoza, Zaragoza, Spain

Abstract: This chapter deals with the legal concept of reasonable accommodation, presenting in a novel way a topic that is not covered in the Spanish doctrine. It analyzes the development of this notion in the jurisprudence of the Supreme Court of Canada and the recent introduction in the European Court of Human Rights, in which some judges have made an explicit reference to this technique and call for their use. The duty to accommodate or adjust is the duty, under the law that managers of institutions and public and private organizations have in order to avoid any form of indirect discrimination for minorities and majorities, taking different harmonization adjustments in the application of certain laws or certain regulations, making norms more flexible or adapting them in its implementation. This allows a fairer management of cultural and religious diversity in public space, according to an intercultural model led by the Council of Europe.

Keywords: Cultural and religious diversity in the European Court of Human Rights, Council of Europe, Reasonable accommodation, Supreme Court Case-Law in Canada.

1. INTRODUCTION

Europe is experiencing not only an economic crisis but also a crisis of accepting its own internal diversity. We are experiencing moments of paradoxes and contrasts [1].

The 47 countries that make up the Council of Europe have their own minorities, the so-called "old minorities". Our countries are and will be increasingly diverse, new groups continue to appear while antiracist political parties are increasing [2].

* **Corresponding author María Elósegui Itxaso:** Faculty of Law, University of Zaragoza, Zaragoza, Spain; Tel: 0034 976 762117, Fax: 0034 976761499; E-mail: elosegui@unizar.es

J. Alberto del Real Alcalà (Ed.)

We live in a society of contrasts: on the one hand racism and xenophobia are on the rise in civil society, especially in sports [3]; on the other hand, public and private institutions are leading best practices in diversity management in public services such as hospitals [4] and schools. In addition, the Council of Europe recommends legislative changes in favour of human rights, including measures to combat racism and intolerance [5].

Amid this climate, this intervention focuses on the legal benefits of making greater use of the case-law in the European Court of Human Rights (ECtHR) and the experience of various public and private institutions by applying the mechanisms of reasonable accommodation.

The concept of reasonable accommodation has entered the fray of the European legal world following the discussion that took place in Quebec in 2007 [6]. The word "accommodation" appeared in the title of the report that was developed and has become famous over the last five years. So much so that the Council of Europe has started to discuss it and has convened study meetings for analysing it [7].

Although, this concept may appear somewhat strange in terms of the techniques applied by the ECtHR, it has recently been referred to in judgments where some judges of the Court, for instance the Belgian Judge Tulkens in the dissenting opinion in the case of *Francesco Sessa v. Italy,* makes explicit reference to such techniques and calls for their use, citing Belgian authors such as Emmanuelle Bribosia [8] and Sébastien Van Drooghenbroeck in his monograph on the principle of proportionality in the European Convention on Human Rights. They in turn are inspired by the Canadian academics, Pierre Bosset or José Woehrling. This technique has also been used in the case of *Thlimmenos v. Greece* and more recently in the judgment *Eweida and Others v. the United Kingdom,* in which the majority voting makes explicit use of the concept, noting in this regard Canadian law.

This paper attempts to provide some brief clues regarding the Canadian jurisprudence and the case-law of the ECtHR, focusing on the use of reasonable accommodation as applied in respect of two issues only: cultural and religious diversity, the latter taken as part of cultural identity. The accommodation focuses primarily on the individual rights of persons, less so in respect of group or collective rights of minorities, although these issues are converging in some cases.

Moreover, in this brief paper only some judgments considered as leading cases or paradigmatic decisions have been indicated. One should not lose sight of the fact that the case-law referred to here is limited to discussing specific situations and reaching general conclusions applicable to everyone, at any time and in all circumstances is not intended.

Although the Canadian technique of "reasonable accommodation" might well serve as a good example for Europe, this does not mean that we should do a direct rollover of this jurisprudential concept.

Regardless of the details of this legal concept, the possibility of the ECtHR applying the concept of accommodation in the future would require a profound change of perspective and attitude towards cultural diversity and its management. Therefore the adoption of these techniques is only possible from an intercultural state model, like the one supported by the Council of Europe. It is impossible to "sympathize" with them from a perspective of cultural assimilation [9], homogenised multiculturalism or closed legal models. This legal method would require, both in the legislator and the citizens, an opening of minds, which in general appears to be a difficult task for human beings [10].

It requires a positive view on freedom, including the right to one's own identity, forged by various elements, such as religious and philosophical convictions, focusing on diversity as an asset and not a problem [11].

The concept is, in essence, a mechanism against indirect discrimination (not only against minorities but also against the majority) and this requires, as a first step, the recognition of identity. To accept the first premise, "this is discriminatory", can be an arduous task. The first step in the search for legally possible solutions (both regulatory and jurisprudential) is being willing to find and to avoid denying the existence of discrimination as a necessary starting point.

It is not a coincidence that many of the recent reports on cultural diversity have been led by intellectuals and/or academics, for instance the Parek report in the United Kingdom [12], the Bouchard-Taylor Commission in Quebec [13], or the Belgian 2010 report 'Assises de l'Interculturalité', led by Marie Claire and Christine Foblets Kulakowski, Director of the Belgian Centre for intercultural action [14].

Accommodations are a very specific jurisprudential technique to be complemented by various other management resources in respect of diversity, both of legal and public policy nature.

2. THE ORIGIN OF THE CONCEPT OF REASONABLE ACCOMMODATION IN CANADIAN JURISPRUDENCE

The idea of reasonable accommodation as a jurisprudential concept was introduced *via* case-law both in the United States and in Canada [15]. This legal practice was first adopted by American law and jurisprudence, being legislated in 1971 through an amendment of Title VII of the Civil Rights Act of 1964 [16].

Years later, it was introduced in Canada through its case-law as of 1985 by the Supreme Court in its ruling. *Ontario Human Rights Commission and O'Malley v. Simpsons Sears Ltd* [17]. This case concerned a saleswoman, a member of the Seventh Day Adventist Church, who asked her employer to excuse her from working on Saturdays because it was incompatible with her religious belief. The Supreme Court of Canada (hereafter SCC) acknowledged that an employer was entitled to open his store on Saturdays. However this normal employment requirement had a discriminatory effect on this employee from practicing her religion. In the absence of "significant inconvenience" or "undue burden" (excessive or undue hardship constraints), the employer was not entitled to prevent the employee from practicing her religion. As a result the employer must try to seek accommodation, by modifying the working hours of his or her employees [18]. Therefore, the court in this judgment ruled in favour of the applicant requiring the employer to compensate.

That same year, in the case of *R v. Big M Drug Mart Ltd* [19]. a company that objected to the validity of the federal law that imposed the closure of all shops on Sundays in accordance with the tenets of the Christian faith [20]. This Sunday Act required all non-Christians to conform to the rule of the majority. The Supreme Court recognised that the effect of this Act was to create inequality between Christians and non-Christians that is between the dominant religion and religious minorities [21].

3. REASONABLE ACCOMMODATION IN EUROPE

As we have seen, in Canada the practice of accommodation is related to the implementation of the right to equality and non-discrimination on grounds of sex, religion, ethnicity or culture.

This concept has been used so far only in the EU Community Law in relation to persons with disabilities, where there is a requirement to adapt structures so as to provide barrier-free access to the equal exercise of human rights. In the Canadian case, it has been clearly established that the employer has in principle an obligation to provide a solution of accommodation to a person who is different so as to enable him or her to exercise his or her rights guaranteed by the Canadian Charter of Rights and Freedoms. In Europe this obligation exists in European Union law and in the Council of Europe in respect of people with disabilities.

Overall, in the European legal world and with the common EU citizenship, the goal has been to achieve a culture of symmetrical equality, to flee from any privilege, even though the European history of discrimination with its many national minorities has been a frequent issue of conflict especially at the European Court of Human Rights. Although due to regionalism, certain collective rights for national or regional minorities are now better tolerated, this is far from the case when it comes to new-coming minority immigration despite the fact that the latter settled in Europe in the fifties and sixties in response to a need for manpower that Europe was experiencing as a result of its industrial development in the sixties [22].

Despite theoretical resistance and prejudice, we are confronted with the reality of cultural diversity generated by immigration. The decision not to face the struggle against discrimination by means of the appropriate legal measures leads to conflicts of far greater social instability. At the level of international and European law constitutional rights, strong legal instruments have been created to pursue the achievement of equality. The challenge is to ensure equality through difference and to create the political and legal levers that will allow for a model of intercultural citizenship. The ECtHR emerges as one of the relevant legal mechanisms in this respect.

The second part of this paper will attempt to answer the question: To what extent can the techniques of reasonable accommodation applied in the Canadian and American context be used to combat indirect discrimination on grounds of race or religion in Europe with similar effectiveness?

4. THE EUROPEAN CONVENTION ON HUMAN RIGHTS AND INDIRECT DISCRIMINATION: REASONABLE ACCOMMODATIONS IN ECHR?

The concept of indirect discrimination allows detecting and prohibiting rules that *a priori* seem acceptable and neutral, but that, in practice, are discriminatory because they pose disadvantages for certain groups, without any objective and reasonable justification. It also prohibits differential treatments that are discriminatory. We will try to show how the jurisprudence of the European Court of Human Rights has introduced reasonable accommodations in cultural identity, and in contrast we will see how it is more reluctant to introduce such flexibility into issues related to the right to religious freedom [23].

We will focus on this second part, showing how the European Court of Human Rights has developed the concept of reasonable accommodation through its jurisprudence, as a parallel model to the CSC. The Court does not use this term, although it does use similar mechanisms. As stated in the case *Gorzelik and others v. Poland,* the Court aims to protect pluralism based on "recognition and genuine respect for the diversity and dynamism of cultural traditions, ethnic and cultural identities, as well as religious convictions" [24].

Let us assume that the European Court of Human Rights had not, until the recent case *Eweida and others against UK* in January 2013, hitherto used the term reasonable accommodation (accommodement) or arrangements or adaptations (amenagement). As we have said before, this concept had only appeared in an explicit way in the dissenting opinion of the case *Sessa against Italy* [25], led by Judge Tulkens.

But even if that judgment is an isolated case, later on, in the case *Eweida v. UK* the European Court of Human Rights uses the techniques of the Supreme Court of Canada. Previously the Court had used a similar reasoning in judgments regarding the right to cultural identity.

The Council of Europe is an ideal place to study cultural diversity, as the 47 member countries of this organization, although all of them are European, have great diversity taken as a whole, with greater contrasts, much more so that than the EU and not only due to the variety created by immigration but due to the existence of its own old minorities, which also includes major cultural and religious pluralism within their national territories.

We must insist on the fact that the European Convention does not explicitly recognize a right to cultural identity, although there is the Framework Convention for the Protection of National Minorities of the Council of Europe [26]. But rather, it does so indirectly in numerous cases before the ECHR. The Court has developed, by means of a dynamic interpretation, a jurisprudence in which it recognises certain contents on cultural rights in a broad sense, in relation to other rights of the Convention, in particular Article 8 (right to private and family life), Article 9 (right to freedom of thought, conscience and religion), Article 10 (right to freedom of expression) and Article 2 of Protocol 1 (right to education) [27].

Another important factor behind the growing jurisprudence in relation to cultural rights has been the number of cases brought before the Court by persons or entities belonging to national minorities, including cultural, linguistic or ethnic minorities. According to the report of the Research Division of the ECHR, "although the Court does not always rule in favour of minority cultural rights, the key principles established in these cases provide a basis for future litigation and its development" [28]. This should also be studied in the context of the White Paper on intercultural dialogue, which, although not a rule of law, has opened, in our opinion, new lines and recommendations for the States, insofar as cultural, ethnic and religious identities are concerned [29], which may have led to progress in the groundbreaking line established by the Court in the case of Thlimmenos against Greece.

a. The case *Thlimmenos against Greece* has been described as the leading case of accommodations [30].
   The European Court in the case Thlimmenos requires the States to make a flexible legislation in its application of a general and typical norm in cases where there is objective and reasonable justification.
   This case is based on a conduct related to a person's conscience, which in this case is pacifist and did not want to comply with the compulsory military service imposed on all citizens.
   In these cases, the Court considers that the state can be open and flexible to the claim of some of its citizens who request different treatment based on serious reasons and grounds.
b. The case of Czech Roma children and the obligation to accommodate a general rule to avoid indirect discrimination based on race or ethnicity.
   Another case before the ECHR that can be framed as reasonable accommodation is the case *DH and Others v the Czech Republic*, which was ruled in 2007 [31]. This would be indirect discrimination based on race, not religion. The appellants alleged that they had been discriminated against in their right to education because of their race or ethnicity (Cf.., Paragraph 3).
c. The case *Orsus et al.* v. Croatia. Demand from Roma and the application of the same criteria as in the case *DH against Czech Republic*.
   The Grand Chamber of the Court wanted to settle the indirect discrimination against Roma children in school in a new ruling. *Orsus et al.* v. Croatia on July 17, 2010 [32], whose decision has split the judges, with nine votes in favour of the existence of discrimination and eight against such discrimination, considering that the state measures were justified in an objective manner and had a legitimate end.
   Although the aim is to present the facts as being similar to the case *DH c. Czech Republic,* close reading of the data provided in the judgment enables us to verify that the cases are not identical, hence the dissension in the ECHR.
d. *Case Glor against Switzerland.* A case of accommodation because of a disability.

Another case that could be considered as reasonable accommodation is the case *Glor against Switzerland* in 2009 [33]. This would be indirect discrimination on grounds of an illness, diabetes. Glor, a Swiss citizen, could not perform military service due to suffering from diabetes. Under Swiss law, he had to pay a fee like all other Swiss citizens who, for other reasons, could not do the military service. In Swiss law, and alternative service can be provided, but only on grounds of conscience objection. On the other hand, only those who are exempt due to having disabilities of over 40% are exempt from paying the tax.

5. ECHR RECENT JURISPRUDENCE ON THE RIGHT TO CULTURAL IDENTITY AND REASONABLE ACCOMMODATIONS TO PROTECT SUCH IDENTITY

We will take a look at some judgments that might be called leading cases of jurisprudence over the last fifteen years in relation to cultural identity [34]. This jurisprudence should be analysed from the perspective of reasonable accommodation with different techniques that we will address later.

5.1. Chapman Case v. United Kingdom

For *Chapman v. United Kingdom* [35], the court has considered the issue of the lifestyle of Roma families and the specific difficulties they have to park their caravans. In this case, a right to that specific mode of cultural identity has been recognised through Article 8 of the Convention, which guarantees the right to privacy, family life and housing, which in turn protects the right to maintain the identity of a minority and to live their private and family lives according to their own tradition.

The Court has stated that "the occupation of their caravan by the applicants is an integral part of their ethnic identity as gypsies, which reflects a long tradition of this minority that has a nomadic lifestyle. This is the case, despite the fact that due to the pressure of development and different policies or by their own choice, many Gypsies no longer live a completely nomadic existence and often stay in one place for long periods to facilitate, for example, the education of their children. Measures affecting the parking of the plaintiffs' caravans therefore cause an impact that goes beyond the law to respect their home. It also affects their ability to maintain their identity as Roma according to their tradition" [36].

The Court maintains that "it must be said that there is an emerging international consensus among member countries of the Council of Europe recognizing the special needs of minorities and an obligation to protect their security, identity and lifestyle... not only with the purpose of safeguarding the interests of the minorities themselves but to preserve a cultural diversity of value to the community as a whole" [37].

An argument is developed below whereby the possible existence of general standards could be the origin of indirect discrimination. For this reason, States have the obligation to establish positive measures to protect some rights, such as, for instance, in this case, the implicit obligation to provide Gypsies with their way of life, in particular taking into account the needs of their different lifestyle, both within the framework of relevant regulatory planning and also reaching decisions in particular situations.

This idea recalls some of the characteristics of the technique of reasonable accommodation that we have highlighted above, because it would sometimes include the following two things: namely, a modification in the rule itself, and in some cases, its different application in certain cases. According to the Court, "although the case of belonging to a minority with a different lifestyle to the majority does not confer immunity with respect to general laws, in order to safeguard the assets of the community as a whole, as well as the environment, this situation may have an impact on how these laws are implemented" [38].

Apart from the right to maintain the culture or the identity of an ethnic minority and organizing one's own life according to that identity and tradition, with the positive obligations that entails for the State, Article 8 of the Convention can also be applied to the right to freedom of choice of cultural or ethnic identity and the right for that decision to be respected when it is based on objective grounds.

5.2. Case Ciubotaru v. Moldova

For example, in the case *Ciubotaru v. Moldova* [39], the Court examined the rejection of the Moldovan authorities to register the ("Romanian") ethnic identity of the plaintiff. The incident occurred following the application to replace his Soviet identity card with the Moldovan identity card. The government's refusal was based on the fact that his parents were not registered as "ethnically Romanian" on their birth or marriage certificates.

The Court held that "the ethnic identity of an individual is an essential aspect of his private life" which falls under the protection of Article 8 and concluded that the Moldovan legislation and enforcement created insurmountable barriers to anyone wishing for a different ethnic identity to be registered to that registered in relation to their parent by the Soviet authorities. The Court accepted that the authorities can reject a request to be officially registered as belonging to a particular ethnic group, when that petition was based on purely subjective and insubstantial reasons.

However, the procedure established by law in Moldova prevents the applicant from providing an objective reason to support their request, such as verifiable links with the Romanian identity, such as language, name, empathy or others (§ 58). Some of the objective foundations of ethnic and cultural identity, like a shared language, religious faith or the origins, and cultural and traditional backgrounds have been recognized by the Court in other rulings [40].

In these cases, this characteristic is related to the cultural origins. Unlike the cases of disability, these are characteristics, which, in part, could be changed voluntarily, and yet that the Court considers worthy of protection. It follows that the person would be entitled to retain them when he or she wishes.

5.3. Case of Sinan Isik v. Turkey

The identity element also overlaps with the religious freedom protected by Article 9 because sometimes religion is part of the cultural identity of the individual. For example, in one case ruled in 2010, *Sinan Isik c. Turkey* [41], the appellant claimed against the denial of his request to replace the term "Muslim" on his identity card, with that of his "Alevi" faith.

The Court recognized a violation of art. 9 on freedom of religion, not because of the applicant's claim, that is, not because t the "Alevi" religion did not feature, but due to the fact that a religion had to appear on the Identity Card, because this forced individuals to give that information related to an aspect of their religion or personal convictions against their will. Because Article 9 protects the right to not testify religion or disbelief, the judgment of the Court leant towards the line of demanding the Turkish state to eliminate religion for the Turkish identity card (Cf., § 60). Some scholars have criticized the fact that the ECHR prohibits any legislation that imposes a non-voluntary declaration of religious conviction because that prevents drawing up statistics based upon religious beliefs, which in turn serve to detect indirect discrimination on grounds of religion [42]. However, we believe this objective could be achieved without requiring the declaration to be made on public identity documents. Moreover, the case would be different if the people themselves were those who wished to make that declaration for different reasons such as achieving work accommodation, for example, or to receive religion classes. For others, there may be an intention in the ECHR to gradually delete individuals' characteristics attached to their religious affiliation, given the line of defence of negative secularism that the ECHR has been conducting sometimes.

As noted above, many rights are interrelated. Freedom of religion, thought and conscience of art. 9 of the Convention is closely connected to the right of minorities to express their belief or religion, together with others, both in the private and public sphere, in areas such as worship, teaching, religious practice and its observance. Being able to exercise religion or cult individually or in group constitutes an elementary form of the right to manifest one's religion collectively. One aspect that is decisively attached to this fact is the possibility of entering the place of worship to take part in the services and observances, which is reflected in the jurisprudence of the ECHR in cases like *Cyprus v. Turkey* [43], which deals with restrictions on the freedom of movement of Greek Cypriots in northern Cyprus. The access of that religious community to food from animals slaughtered in accordance with religious specifications was not guaranteed and the ECtHR considered that this restriction interferes with their right to express their own religion, protected by article 9.

5.4. Case of Chaare Shalom ve Tsedek v. France

Another similar case is observed in the judgment *Chaare Shalom Ve Tzedek c. France* [44], referred to Jews in France who were prevented from having access to animals slaughtered according to their religious rules.

5.5. Case of Sidiropoulos and Others v. Greece

Sometimes the ECHR has indirectly protected the right to identity through the right of minorities to form partnerships to promote their culture, under Art. 11 of the Convention, for example in the case *Sidiropoulos et al.* v. Greece [45]. The plaintiff claims that he has Macedonian ethnicity and that he has a "national Macedonian conscience". He decides to establish a non-profit organization called "The House of the Macedonian civilization ". National courts deny him the opportunity to register this association.

The ECHR states that there is a violation of Art.11 of the Convention. The aims of the association were exclusively to preserve and develop the cultural traditions and folklore of the region of Florina. The Court considers these ends to be legitimate: "the inhabitants of a region in a country have the right to form associations to promote the special characteristics of the region, both for historical and economic reasons" (§ 44). The plaintiffs also allege in their favour that they have a an awareness of minority rights protected by international treaties such as the "Document of the Copenhagen Meeting of the Conference on the Human Dimension of the CSCE (Section IV)" from June 29, 1990 and "charter of Paris for a New Europe" of 21 November 1990, that Greece has signed and which gives them the right to protect their culture and spiritual heritage (§ 44).

5.6. Case of Gorzelik and Others v. Poland

Furthermore, in the case *Gorzelik et al.* v. Poland [46], the ECtHR stressed the importance of freedom of association for persons belonging to ethnic and national minorities. Apart from the protection that the Court has given to political parties as a part of the existing pluralism in a society, which is not now the subject of our study, as we are discussing, special protection has similarly been granted to associations whose purpose is to protect the cultural or spiritual heritage, whilst pursuing economic and social goals, or teaching religion, seeking their ethnic identity or asserting their sense of belonging to a minority, or their religious, religious, artistic, literary and linguistic identity. This is linked to the protection of the plural functioning of a democracy. The harmonious interaction of people and groups is essential in order to achieve social cohesion (cf. § 92).

In developing these principles, the Court protected the right to express one's own point of view through the freedom to form associations and through the notion of personal autonomy in order to express their ethnic identity and belief. This kind of association should be possible within the legal framework (see *Tourkiki Enosi Xanthis et al.* v. Greece).

5.7. Case of Stankov and Organization of Macedonia United Ilinden v. Bulgaria

Regarding history, Article 11 of the Convention protects the right of minorities to celebrate historic events of singular importance to this minority (see *Stankov and the United Macedonian Organisation Ilinden v. Bulgaria*) [47].

The question of teaching history in official curricula, which is always controversial, has led to a clear resolution of the Committee of Ministers of the Council of Europe, called "Recommendation REC (2001) 15 of the Committee of Ministers of the Member States relating to teaching European history of the XXI century" [48].

6. LIMITS IN THE EXERCISE OF RIGHTS PROTECTED BY THE EUROPEAN CONVENTION ON HUMAN RIGHTS AND THE TEST OF PROPORTIONALITY

We now proceed to examine the techniques used by the ECtHR to set some limits on the claims filed by individuals against their states, justifying a denial of the exercise of a right by observing that there is no violation of law or that the restriction is justified. The functional and social limits set by the Supreme Court of Canada are similar to the current techniques of the ECHR.

A first technique consists of using the test of proportionality, which the ECHR also applies, using both (legal) social and functional boundaries as limits to the exercise of an individual's right.

The jurisprudence of the ECtHR has three criteria: first, the State must prove in the case of a rule at issue that such a measure pursues a legitimate right [49]; second, that there is a reasonable relationship of proportionality between the means used and the aim sought; and third, that there is no other measure, which, achieving the same end, may damage the individual right to a lesser extent, namely, that it is less burdensome for the individual to whom the exercise of a legitimate right is restricted. The ECHR limits itself to examining the second criteria and avoids the analysis of the first and third ones.

In all three cases, all of these criteria are encompassed within the other known mechanism of "margin of appreciation of states" of the ECHR, which we will examine later, and which we have described as an equivalent notion to that of "overriding interest of the state" in Canadian law.

With regard to the first criterion, the vague concept of "objective and legitimate purpose" will be interpreted by the judge and will be implemented in light of the specific circumstances [50].

The same applies to the second criterion: judges will decide, using the usual methods of legal reasoning, such as proportionality and balancing, if there is a reasonable relationship of proportionality between the means used and the aim sought.

Regarding the third criterion, too, as part of the concept of proportionality, the Court examines whether the restriction of the right for the citizen or the application of that rule represents excessive sacrifice of his right, as mentioned in the case of Glor against Switzerland.

Therefore, coupled with the concept discussed above of indirect discrimination, the principle of proportionality helps to detect if the effect of the rule is disproportionate, when, if so, would then force the State to adopt a solution that would relax the rule in order to avoid adverse impact on those citizens. The rule can be formulated in a neutral way (consisting of a restriction or not), but it would be indirectly discriminatory if its effects impose particular difficulties for some people [51]. The goal of the proportionality test is to detect and prevent unwarranted negative differential (discriminatory) treatment based on the indirect discriminatory effects of the neutral rule.

To avoid this, it is necessary to give the citizen, paradoxically, a special positive treatment, based on the principle of equality that requires treating different people differently (see Thlimmenos v. Greece), by making an adaptation of the rule.

7. THE MARGIN OF APPRECIATION AS A LIMIT TO STATES RIGHTS. PARALLELS WITH THE CANADIAN CONCEPT OF COMPELLING STATE INTEREST

A similarity is noticeable, in turn, between the margin of appreciation possessed by each State and the limits to the rights established in the European Convention of Human Rights with the Canadian notion (taken in turn from American jurisprudence) of the compelling state interest.

As a result of the analysis carried out in the case law of the ECHR, it can be concluded that the ECHR is being more inclined to defend cultural rights in support of certain minorities such as the Roma among others, and yet does not seem too inclined towards the defence of religious freedom, when the states have violated this right, with the recent exception of Eweida [52].

In my opinion, the jurisprudence of the ECtHR is very promising in respect of the protection of minorities and of their cultural rights, but in contrast it shows little hope regarding reasonable accommodations to protect the positive freedom to manifest one's religion. Although there have been some judicial cases that have differed from the general line, and the ECtHR absolutely refuses to grant reasonable accommodations, for instance to parents due to religious beliefs in educational matters. It does not accept the dispensation or objection to certain teaching programmes, with the exception of some positive judgements such as the *cases of Folgerø and other v. Norway* [53] and *Hassan and Eylem Zengin v. Turkey* [54].

In contrast to the previous cases, the ECHR has ruled in favour of Eweida, an employee of British Airways, in the famous case, *Eweida v. British Airways* [55]. She was not allowed by her employer to wear a small cross on her uniform and was finally thrown out of the company. In addition, there was the case of the nurse, Chaplin, who was forbidden to wear a small chain around her neck with the crucifix, The ECHR judgment of 15 January 2103 decided in favour of the stewardess, Eweida, but not so in favour of the nurse, Chaplin [56].

8. A NEW CHALLENGE: CONCERTED ADJUSTMENTS AND PREVIOUS HARMONISATION PRACTICES: A CHANGE IN PARADIGM

In Canada jurisprudence and legal arguments have created a new mindset that fosters previous measures in terms of concerted adjustments and adaptations provided for or negotiated in advance between the parties without going through situations of bitterness, which may end up in court. As noted by many authors [57], this leads to a preventive and proactive attitude and not just a corrective attitude.

In that sense, the lesson learnt leads to a change in attitude and an analysis of the general rules in a proactive manner so as to allow for a possible adaptation, taking into account the citizens' needs or capabilities. The jurisprudence of the Supreme Court of Canada has led the government to take an active approach in response to what is part of its obligation. Instead of waiting for conflicts to occur and seek solutions *a posteriori* it has anticipated problems by establishing guidelines and best practices. It would not be necessary, then, to wait for legal remedies to be taken against indirect discriminations, but rather to prevent them from arising in the first place. Implementation of employment policies and standards that avoid structural and institutional barriers for people who are different to the majority of the population will enable them to integrate.

The application of this new attitude leads to different types of solutions; in some cases, the general rule requires only a minor adjustment, in others, a different, and therefore, special standard, would be necessary. We are not talking about applying a system of exceptions [58] that would lead some people to benefit from an advantage or privilege (favouritism) over others (workers or users), but about legal measures that will enable a person to occupy the same post as other citizens. Therefore, it is not a system of exceptions, but of flexibility built into the rule itself to prevent it from producing unintended discriminatory effects. It is about providing flexible modes to execute the rule. It is a way of accepting the difference in situations of ordinary citizens who thus have different needs [59]. All of this permits us to stick to the obligation of complying with the rule, whilst, at the same time, it enables us to avoid a discrimination that cold otherwise occur if the rule were to be applied in a rigid manner. Moreover such adjustments do not affect the essential objective of the rule itself, for instance, compliance with a work schedule, wearing a uniform, customer care, teaching in schools and universities, *etc.*

As societies are becoming more and more pluralistic, from the cultural point of view, too, there will be an increasing need for applying accommodations [60]. This new mindset opens up valid perspectives for managing cultural and religious diversity. So far this has been a technique that has been used to prevent indirect discrimination of historically stigmatized minorities, including African Americans and indigenous minorities, people with disabilities (today imposed as a clear duty) or indirect discrimination against women. However, there is still a long way to go to avoid discrimination on grounds of culture and to be able to embrace diversity as a result of immigration and to accept differences in colour, visions of life or worldview, philosophy and religion, differences between the citizens of origin and newcomers, between believers and non-believers. It is about using legal techniques to promote inclusive citizenship that balances the advantages of the dominant culture and those of other groups in society. An example would be the possibility of providing newcomers, who have not yet had time to learn the language of the host country, with interpreters, thereby facilitating access to services and communication.

These techniques to detect indirect discrimination in different minorities or adverse impact also originate in American jurisprudence. It is about studying how regulations will affect certain specific groups in the access to public services or new business niches. *A fortiori* this criterion is used to promote the employment of immigrants.

The underlying philosophy of the legal need for reasonable accommodations is based on a conception of distributive social justice, from the perspective of inclusive citizenship. It is based on a specific intercultural model, as already mentioned, and upon previous works to which we have referred [61]. The building of an inclusive citizenship requires, as a starting point, sharing some ethical-legal civic values that also allows for differences. Moreover, both cultural and religious freedoms are part of such values.

Integration of the difference must be carried out without compromising fundamental constitutional values, but in turn it requires the flexibility to distinguish between what is essential and what is not and therefore it need not be a homogeneous requirement for all [62]. That is the task of the legislator, the judiciary and intellectuals [63].

Although the Canadian or Quebec model is not directly transferable to Europe, it holds many parallels to the situations occurring in our European countries. European societies like the Quebec society are in a dilemma between tradition and renovation of their past identities and integration of themselves and others in a new era of greater local autonomy and the acceptance of foreign elements.

Individuals and governments should manage diversity, both through legislation and applying exceptions provided in the general laws (through other ordinary laws), and through concerted agreed adjustments (between the state administration and the citizens, as well as among individuals), and also through jurisprudence, adopting reasonable accommodations whenever such cases are appealed to the courts.

In recent years, the phenomenon of religion in Europe has perhaps focused to a great extent on the state's relationship with the Churches as institutions, however, today, it is essential to draw attention to the idea that the welfare state is also comprised of individual citizens who have their own convictions, beliefs and philosophies in life. In this regard, the State, public authorities, private enterprises and individuals must be able to manage the diversity emanating from its own citizens and civil servants as well as workers in the private sector.

It is a matter of governance and the management of diversity being tackled by public and private authorities with a healthy amount of realism, which would involve providing small feasible, legal and administrative solutions as contained within the concept of "reasonable accommodation" and "agreed or concerted adjustments" that have emerged in American and Canadian jurisprudence. This concept could be very useful for promoting inclusive citizenship for groups and individuals, in addition to the state's relations with minority cultures and religious faiths. The focus here has been to tackle diversity from the perspective of the individual citizen - less so from the group perspective - and the specific practices adopted by various public authorities in order, from the legal point of view, to tackle the challenge of diversity when managing social services in municipalities and different neighbourhoods.

In summary, the concept of reasonable accommodation as developed in Canada and the new mindset which this has brought about, could be used as a model in current European debates on diversity which appear to be somewhat frazzled. Indeed, the concept appears to be very relevant in the context of the relationship between the State and the religious phenomenon, which should not be managed from a distance, but by administrations that take into account the moral and spiritual diversity of its citizens, even in the religious and philosophical sphere. The governments and the attitude adopted by the judges of the Supreme Court of Canada show the example that governance or management of diversity from the state's perspective should and can be done on the basis of broadmindedness, using, among others, the mechanisms of reasonable accommodation and agreed adjustments.

JURISPRUDENCE

ECHR (Grand Chamber)	Cha'are Shalom Ve Tsedek v. France, no.. 27417/95, 2000- VII.
ECHR (Grand Chamber)	Chapman v. United Kingdom, no.. 27238/95, ECHR 2001-I.
ECHR (Grand Chamber)	Cyprus v. Turkey, 2001-Is, no.. 27417/95, ECHR 2000-VII.
ECHR (Grand Chamber)	D.H and others v. Czech Republic, no. 57325/00, 13 November 2007.
ECtHR (Grand Chamber)	Folgerø and Others v. Norway, no. 15472/02, § 84, CEDH 2007-VIII.
ECtHR (Grand Chamber)	Gorzelik and Others v. Poland, no. 44158/98, 17 February 2004.
ECtHR (Grand Chamber)	Orsus and Others v. Croatia, no. 15766/03, 17 July 2008.
ECtHR Ciubotaru v. Moldova	no.. 27138/04, 27 April 2010.
ECtHR Eweida and Others v. UK	no. 48420/10 and 59843/10.
ECtHR Glor v. Switzerland	no. 13444/04, 30 April 2009.
ECtHR Hassan and Eylem Zengin v. Turkey	no. 1448/04, 9 October 2007.
ECtHR Inze v. Austria	serie A, no. 126, 28 October 1987.

ECtHR Rasmussen v. Denmark	serie A, no. 87, 28 November 1984;
ECtHR Sejdic and Finci v. Bosnia-Herzegovina	nos. 27996/06 and 34836/06, § 43, 22 December 2009.
ECtHR Sessa Francesco v. Italy	no. 28790/08, 3 April 2012.
ECtHR Sidiropoulos and Others v. Greece	10 July 1998, Reports of Judgments and Decisions 1998-IV.
ECtHR Sinan Isik v. Turkey	no. 21924/05, 2 February 2010.
ECtHR Thlimmenos v. Greece	no. 34369/97, 6 April 2000.
ECtHR Tourkiki Enosi Xanthis and Others v. Greece	no. 26698/05, 27 March 2008.
SCC (Canadian Supreme Court); official site	www.scc-csc.gc.ca/court-cour/ju/cory/index-fra.asp.
SCC Colombie-Britannique (Superintendent of Motor Vehicles) c. Colombie-Britannique (Council of Human Rights)	[1999] 3 RCS 868 (caso Grismer).
SCC Commission ontarienne des droits de la personne et Theresa O´Malley (Vincent) c. Simpsons-Sears Ltd (1985) 2 RCS 536.	En su versión inglesa, Human Rights Commission y O´Malley v. Simpsons Sears Ltd. Available at scc.lexum.org/fr/1985/1985rcs2-536/1985rcs2-536.html
SCC R. v. Big M. Drug Mart Ltd	[1985] 1 RCS 295.
SCC Syndicat Northcrest v. Amselem	(2004) 2 SCR 551.

CONFLICT OF INTEREST

The author declares no conflict of interest, financial or otherwise.

ACKNOWLEDGEMENTS

Declared none.

REFERENCES

[1] This intervention reflects some of the results of an extensive research conducted as part of the IDEA Research Group, University of Zaragoza, with the assistance of the Government of Aragón (DG Research and Innovation) grant programme to encourage the mobility of researchers - in this context a three-month stay in Strasbourg at the Council of Europe, Directorate General of Human Rights and Rule of Law, DG HR, and at the European Court of Human Rights - and other aid from the Ministry of Foreign Affairs of Canada and the International Council for Canadian Studies (ICCS), for a fellowship in Canadian studies on understanding Canada's programme for the preparation of the report of the Bouchard-Taylor Commission at the University of Laval in 2009. This research has resulted in a monograph published in March 2013: The case-law concept of reasonable accommodation. Cizur: Aranzadi Editorial 2013. All websites are updated until October 2014.

[2] European Commission against Racism and Intolerance (ECRI). Report on Spain. Published on 8 February 2011. Available from http://www.coe.int/t/dghl/monitoring/ecri/Country-by-country/Spain/

ESP-CBC-IV-2011-004-ENG.pdf.

[3] See the numerous sanctions imposed at the meeting of the State Commission against Violence, Racism, Xenophobia and Intolerance in Sport (28/02/2013). Available from http://www.csd.gob.es/csd/documentacion/01GabPr/Noticias/reunion-de-la-comision-estatal-contra-la-violencia-el- racismo-la-xenofobia-y-la-intolerancia-en-el-deporte-28-02-2013/.

[4] Guide Management of Religious Diversity in Hospitals. Guide for Public Management of Religious Diversity. Observatory of Religious Pluralism in Spain. Madrid: Ministry of Health, Social Policy and Equality 2011. Available in Spainsh only: Guía de gestión de la diversidad religiosa en los centros hospitalarios. Guía para la gestión pública de la diversidad religiosa. Observatorio del pluralismo religioso en España. Madrid: Ministerio de Sanidad, Política social e Igualdad 2011.

[5] See Proceedings of ECRI´s Expert Seminar. Combating Racism while Respecting Freedom of Expression. Strasbourg: Council of Europe 2007.

[6] Report of the Bouchard-Taylor Commission. Building the future: A time for reconciliation. Final Report of the Consultation Commission on Accommodation Practices Related to Cultural Differences. Quebec 2008. Available in English and French at www.accommodements.qc.ca.

[7] Institutional Accommodation and the Citizen: Legal and Political Interaction in a Pluralist Society. French version: Accommodements institutionnels et citoyens: cadres juridiques et politiques pour interagir dans des sociétés plurielles. Strasbourg: Conseil de l´Europe/Council of Europe 2009.

[8] Bribosia E, Ringelheim J, Rorive I. Aménager la diversité: le droit de l'égalité face à la pluralité religieuse. Revue Trimestrielle des droits de l´homme 2009; 78: 325-333.

[9] Leitkultur with the meaning of "dominant culture" was a term invented by Bassam Tibi in Europe ohne Identität? Leitkultur oder Wertebeliebigkeit. Munich: Pieper 1998, related to German culture, as recorded by Bielefeldt H. Challenges faced by culturally diverse societies in Europe. In: CoE. Human Rights in Culturally Diverse Societies. Challenges and Perspectives. Netherlands: The Hague 2008 November, 12-13. Proceedings. Directorate General of Human Rights and Legal Affairs. Council of Europe. Netherlands 2009 October; p. 38, note 10. See also, Barbara J, *idem,* p. 76.

[10] Stavros S. Freedon of Religion and Claims for Exemption from Generally Applicable, Neutral Laws: Lessons from Accross the Pond? *EHRLR* 1997; (Issue 6): 607-627.

[11] In this regard I fully share the vision of Malcolm Evans in his article Advancing Freedom of Religion or Belief: Agendas for Change. Oxford Journal of Law and Religion 2012 April; 1(Issue 1).

[12] Parekh BC, Ed. The Future of Multi-Ethnic Britain: The Parekh Report. In: Commission on the Future of Multi-Ethnic Britain. London: The Runnymede Trust 2002.

[13] Building the future. A Time for Reconciliation. Report of the Bouchard-Taylor Commission. Building The Future: A Time For Reconciliation. Final Report of the Consultation Commission on Accommodation Practices Related to Cultural Differences. Quebec 2008. Available in English and French at: https://www.mce.gouv.qc.ca/publications/CCPARDC/rapport-final-integral-en.pdf

[14] Rapport Belge: Assises de l'Interculturalité 2010. Rapport remis à Joëlle Milquet, Vice-Première Ministre, Ministre de l'Emploi et de l'Égalité des Chances, en charge de la Politique de migration et d'asile, lors de la cérémonie de clôture des Assises de l'Interculturalité, le 8 novembre 2010 à Bruxelles. Available from www.milquet.belgium.be/sites/default/files/Télécharger%20le%20rapport %20des%20Assises%20de%20 Interculturalité.pdf See also Foblets MC. Le droit face à la multiplication des revendications identitaires. Pluriculturalité et pluralisme juridique au départ de l´experience belge. In: Ringelheim J, Dir. Le droit et la diversité culturelle. Bruxelles: Bruylant 2011; pp. 877-906.

[15] Maclure J, Taylor C. Laïcité et liberté de conscience. Montréal: Les éditions du Boréal 2010. Elósegui M. El fundamento filosófico de la laicidad abierta en Taylor y Maclure *versus* las leyes de neutralidad en Alemania. Anuario de Derecho Eclesiástico del Estado 2011; 27: 209-254. See Elósegui M. El modelo de interculturalidad en el informe de la Comisión Bouchard-Taylor. Anuario de Derechos Humanos 2010 June: 129-164. Available from www.ucm.es/BUCM/revistas/der/02120364/

articulos/ANDH1010110129A.PF.

[16] About the evolution in Unites States, see Bribosia E, Ringelheim J, Rorive I. Aménager la diversité: le droit de l'égalité face à la pluralité religieuse. *cit.*, pp. 325-333.

[17] SCC, Ontario Human Rights Commission and O'Malley v. Simpsons-Sears Ltd (1985) 2 R.C.S 536, 17 December. This case is sometimes referred to as 'Human Rights Commission', 'O'Malley', 'Simpsons-Sears', and 'Vincent', which is the maiden name of Mrs. O'Malley. Available from http://scc.lexum.org/fr/1985/1985rcs2-536/1985rcs2-536.html. See report of the Bouchard-Taylor Commission. Building The Future: A Time For Reconciliation. *cit.*, p. 48.

[18] Jézéquel M. The Reasonable Accommodation Requirement: Potential and Limits. CoE. Institutional Accommodation and the Citizen: Legal and Political Interaction in a Pluralist Society. *cit.*, pp. 21-36. Here p. 21.

[19] Decision of the Supreme Court of Canada, SCC Cases Lexum, R. v. Big M. Drug Mart Ltd, [1985], (24 April 1985), 1 R.C.S. 295, Case Number 18125. Available at https://scc-csc.lexum.com/sc--csc/scc-csc/en/item/43/index.do

[20] In most European countries there are disputes on laws governing business hours. The use of Sunday as a day of rest is not only used in Christian and/or Western societies but also remained in the Russian Federation during the communist period, and is used today in the People's Republic of China; See Ferrer J . The Crucifix in Public Schools. In: Elósegui M, Coord. State Neutrality and the Role of Religion in the Public Sphere in Germany. Zaragoza: Fundación Giménez Abad and Fundación Alexander von Humboldt 2012; p. 54. Avaiblable in Spanish only: El crucifijo en la escuela pública. In: Elósegui M, Coord. La neutralidad del Estado y el papel de la religión en la esfera pública en Alemania. Zaragoza: Fundación Giménez Abad y Fundación Alexander von Humboldt 2012; p. 54.

[21] See opinion of Woehrling J. L'obligation d'accommodement raisonnable et l'adaptation de la société à la diversité religieuse. Revue de droit de McGill 1998; 43: 325-401: "C'est le point de vue très clairement adopté par la Cour suprême dans ses deux premières decisións sur la liberté de religion, les arrêts R. c. Big M. Drug Mart Ltd., [1985]1 R.C.S. 295 et R.c.Edwards Books, [1986]2R.C.S.713, décisions rendues à un moment où l'article 15 de la Charte canadienne, portant sur le droit à l'égalité, n'était pas encore en vigueur. Dans l'arrêt Big M.Drug Mart Ltd., pp. 336 et 337, le juge Dickson considère qu'une atteinte à la liberté de religion peut résulter soit d'une coercition étatique qui oblige ou empêche quelqu'un de se conformer à une prescription religieuse, soit d'une inégalité de traitement d'une religion par rapport aux autres".

[22] For an study on the protection of cultural minorities in the European Convention of Human Rights, see Marschall J. Personal Freedom through Human Rights Law?: Autonomy, Identity and Integrity under the European Convention of Human Rights. Boston: Martinus Nijhoff 2009.

[23] See Ast F. La discrimination indirecte comme outil de protection du pluralisme: enjeux et limites. In: COE. Accommodements institutionnels et citoyens: cadres juridiques et politiques pour interagir dans des sociétés plurielles. *cit.*, p. 90.

[24] Judgment of the European Court of Human Rights, ECtHR (Grand Chamber), Gorzelik et al. v. Pologne, no 44158/98, 17th February 2004. Available at: https://studentportalen.uu.se/uusp.../download.action?.

[25] Judgment European Court of Human Rights, ECtHR, Sessa Francesco c. Italie, no 28790/08, 3rd March 2012.

[26] See Basta Fleiner LR. Les droits de participation prévus par la Convention-cadre pour la protection des minorités nationales (CCPMN): évolution vers un cadre juridique rejetant la discrimination sociales et économiques". In: COE. *cit.*, pp. 69-87. Also Meda-Windischer R. The European Court of Human Rights and minority rights. Journal of European Integration 2003 Sept.; 25(3): 249-271. Breitenmoser S. The Protection of Groups and Groups Rights in Europe. In: Koen de Feyter, Pavlakos G. The Tension between Group Rights and Human Rights: a Multidisciplinary Approach. Oxford, Portland-Oregon: Hart 2008; pp. 245-269.

[27] Research Division; Cultural rights in the case-law of the European Court of Human Rights. Council of Europe/European Court of Human Rights, January 2011. This report has been prepared by the Research Division of the ECHR in English and is not binding on the ECHR. It is published and available on the following website: www.echr.coe.int (Case-Law / Case- Law Analysis / Research Reports), p. 4.

[28] Research Division; Cultural rights in the case-law of the European Court of Human Rights. Council of Europe/European Court of Human Rights, January 2011. This report has been prepared by the Research Division of the ECHR in English and is not binding on the ECHR. It is published and available on the following website: www.echr.coe.int (Case-Law / Case- Law Analysis / Research Reports), p. 4.

[29] COE. White Paper for an intercultural Dialogue: Living Together with Equal Dignity. CM (2008) 30 final. 2 de mayo de 2008. Available from www.coe.int/t/dg4/intercultural/Publication_ White Paper_ID_en.asp.

[30] Some authors believed that the argument somehow opened in *the case Thlimmenos against Greece* had not been continued thereafter. However, the ECtHR has shown in the subsequent case for 2000 a new sensitivity towards cultural identity that could well be seen in continuity with that case.

[31] TEDH (Grand Chamber), D.H and others v. Czech Republic, nº 57325/00, 13the November 2007. See the dissenting opinion of Judge Borrego Borrego in this ruling and comment on it in Flauss JF. Actualité de la Convention européenne des droits de l'homme (septembre 2009-février 2010). L´Actualité juridique droit administratif (AJDA) 2010 May; 18: 997-1009. According Flauss, dissenting opinions have become increasingly virulent (see p. 998) and sometimes are more aggressive than those made by academic doctrine.

[32] ECHR (Grand Chamber), Orsus and others v. Croatia, nº 15766/03, 17th July 2008.

[33] ECHR, Glor c. Switzerland, nº 13444/04, 30th April 2009.

[34] RESEARCH DIVISION/DIVISION DE LA RECHERCHE: Cultural Rights in the Case-Law of the European Court of Human Rights. Council of Europe/European Court of Human Rights 2011 January; 9-12.

[35] ECHR (Grand Chamber), Chapman v. United Kingdom, nº. 27238/95, ECHR 2001-I.

[36] ECHR (Grand Chamber), Chapman v. United Kingdom, nº. 27238/95, ECHR 2001-I), § 73.

[37] ECHR, Chapman v. United Kingdom, § 93.

[38] *Idem*, § 96.

[39] Judgment European Court of Human Rights, ECtHR, Ciubotaru v. Moldavia, no. 27138/04, 27th April 2010.

[40] See the concept of ethnicity in judgments of the Grand Chamber of the ECHR, Sejdic and Finci v. Bosnia-Herzegovina, nºs. 27996/06 y 34836/06, § 43, 22 December 2009.

[41] Judgment European Court of Human Rights, ECtHR, Sinan Isik v. Turkey, no. 21924/05, 2nd February 2010.

[42] Flauss JF. Actualité de la Convention européenne des droits de l´homme (septembre 2009-février 2010). L´Actualité juridique droit administratif (AJDA) 2010 May; 18: 1002.

[43] Judgment European Court of Human Rights, ECtHR (Grand Chamber), Cyprus v. Turkey, no. 25781/94, §§ 241-247, 2001-IV, no. 27417/95, ECHR 2000-VII.

[44] ECHR (Grand Chamber), Cha'are Shalom Ve Tsedek v. France, nº. 27417/95, 2000- VII. See Martín-Retortillo L. Sacrifices rituels d´animaux, autorisation administrative et liberté religieuse de la Cour européenne des droits de l´homme, Cha´are Shalom ve Tsedek c. France, du 27 juin 2000. In: Mouvement du droit public: du droit administratif au droit constitutionnel; du droit français aux autres droits/mélanges en l´honneur de Franck Moderne, Paris: Dalloz 2004; pp. 1235-1252.

[45] ECHR, Sidiropoulos and Others v. Greece, 10th July 1998, Reports of Judgments and Decisions 1998-IV.

[46] Judgment European Court of Human Rights, ECtHR (Grand Chamber), Gorzelik and others v. Poland, no. 44158/98, 17th February 2004, § 92.

[47] Judgment European Court of Human Rights, ECtHR, Tourkiki Enosi Xanthis and others v. Greece, no. 26698/05, 27th March 2008, § 56.

[48] Recommendation REC (2001) 15 of the Committee of Ministers of the Member States relating to the teaching of the history of Europe of the XXI century. On recent jurisprudence of the ECHR regarding the right to seek historical truth, see RESEARCH DIVISION / DIVISION OF RECHERCHE, Cultural rights in the case-law of the European Court of Human Rights, Council of Europe / European Court of Human Rights, January 2011, pp. 21-22. The issue of teaching history, of government programmes and manuals has been the subject of much academic research by professional historians. Logically, they are highly controversial issues, also in the countries of the Council of Europe and that lend themselves to consdierable manipulation when rigor and professional ethics are lacking. The establishment of nine States after the political changes in the former Soviet Socialist Republic and the regime change in other former communist countries has led to demand related to national minorities filed with the ECHR. This far exceeds the specific purpose of these pages.

[49] Commission (Plenary), European Court of Human Rights, ECtHR, Thlimmenos v. Greece, Application no. 34369/97, 12/01/1998 and Judgment Chamber First Section, ECtHR, Glor v. Switzerland, Application nº 13444/04, Judgment 30 April 2009, Final 06/11/2009. Available at: www.legislationline.org/.../ECHR_Glor_v._Switzerland_2009_en-2.pdf.

[50] Judgment European Court of Human Rights, ECtHR, Rasmussen v. Denmark, Series A, n° 87, Case No 9/1983/65/100, App No ... ECHR 17, (1985) 7 EHRR 371, IHRL 50 (ECHR 1984), 28th November 1984; European Court of Human Rights, ECtHR, Inze v. Austria, Series A, n° 126, 28th October 1987.

[51] Bosset P, Foblets MC. "Le Québec et LÉurope face au besoin d´accommoder la diversité: disparité des concepts juridiques, convergence des résultats?", in Accomodements institutionnels et citoyens: cadres juridiques et politiques pour interagir dans des sociétés plurielles, Publishing Editions Council of Europe, 2009, p. 63. English versión Institutional Accommodation and the citizen: legal and political interaction in a pluralist society. Available at: https://www.coe.int/t/dg3/socialpolicies/socialcohesiondev/source/Trends/Trends-21_fr.pdf (French version) and https://www.coe.int/t/dg3/socialpolicies/socialcohesiondev/source/Trends/Trends-21_en.pdf (English version).

[52] See Elósegui M. El concepto jurisprudencial de acomodamiento razonable. Cizur-Menor: Thomson Reuters-Aranzadi 2013.

[53] ECHR (Grand Chamber), Folgerø and others v. Norway, no 15472/02, § 84, CEDH 2007-VIII. See, Ducoulombier P. Folgero v. Norway: Dispensation from Religious Education: from the United Nations Human Rights Committee to the European Court of Human Rights. European Human Rights Law Review 2008; (issue 3): 391-399.

[54] Judgment European Court of Human Rights (former Second Section), ECtHR, Hassan and Eylem Zengin v. Turkey, no 1448/04, 9th October 2007 . Available at: http://www.aihmiz.org.tr/?q=en/node/94.

[55] ECHR, Eweida v British Airways [2010] EWCA Civ 80, together with the case of Chaplin´s nurse, See App Nos 48420/10 y 59843/10.

[56] *Idem.* For a comment about the atmosphere in UK, see McGoldrick D. Religion in the European Public Sphare and in European Public Life. Crucifixes in the Clasroom? Human Rights Law Review 2011; 11(3): 451-502. About United Kingdom pp. 456-457.

[57] Jézéquel, Bosset, Ast, Foblets, Woehrling, Kymlicka, already quoted. Namely, it could be better to take measures in advance, instead of waiting until individual demands for adaptation are requested, following the suggestions of Jézéquel, Bosset and Foblets. *cit.,* p. 46.

[58] Stavros S. Freedom of Religion and Claims for Exemption from Generally Applicable, Neutral Laws: Lessons from Accross the Pond? EHRLR 1997; (Issue 6): 607-627.

[59] See, opinion of arbitor Blais F. In: Soleno inc. v. Métallurgistes unis d'Amérique 2005, Canlii. 55297, § 196 (2005T-1114).

[60] Supreme Court of Canada, British Columbia (Superintendent of Motor Vehicles) v. British Columbia (Council of Human Rights), [1999] 3 RCS 868 (Grismer´s case).

[61] Elósegui M. El derecho a la identidad cultural en la Europa del siglo XXI. Pamplona: Eunsa 2012.

[62] Elósegui M. Derechos Humanos y pluralismo cultural. Madrid: Iustel 2008.

[63] Ramadan T. Accommodations for Minorities or Accommodations for All – Bringing about Harmonious Coexistence in Pluralist Societies. In: CoE. *cit.*, pp. 161-169, where he says that "Mistrust, fears, repeated controversies, the nagging question of immigration all create an atmosphere requiring legal professionals – usually discrete and calm – to take measures, both preventive and ongoing, to clarify and openly explain matters to the political class and journalists".

CHAPTER 3

Language Rights and Linguistic Groups: From International Law to Domestic Legal Protection (The Case of Spain)

Eva Pons-Parera[*]

Faculty of Law, Department of Constitutional Law and Political Science, University of Barcelona, Barcelona, Spain

Abstract: In this chapter, we address the relationship between international law and domestic legislation to protect language rights and groups speaking sub-state's languages. In the first part, the contribution of international and European instances is analyzed through the identification of three great models of protection applicable to the idiomatic field: the human rights model, the protection of linguistic minorities and the protection of linguistic diversity, highlighting their respective reception by the Spanish State. In the second part, after the definition of the general characteristics of the protection of language rights and linguistic groups in Spain, the different legal systems applicable to the Catalan language in four regions and the current legislation and its jurisprudential application are compared from the perspective of the *normalization* aim of the local language. Finally, the recent jurisprudence of the Constitutional Court on the of languages in the Statute of Autonomy of Catalonia of 2006 and its limitative impact on the language policies aimed at protecting and promoting the local language is analyzed.

Keywords: Constitutional jurisdiction, International law, Language rights, Linguistic groups, Official status.

1. INTRODUCTION

International regulations on linguistic matters have developed a number of general standards that frame state's action on this field. According to this perspective, the international framework not only protects linguistic minorities but influences the legal covering languages that enjoy a legal status within a given state, as the case of Spain, where an official status is also recognized to other languages different from Castilian/Spanish (the official language of the State). In the first part, this article reflects on the contribution from international organizations to the

[*] **Corresponding author Eva Pons-Parera:** Faculty of Law, Department of Constitutional Law and Political Science, University of Barcelona (UB), Barcelona, Spain; Tel: 0034 93 4024408; Fax: 0034 93 4024354; E-mail: evapons@ub.edu

J. Alberto del Real Alcalà (Ed.)

protection of languages rights and linguistic groups, by identifying the current focuses of international legislation on linguistic questions and the general scope of the instruments in force. The position adopted by state bodies in view of this international framework is analyzed concerning its reception under Spanish Constitution.

The second part of the article focuses on the protection of language rights and language groups under the Spanish legislation. The legal system for Spanish languages, based on the Constitution of 1978 (SC), recognizes an important role to Statutes of autonomy of various regions to define the official status -or other legal recognition- for languages different from Castilian. This feature implies also a fragmented legal, where a unique language, as Catalan, can enjoy different levels of protection according to the situation of different autonomous communities where it is traditionally spoken. In general, the Statutes of autonomy (SA) and the legislation passed by regional parliaments in the 1980 respond to a normalization aim of the local language, aimed at give it real the formal official status and to adopt positive measures in order to bring about a change of direction to a situation of monolingual predominance of Castilian that has been remaining for centuries. That implies that the local language, named by Statues of autonomy as the 'own' language of the autonomous community benefits from an asymmetrical treatment. The jurisprudence of the Constitutional Court (CC) and ordinary courts have supported the constitutionality of this kind of asymmetrical legal concerning the 'own' language, in accordance with the normalization aim. However, the recent jurisprudence about the 2006 reform of the Statute of autonomy of Catalonia seems to impose a more restrictive limits to the language policies aimed at foster and safeguard the local language, and reopen a political and legal conflict around the language rights of the different groups that coexist in the framework of the *Autonomic State*.

2. INTERNATIONAL LEGISLATION ON LANGUAGES: DIFFERENT MODELS OF PROTECTION

International law has been consolidated as one of the mainstays of languages and linguistic minority communities [1]. International and European organizations deal with a great number of dimensions of language. This intervention has given rise to an international doctrine and regulations increasingly widespread were languages, most commonly, are not directly addressed, but benefits from the protection of other related objects.

Historically, the origin of this intervention within the Society of Nations (1919-1945) was directed to the protection of linguistic minorities within the framework of a deep reorganization of the world political map. When the United Nations were created (1945), the idiomatic question was redirect towards the human rights protection model. A new step was done in the 1990', in the new geopolitical scene arising after the disappearance of East-West blocks, when the human rights perspective was enriched and complemented through new instruments regarding the minorities' rights and linguistic diversity.

According to that, the current situation of the international law enables the identification of three great models of protection applicable to the linguistic field: [2]

a. The human rights model, *via* the formulation of linguistic rights or the identification of a linguistic content implicit in other non-linguistic human rights;
b. The protection of minorities, and in particular those of a linguistic and national nature;
c. The protection of linguistic diversity, which is linked at universal level with the diversity of cultural expressions, and at the European level with the protection of regional or minority languages.

In substantive terms, these three protection models can't be conceived as watertight, but they interrelate and reinforce each other, *e.g.* when the link between the protection of minorities and human rights is highlighted. At other times, different models can oppose or neutralize each other, *e.g.* when some states adopt the model of diversity as a way to elude the recognition of collective rights for minorities existing in their territories.

Another general feature of the current international and European arena is the cohabitation of distinct protection systems, according to the particular approach to the linguistic phenomenon by each individual organization. Inside UN linguistic matters are mainly carried out according to the human rights perspective under the International Covenant on Civil and Political Rights of 1966 (ICCPR) and the International Covenant on Economic, Social and Cultural Rights of 1966 (ICESCR); but this approach coexists with the minorities model in the Declaration on the Rights of Persons Belonging to National or Ethnic, Religious and Linguistic Minorities of 1992, adopted by the UN General Assembly on 1992 (UN Declaration on Minorities). The protection of linguistic and cultural diversity perspective prevail in UNESCO, under the Convention on the Protection and the Promotion of the Diversity of Cultural Expressions of 2005.

The conjunction of this triple model can also be found, inside the European regional system, in the action carried out by the Council of Europe: human rights, under the European Convention of Human Rights (ECHR) and its protocols; the minorities rights, under the Framework Convention for the Protection of National

Minorities of 1995 (FCPNM); and, finally, the safeguard of linguistic diversity, under the European Charter for Regional and Minority Languages of 1992. In a more limited way, mainly inscribed in the second model, the Organization for Security and Cooperation in Europe (OSCE) also has a certain role in the linguistic matters, through the action of the High Commissioner on National Minorities (created in 1992), who has adopted in 1998 the Oslo Recommendations Regarding the Linguistic Rights of National Minorities.

A last analytical perspective of this international legislation emphasizes the particular scope of the current international instruments and its binding effects. Nowadays, there is not a universal multilateral treaty addressed to the protection of linguistic rights. Legally binding multilateral instruments can be found only in the framework of the Council of Europe (ECRML and FCPNM). Additionally, in this organization, some linguistic rights derived from the ECHR and its protocols receive a jurisdictional guarantee by the European Court for Human Rights (ECfHR). Diversely, the protection of linguistic rights in the UN and UNESCO international treaties on human rights (among them, see the Convention in the Rights of the Child of 1989) covers only a rather portion of the international doctrine on linguistic matters derived from this institutions, that is mainly included in non-binding documents and recommendations, as soft law, with an indicative value for the states.

The reception by the states of this international framework diverges, despite general ratification of basic instruments (as the ICCPR, ICESCR, or in Europe ECHR). Spain is, at this sense, on the advantaged states, as it takes part of more specialized instruments, as the ECRML or the FCPNM, contrary to other countries that have signed but not ratified both treaties (as example, neighbor countries as France or Italy). Additionally, in the case of the European Charter, the high level of undertakings exceeds the average of the states' parties. But political and juridical controversies arise - especially between the central State and autonomous political institutions- on the interpretation and application of this treaties, particularly by different views on its transformative potential of domestic legislation regulating the status and use of languages as Catalan specially protected by this international framework as minority or regional languages.

2.1. Human Right to Use the Language

The existing legal international right to use the language in public and private life is proclaimed as an "inalienable right" by the preamble of the ECRML (a typical instrument of protection of the linguistic diversity) "conforming the principles embodied in the United Nations International Covenant on Civil and Political Rights, and according to the spirit of the Council of Europe Convention for the

Protection of Human Rights and Fundamental Freedoms." In that way, the connexion of the right to use the language with principles and human rights recognized by general international instruments determines its inalienable character, that precedes and it is not dependent on the internal official status of languages [3].

International grounds of this linguistic freedom must be found in the non-discrimination principle due to language (Articles 2.2 ICCPR and 14 ECHR). In a negative sense, the interdiction of discrimination excludes all discriminatory treatment which implies the denial or deprivation of rights from using a specific language. This principle does not confer an autonomous protection to language and linguistic rights, but rather a protection linked to exercising other rights recognized by the treaties. The UN Human Rights Committee states that the term *discrimination* refers to "distinction, exclusion, restriction or preference which is based on any ground such as (...) language (...) and which has the purpose or effect of nullifying or impairing the recognition, enjoyment or exercise by all persons, on an equal footing, of all rights and freedoms" [4]. But also non-discrimination principle act as a source of positive obligations for the states, especially where applied to the protection of minorities (see *infra*).

In general, authors tend to stress the limited scope on international instruments concerning linguistic rights. As noted before, there is not an international binding instrument that list linguistic rights that must be universally respected, but it is not unusual that other human rights present a linguistic content (or a guarantee of subjective linguistic positions), that limit the states action in the material domain covert by the right. By this way, states can be confronted to certain minimum standards that limit the scope and the extent of their legislation [5]. In the case of Spain, this consequence is assumed by Article 10.2 SC, when stating that "Provisions relating to the fundamental rights and liberties recognized by the Constitution shall be construed in conformity with the Universal Declaration of Human Rights and international treaties and agreements thereon ratified by Spain". But the capacity of human rights to determine the status and use of languages in a statistic context remains quite limited, as it does not cover their collective dimension or specify the type of positive measures required to preserve the individual or group idiomatic identity [6]. Last considerations do not impede the efficacy of human rights as a minimum threshold of linguistic rights that can be alleged by persons who speak a language deprived of any internal legal statute.

Concerning the internal reception of the non-discrimination principle, lots of the constitutions explicitly recognizes the right not to be discriminated on the grounds of language, and some other constitutional text –as in Belgium or Switzerland- individuates a right to 'linguistic freedom'. This is not the case in Spain where the anti-discrimination clause (Article 14 Spanish Constitution, SC) does not refer expressly to the language, although it admits including the idiomatic dimension in the final reference to "other personal or social condition or circumstance". In any case, the reception of such rights at the constitutional level must be framed by the constitutional language, which, by attributing a legal status to some specific languages, legitimizes the recognition of specific rights and duties in relation to them. This different meanings derive from the Statute of Autonomy of Catalonia (SAC), where the non-discrimination principle is linked to official languages in Articles 6.2 ("All persons have the right to use the two official languages and citizens of Catalonia have the right and the duty to know them…In keeping with the provisions of Article 32, there shall be no discrimination on the basis of use of either of the two languages") and recognized with a more general scope in Article 32 "Each individual has the right not to be discriminated against for linguistic reasons". In Spanish linguistic internal debate the non-discrimination principle has not had a very prominent judicial role. As example, Constitutional Court has declared not been violated Article 14 by the education system education –applied in Catalonia and other autonomous communities- where official language of instruction is not determined by individual languages of pupils (CC Sentence 337/1994).

The human right of freedom of expression (Articles 19 ICCPR and 10 ECHR) presents also a linguistic dimension. Where constitutional or legal provisions retain the official status of one or more language the use of these can be subject to internal rules of law in public spheres and, under certain conditions, in private spheres. In this way, the official status of a given language legitimizes the obligatory nature of its use in the public service and in education, as well as the requirements for linguistic qualification for public agents. Diversely, freedom of expression stands out as a limit for constrictive linguistic interventions in the private sphere that must be adopted under the conditions required on the limits to freedom of expression [7]. Also with regard the right to access to the mass media, freedom of expression is configured broadly but it is a relative -rather than an absolute- right whose scope must be balanced so that this freedom can coexist with other values and rights that also deserve protection [8].

The right to private life involves also a linguistic content that tend to reduce the possibilities of limiting freedom of linguistic expression when privacy, family, home or correspondence is affected. In the European system, this right is conceived in quite broad terms, which reach the individual self-determination which is deemed necessary in order to lead a decent life [9]. Courts have prevented public authorities from conditioning the individual linguistic option set out in the individual or familiar private sphere. Spanish Constitutional Court (CC), as example, argues fundamental right to family privacy (Article 18 SC) to cover the right to communicate with family in Basque language, in the case of an inmate subject to the penitentiary regime (Sentence 201/997, of 25th November).

Right to private life also includes the right to choose a personal name, without idiomatic restrictions. The ONU traditional approach to the right to have a name (art. 24(2) ICCPR) is based on the interest to identify a person, whereby the imposition of legal restrictions justified by reasons of public interest –including linguistic ones- is expressly admitted. In the European context, EctHR shows another perspective when balancing the states' public interest in naming, such as the preservation of a national name practice related with the preservation of the cultural and linguistic identity of a given country, with the right of parents to choose a name for their children in a non-official language, that in the case must prevail [10]. A similar evolution is seen in the Spanish Context, where legislation on naming has evolved to a more liberal approach, and existing legal limitations tend to be interpreted restrictively, by contrast with a past not far where only Castilian names were admitted [11].

Another linguistic right, directly specified by international law, is that everyone who is arrested or accused of a crime shall be informed, is a language which he or she understands, of the reasons for his arrest and the nature and cause of the accusation against him, and have the free assistance of an interpreter if he cannot understand the language of the authorities (art. 9(2) and 14 (3) ICCPR and art. 5(2) and 6(3) ECHR). As individual human right, the protected interest is the right to a fair trial of persons seeking justice or the detained who do not speak or understand the language used by the state authorities. The same right, but with different grounds, is formulated as a minorities' right to use their language before the administration of justice (art. 10(3) FCPNM). The first linguistic right is, probably, the only human linguistic rights with a general reception by state's legislation (normally, by legislation on criminal proceedings). An interesting judicial case where both dimensions –individual and collective- of this rights seems to have been considered, was the recognition by a central Spanish court (*Audiencia Nacional*) of the right of defendants of Spanish nationality, but Catalan-speaking people, to testify in their mother tongue in criminal proceeding, even if these proceedings are conducted outside of the territories where the Catalan language is official and regardless of whether they understand the language of the state [12].

Finally, the linguistic content of the right of education is one the most controverted issues, due the vagueness and ambiguity of the existent international instruments. The Convention on the Rights of the Child, approved in 1989, establishes that education should be aimed at instilling into the child the respect "for his or her own cultural identity, language and values" (art. 29). This clause discredits the homogenizing linguistic-school policies and models, which ignore or underestimate the child's language. Other general instruments (as example, Article 13 of the International Covenant on Economic, Social and Cultural Rights, ICESCR), doesn't identify any linguistic dimension of the education right. In Spain, legal doctrine has identified as the basic content of the right, on the basis of international law and comparative law, the right to receive the education in a language that results understandable by pupils [13]. But only in international instruments regarding minorities can be found, in that field, the formulation of concrete positive obligations for the states.

2.2. The Protection of Linguistic Minorities

Language is an essentially collective phenomenon, which not only serves the purpose of communication but also the safeguarding and creation of collective identities. The connection between linguistic rights and the models of minority protection systems is therefore of special relevance. At the same time, some of the vagueness and weaknesses of the current systems of protection of minorities (although certain binding rules exists at the universal and European levels, this protection is partially included in non-binding dispositions) show their effects in the linguistic field. Specially, an open question remains in the international sphere about the definition of *linguistic minorities,* a term used by some European constitutions (as example, in Italy or Eastern countries), but refused by others (as Finland or Spain). The related concept used in the European regional system is that of *national minorities,* in which the linguistic dimension is included (for instance, the Preamble of the FCPNM mentions the respect of the "ethnic, cultural, linguistic and religious identity of each person belonging to a national minority"), but not necessary as a determining factor of the particular group identity.

According to Article 27 ICCPR, the main international norm regarding the minority status:

> "In those states in which ethnic, religious or linguistic minorities exists, persons belonging to such minorities shall not be denied the right, in community with the other members of their group, to enjoy their own culture, to profess and practice their own religion, or to use their own language."

The right of the members of the minority to use their own languages is broader than the individual right to use the language derived from the non-discrimination principle and human rights (see *supra* 2.1). The international action for the protection of minority groups is conceived as a new dimension of human rights, basically focusing on their protection from the perspective of non-discrimination [14]. In that sense, in spite of its negative formulation ("shall not be denied"), Article 27 ICCPR does not only entail the public authorities' obligation to refrain from establishing unjustified differences, but it also includes a sense of positive equality in reference to the protection and promotion of the linguistic and cultural identity of the minority. Human Rights Committee states that the concrete content of this minorities rights depend on the minority group's capacity to preserve their language, to the extent that

> "measures by states may also be necessary to protect the identity of a minority and the rights of its members to enjoy and develop their culture and language (…) in community with the other members of the group (…) as long as those measures are aimed at correcting conditions which prevent or impair the enjoyment of the rights guaranteed under article 27, they may constitute a legitimate differentiation under the Covenant, provided that they are based on reasonable and objective criteria" [15].

A cornerstone of the Human Rights Committee doctrine is that the presence of minorities for the purpose of the application of ICCPR does not depend upon their recognition by the state and the applicability of the protective measures set out by this precept is general in all those states in which minorities exist. The situation of the languages spoken by this minorities can be of two types: first, a situation of non-recognition of its official status by internal legislation, that implies been protected substantially through international provisions; and second, the recognition of the incidence of minority rights in the sphere of official status, traditionally conceived as a State' sovereign decision [16]. In Spain, the capacity of international provisions to influence an internal decision in terms of recognition of an official status to all Spanish languages spoken in different autonomous communities (as example, Asturian in the autonomous community of the Principality of Asturias or Catalan in Aragon) has been neglected by Constitutional Court, as example in recent Sentence 56/2017, 17th Mars, related to the legal of Aragon.

Regarding the scope and content of linguistic rights of minorities, a more complete enumeration of these rights can be found in the FCPNM and especially in the 1998 Oslo Recommendations regarding the linguistic rights of national minorities by the OSCE High Commissioner on National Minorities. Both instruments specify the areas of projection of the right to use a language and the positive measures that the states must apply to guarantee they are exercised by members of minorities [17]. As regards the right to use the language in the public sphere, it directly protects the linguistic interactions that take place in the public (or external) space, among people belonging to the minority or in the presence of other people, through the circulation of publications and the commercial signs, *e.g. via* private media or in the framework of public meetings. The use of the minority languages in dealing with the public authorities is not generally assured –particularly where the language lacks internal legal recognition- but it is usually conditioned by the existence of a demand and a significant number of speakers (Article 10.2 FCPNM) [18]. And with regard to education, the presence of the minority language at school is guaranteed by a double alternative possibility: enabling the pupils to learn the language or establishing its vehicular use in teaching. Some international texts also include a right for the minority to create private schools in which their own language is taught or used. Other linguistic rights of members of national minorities cover the following areas: people's first name and surnames; practicing religion; setting up of non-governmental associations and organizations; creation of own media sources and presence in publicly-owned media; private companies; and penitentiary institutions.

In any case, considering this international framework from the perspective here adopted, that is the interrelationship between international legislation and domestic law, the practical consequences on the Spanish legal system appear very limited and disappointing. On one hand, the official status recognized under 3.2 SC to of Catalan, Basque and Galician languages in most of their traditional territory reduces the potential of this protective focus (and, as said before, the Constitutional Court doesn't support the doctrinal opinion that derives from the protection of minorities some implications in terms of the recognition of a legal official status to this languages in some autonomous communities where they don't enjoy it). The ratification by the Kingdom of Spain of the FCPNM doesn't refer to this languages for the purpose of the commitments assumed in Article 10[ ], according to the interpretation of existing national minorities made by state authorities. In that sense, and answering the explanations that had been required by Council of Europe about the role of language as a fundamental element of the identity of "peoples of Spain" (Preamble) or "nationalities" (art. 2) referred to in the Spanish Constitution, the Spanish government answer was:

> "However, there is in any event in the Spanish legal-political reality a concept of people as an entity as such, with differentiated characteristics if ethnicity, religion or identity (...) the populations of the various Autonomous Communities have in common the existence of historical-cultural and linguistic links, but there are not significant ethnic components."

As a result of this restrictive vision of the scope of the FCPNM in its application to Spain reality, the only one minority included in the Convention is the Gipsy community, despite acknowledging that it does not constitute a national minority. The Autonomic State (that is the decentralization or articulation of the state into autonomous communities) remains as the main basis of the linguistic protection system (see below 3). The Spanish government comments on the application of this instruments also stress the inclusion of autonomous communities in the Spanish nation, rejecting the conception of a State including a plurality of nations. And finally added, with reference to the next international model of protection here examined (see 2.3), that "In linguistic terms, the Spanish state complies with the protection established in the European Charter for Regional and (sic) Minority Languages, duly signed and ratified by Spain."[ ] Indeed, although the official status of Catalan, Basque and Galician grants some superior linguistic protection, the recognition as national minorities would enable to subject to international scrutiny the treatment that minority linguistic groups receive from the State [19].

2.3. The Protection of Linguistic Diversity

As mentioned above, in the 1990' international law incorporated new avenues to the linguistic matters and the protection of linguistic interests is set within the protection of cultural rights and languages as an expression of cultural heritage. In this context, emphasis is made in principles of democracy and pluralism that foster the protection and promotion of different languages (see, for instance, the ECRML Preamble). The concepts of *linguistic diversity* and *cultural diversity* take on greater relevance and are sanctioned by international text in a universal (UNESCO) and European context (firstly, in the Council of Europe, and later inside the European Union).

In the UNESCO, the 2005 Convention on Protection and Promotion of the Diversity of Cultural Expressions protects cultural policy measures applied by state authorities aimed at guaranteeing the presence of a certain language in cultural activities, goods and services. In concrete terms, second paragraph of Article 6 establish that measures aimed at protecting and promoting the diversity of cultural expressions in a given country (as example, the existence of different official languages or other languages legally protected), taking into account its particular circumstances and needs, may include the following: "b) measures that, in an appropriate manner, provide opportunities for domestic cultural activities, goods and services among all those available within the national territory for the creation, production, dissemination, distribution and enjoyment of such domestic cultural activities, goods and services, including provisions relating to the language used for such activities, goods and services". The scope of this provisions remains limited to this sectors, but expressed a major concern about the effects of globalization on the preservation of linguistic heritage and the cultural diversity.

In the Council of Europe, the European Charter for Regional or Minority Language (ECRML), nowadays the only multilateral treaty devoted to the protection of languages, stands out for the level of detail with which the positive measures to be adopted by the states are set, and also due to the design and dynamism of the international mechanisms for supervision and control provided [20]. A priori, these features enlarges the opportunities for the protection of regional or minority languages under this instrument, but the Charter voluntary ratification (as example, Italy and France, with an important linguistic heritage, haven't ratified yet, and in the last case a substantive contradiction with main constitutional principles is alleged by the Constitutional Council to do not this) and the implementation by states is subject to different constraints derived for their legal architecture and political position of different governments.

Conceptually, the Charter does not establish collective rights for linguistic communities, but rather duties for the protection of European linguistic diversity represented by regional or minority languages. However, as has been noted, the specific Charter orientation towards languages –and no to their speakers' rights- does not prevent that the cumulative action and a crossed interpretation of CMPN an ECRML drives to some European standards for protection of linguistic rights. Council of Europe, with this double approach, open new possibilities for the states to recognize individual and collective linguistic rights concerning their speakers, despite certain imbalances resulting from the different perspectives of both treaties [21].

The *regional* or *minority* languages -a conceptual distinction with no direct legal consequences- are defined as those that are "traditionally used within a given territory of a state by nationals of that state who form a group numerically smaller than the rest of the state's population (Article 1(a) ECRML). The concept of historicity is important in that context, but admits flexible interpretations [22]. The delimitation of the territorial area is in line with the presence of a number of specific language-speaking people justifying the adoption of the various protective and promotional measures provided for (Article 1.b ECRML). And it does not only include that territories in which the regional language persists as the majority language, but rather it can be extended to other areas in which it has traditionally been installed and it has become a minority language [23].

The structure of the Charter distinguishes basic protection based on Article 7 (Part II) and enables the states to shape the commitments assumed in the framework of Part III, whilst respecting the established minimum of 35 paragraphs. Kingdom of Spain ratified the Charter in 2001 [24]. The ratification formula used at that time refers to the languages recognized in the Statutes if Autonomy of the autonomous communities and provides the application of two levels of protection to the minority languages in presence: in the territories where the regional language is declared official, not only Part II is applied, but also the specific commitments taken on by Spain in the framework of Part III in the areas of education, judicial authorities, administrative authorities and public services, media, cultural activities and facilities, economic and social life, and transfrontier exchanges (Articles 8 to 14); in other territories where a statutory protected language exists, only Part II is applied, according to the interpretation given by Committee of Experts to the declarations contained in the instrument of ratification.

In the area of objectives and principles (Article 7 ECRML), a general commitment is made by the states to eliminate any restrictive measures, which have the objective of discouraging or endangering the use and development or regional and minority languages. The principle of non-discrimination is established by Article 7.2 ECRML also in its positive, discarding the discriminatory character of the "special measures in favor or regional or minority languages aimed at promoting equality between the users of these languages and the rest of the population, or which take due account on their specific conditions." The implications derived from Article 7 for states implies reviewing legal texts and administrative actions to that place minority or regional languages in a disadvantaged position. Furthermore, a mandate is established to promote understanding among all linguistic groups inside the state. The last aspect is underdeveloped in the Spanish context. Despite the positive assessment of the linguistic model in Spain, the Committee of Experts considers that:

> "More efforts therefore seem to be needed in education for the majority Castilian-speaking population and in the national media with a view to fostering a greater acceptance and respect by the majority vis-à-vis the specificities of regional identities as an integral part of the Spanish heritage. There is also a need to improve mutual understanding, with a view to promoting the virtues of plurilingualism and linguistic diversity and, in both majority and minority language groups, the fundamental idea of peaceful and harmonious co-existence"[25].

Secondly, the Charter establishes the objective of a resolute action to promote regional or minority languages, their teaching and study at all stages, their use in public and private life, the maintenance and development of links between groups using a regional or minority language and other groups in the state employing a language used in identical or similar form and the promotion of appropriate types of transnational exchanges. In all these aspects, the affirmative action or promotion policies developed by the autonomous communities –also called policies of *linguistic normalization*- become legitimated with additional international regulatory coverage. But also another transformative effect can be observed from this mandate concerning a larger conception of language policy in

Spain. In that sense, Spanish State authorities tend to interpret, and also expressly defend the idea, that the protection of the Spanish languages different from Castilian is a responsibility exclusively offload to the authorities of the autonomous communities where they receive an official status or other legal recognition [26]. This vision, that also affect the interpretation of third paragraph of Article 3 SC (see below 3.1), seems far from the comprehension of the Article 7 ECRML by the Committee of Experts charged of its interpretation.

Thirdly, another important general objective within the Charter is the respect of the geographical area of each regional or minority language in order to ensure that existing or new administrative divisions do not constitute an obstacle to the promotion of the regional or minority language in question. The legal-political fragmentation of the Basque-speaking and Catalan-speaking linguistic areas awards special interest to this provision. In the first, restrictive effects on the linguistic rights of internal linguistic divisions of the Community of Navarre have been repeatedly highlighted by the Council of Europe [27]. In the Catalan-speaking areas, the Council of Europe has questioned -albeit timidly- some of the consequences of secessionism policies promoting the development of Valencian as a language other than Catalan [28].

Concerning Part III of the Charter, the control process on the application of the Charter in Spain has enabled the Council of Europe to note certain shortcomings in the internal legislation and in the action of the public powers in order to guarantee compliance with the obligations assumed. In those aspects that affect the entire linguistic model and not only to particular regions –that we will examine later-, and regarding judicial authorities (Article 9 ECRML), the Council of Europe has noted that the compliance of the commitments would require the modification of the state legal framework to ensure it remains clear that the judicial authorities will carry out the procedures in the minority language on the request of any part involved in the process and the necessary legal and practical measures to ensure that a percentage of judges and magistrates –and also percentage of officers in the state administration in the autonomous communities concerned by Article 10 ECRML- have practical knowledge of that language [29]. However, to this date, the Spanish state has not made the above-mentioned reforms alleging the unity of the judiciary power and the mobility of the judicial staff as the main raison for this. This matter was raised before the Constitutional Court, that rejected the ignorance of the Basque language by the judges or magistrates infringe Articles 3.2 (official status of the language) and 24 (principle of immediacy) of the Spanish Constitution (CC Sentence 166/2005, 19 April 2005).

Finally, in the European Union, the process of drafting the Charter of Fundamental Rights of the EU at the turn of the century (1999-2000), allowed to highlight certain vagueness of the discourse within this organization. When defining the European commitment towards languages, finally embodied in Articles 21 (commandment of respect for linguistic diversity) and 22 (prohibition of discrimination on grounds of language) of the Charter, there were attempts to circumscribe its meaning and scope to the official languages or langue of the treaty, without including other European languages that also express this diversity [30]. Finally, the text adopted of Article 22 avoided the mention of "minority rights", as demanded by representatives of linguistic minorities during the debates, although with this does not preclude an interpretation of the mandate of respect for linguistic diversity in accordance with the standards of legal protection emanating from the Council of Europe. Some authors have observed in the process politicization of "linguistic diversity" (which also appears in Article 3 of the Treaty on the European Union, just after the guarantee of the market unity) important tactical reasons, as far as avoiding divisions between states members based on the language –due to its symbolic and political relevance- is seen as a condition to advance in the economic and political European integration [31]. Recent final judgment of the Court of European Union of 21th June 2016, on the legal protection in the field of commercial Dutch, exemplifies the subordination of linguistics interests to the prevailing economic integration objectives.

Concerning de positive consequences derived from the linguistic diversity for Spanish languages different from Castilian -the only with an official status at the UE level- a reference must be done to the Luxembourg European Council Conclusions of 13 June 2005. Under the mentioned principle, some limited official uses were recognized to Catalan, Basque and Galician, by means of administrative agreements between the State and concerned European institutions and bodies. The same Conclusions ratify the exclusion of these languages of the European legal system, with the argument that they were not languages of the treaties, as a previous condition to access and Regulation 1/1958 on the official languages of the UE.

3. THE PROTECTION OF LANGUAGE RIGHTS AND LINGUISTIC GROUPS UNDER THE SPANISH LEGISLATION

3.1. Constitutional and Statutory Provisions on the Spanish Languages

The Spanish Constitution establishes the official status of Castilian (referred as *Spanish* in international and European spheres) and specifies "the right to use and the duty to know" the language as contents inherent to this declaration (Article 3, first paragraph). The second paragraph of Article 3 SC provides that other Spanish languages shall also have official status in accordance with the corresponding 'Statutes of autonomy'. The *Statutes* are "the basic institutional legislation of the autonomous community" (Article 147 SC), and may be considered similar to sub-state or regional constitutions, with a legal rank of state organic law, which is directly subordinate to the Constitution and subject to a special process of reform (Article 81 SC).

During the 1980s, the Catalan language has been declared official by the Statutes of Autonomy of three autonomous communities (Catalonia, Balearic Islands and the Community of Valencia), the Basque language in other two autonomous communities (Basque Country and Navarre, in the last restricted in the Basque-speaking area and mixed area) and Galician in the autonomous community of Galicia. The Occitan language, in its *Aranese* variety, has been declared official more recently by the 2006 Statute of Autonomy of Catalonia [32].

For its part, Article 3.3 SC determines that "the richness of different *linguistic forms* in Spain is a cultural heritage and shall be protected and respected in a special way". Default of a unanimous doctrinal interpretation, this paragraph covers all the Spanish languages, including their dialectal variations. Simultaneously, the legal protection of some official languages within the territories where the language does not have an official status (*e.g.* Catalan in the east of the Autonomous Community of Aragon), but also other languages (*e.g.* Asturian/Bable, language recognized by the Statute of Autonomy of Asturias) or traditional linguistic varieties (Leon or Andalusian, as linguistic varieties of Castilian protected by Statutes of Autonomy of Castile and Leon and Andalusia, respectively) spoken in some parts of Spain that do not have an official status must be included under the protection of third paragraph of Article 3.

However, in the framework of Article 3.2 SC, and after Franco's Dictatorship (1939-1975) where these languages were banished from official and public spheres, a mere declaration of the official status of languages other than Castilian Spanish was on its own wholly insufficient to reverse this historical situation. In all this historical past, covering the constitutional period (that begins in Spain in 1812), the use of Spanish languages other than Castilian was at certain times simply tolerated or also expressly banned. Only during the brief Second Republic (1931-1939) Catalan, and in a way much more limited Euskera and Galician, had some official uses in legislation, administration or jurisdiction. For that, the term *linguistic normalization* recall a process that "involves the adoption of a series of legislative, administrative measures, applicable at different moments in time, aimed at promoting a specific language that is considered to suffer from discrimination and/or requires special protection - or which, in any case, find itself in a disadvantageous or undesirable situation- by the legislator."[33]

Linguistic legislation was initially passed in the early 1980s by autonomous communities (Catalonia, Community of Valencia, Balearic Islands, Galicia, Basque Country and Navarra). This legislation recognize specific linguistic identities linked to the 'own' languages and try –with different degrees of political commitment- to guarantee an equal status for both official languages. To reach this objective, fostering the knowledge of the local language between population and its social uses in strategic public sectors, such as education, autonomous and local administrations and the media, was imperative. The majority of this laws adopted by autonomous communities during 1980s is still in force, but their implementation has not always been consistent, especially when the political majorities in the regional government are not favorable to the normalization discourse and neglect the adoption of the political and administrative measures needed to promote the use and learning of the language.

Only in Catalonia (but not in other political regions) a second stage in the normalization process is clearly distinguishable, under the linguistic legislation passed in 1990s (Catalan Language policy Act of 1998) and the 2006 Statute of Autonomy. These norms try to extent the promotion of the use of Catalan in less normalized sectors, in particular the peripheral state administration, the judiciary power and the socio-economic sector. This new legislation also addresses new phenomena as the immigration or technological changes. Specially in that case, when legislative or administrative measures are specified in such a number of relevant social sectors (including labeling, advertising or linguistic requirements for public employees), the normalization process is more exposed to criticism. In most cases, such critical discourses came from a position of monolingual predominance, in a general framework where the State agents and institutions operate only in Castilian [34]. But, in general terms, the need for this type of special measures, concerning languages that have been historically marginalized in their own territory, is confirmed by Part II of the European Charter for Regional or Minority Languages: "The adoption of special measures in favor of regional or minority languages aimed at promoting equality between the users of these languages and the rest of the population or which take due account of their specific conditions is not considered to be an act of discrimination against the users of more widely-used languages" (Article 7.2 of the Charter).

3.2. Legislations on Catalan Language in Various Regions

Catalan language regime is fragmented in different legal-linguistic systems in various Spanish regions (and also in the south of France and the Italian population of Alghero). Such distinct legislations derives from the political territorial organization of the *Autonomic State*, where the same autochthonous language is spoken in different Autonomous Communities. This legal and administrative fragmentation can have some negative impacts in terms of cohesion of the linguistic groups and coherent action to promote regional or minority languages in order to safeguard them, as it was pointed when analyzing the application of the ECRML in Spain. In this section we will discuss synthetically the concrete legislation on the Catalan language (spoken in four regions) approved by Autonomous Parliaments and its jurisprudential application. In that exam we will distinguish a region where the Catalan language has not an official status (*a*) [35] from other territories with two official languages (*b* to *d*).

a) Aragon has a traditionally speaking Catalan are in the eastern part of its territory. According to the Statute of Autonomy (SAA), amended in 1996, "the languages and linguistic forms native to Aragon shall enjoy protection" and "their teaching and the speaker's right to use them shall be guaranteed in the manner established by a law of the Parliament of Aragon in the regions in which they are predominantly used" (Article 7). Catalan and Aragonese, although not explicitly mentioned, were the languages concerned by this statement. A new statutory reform on 2007 reinforces the mandate to legislator by stating that it shall regulate "the speakers' rights" to use the language in those regions and it shall favor "the use of local languages in the relations between Aragonese citizens and public administrations" (new Article 7.2 SAA).

Prior to the legislative development of this Statutory provisions, Law 3/1999, of 10 March, on cultural heritage, identifies Catalan and Aragonese in its final provision as the "own languages of Aragon". In spite of the repeated demands of public and social instances, and after several recommendations of the Council of Europe in the monitoring cycles on the application of Charter in Spain, the first general linguistic law approved by Autonomous Parliament was Aragonese Law 10/2009, of 22 December, on the use, protection and promotion of Aragon's own languages. The progressive approach of this Law implies that some linguistic rights to use Catalan an Aragonese were recognized in relationships with local administrations in their "areas of predominant historical use" or "mixed areas". But only three years after, and without practical advances on the situation of the minority languages of Aragon, Popular Party gained autonomous elections and abrogated previous legislation by the Aragonese Law 3/2013, of 9 May, on the use, protection and promotion of languages and linguistic modalities of Aragon.

The Law 3/2013, still in force, has been criticized from all political and social sectors that support the normalization of Catalan and Aragonese. In the first place, the name of the languages different from Castilian are eliminated and substitute by a cardinal geographical identification (as example, Catalan is now in the Law the "Aragonese language near the Eastern area" of the Autonomous Community), which should be put in relation with the aim of enabling a secessionist policy toward Catalan. Secondly, individual rights were absent from the new Law. Thirdly, the Law contains only general and ambiguous mandates of promotion, which in practice have not been applied during the last two years. The 2013 Law was appealed of unconstitutionality by the Spanish Socialist Party alleging that it undermines the prior legal protection of Catalan (and Aragonese), threatens legal certainty principle and violates the ECRML. The Constitutional Court reject this type of argumentation and confirms the constitutionality of this regressive legislation (Constitutional Court Sentence 56/2016, 17 of Mars), but new political majorities emerging after regional elections of May 2015 may facilitate a return to the linguistic principles inspiring the legislation adopted in 2009.

b) The legal situation of the 'own' language in the Community of Valencia remains substantially unchanged after the entry in force of the Article 7 of Statute of Autonomy of the Community of Valencia (SACV 1983) and Valencian Law 4/1983, of 18 April, for the use an teaching of Valencian (LUTV). Under Article 3.2 SC, Valencian and Castilian have recognized an official status in this region, the first subjected to territorial modulations in the internal geographical area traditionally Castilian-spoken (that means that Valencian can be excluded from the teaching and administrative use in this part).

In general terms, the *normalization* aim of the LUTV seems much more limited than in other Autonomous Communities (as Catalonia or Balearic Islands), despite of the political will –as stated in the Preamble of the Law- "to restore *our language* to the category and place it deserves, bringing an end to the situation of neglect and deterioration in which it finds itself." Historical roots of the general legal situation can be found in the identity conflict that precedes the creation of the Autonomous Community (the so called *"batalla de València)*, including political cleavages that reaches the language, the symbols and the name of this community. In legislative terms, in the LUTV, on the one hand, Valencian and Castilian tend to be treated on equal footing, as example in education or linguistic rights of use (Articles 17 and 19 LUTV); but, on the other hand, some provisions recognizes Valencian as the object of special promotion action (Articles 25 or 27 LUTV), or recognize its singular position in local administrations in stating that Valencian "is also the language" of these administrations. Castilian seems favored by other provisions, as example when legislator establishes that regional government will encourage the teaching of Valencian to civil servants (Article 30 LUTV), which, therefore, were not obliged to know this language, but were constitutionally obliged to know Castilian (Article 3.1 SC). The main point is, however, the absence of a consistent and continuous political will, expressed through the necessary normative and administrative measures to apply the different kind of legal provisions.

The 2006 reform of the Statute of Autonomy doesn't mean a real shift from the first Statute of 1982. According to Article 6, first paragraph, Valencian is defined as "Valencia's *own language*". This reference hasn't have, in the Valencian legislative context, the same consequences as in other regions. Otherwise, it is primordially connected with the controversial political question on the unity of the Catalan language or its segregation in a new language. The linguistic unity is pacific in the academic sphere (where was ratified by Constitutional Court Sentence 75/1997, of 21 April, about the equipollence between the official name 'Valencian' with its the academic denomination as 'Catalan'), and even the Valencian Academy of the Language -created by Valencian self-government institutions-, has defined Valencian as a variety of the Catalan language [36]. But political discourse and administrative actions had continued to focus on the question of the language identity [1], with scarce measures for linguistic normalization (basically economic subsidies for local administrations and some social and academic entities) and a certain degree of political and institutional neglect during most of the democratic period. Similar to what happened in Aragon, the regional elections of May 2015, which put an end to over a decade of government of the Popular Party in Valencia, seem to offer new opportunities for the normalization of the local language. As a significant symbol, the new socialist president delivered in Valencian his first discourse, and its new political project includes to reopen the autonomous television in Valencian (that was closed during the previous political mandate) and to regulate linguistic requirements for civil servants.

c) In the Balearic Islands the legal system of the Catalan language derives from the Statute of Autonomy of 1983 (SABI) and Balearic Law 3/1986, of 29 April, for the linguistic normalization of the Balearic Islands (LLNIB). The current Article 4 of the Statute (reformed in 2007) stated that Catalan as the 'own' language of the Balearic Islands, together with Castilian, shall have the status of official language and that everybody has the right to know and use Catalan. It also maintains the provision, according to which "the institutions of the Balearic Islands shall guarantee the normal and official use of both languages, take the necessary measures to ensure the knowledge of them, and create the conditions that allow the full equality of both languages with regard to the rights of the citizens of the Balearic Islands" (art. 4 (3) SABI). Other linguistic provisions can be found in Articles 35 (Education), 97 and 99 SABI (knowledge of Catalan as a preferential merit for access to posts of judges and magistrates, notaries and public registrars). In 2007 were added to Article 35 of the Statute the forms or *modalities* of Catalan, based on a geographical reference to the islands, which "have to be object of study and protection, without prejudice to the unity of the language".

The 1986 Balearic Law of Normalization proposes a sector-based objective to implement the progressive and normal use of Catalan in the official and administrative domains, to guarantee the knowledge and progressive use of Catalan as a vehicular language in teaching, to promote the use of Catalan in all domains of social communication and to increase social awareness of the importance of its knowledge and use by all citizens (Art. 1.2 LLNBI). The text sets out the linguistic rights and their protection by the courts, as well as the regulation of the Catalan language in the administration, education and the media, among others.

During the autonomic period, the Balearic linguistic policy in the action to promote the use of Catalan language was fluctuant depending on the government majority. Under the early governments of the People's Party, even though the law of normalization was passed, linguistic policy neglected its duties to a certain extent. One important factor was the absence of autonomous powers for education, only granted in 1996, when the so-called *decree of minimums* adopted the model of linguistic conjunction, aimed at ensuring that at last 50 per cent of education was in Catalan (a percentage that could be increased by the school board at each education establishment, according to the normalizing aim). During the periods1999-2003 and 2007-2011 centre-left governments introduce new and more decided linguistic provisions in sector-based laws: by way of example, Balearic Law 3/2003, on autonomous administration (articles 43 and 44); Law 5/2003 on Health; and Law 11/2001 governing commercial activity. From mid-2003 to 2007 Popular Party passed legislation covering education and public office that, in a different way, doesn't favors the normalizing process.

Before the regional elections of May 2015 returned the regional government of leftist parties, the situation worsened during the last government of Popular Party (2011-2015), which promoted a clearly regressive set of legal and administrative measures concerning the official status of Catalan: in education, the introduction of a controversial trilingual model (Balearic Decree 15/2013), which was contested by massive street demos and prolonged strikes by primary and secondary teachers; in local and regional administrations, the elimination of the linguistic requirement for the majority of public employees (Law 9/2012, of 19th July, on the regional civil service); the abrogation of previous linguistic guarantees for consumers in an economic context driven by high taxes of immigration from the rest of Spain and other European countries and tourism activity (Law 11/2014, of 15th October on commercial activity); and the decreased use of Catalan in public media. Some of this norms were successfully challenged before courts for violating the Statute of Autonomy and the Law of linguistic normalization (*e.g.* the Decree on trilingualism), but other were sanctioned by the Spanish Constitutional Court (the elimination of the linguistic requirement was accepted by CC Sentence 165/2103, of 26 September). The new leftist government has repeal last linguistic rules, returning to prior legislation concerning administrations and trying to discuss with the participation of education community the reforms required by the educational model.

d) In Catalonia, linguistic legislation has evolved in different stages according to the *normalizing* aim. Article 3.3 of the 1979 Statute of Autonomy of Catalonia (SAC) describes normalization as a process which must culminate in full equality as far as linguistic rights and obligations of the citizens of Catalonia are concerned. Afterwards, Catalan Act 7/1983, of 18 April, for normalization (LLNC) states in its Preamble that "the reestablishment of Catalan to its rightful place as the own language of Catalonia is an irrefutable right and obligation of the Catalan people, which must be respected and protected". And it continues: "For this reason this Law proposes to overcome the current linguistic inequality by promoting the normalization of the use of Catalan throughout Catalonia." The content of this Law, similar to other texts passed during the 80', focused this action in education, public administration and public media, and regulates certain forms of language political promotion. The Constitutional Courts, in Sentence 337/1994, of 23rd December, describes the Catalan legislator general aim:

> "to guarantee respect for and encourage the use of the local and joint-official language for the Autonomous Community and, to this end, to remedy in a positive way a historical situation of inequality regarding Castilian Spanish. Thus it allows, in a progressive way and within the demands imposed by the Constitution, an increased knowledge and use of the aforesaid language in this region" (SCC 337/1994).

Another important judgment, in the CC Sentence 46/1991, 28th February, declares that the 'normal' use of Catalan on the part of the Catalan institutions was compatible with the Spanish Constitution, provided this option does not exclude the possibility of using the other official language, and acknowledges the citizens' freedom of choice.

The new LPL reaffirms, in its preamble, the objective of "consolidation of the statutory commitment to reach full equality in terms of linguistic rights and obligations. In particular, those of knowing both official languages and using them". The first chapter of this norm includes a legal definition of the concepts "*own* language" and "official language" (art. 2 and 3), and a first list the citizens' linguistic rights and duties (art. 4). Next chapters regulates the classical sectors yet included in LNL, but also other areas where the presence of the Catalan language progress very slowly, as the judicial power, leisure or advertising [37].

The 2006 reform of the Statute of Catalonia (Organic Law 6/2006, of 19 July 2006), which has been defined as a third stage in that normalization process, was adopted with the aim of consolidating this previous linguistic. For that, Article 6, first paragraph, includes definitions on the main legal notions, as Catalan as the Catalonia's 'own' language, in stating: "As such, Catalan is the language of normal and preferential use in Public Administration bodies and in the public media of Catalonia, and is also the language of normal use for teaching and learning in the education system". Other significant provisions refer to the enumeration of linguistic rights and duties (in chapter III of its first title, devoted to citizens' rights and duties), including the duty to know both official languages, for which "the public authorities of Catalonia shall establish the necessary measures to enable the exercise of these rights and the fulfillment of this duty. In keeping with the provisions of Article 32, there shall be no discrimination on the basis of use of either of the two languages" (Article 9, second paragraph). According to the special nature of the Statute of Autonomy, formally adopted for Spanish parliament, also some provisions concerning State public administration and justice, as sectors where the improvements of the normalization process had found more difficulties, were adopted in the context of the new Statute (see Articles 33.4 and 102). Finally, Article 6, paragraph 5, of the new Statute establishes the official status of the Aranese, previously recognized by Catalan legislation, with this terms: "The Occitan language, known as Aranese in Aran, is Aran's own language and is official in Catalonia, as established by this *Statute* and by the acts of linguistic normalization".

3.3. Recent Jurisprudence and Pending Issues before the Constitutional Court in Linguistic Matters

The new Catalan Statute of Autonomy was the result of a complex reform proceeding with the intervention of Autonomous and State parliaments and a final referendum by the people of Catalonia. Near half of the linguistic provisions proposed by the Parliament of Catalonia were amended by the State Parliament when passing the Statute [38]. After the entry into force in August 2006, the SAC was subject of two appeals alleging general unconstitutionality filed by People's Party and the Spanish Ombudsman (*Defensor del Pueblo*), which affected a similar percentage of its linguistic provisions.

Constitutional Court Sentence 31/2010, dated 28 June 2010, which ruled on the appeal submitted by People's Party, declared unconstitutional a number of important statutory provisions and interpreted in a restrictive way key aspects of the Catalan Statute as political and administrative powers, financial aspects and community definition of Catalonia as a nation. These consequences must be linked to the general position recognized to Statute of Autonomy, previously defined by CC as a crucial legal instrument in the configuration of the matters regulated by Article 3.2 SC (Sentence 247/2007), that also contributes to definition of the Spanish model of "linguistic pluralism" (Sentence 82/1986) [39]. Diversely, with a very more restrictive approach to the scope of this norm in the linguistic field, its role seems now limited to concrete the effects of the official status of Catalan inside the Autonomous Community. In fact, in last Sentence Statute of Autonomy is treated more like a regional or autonomous linguistic norm, neither than a nearly 'constitutional' legal instrument concerning the definition of the decentralization territorial model and the linguistic pluralism as one of the main features. Within the described conceptual framework, CC expands the scope of its control (opposite to a principle of self-restraint) and interpretatively manipulates the meaning of certain linguistic statutory provisions, discard preventively certain interpretations of other precepts and uses ambiguous terms to fix the limits affecting future legislations in linguistic matters. In doing that, CC tends to introduce legal insecurity for lawmaking bodies and political and administrative actors that affect some basic grounds of the linguistic (see below).

In the same ruling, CC declares unconstitutional the Article 6.1. SAC clause "and preferential", directed to describe some effects of the definition of Catalan as the "own language". Under this decision one can see the influence of Spanish doctrinal sectors, opposed to the Statutory reform, that defend Castilian the as shared or common language (in fact, a concept non explicit in SC) and argue against a territorial linguistic model grounded upon the concept of the 'own' language. Actually, this concept belongs to a long legal tradition in Catalonia (since it came from the *Interior Statute* of 1933, a Catalan basic law adopted during the Second Republic), where it retains a triple meaning: Catalan as an element of the collective identity of Catalonia (which is linked to Article 5 SAC, by proclaiming the historical rights of Catalonia with regard to language); a mandate to use this language in the Catalan institutional spheres; and the expression of the political will to normalize the Catalan language.

This legal conception seems far from the Sentence 31/2010 reduced vision about the 'own language' legal notion. First, in equating it with the "peculiar or primitive language of Catalonia, in contrast to Spanish, a language shared with all the autonomous communities", without taking into account that is also shared with other communities inside the sate (see 3.2). Second, trying to identify this concept with a conditioning or limiting element of discretion of the statutory lawmaker, which can only declare language that coincides with the history of a region as a second official language (but without convening of the necessity, deriving from this argument, to declare official this languages in communities like Aragon, were Catalan, as one of the "own languages" doesn't enjoy of this character); and third, with the attempt to reduce the notion to a descriptive character of a "reality of normal and habitual use". In fact, with the aim of devaluating the legal effects of this notions, Sentence 31/2010 seems to partially identify it with the separate notion of official status, by saying: "The definition of Catalan as the 'own language of Catalonia' cannot entail an imbalance in the constitutional of co-official status of both languages at the expenses of Castilian".

Until now, the concrete consequences of this interpretative and nullifying statements of the Sentence 31/2010 are not clear, but their impact rest evident in the increased linguistic conflict, in an scenario where all the new laws adopted by Catalonia's Parliament after 2006 (concerning the education sector, immigration, consumers rights and the Aranese language) are applied before the Constitutional Court; and also visible in the interpretative shift in a more restrictive jurisprudence concerning legal measures with a normalization aim.

In the later sense, two relevant examples, concerning linguistic rights and duties in public administrations and education, serve to illustrate this recent jurisprudential evolution. In the first domain, CC Sentence 31/2010 endorses the constitutionality of the principle of language proficiency of civil servants as a consequence of the citizens' linguistic right to choose the official language used in the relationship with public institutions located in the territory of the Autonomous Community. But the link established between language rights and language duties for officials appears weakened in this jurisprudence (in contrast with precedent CC Sentence 46/1991), as statutory precepts that formulate linguistic rights (Articles 33 and 102 SAC) are endowed with a "declarative nature as a constitutionally inherent consequence of co-official status", with the striking assertion of "the exclusive and excluding competence" of the state legislator concerning state and judiciary servants (see the contrast with previous CC Sentence 56/1990).

These restrictive interpretations of the CC have expanded to other territories where a double official status of Catalan and Castilian. For example, in Sentence 165/2013, regarding Balearic Act 9/2012 which eliminated the general requirement for a specific level of knowledge of Catalan for getting a job in the Balearic civil service, the CC did not detect any cause for unconstitutionality, because the aforementioned legislative change took place in a context of "the development of a widespread knowledge of Catalan in the region's civil service and in society", and "because there exist no cases where Spanish has been granted preferential treatment over Catalan." At the same time, the Constitutional Court ruling expressly called for "achieving full equality between the two languages" [Catalan and Spanish]. But, as warned by the dissenting opinions formulated by some constitutional magistrates, this decision deprive linguistic rights of guarantees in the case of those citizens who intend to make use of Catalan before public administration.

Also regarding the administrative use of languages, the CC Sentence 31/2010 contained ambiguous statements when constitutionally interprets Article 50.5 of the Statute of Autonomy: "The Generalist, the local administration and other public corporations in Catalonia, the institutions and companies answerable to them and the franchisees of their services, shall use Catalan for their internal proceedings and for relations among themselves. They shall also use it in communications and notifications addressed to natural or legal persons resident in Catalonia, without prejudice to citizen rights to receive them in Castilian should they ask for this." The effects of these pronouncements of the CC have materialized in several judgments of the courts which nullify the regulatory provisions of local authorities that established the preferential or by default use of the Catalan language in its operation (Sentence of Supreme Court of 5 May 2015, regarding provincial Council of Lleida and Council of Girona).

In the second proposed example, education, the influence of Sentence 31/2010 on the jurisprudential shift concerning the legal position of the Catalan language is still more accentuate. Constitutional Court considered, when analyzing Article 6.1 (Catalan language "is the language usually used for instruction and learning in education") and Article 35 SAC (on the education language rights), that the stipulated 'usual' or 'normal' use of this language in education is legitimate as long as it is "equally declared for Spanish" and does not violate the ban on excluding Spanish as language of instruction. Although CC maintains in this judgment the main pillars of its previous jurisprudence (STC 337/1994), that denies the existence of a constitutional or fundamental right to receive instruction in one of the two official languages, at the same time adds, as a new limit, that public administrations "do not impede the free and effective exercise of the right to receive education in Castilian as the language of instruction and learning in education" when determining the language of instruction.

Based on this statements, the Spanish Supreme Court, on a jurisprudence which has been criticized by excessive jurisdiction, has understood that the doctrine of the Sentence 31/2010 implies a requirement for a certain percentage (in any case superior to that of a subject) of vehicular use of Castilian (see for all, Sentences of 23 and 28 April 2015). In response to individual requests of parents, under this reinterpretation of the Supreme Court, lower courts in Catalonia have forced several schools to provide 25 per cent of classes in Castilian for the whole group or class of students whose parents have asked for more Castilian. These resolutions do not understand that the requirement affects the whole education system. However, a new State Education Act (Organic Act 8/2013, of 9

December) intends to frame the Catalan educational linguistic model between two existing in other regions (separation model or model with similar percentages of use of each language) without taking into account the legal in force in Catalonia concerning education (Catalan Act 12/2009, 10 July, on education) and nor the requirements of the European Charter for Regional or Minority Languages but with the intention of guaranteeing the position of Castilian in this sphere based on an expansive interpretation of article 3.1 SC.

In the second sense, one of the law challenged before the CC is the Catalan Act 10/2010, of the 7th May, on reception for immigrants and returnee to Catalonia, was also challenged in the part related to the basic linguistic skills of this persons. Article 9 establishes that "the first reception service shall provide the training and resources needed to acquire basic skills in Catalan to people holding the right of access to first reception services and who do not speak the language, wherever possible through the Consortium for Language Normalization" (Article 9.2). According to the same Act, people holding the right of access to first reception services must acquire basic language skills in Catalan and Spanish, and that reception service previously offer Catalan language training and, once it has been completed, shall offer training to acquire basic skills in Spanish to those people who request or require it (it must be said that a large part of immigrants come from Latin America and know yet Castilian). The State Ombudsman (*Defensor del Pueblo)* has challenged this Law considering that establish a language –the appeal was also founded on the distribution of powers on immigration– contrary to CC Sentence 31/2010. In concrete, the appeal retain that regional legislator violates the official status of Castilian and tries to enshrine a constitutional imbalance to the detriment of this language, when establishes a priority in the use of Catalan over Spanish in administrative services for reception of immigrants; considers Catalan as the 'own' language of this services in relation to users; establishes absolute preference of Catalan over Spanish that the override any power of choice; and considers access to knowledge of Spanish as an option subject accreditation of prior knowledge of Catalan.

In front of these criticism, a different interpretation of the effects of CC Sentence 31/2010 in the immigration sector has been supported by the *Generalitat* of Catalonia [40]. From that vision, Act 10/2010 develops the characterization of Catalan as the 'own' language and doesn't impede, in stating that linguistic training begins in that language, its continuity in Castilian. Article 9, according to this interpretation, doesn't create any obstacle for immigrants to reach basic skills in Castilian, neither a discrimination or exclusion, when establishing a temporary priority as a proportionate measure for that a language as Catalan, that is subject to a normalization process. The statutory mandate for protection and dissemination of the Catalan language (Article 50.1 SAC: "The public authorities shall protect the Catalan language in all fields and sectors and shall foment its knowledge, use and dissemination") also supports this thesis. Further, the specific for immigration service allows the instrumental use of other non-official languages in information and training actions addressed to immigrants; and, as a voluntary option of regional legislature in the exercise of their competences, it can be justified by the current situation of disadvantage of the language Catalan in this area, and not only for historical reasons but by the demographic reality of migration flows (most immigrants even doesn't know, when they arrive at this territory, the existence of a second official language, different from the language of the State).

A second example of the current judiciary conflict affects consumers' language rights. Act 22/2010, of 20th June, on the Consumer Code of Catalonia, stipulate in its Article 128 the right of persons, in their consumer relationships: "to be served orally and writing in the official language they choose". This legal provision also stipulates some documents that can be asked by consumers in Catalan (as example, offers to buy, fixed information, contractual documents, information necessary for consumption or adhesion contracts).). This provisions were the object of two constitutional appeals, from deputies of the Popular Party and the Spanish Ombudsman, always founded in legal grounds of the Sentence 31/2010. In that field, concrete effects of the repeated ruling on language rights of consumers and users recognized by Article 34 SAC ("Each individual, in his or her capacity as a user or consumer of goods, products and services, has the right to be attended orally or in writing in the official language of his or her choice. Bodies, companies and establishments that are open to the public in Catalonia are bound by the obligation of linguistic availability within the terms established by law") remain controversial due the ambiguous and contradictory CC statements. The debate concerns the possibility and the legitimate extent of linguistic duties for private agents, as enterprises or other commercial establishments. In that sense, the *Generalitat* had considered that that provisions of the mentioned Article 128 of the Consumers Code "Partially delimit the scope of the right of linguistic attention (and therefore of the duty of availability, which acts as guarantee of the first) with respect to documentation and information in consumer relations", considering that the legal precept is covered by Article 34 SAC, when it provides for a subjective right that grants people the language option previously provided by the duty also provided in the same article [41].

Specific questions on the cinema consumer's rights arise around the Catalan Act 20/2010, of 7 July, on cinema, also challenged by the State government in several provisions that try to guarantee a similar offer in both official languages in Catalonia. Concretely, the provisions challenged establish some duties to cinematographic distributors and exhibitors with the aim to advance in the normalization of Catalan in this sector. The State argument of violating free enterprise of Article 38 SC does not take into account the clear disadvantage that conditions the use of the local language in cinema.

Finally, a third judiciary conflict touches the position of Occitan language, declared officially in Catalonia by SAC 2006 in its Article 6, paragraph 5. After been banned by contemporary Spanish legislation, since 1979 SAC all the linguistic laws in Catalonia deserve a special protection to Aranese. The legal situation evolved from recognizing the 'aranese speaking', to formally recognizing Aranese itself (LNL 1983) and the Occitan cultural background (LPL 1998) under an "official status" (SAC 2006). In that context, Catalan Act 25/2010 regarding Occitan language, called Aranese in Aran, regulates its official status and adopt this legislation to new undertakings derived from de ECRML (due to the Spanish ratification that cover provisions of the Part III of the Charter for all those language with an official status declared by the Statutes of autonomy). This Act was challenged before the Constitutional Court by State Government, always on the grounds of 31/2010 CC Sentence, in all those provisions that establish a "preferential" use of Aranese, as the own language of Aran, by local or autonomous public bodies operating in this territory (articles 2.3, 5.4, 5.7 and 6.5).

Pending a resolution of the CC on the Act 25/2010 (in the meantime, the Court has suspended the contested precepts), it must be note that before to that law, the preferential position of the Aranese language in public authorities of this territory derived indirectly from Article 7 LPL. The justification of this special treatment can be found in the weak social use and delicate position of this autochthonous language, that is also the object of Statutory mandates of promotion and dissemination of knowledge under 50.1 SAC (according to this precept, the same principles applied to Aranese) [42]. The current opposition of central Spanish authorities to this special legal treatment reaches also the provision that determines the preferred position of Aranese in administrative forms or documents that could be bilingual or trilingual forms. From this point of view, the obstructive attitude shown before the CC must be retained inconsistent or disproportionate to the objectives of protection sought by legislator.

In conclusion, the Spanish model of linguistic rights, which in principle conforms to international framework, is characterized in its practical development for an inconsistent use of international law, jurisprudential oscillations of courts and frequent political shortcomings, so depriving the languages other than Castilian of solid guarantees to advance in their normalization. This linguistic model remains under a constant tension between the center –resistant to leave the Castilian monolingualism from state institutions- and the periphery, that are a manifestation of most profound political tensions about the territorial model.

CONFLICT OF INTEREST

The author declares no conflict of interest, financial or otherwise.

ACKNOWLEDGEMENTS

Declared none.

REFERENCES

[1] See Pons-Parera E. International Legislation and the Basque Language. In: In Totoricagüena G., Urrutia, I; ed. The legal status of the Basque Language Today: One Language, Three Administrations, Seven Different Geographies and a Diaspora. Bilbao: Eusko Ikaskuntza-Sociedad de Estudios Vascos 2008: 74-75..

[2] See Pons-Parera E. Los derechos lingüísticos en el ámbito internacional y comunitario europeo. In: Pérez-Fernández JM, Ed. Estudios sobre el estatuto jurídico de las lenguas en España. Barcelona: Atelier 2006: pp. 65-86. See also Arzoz X. The Nature of Language Rights. Journal on Ethnopolitics and Minorities Issues in Europe 2007: 6..

[3] See Fabeiro P. El derecho a la lengua propia en el ordenamiento internacional y de la Unión Europea. Barcelona: Bosch Editor 2014..

[4] Human Rights Committee General Comment Number 18: Non-discrimination: 10/11/89, paragraph 7..

[5] Paz M. The Failed Promise of Language Rights: A Critique of the International Language Righs. Harvard Law Review 2013; 54, 1: 157-217..

[6] Kymlikca W, Patten A. Linguistic Rights from Political Theory. Cambridge: Cambridge University Press 2003; pp. 2-16..

[7] Human Rights Committee, Ballantyne, Davidson, McIntyre v. Canada, Communication Nos. 359/1989 and 385/1989, UN Doc CCPR/C/47/D/359 and 385/1989/Rev.1, of 31st March 1993, which considers Article 19 ICCPR applicable on language on commercial signs. More specifically, it requires that the limitations be established by law, that they pursue any of the objectives listed in Article 19 (3, a or b) ICCPR and that they are necessary in order to achieve the legitimate purpose established..

[8] See in this volume, Urrutia I. The right to access by non-dominant linguistic communities to the mass media..

[9] See inter alia ECfHR *Evans v. The U.K.*, Sec 4a., Judgment of 19th March 2006..

[10] ECfHR *Johansson v. Finland*, Sec. 4a., 6th September 2007. The progressive liberalisation of Spanish legislation in this matter has also reached the linguistic dimension through 1999 and 2007 reforms of the Act on Register of Births, Deaths and Marriages of 8th June 1957 (in force until July 15, 2015), which initially forced people to translate the personal names to Spanish..

[11] Pons-Parera E., Pou-Pujolràs A. Jurisprudència del Tribunal Suprem. Revista de Llengua i Dret/Journal of Language and Law 2013; 59: 15-19..

[12] Sentence of the Audiencia Nacional, Criminal section, 24th April, 2008. In the case, the accused use the Catalan language, which is an official language in the territory of certain autonomous communities in Spain, but it is not official in Madrid, where are located supreme courts..

[13] Milian A. Derechos lingüísticos y derecho fundamental a la educación. Un estudio comparado: Italia, Bélgica, Suiza, Canadá y España. Madrid: Civitas 1994..

[14] Francesco Capotorti pointed out in his classic study that "the struggle against discrimination, on the one hand, and the application of special measures aimed at the protection of minorities, on the other, are just two aspects of the same problem, that is, defending human rights." See Rights of Persons Belonging to Ethnic, Religious and Linguistic Minorities. Human Rights Series 5. New York: United Nations..

[15] Human Rights Committee. General Comment Number 23 on Article 27, 8th April 1994..

[16] Thornberry P. International Law and the Rights of Minorities. Oxford: Clarendon Press 1991, 199-200; Hernrard, K. Devising and Adequate System of Minority Protection. Individual Human Rights, Minority Rights and the Right to Self-Determination. The Hague: Kluwer Law International 2000, 170, 247..

[17] The participation of the people in the decision making regarding the adoption of policy at the state and regional levels is highlighted by Article 2(3) UN Declaration on Minorities..

[18] See De Varennes F. Language, Minorities and Human Rights. The Hague: Kluwe Law International 1996..

[19] See, as example, the matter raised by the Committee responsible for supervising compliance with the FCPNM on the proportionality of the Spanish authorities' measure in 2003 closing down of the Euskara language newspaper *Euskaldunon Egunkaria.* Consultative Committee, Opinion on Spain, paragraph 53, Document ACFC/INF/OP/I(2004)..

[20] According to Part IV of the Charter, state parties must submit periodical reports to the Secretary General of the Council of Europe, which are examined by a Committee of Experts charged to prepare the recommendations finally adopted by Committee of Ministers. See Nogueira A, Urrutia I, Vieytez E, Eds. Shaping Language Rights. Commentary on the European Charter for Regional or Minority Languages in light of Committee of Experts' evaluation. Strabourg: Council of Europe Publishing 2012. Documents on monitoring are available from http://www.coe.int/t/dg4/education/minlang/..

[21] See Fabeiro P. cit. *supra*, 141-170..

[22] See Vieytez E. Constitutions, Languages, Definitions and the European Charter for Regional or Minory Languages. Revista de Llengua i Dret/Journal of Language and Law 2009; 51: 251-252..

[23] Explanatory Report, paragraphs 59 and 60. http://conventions.coe.int..

[24] See the instrument of ratification in http://conventions.coe.int..

[25] In this regard see Committee of Experts' Report on Application of the Charter in Spain. 1st monitoring cycle, April 2005, General findings, paragraph T..

[26] This type of discourse vas mainly present in the Initial Periodical Report submitted by Spain in 2002..

[27] Committee of Experts' Report on Application of the Charter in Spain. 1st monitoring cycle, April 2005, paragrapf 64 to 74; and Committee of Expert's Report on Application of the Charter in Spain. 3st monitoring cycle, December 2012, paragraph 330..

[28] Committee of Experts' Report on Application of the Charter in Spain. 3st monitoring cycle, December 2012, paragraph 878 to 880, concerning the administrative closure of the retransmission of the Public Catalan Television in the Autonomous Community of Valencia" it underlines the necessity for the Autonomous Communities sharing the same or a similar language to co-operate, for the benefit of the language, respecting the identity of each community."..

[29] Valencian Academy of Language. Diccionari normatiu valencià 2014. The definition of "Catalan" is: "Romance language spoken in Catalonia and the Balearic Islands, the French department of the Eastern Pyrenees, the Principality of Andorra, the eastern strip of Aragon, the Sardinian city Alghero and the Valencian Community, where it is called Valencian." http://www.avl.gva.es/dnv..

[30] Arzoz X. The protection of linguistic diversity through Article 22 of the Charter of Fundamental Rights. In: Arzoz X, ed. Respecting linguistic diversity in the European Union. Amsterdam: John Benjamins Publishing Company 2008: 145-176)..

[31] Krauss P. A one-dimensional diversity? European integration and the challenge of language policy. In Arzoz X, ed. Respecting linguistic diversity…, cit.: 85-107..

[32] Although Article 6.5 SAC establishes that "Occitan is official in Catalonia" subsequent legislation has restricted the full official status to the territory of Aran Valley, recognizing at the same time some language rights and official linguistic uses before other Catalan administrations (The Occitan, Aranese in Aran, Act 35/2010, dated 1 October)..

[33] J, Pons E. The Legal Systems of the Catalan Language. In: Strubell M, Boix-Fuster E, ed. Democratic Policies for Language Revitalisation: the Case of Catalan. London: Palgrave Macmillan 2011: 59..

[34] One exception is the Regulation of the Spanish Senate, where following the reforms of 2005 and 2007, allows citizens to send communications there and use such official languages in the debates of the chamber (excluding those where members of Government are subject to parliamentary control) and in some texts (excluding legislative proposals)..

[35] From the Middle Ages, Catalan language had been also present in the present Autonomous Community of Murcia, in the Carxe area (municipalities of Yecla, Jumilla and Albanilla), which borders with the Valencian Community. The Statute of Autonomy of Murcia (Organic Act 4/1982) establishes "The Autonomous Community (…) shall promote peculiarities, as well as its popular customs and traditions, respecting loal and regional variants in all cases" (Article 8)..

[36] Valencian Academy of Language. Diccionari normatiu valencià 2014. The definition of "Catalan" is: "Romance language spoken in Catalonia and the Balearic Islands, the French department of the Eastern Pyrenees, the Principality of Andorra, the eastern strip of Aragon, the Sardinian city Alghero and the Valencian Community, where it is called Valencian." http://www.avl.gva.es/dnv..

[37] See Law 1/1998, articles 13 (judicial actions), 15 (civil and commercial documents), 16 (collective work agreements, 17 (public registers), 28 (cultural industries) and 32 (commercial establishments)..

[38] See Pons E. and Pla A. La llengua en el procés de reforma de l'Estatut d'autonomia de Catalunya (2004-2006). Revista de Llengua i Dret 2007, 47, 183-226..

[39] See a more detailed commentary in Pons, E. The effects of Constitutional Court ruling 31/2010 dated 28 June 2010 in the linguistic of the Statute of Catalonia. Catalan Social Sciences Review 2013, 3, 67-92..

[40] Generalitat de Catalunya, Consell de Garanties Estatutàries, Opinion 6/2010, of 6 April..

[41] Generalitat de Catalunya, Consell de Garanties Estatutàries, Opinion 9/2010, of 21 June..

[42] Generalitat de Catalunya, Consell de Garanties Estatutàries, Opinion 22/2010, of 5 August..

CHAPTER 4

A Human Rights Perspective on the Vulnerability of Migrants

Ángeles Solanes Corella*

Department of Philosophy of Law and Political Philosophy, University of Valencia, Valencia, Spain

Abstract: The universality, which paradigmatically characterises human rights, becomes especially significant when linked to the field of migrations. In order to prevent and combat migrant vulnerability, migration policies and legal statutes need to respect certain inviolable limits. This paper proposes an analytical and critical review of the international framework of migrant rights, starting with the basic instruments of the United Nations and then delving into the European and Inter-American systems for the protection of human rights in the case of migrants. The aim of this paper is to show why it is imperative to strengthen international human rights law –by invoking and exercising it in an environment that systematically distorts it– in order to overcome the vulnerability that recurrently affects migrants.

Keywords: Human rights, International human rights law, Legal systems of protection, Migrants, Public policies, Vulnerability.

1. PRELIMINARY REMARKS

Human mobility in the form of migration subjects the values and principles which are the pillars of human rights to an ongoing revision. Both the idea of human dignity that underpins them and the characteristics of universality, indispensa-bility and inalienability that define them are blurred in certain situations where other variables come to the fore. Human rights are not always respected as liberties, immunities, claims or powers that belong to every human being as a necessary condition to attain self-fulfillment as a moral subject. To the extent that human rights are questioned or violated, the necessary and sufficient condition for the justification of the existence, origin and content of a legal system is weakened [1].

* **Corresponding author Ángeles Solares Corella:** Department of Philosophy of Law and Political Philosophy, University of Valencia, Valencia Spain; Tel: 0034 629070668; Fax: 0034 962839196; E-mail: angeles.solanes@uv.es
This study was carried out within the project "Human Rights, Multicultural Societies and Conflicts" (DER 2012-31771), funded by the Spanish Ministry of Economy and Competitiveness as part of the VI National Plan of Scientific Research, Development and Technological Innovation (Plan Nacional de I+D+i); and by the project PROMETEO/2014/078, "Social justice, enforceability of human rights and integration", Grant for the implementation of R&D projects in research groups of excellence, Generalitat Valenciana.

J. Alberto del Real Alcalà (Ed.)

Human rights and realities, such as migratory mobility, are often presented as unrelated issues since the discourse of human rights is deemed to be compatible with all the differentiations established in the regulations on immigration and the status of foreign nationals, thus transforming the immigrant into a subject with limited rights. Human rights, understood as a set of requirements and ethical pretensions belonging to all human beings, thus seem to be redefined. In those parallel contexts, the invisibility of immigrants as subjects of the law takes root, progressively turning them into objects, with highly questionable normative gradations on the basis of their administrative status [2].

The vulnerability of migrants arises and perpetuates itself through to them being politically, legally and socially perceived as "different" and therefore distinguished from the locals, who are citizens with a full legal status. In the current debate, the notion of foreign nationals is renewed as a consequence of migrations but its different aspects and underlying emphases are connected with issues of major, and well-known, unphilosophical relevance, such as global justice [3].

These approaches are hardly compatible with the idea of human dignity that took shape with the transition to modernity and constitutes the foundation of human rights. Such dignity was linked to the ideology of rationalist iusnaturalism, where human rights are configured as universal and inalienable. As implied by these characteristics, those rights belong to all persons by the mere fact of being human beings, since human rights are connected to a common human dignity -in other, the equal value of all human beings [4].

However, against this Universalist nature of human rights, the legal status of foreigners and, among them, immigrants, takes shape within the framework of a specific state and within the specificity of its legal system. Thus, the state determines their rights and duties by exception or in opposition to those of citizens. As Habermas recalls [5], the nation state is the organism that, through its laws, includes the democratic rights that subjects can use to reflectively change their substantive legal status, position or condition. If certain individuals are denied those rights, *e.g.* political rights, the ability of these individuals to ensure equal treatment and to influence decision-making is limited, thus closing the circle of exclusion. Thereby, Benhabib's [6] so-called "paradox of democratic legitimacy" gains particular relevance: the republican sovereign subjects its will to human rights, thanks to which other claims can be negotiated, so that we find ourselves in a field that is circumscribed by human rights and sovereignty. However, when foreign nationals enter this scenario, the universality of such rights comes under strain.

The modern, restrictive legal view of foreign nationals is but a constantly revised version of their historical differentiation from citizens. Nevertheless, the intended aim of blurring the foreign nationals is not always achieved. Indeed, as pointed out by Balibar based on a reading of Arendt [7], "those human beings that seem to be in some way superfluous" do not cease to exist physically just because the state limits or does not recognise their liberties. Quite on the contrary, they are still physically present in the global space and have one thing in common: all of them are generally, either totally or partially, deprived of any protection beyond the efforts of international agencies. This means that every time we find persons whose rights are conditioned, this should be seen as one of the perverse consequences of the history of the nation state. Without a doubt, this model served as a historical framework for the universal proclamation of certain basic human rights but, at the same time, it contributed to rigorously identify community membership with the possession of a nationality or with the status the national citizen [8].

As stated by Bauböck [9], migration also produces a difficult relationship between territory and citizenship. On the one hand, we have emigrant citizens living outside their countries of origin, and on the other hand, foreign immigrants living in host states. From this dual situation, different problems may arise. On the one hand, there is the attribution of rights and duties by sending states to their emigrants, without interfering in the sovereignty of the countries where emigrants live. Although difficulties may occur in this field, the element of conflict will most commonly arise in relation with immigrants rather than emigrants. On the other hand, all the problems stemming from the liberal and democratic legitimation of political authority appear in relation to immigrants in the host country. In liberal democracies, alternatively, some privileges traditionally linked to citizenship have been decoupled from nationality and associated either to universal human rights or to residence and work. Civil rights and freedoms are found in the former group, while social rights and those that are specific to immigrants (such as family reunification) increasingly tend to be included in the latter group, thus graduating their enjoyment on the basis of foreign nationals' administrative status and, in many cases, without achieving full equality with citizens.

The stereotypes associated with the immigrant are diverse and have been strengthened by constant regulations. Laws are often formulated from an instrumental, utilitarian perspective: the immigrant is a worker (preferably a temporary one), bound to fill niches or job vacancies, initially alone (without a family), whose aspirations cannot include claiming rights (since obligations are presupposed) or accessing the privileged status of citizenship, unless by means of naturalisation. Needless to say, the way in which immigration affects citizenship is intimately connected with the way in which states and their citizens perceive immigrants and how they construct the meaning of citizenship.

The legal creation of infra-subjects, *i.e.*, persons whose rights are legally limited in function (basically) of their administrative status, involves the implicit classification of the freedoms provided by the regulations. Indeed, some rights are usually denied to foreign nationals, such as voting and standing for election. Even in those countries largely in favour of granting voting rights to foreign residents, such claims were responded only at a local or municipal level. Along with these, other rights deemed to be basic, including social rights (education, health or housing) and, undoubtedly, labour rights (joining unions, associations, demonstrations or strikes) depend on the legal regulations of specific states. This creates significant differentiations, for instance, between regularity and irregularity in the assertion, enjoyment and protection of those rights [10].

The requirement for such differences to respect the principle of legality aims to ensure democratic deliberation on any restriction, thus respecting the relevant constitutional parameters. However, this does not prevent the result from being a downgraded legal status for denizens. Likewise, the national laws of democratic constitutional states include substantive guarantees on the reasonableness of the norms and/or policies establishing this differential treatment. Policies and regulations on immigration and the status of foreigners must strive to demonstrate that they are not merely the fruit of the discretion or arbitrariness of public authorities but follow objective criteria seeking certain legitimate purposes and that these differences are, therefore, necessary [11].

The vulnerability that stems from a limited legal status does not exclude the possibility for migrants to be vulnerable as subjects of human rights in their countries of origin. The first type of vulnerability –the one that takes place in the country of origin– is regarded as an internal issue under international law; whereas the vulnerability of international migrants exceeds national borders, thus involving other institutions as well. This distinction determines the rights of migrants as human beings and their access to enforcement bodies, as well as the lack of both.

It is precisely the limitation of both rights and access to enforcement bodies that can be understood as the vulnerability of migrants as subjects of human rights. This problem lies in the legal distinction between foreigners and nationals, which becomes a criterion to justify the less favourable treatment of foreign nationals.

On a second –social– level, the concept of migrant and, particularly, immigrant is, from the perspective of the receiving state, a useful device to operate a social discrimination that starts at the semantic level, since not all foreign nationals are included in this category. The notion of immigrant involves different stereotypes that mark social distance and cultural differences. The relation of otherness is basically understood as a position of inequality with respect to the leading and dominant host society, as well as a rupture with the society of origin. Due to this set of representations, immigrants appear as excluded and suffering important social and cultural limitations, so that policies in favour of their insertion seem justifiable, at least in principle, whenever they are compatible with the aim of seeking to overcome inequalities.

As stated by Cachón [12], the stable presence of new populations, especially when such populations are ethnically different, activates new collective problems. Beyond access to rights and the management of relations among competing social groups, there appears what may be called "co-inclusion": all parties concerned are induced to include the others, but they do not find themselves on an equal footing at the point of departure. At this moment, the new populations are very differentiated due to different elements, but especially due to the absence of power in the aforementioned terms of vulnerability. As a result, migrants are *de facto* treated as inferior.

The conceptual link between immigration and exclusion is sometimes abusive in the sense that, by emphasising cultural explanations, it simplifies a plethora of phenomena that have nothing to do with immigration. Moreover, the term immigrant is, by itself, excessively ambiguous. Multicultural societies with a strong immigrant presence clearly require neutral public authorities that assess cultural diversity in conceptual concretions rather than vague remarks.

In these contexts of immigration, a lack of legitimacy can be observed in the decoupling of civil and political society. A satisfactory notion of liberal democracy, from a national dimension, should aim to build a *demos* that includes all those individuals who are subject during a relevant period of time to the political authority of the state, regardless of their affiliation to other political units or specific cultural features [13].

At the international level, overcoming migrant vulnerability is essential to strengthen the instruments that protect and implement human rights, together with proactive policies. As pointed out in the Human Development Report, published by the United Nations Development Programme in 2009, it is necessary to question the stereotypes that are linked to migrations –associating them with negative realities– in order to expand and balance perceptions. About a quite complex and highly variable phenomenon that, in any case, cannot be understood separately from human rights.

2. THE INTERNATIONAL FRAMEWORK OF MIGRANT HUMAN RIGHTS IN UNITED NATIONS INSTRUMENTS

In order to counteract the vulnerability affecting migrants as subjects whose legal status is constructed at the national level, international law and, within it, international human rights law, plays an inescapable role.

It may be advisable to start by recalling the aforementioned emancipatory and Universalist origin of human rights. The United Nations Charter (1945) already stated the objective "to reaffirm faith in fundamental human rights", establishing for the United Nations the goal to achieve international cooperation in promoting and encouraging respect for human rights and fundamental freedoms for all without distinction as to race, sex, language, or religion.

As highlighted in the Preamble of the Universal Declaration of Human Rights (1948), these rights are to be protected by the rule of law "if man is not to be compelled to have recourse, as a last resort, to rebellion against tyranny and oppression". It is also essential to avoid confusion between globalisation and universalism, since the logic of the global market –with its implicit despotism– is against the universality of human rights in a complex reality that ultimately relegates persons to a secondary status [14].

International human rights law can be understood as a sector that aims to develop a legal and institutional framework for the protection of individuals at the international level, thus guaranteeing the enjoyment and respect of those common values we establish as rights. In that sense, it has insisted on the respect and protection of those freedoms linked to the dignity of all persons. Some instruments with a strong foundational character, such as the Universal Declaration of Human Rights (1948), have been created as a response to socio-historical struggles in national spaces. The Declaration emphasises the discourse of rights from the perspective of "equality-decolonisation", *i.e.* from the necessity of guaranteeing the emancipation of communities and peoples that had been subjected to conditions of colonisation and utter atrocities. This situation required to search for a new horizon, a rights-based reinterpretation of human dignity [15].

From the United Nations Charter to the Universal Declaration of Human Rights and the 1966 Covenants, the international human rights code comprises more than 150 international treaties and protocols. They all impose obligations on the ratifying states, including the right to respect, protect and fulfil these rights; and, concurrently, the obligation to promote and guarantee them. Among the main commitments taken by states through the international covenants on human rights is the adoption of (legislative and other) measures to form a legal system that conforms to the provisions in the treaties. At the same time, states have to establish, facilitate and guide the development and implementation of policies to allow the rights recognised in such treaties to be effectively exercised by all persons under the jurisdiction of the state concerned [16].

These covenants and treaties are supplemented by declarations and principles of interpretation which aim to balance situations of inequality or discrimination [17], including:

1. The *pro homine* principle (or, in this context, *pro personae*), understood as a hermeneutic criterion for the whole international human rights law, under which the broader norm –the one with the most expansive interpretation– is to be applied when recognising rights "always in favour of the person"; restrictions must be justified and not the other way around.
2. The non-discrimination principle: recognised as a peremptory norm of international law (*ius cogens*) that, as such, does not admit any legal act which may come into conflict with it. According to this principle, it is prohibited to make any distinction, restriction or exclusion in the recognition or exercise of any human right based on the so-called "prohibited grounds" or "suspicious categories", such as race, ethnic or national origin, age, sex, economic status, *etc.*
3. The principle of the dynamic interpretation of human rights: it includes both progressivity, understood as the increasingly broader protection of human rights on the international and national dimensions, as well as dynamism and non-regression, referring to the obligation of states not to adopt measures that may reduce the level or recognition and protection of human rights in their national jurisdiction.
4. The *pacta sunt servanda* principle, alluding to the fact that all commitments taken by the states in the treaties (even when taking account of the *rebus sic stantibus* doctrine) have to come into force in the domestic legal system.

Within the framework of the United Nations, the international human rights standard explicitly concerning immigrants is established by three basic instruments: the United Nations Convention on the Protection of the Rights of All Migrant Workers and Members of Their Families, adopted by resolution 45/158 of the General Assembly on 18 December 1990 and in force since 1 July 2003; and two International Labour Organisation (ILO) Conventions on migrant workers: Convention No. 97 of 1949 and Convention No. 143 of 1975, together with recommendations No. 86 of 1949 and No. 151 of 1975 [18].

These three international references have in common an aspect that is key to understanding the configuration of immigrants' rights: the underlying exclusiveness of this term, a subclass of the concept of foreigner, and the exclusive depiction of immigrants as workers. Indeed, the United Nations instruments are specific to migrant workers, not immigrants in general, although family members and irregular immigrants are included. Participation in the workforce and foreigner status are, therefore, the two fundamental characteristics of the legal concept of immigration on the international level.

On this basis, it is no surprise that the two conventions within the multilateral framework of the ILO were precisely the first to guarantee the elemental rights of migrant workers. Convention 97 concerning migration for employment of 1949 provided the basis for a modern normative framework. Convention 143 concerning migrant workers of 1975 addressed issues related to irregular migration and explicitly referred to the application of human rights norms.

Both ILO conventions provide the basis for the development of legislation on labour migration at the national level. Among other things, they stipulate that states must facilitate practices for fair recruitment, a transparent consultation process with social partners, reaffirm non-discrimination and establish equal access between local and migrant workers in questions such as social security, working conditions, wages or union membership. These conventions were the basis for what was arguably the most important of the instruments within the international standard on this topic: the aforementioned United Nations Convention, which also includes migrant family members among the subjects of protection.

The Committee on the Protection of the Rights of All Migrant Workers and Members of their Families (CMW) is the body of independent experts charged with monitoring the implementation of the Convention by states parties. They must submit reports to the Committee on the way the rights are exercised. Initially, states must submit a report one year after their adherence to the Convention and then every five years. The Committee examines each report and expresses its concerns and recommendations to the state party in the form of "concluding observations". In certain circumstances, the Committee may examine complaints or communications from individuals stating that their rights under the Convention have been violated [19].

As the UN Convention is a provision of significant relevance for the protection of the human rights of migrants, it is important to highlight that no member state of the European Union has ratified it. The arguments put forward to object to the Convention are not very convincing: that it is superfluous (insofar as member states already include guarantees for immigrants within their national legislations, which would be an argument in favour of the ratification rather than against it) as well as incompatibilities between the Convention and the guidelines of the

European immigration policy. In practice, this means recognising the impossibility of addressing the practical implications of such a ratification for the states that receive significant migratory flows. The fact that the Convention has not been ratified by any of the EU member states, which are committed to the defense and protection of human rights, makes it interesting to highlight the most emblematic points of the Convention in order to examine whether they are compatible, *e.g.*, with the legislations of the member states [20].

The significant progress that the Convention represents contrasts with the impossibility of realising its underlying aspirations. Although it has finally come into force, there remain numerous doubts on its effectiveness, since the negotiation process caused the final text to contain several ambiguities and contradictions.

The Convention is conceived from a minimalist perspective. A large part of its specifications are optional and not imperative for the states, and the rights it regulates cannot be considered innovative in democratic countries. In any case, it reflects a growing concern about the problems and discriminatory treatment of many migrant workers and their family members, simultaneously recognising irregular migration.

From its wording, it is clear that this international instrument pursues basic objectives such as the incorporation of the non-discrimination principle in the recognition of rights, recognising a set of minimum rights to undocumented migrant workers, granting additional rights (economic, social and cultural) to documented migrant workers and preventing and eliminating irregular migration and employment. To that end, it includes the imposition of sanctions on persons organising irregular movements and employers of undocumented workers, in order to promote equal, human and legal conditions.

It is essential to emphasise that the Convention neither creates new rights for immigrants nor interprets rights in a way that is incompatible, as will be discussed later, with immigration policy. Rather on the contrary, it vindicates rights that are already provided in other instruments of international human rights law, only to highlight their relevance in relation to migrants [21]. For instance, it incorporates rights, such as the right to leave any state, including the state of origin, the right to enter and remain in the country of origin (article 8), the prohibition of torture or any other cruel, inhuman or degrading treatment (article 10), the prohibition of slavery, servitude, forced or compulsory labour (article 11), the right to freedom of thought, conscience and religion (article 12), the right to liberty and security of person and prohibition of arbitrary arrest or detention (article 16) and the prohibition of collective expulsions (article 22) [22].

Likewise, as in article 2 of the Universal Declaration of Human Rights, the UN Convention refers to the so-called prohibited grounds that cannot be used to differentiate rights. These include national origin, which is precisely the pillar on which differentiations in the regulations on the status of foreigners are constructed, as noted earlier. However, the Convention expressly states that this is applicable "except as otherwise provided hereafter (within the Convention)". That is to say, the Convention does not establish equal rights for all migrants. Therefore, Part III is devoted to the "human rights of all migrant workers and members of their families" while Part IV refers to the "other rights of migrant workers and members of their families who are documented or in a regular situation".

Regarding the immigrants who are eligible to the provisions of the Convention, article 2 is essential as it defines the "migrant worker" as a person who is to be engaged, is engaged or has been engaged in a remunerated activity in a state of which he or she is not a national. Therefore, if such an activity has never existed, the subject is not categorised as a 'worker'. Thus, it is possible to differentiate between these foreigners and other types such as asylum-seekers, refugees or stateless persons. With regard to family members, article 4 defines them as persons who are married to migrant workers or maintain with them a relationship that, according to applicable law, produces effects equivalent to marriage. It also includes their dependent children and other dependent persons who are recognised as members of the family under the applicable legislation or applicable bilateral or multilateral agreements between the states concerned.

The leeway provided in the Convention to encourage the ratification by states, specified in article 79, is sufficiently broad to avoid affecting the right of each state to establish the criteria governing the admission of migrant workers and members of their families. The entry of immigrants and the possibility of regularising foreign nationals thus remains under strict state control.

However, many factors have caused the Convention, which is the paradigmatic instrument for the international defense of the rights of migrants, to display a very low rate of ratification. Among the most decisive ones is political reality and the interests of states, which are sometimes presented as diverging from those embodied in previous agreements. In general, the Convention is described as having a limited effect on the improvement of migrant rights, especially in the case of irregular migrants. This shows that the central idea of human rights –universality– is still restricted by the powers of national sovereignty.

3. THE EUROPEAN SYSTEM OF HUMAN RIGHTS AND ITS APPLICATION TO MIGRANTS

The guidelines set by the European Union in the field of migration are strongly conditioned by the will of each particular state. National discourses and practices are focused on immigration, and the space of the EU is permeated by state structures. As a result, Community proposals articulate minimal standards for common action on human mobility and national sovereign powers enjoy a wide freedom of action. The basic premise of the so-called immigration policy is the promotion of regular immigration, so the enjoyment of rights is limited to this modality. The impossibility of accessing the formal labour market thus caused the negation of rights or, in other words, modern forms of slavery. Irregular immigrants share the condition of remaining concealed, denied or ignored, disseminating through local systems of production. As a result, their presence only becomes evident in the most extreme circumstances, such as xenophobic episodes or catastrophes [23].

There is no European-level instrument designed specifically for the protection of the human rights of migrants, so that the European Convention for the Protection of Human Rights and Fundamental Freedoms (1950) has become the protection mechanism *par excellence*. Despite the limited number of rights and freedoms included in the Convention, it can be argued that the regional system of human rights protection has been especially effective thanks to the work of the European Court of Human Rights (ECHR). Since the reform carried out by Protocol No. 11, this is the only international court that has binding effect in the field of human rights [24]. The rights guaranteed by the Convention are expanded in its additional protocols [25].

Additionally, the Charter of Fundamental Rights (2000) defines the rights applicable at the Community level, in particular those concerning dignity, freedom, equality, citizenship and justice. It now has the same binding nature as the treaties.

The importance of the Convention, considering the moment when it was approved, lies in it being arguably categorised as a pan-European instrument for the consolidation of democratic public order in the field of human rights and, at the same time, a collective mechanism for the safeguarding of this order.

The vulnerability of the legal status of migrants at the European level has made it indispensable to resort to the ECHR, taking as well in account the diversity of migratory flows [26]. After decades aiming at a model of immigration categorised as unqualified, intended to fill vacancies at the bottom of the "career ladder" and with an assumed intention of non-permanence based on the classic model of the guest worker [27], EU member states have introduced a second dimension of differentiation for highly skilled immigration. Measures have been taken to further narrow the list of rights and freedoms of migrants residing in the EU, such as Directive 2008/115/EC of the European Parliament and of the Council of 16 December 2008 on common standards and procedures in Member States for returning illegally staying third-country nationals; Council Directive 2009/50/EC of 25 May 2009 on the conditions of entry and residence of third-country nationals for the purposes of highly qualified employment [28]; and Directive 2011/98/EU of the European Parliament and of the Council of 13 December 2011 on a single application procedure for a single permit for third-country nationals to reside and work in the territory of a Member State and on a common set of rights for third-country workers legally residing in a Member State.

Together with these directives, the European Pact on Immigration and Asylum (2008) [29] consolidates the common European immigration policy. Under this agreement, member states undertake to steer migration policies toward five objectives: organising legal immigration by taking into account the priorities, needs and reception capacities of EU countries, and encouraging integration; controlling irregular immigration, especially to ensure that migrants without a legal authorisation to reside return to their country of origin or transit; improving border controls; creating a Europe of asylum; and collaborating with countries of origin and transit to encourage synergy between migration and development. Measures to give effect to these commitments must be both national and European [30].

Within this context, marked by restrictive policies, largely symbolic elements (such as the preservation of national identity, constitutional values, *etc.*) take on special relevance and the immigrants are stigmatised, which affects their rights. Therefore, the aforementioned European Convention on Human Rights is an extremely important instrument of protection.

The Convention includes some specific provisions on the status of foreigners. At any rate, the absence of a desirable reference has not been compensated for by additional protocols. Precisely for that reason, the role played so far by the ECHR is highly significant [31]. Based on the general statement in article 1, under which human rights are recognised to "everyone", the Court has used textual references related to foreign nationals. First, article 3 has enabled the protection of the mental integrity and dignity of foreign nationals, especially in cases of expulsion to third countries. Article 5.1.f), on the right to liberty and security, allows the lawful arrest or detention of a person who is attempting an unauthorised entry into the national territory or is undergoing a procedure of deportation or extradition. Likewise, article 16 on the restriction of aliens' political activities states that "nothing in Articles 10 (freedom of expression), 11 (freedom of assembly and association) and 14 (prohibition of discrimination) shall be regarded as preventing the High Contracting Parties from imposing restrictions on the political activity of aliens".

On this point, the Convention is completed by the specific provisions of Protocol no. 4 (1963), particularly regarding two aspects. Article 2 on freedom of movement establishes that anyone who lawfully finds theirself within the territory of a state has the right to liberty of movement and freedom to choose his residence as well as to leave any country, including their own; and article 4 prohibiting the collective expulsion of aliens.

Procedural safeguards, from which migrants stand to benefit, are set out in Protocol No. 7 (1984). On expulsion specifically, article 1 establishes that an alien lawfully resident shall not be expelled therefrom, except in pursuance of a decision reached in accordance with law and shall be allowed "to submit reasons against his expulsion; to have his case reviewed, and to be represented for these purposes before the competent authority or a person or persons designated by that authority". Only in the interest of public order or on grounds of national security may the aforementioned rights of foreign nationals be suspended in order to proceed to expulsion.

Since the protection provided by the Convention, even when we include the protocols, does not offer but weak guarantees of the rights of foreign nationals, the ECHR has compensated by showing remarkable innovation and dynamism in its case law in order to protect the human rights of foreign nationals in terms of forcible displacement and the right to family life. The protection of the Court is based on three key principles that repeatedly come up in its case law:

1. The Court systematically points out that states parties have a right, under international provisions and without prejudice to their treaty obligations, to control the entry, residence and expulsion of aliens.
2. However, when the consequences of an expulsion order undermine the exercise of a right guaranteed under the Convention, the Court can make a state respect its obligations under the relevant provision – provided that it does not lead to far-reaching implications–, as has been sustained since 1985 in the field of immigration.
3. Additionally, each state party should ensure respect for the obligations undertaken upon ratification of the Convention when exercising its powers on the control of foreign nationals; for instance, discrimination must be prevented [32].

The dynamism of ECHR case law and its commitment to implement the Convention was evident, for instance, in the decision of the Grand Chamber of 23 February 2012 (Affaire Hirsi Jamaa et autres c. Italie) confirming the extraterritorial effect of the prohibition of collective expulsions and concurrently reminding that the Convention must be a living instrument and therefore interpreted in the light of the current circumstances so that concrete and effective guarantees are provided, not just theoretical and illusory ones [33].

4. THE INTER-AMERICAN SYSTEM FOR THE PROTECTION OF HUMAN RIGHTS AND ITS APPLICATION TO MIGRANTS

The Inter-American system for the protection of human rights incorporates the universality of these rights and is part of the *corpus juris* of international human rights law [34]. Within the Inter-American system, a series of legal principles and standards have been developed, intended to strengthen the minimum content of the fundamental and human rights of migrants. The Rapporteur on Migrant Workers of the Inter-American Commission on Human Rights (through its reports), the Inter-American Commission on Human Rights (in its reports by country and by case) and, significantly, the Inter-American Court of Human Rights (IACHR, through some contentious cases and certain advisory opinions) have all contributed to reaffirming the guiding principles that should guide migration-related policies [35].

In general, within this system and, as already noted for the European system, states enjoy considerable leeway regarding the definition and implementation of their migration policies based on objectives that are deemed legitimate, such as the aforementioned regulation of the labour market. Likewise, this system recognises their ability to regulate immigration control on the basis of their territorial sovereignty. However, human rights standards establish a minimum framework that states must respect and that, in the field of migration, hinges on the principles of equality and non-discrimination. Thus, human rights bodies within this system admit that states may establish some distinctions between citizens and regular or irregular foreigners in relation to certain rights or access to certain goods or services. However, this power can only be exercised if such differential treatment is established by a formal law and is reasonable, objective and proportionate so that persons are not deprived of substantial dimensions of human rights [36].

As in the European context, such differences in treatment must comply with the principle of legality, establishing an irreducible core of rights that are linked to the status of human being. Yet in Latin America and the Caribbean, as in Europe, utilitarian and instrumental logics have prevailed in the perception of migrants and their legal status. Some problems relate in different ways, in several countries of the region, to exclusionary approaches that rely on an idea of national sovereignty that forecloses economic and commercial openings, thus generating greater poverty and emigration. These problems include: the invisibility of children and the gender perspective in migration policies; the ignorance of basic guarantees of due process; international conflicts that make it more difficult to address the migratory phenomenon and exacerbate xenophobic attitudes; the absence of social integration policies; weak mechanisms for protection and consular assistance; and the electoral or political instrumentalisation of immigration [37].

The identification of a basic core of non-derogable rights based on migration status remains the most problematic issue in the Inter-American system of human rights, since state laws deny or restrict rights according to the situation of irregularity, with similar parameters to those used in the European system. For this reason, it is IACHR case law that responds to the challenge of a conception that understands fundamental rights as mere attributes of political citizens and insists that "human rights are universal and inherent to all human beings, while the rights of citizenship vary from country to country and encompass only those which the positive law of the state considers citizens, not protecting, thus, undocumented migrants" [38]. The IACHR thus establishes the first general comment on the human rights of migrants, maintaining that states have the general obligation to respect and guarantee the exercise of human rights, regardless of immigration status [39].

States thus have the capacity to act at the normative level in order to restrict certain rights, but not under the migration status; in other words, it is not permissible to deprive a group of persons under the jurisdiction and control of a state of the protection granted by international human rights law. In the Inter-American sphere, just as in Europe, there is a continuous tension between the perception of migration as a problem to be solved according to paradigms such as national security and a new perspective based on the process of regional integration, where the human rights dimension is gaining prominence and migration is seen as a factor of social development [40].

The limitation of migrant rights, particularly for those in an irregular situation, is a recurring theme that the IACHR has increasingly been specifying in the exercise of its advisory function. A series of minimum standards have been defined, which, within the Inter-American Human Rights System, constitute a minimum core that must be respected and guaranteed regardless of migration status [41].

With respect to civil rights, the American Declaration and the American Convention establish that a number of them cannot be denied on the basis of migration status, including the right to life, physical integrity and personal freedom. These rights apply both to irregular immigrants and those who are under the state's authority but have not, from a legal perspective, formally entered its territory [42]. Indeed, the Inter-American Commission of Human Rights and the IACHR have insisted on the need to make migration policies compatible with international obligations on human rights. The Commission has issued specific recommendations to OAS member states in order to promote compliance with their international obligations, including issues related to non-discrimination, due process and basic procedural safeguards, detention conditions in immigration facilities and the obligation to ensure that people at risk of persecution are not returned to their country [43].

The right to due legal process is yet another guarantee claimed for immigrants regardless of their administrative status. This right is understood in a broad perspective that comprises the judicial and administrative spheres at different levels. The IACHR has indicated that "due legal process refers to all the requirement that must be observed in the procedural stages in order for an individual to be able to defend his rights adequately vis-à-vis any [...] act of the State that could affect them. That is to say, due process of law must be respected in any act or omission on the part of the State bodies in a proceeding, whether of an administrative, punitive or jurisdictional nature" [44].

Social rights, and particularly their protection for migrants in an irregular situation, are still among the unresolved issues. In any case, gradual progress has been made in certain definitions that recognise irregular migrants as a social group facing extreme conditions of vulnerability to institutional and social abuse. The IACHR has insisted precisely on this extreme vulnerability in order to mandate significant protection in situations of irregularity [45]. The existence of groups in situations of high vulnerability certainly affects the human rights obligations of the state; for this reason, the Inter-American Human Rights System has drawn attention to the need to take positive, concrete and targeted measures in order to ensure the exercise of some economic, social and cultural rights. Nevertheless, levels of vulnerability vary within the aforementioned groups, affecting in an especially significant way, for instance, migrant children.

With regard to labour rights, the IACHR in the exercise of its advisory function has stated that rights arising from the employment relationship must be recognised regardless of immigration status. According to the IACHR, labour rights necessarily arise from the status of worker, understood in a broad sense as any person who is to be engaged, is engaged or has been engaged in a remunerated activity. A person having the status of worker acquires the rights linked thereto. The right to work, either at a national or international level, is part of workers' legal status and, as such, regulates the rights and obligations of the employee and the employer regardless of any other economic or social consideration. All persons entering a state and engaging in labour relations acquire human labour rights regardless of their immigration status, since the respect and guarantee of the enjoyment of these rights should be made without any discrimination whatsoever [46].

In the light of this interpretation, states are obliged to act in order to prevent contractual relations or the actions of employers to violate international minimum standards on labour matters. Having the status of an irregular immigrant or even, as the case may be, being subjected to a procedure of expulsion cannot deprive the person of labour rights arising from the work actually carried out for an employer. Furthermore, migrant workers in an irregular situation have the right not to be discriminated against. Therefore, the state is bound to penalise any employer who violates such rights. Non-discrimination in employment entails the recognition to work under decent conditions and to receive an adequate remuneration as legally established.

The IACHR has expressed its concern on the violations of the rights arising from situations of labour exploitation of migrants in an irregular situation, including the prohibition of forced labour, the prohibition of child labour, an attention to working women, freedom of association, collective bargaining and fair wage, social security, judicial and administrative guarantees, and adequate working conditions [47].

Along the lines established by the IACHR, most laws expressly recognise the respect for labour rights. However, with regard to the right to work, they obviously do not allow migrants without legal residency to work. This prohibition aims at countering informal work and economy and their negative impact on workers and the social security system, as is the case in Europe. What happens in practice is that, in the absence of flexible mechanisms to regularise migrants and, despite the recognition of such labour relations, the prohibition to work contributes to job insecurity, social exclusion and the formal impossibility to improve one's living conditions.

5. HOW TO OVERCOME VULNERABILITY? CHALLENGES FOR THE FUTURE

As the vulnerability which migrant persons face originates largely from the legal differentiations incorporated in national systems, the essential precondition to erase this disadvantage is the redefinition of such legal definitions. As previously pointed out, the notion of foreign national and consequently of immigrant explicitly assumes a downgraded legal status. Thus, the challenge lies in foreclosing attacks or violations of the human rights of migrant persons. These rights, within a questionable model of globalisation and from a normative logic, impose duties on national and international bodies to ensure their protection. In practice, it seems that human rights are limited by state laws and, in the context of an anti-universalist globalisation, end up taking shape as a basis upon which to claim individual liberties linked to human dignity, without finding their place in the current economic context. The duality of the human rights discourse is getting ever greater: on the one hand, human rights are presented as universal in the international instruments, but on the other hand, restrictive measures against human mobility proliferate by negations of rights which are not compatible with international human rights standards [48].

These practices can be seen as spreading the "society of contempt" [49] as, if the integrity of human beings –their dignity– is reached by establishing adequate protection against possible offences and personal disrespect, such integrity depends on an intersubjective recognition that is not granted in the case of migrants. In societies that place migrants in situations of vulnerability, at most a minimum core of rights maintain their universal character while others become mere options and, for a part of the population, impossible privileges rather than long-term expectations.

What could be seen as process of nationalisation of human rights has reduced their universality to a rather theoretical level, where it is asserted that human beings are equal in dignity and therefore entitled to these rights. This is stated in various instruments of international human rights law, where signatory states undertake to recognise, respect, guarantee and promote such rights. However, when they are incorporated into the domestic law of modern states, condensed in their constitutions and then specified in laws, modulation becomes limitation. In such laws, human rights are subjected to dominant models that involve a strong cultural background and introduce constraints such as the requirement of legal residence. This hampers, when it does not annihilate, the exercise of such freedoms.

Despite the aforementioned guarantees, it should be acknowledged that the invocation and application of international human rights law is not as frequent as would be desirable, since it often goes unnoticed. This is due to the lack of information, but also to the fact that national jurists are faced with legal categories that differ from their domestic laws. Hence the scarce and unsatisfactory implementation of human rights law.

It is imperative to strengthen international human rights law, invoking and exercising it in an environment that systematically distorts it, in order to overcome the vulnerability that affects migrants. Indeed, such rights are not compatible with modern forms of human exploitation such as forced prostitution, child trafficking or forced and slave labour; they are also incompatible with the gradual increase of poverty, social exclusion and marginalisation. As pointed out by Cançado Trindade, this does not mean that greater regulation is necessary or that the law does not exist, but "it rather means that law is being ostensibly and flagrantly violated, from day to day, to the detriment of millions of human beings, among whom undocumented migrants all over the world" [50].

On this basis, the ratification of the International Convention on the Protection of the Rights of All Migrant Workers and Members of their Families should not be further postponed. This Convention is the international standard *par excellence* to guarantee and protect the rights of migrants and their family members; the legal systems of the states that keep postponing its recognition are taken back to historic moments that seemed to have been overcome with other instruments of international human rights law, such as the Universal Declaration of Human Rights and the 1966 Covenants, which complement the Declaration. The Convention establishes a series of obligations for states, both in origin countries and in countries of transit and destination, as well as on the employment of migrants, which states must take into account since it is the first international legal instrument that encodes the human rights of migrants.

Harmonising national-level public policies with the provisions of the Convention may allow governments to provide responses on migration issues in accordance with international standards of protection and, at the same time, strengthen the rule of law. To this end, it is essential to publicise the Convention so that it is known both by migrants and the various actors involved. Now more than ever, international security and stability depend also on the ability of states to adequately manage migrations. To avoid political setbacks and anti-migration activities, it is essential for states to cooperate in the creation of an international migration regime, or regional migration regimes, including the crucial component of respect for the human rights of migrants.

Furthermore, jurisprudential control continues to be essential, as is evident from the two systems analysed. Both the ECHR and the IACHR will undoubtedly continue to play a key role in the protection of migrant rights, especially in the attempt to find a balance between mandatory international guidelines and the sovereign capacity to legislate on the various issues related to migration policies.

In this sense, these courts will be called upon to keep preserving those insurmountable limits that the ECHR has designated as "red lines", regardless of the context but without distorting the margin of appreciation that provides states with some leeway. However, this is to be done by complying with the procedural obligations that ensure and give effect to the guaranteed rights [51]. As stated by the IACHR, "states may not subordinate or condition observance of the principle of equality before the law and non-discrimination to achieving their public policy goals, whatever these may be, including those of a migratory character" [52].

It cannot be overlooked that, after all domestic remedies have been exhausted, it is imperative to resort to international judicial and quasi-judicial protection mechanisms; within the European system, through the ECHR; within the Inter-American system, through the IACHR; and in the context of the United Nations, through the committees established in international human rights treaties. These international bodies can receive individual claims or complaints for the violation of any right enshrined in the different treaties ratified by the relevant states. After reporting the violation, such international bodies will establish the measures that must be taken by the state in order to compensate victims. Of course, this proposal of strengthening the application of international human rights law, with the correlative prominence of case law in order to overcome migrant vulnerability, may be seen as a utopia by the reluctant and the sceptic. Nonetheless, Sartre was certainly right when he said that an idea, before it comes true, eerily resembles utopia.

CONFLICT OF INTEREST

The author declares no conflict of interest, financial or otherwise.

ACKNOWLEDGEMENTS

Declared none.

REFERENCES

[1] Peces-Barba G. La dignidad de la persona desde la Filosofía del Derecho. Madrid 2002; Hierro L. ¿Qué derechos tenemos? Doxa. 2000; 23: 351-75.

[2] De Asís R. Concepto y fundamento de los derechos humanos. In: Tamayo, J. J. (coord.) Diez Palabras clave sobre derechos humanos. Navarra 2005; De Lucas J. La herida original de las políticas de inmigración: A propósito del lugar de los derechos humanos en las políticas de inmigración. Isegoría. 2002; 26: 59-84.

[3] Peña J. Los orígenes del debate sobre la justicia global. Isegoría. 2010; 43: 363-86.

[4] Ansuategui FJ. Derechos humanos: entre la universalidad y la diversidad. In: Ruiz E, Urrutia G, Eds. Derechos Humanos en contextos multiculturales ¿Acomodo de derechos o derechos de acomodo? Donosti 2010; Barranco MC. Diversidad de situaciones y universalidad de los derechos. Madrid 2011.

[5] Habermas J. Tiempo de transiciones. Madrid 2004.

[6] Benhabib S. The rights of others: Aliens, Residents and Citizens. Cambridge 2004.

[7] Balibar E. Impolítica de los derechos humanos. Arendt, el derecho a tener derechos y la desobediencia cívica. *Erytheis* 2007.

[8] De Lucas J. El mito de la interculturalidad. In: Añón MJ, Solanes A, Eds. Construyendo sociedades multiculturales. Espacio público y derechos. Valencia 2011; 17-41.

[9] Bauböck R. How migration transforms citizenship: International, multinational and transnational perspectives. Österreich 2002.

[10] Solanes A. Sobre la necesidad de garantizar los derechos humanos en el contexto migratorio español. In: Peña J, Coord. Inmigración y derechos humanos. Valladolid 2012; pp. 33-60.

[11] Añón MJ. Integración: una cuestión de derechos. Arbor 2010; 477: 625-38.

[12] Cachón L. Conflictos e inmigración en Europa: presentación de una problemática para reforzar la convivencia. Cachón L, Coord. Inmigración y conflictos en Europa. Aprender para una mejor convivencia. Barcelona 2011; pp. 7-46.

[13] Rubio R. Immigration as a Democratic Challenge. Citizenship and Inclusion in Germany and the United States. Cambridge 2000.

[14] De Lucas J. Las globalizaciones y los derechos. Enrahonar 2008; 40/41: 55-66.

[15] Martínez A. Derechos humanos y diversidade(s) culturale(s): los retos de la interculturalidad. Derechos y Libertades. 2012; 26: 109-44.

[16] Villán C. Los derechos humanos y la inmigración en el marco de las Naciones Unidas. In: VVAA. Derechos Humanos de los Migrantes. México 2005.

[17] De Vergottini G. Jornadas con motivo del 60 aniversario de la Declaración Universal de Derechos Humanos. Ponencia inaugurali. Revista Europea de Derechos Fundamentales 2008; 11/1: 17-38; Canosa R. Igualdad y discriminación en el derecho internacional de los derechos humanos. Revista Europea de Derechos Fundamentales 2008; 39-66.

[18] Aparicio M. Inmigración y DESC. In: Pisarello G, Valiño V, Coords. Herramientas para la defensa de los DESC. Derechos Económicos, Sociales y Culturales. Barcelona 2006; pp. 91-110.

[19] Grange M. Importancia e impacto de la Convención internacional para la protección de todos los trabajadores migratorios y sus familiares. In: VVAA. Derechos Humanos de los Migrantes, Mexico, 2005; p. 43.

[20] De Lucas J, Ramón C, Solanes A. Informe sobre la necesidad y oportunidad de la ratificación por España de la Convención Internacional de la organización de Naciones Unidas de 1990 sobre la protección de los derechos de todos los trabajadores migratorios. Barcelona 2008.

[21] Alba F. La Convención Internacional sobre los Derechos de los Trabajadores Migratorios: algunas implicaciones. In: VV. AA. Derechos Humanos de los Migrantes, Mexico, 2005; p. 35.

[22] La Spina E. Familias transnacionales, sociedades multiculturales e integración: España, Italia y Portugal en perspectiva comparada. Madrid 2011.

[23] Lynch E. La nueva esclavitud y sus cómplices. Claves de Razón Práctica 2005; 149: 64-67.

[24] Bondia D. El sistema europeu de protecció dels drets humans. In: Bonet J, Sánchez VM, Dirs. Els drets humans al segle XXI: continuïtat i canvis. Barcelona 2007.

[25] The additional protocols intended to expand the initial list of rights include: Protocol No. 1 (1952) on rights to property, education and freedom of election; Protocol No. 4 (1963), regulating freedom of movement and prohibiting expulsion of nationals of a State and collective expulsions of aliens; Protocol No. 6 (1983) prohibiting death penalty except in the case of war; Protocol No. 7 (1984) establishing the procedural guarantees in case of expulsion of aliens, equality between the spouses, right to a double degree of jurisdiction in criminal matters, right to compensation in the event of

judicial error and right not to be tried twice for the same cause; Protocol No. 12 (2000) incorporating the prohibition of discrimination in the enjoyment of any right provided by law; and Protocol No. 13 (2002) extending the prohibition of death penalty even in wartime. Furthermore, the procedural protocols pose important modifications in the system of protection of rights, including: Protocol No. 11 (1998) revising the text of the Convention to modify the procedure of protection of rights, suppressing the European Commission of Human Rights and reforming the ECHR so that individuals can bring causes directly before it; and Protocol No. 14 (2004, extended by the Madrid Agreement of 2009) completing the control mechanisms of the Convention. With regard to the provisions of Protocol No. 2, No. 3, No. 5, No. 8 and No. 9 (which never came into force), they were replace by Protocol No. 11).

[26] In the European Union, we find a multilevel system for the protection of fundamental rights that would make it necessary to consider not only the function of the ECHR but also the role of the Court of Justice of the European Union (CJEU). Although at first the protection of fundamental rights was considered to be at the respective national constitutional courts and the ECHR, the fact is that the CJEU assumed the safeguard of such rights by interpreting and applying the EU Law. The analysis of this interesting function has been excluded from this study in order to focus on the extra-Community dimension affecting migrants from a human rights perspective (based on the ECHR and aiming at establishing parallels with the Inter-American system), despite assuming the significant links existing between the ECHR and the CJEU. Sarrión J. El Tribunal de Justicia de Luxemburgo como garante de los derechos fundamentales. Madrid 2013.

[27] Castles S. Guestworkers in Europe: a Resurrection? Internacional Migration Review 2006; 4: 741-66.

[28] Carrera S, Pinyol G. Autoridades locales y regionales en el Espacio de Libertad, Seguridad y Justicia. ¿Hacia una estrategia de multigobernanza para el Programa de Estocolmo? Barcelona 2010.

[29] *European Pact on Immigration and Asylum*, Council of the European Union, 13440/08, Brussels 24 September 2008; approved by the European council on 15 and 16 October 2010. Follow-up of the plan has been performed through different instruments; the most recent ones include: COM (2014) 288 final, Communication from the Commission to the European Parliament and the Council, of 22 May 2014, *5th Annual Report on Immigration and Asylum (2013)*..

[30] Trujillo JA, Ortega JM, Coords. Inmigración y asilo: problemas actuales y reflexiones al hilo de la nueva Ley reguladora del derecho de asilo y de la protección subsidiaria y de la entrada en vigor del Tratado de Lisboa. Madrid 2010.

[31] The ECHR issued 1157 sentences in 2011, producing 50 677 decisions of inadmissibility or removal. Precisely this imbalance gives a special sense to the series of sentences on asylum and immigration. Thus, in 2011, 78 judgments on asylum and immigration can be considered just as the tip of the iceberg, especially when compared with the number of request for "interim measures" presented the same year. This indicates that between 3000 and 4000 records of immigration-related cases were subject to revision in Strasbourg. Parlement Européen, Direction Generale des Politiques Internes, Departement Thematique C, Droits des Citoyens et Affaires Constitutionnelles, Libertes civiles, Justice et Affaires Interieures, Impact de la jurisprudence de la CEJ et de la CEDH en matiere d'asile et d'immigration. Bruxelles. 2012.

[32] García Añón J. Discriminación, exclusión social y conflicto en sociedades multiculturales: la identificación por perfil étnico. In: García Añón J, Ruiz M, Eds. Discriminación racial y étnica. Valencia 2012; pp. 281-16.

[33] Parlement Européen, Impact de la jurisprudence de la CEJ et de la CEDH en matiere d'asile et d'immigration…, Feb 2013.

[34] Cançado Trindade A. El sistema interamericano de protección de los derechos humanos (1948-2002). In: Gómez F, Dir. La protección internacional e los derechos humanos en los albores del siglo XXI. Bilbao 2004; pp. 549-91.

[35] Particularly important in the Inter-American sphere are the different editions of the South-American Conference on Migration (SACM). These events bring together different States to discuss on

migratory movements within the region. Declarations establishing guidelines on policies from human mobility have been approved in the framework of these conferences. The South American Conference on Migration has counted with several editions: I SACM in Buenos Aires, Argentina (2000); II SACM in Santiago de Chile, Chile (2001); III SACM in Quito, Ecuador (2002); IV SACM in Montevideo, Uruguay (2003); V SACM in La Paz, Bolivia (2004); VI SACM in Asunción, Paraguay (2006); VII SACM in Caracas, Venezuela (2007); VIII SACM in Montevideo, Uruguay (2008); IX in Quito, Ecuador (2009); X in Cochabamba, Bolivia (2010); XI in Brasilia, Brasil (2011); and XII in Santiago de Chile, Chile (2012). Particularly relevant are two of the documents emerging from these Conferences: the *South American Plan for Human Development of Migrations, context and perspectives*, document approved in the 10*th* South-American Conference on Migrations, Cochabamba, Plurinational State of Bolivia, 25 and 26 October 2010 and the Brasilia Declaration. Towards the South American Citizenship, approved in the 11th South-American Conference on Migrations, Brasilia, 19-21 October 2011.

[36] IACHR, Advisory Opinion OC-18/03, of 17 September 2003, Legal Status and Rights of Undocumented Workers, paragraph 19.

[37] Ceriani P. Luces y sombras en la legislación migratoria latinoamericana. Nueva Sociedad 2011; 233: 549-91.

[38] IACHR, Advisory Opinion OC-18/03, of 17 September 2003, paragraph 55.

[39] Ceriani P, Fava R, Morales D. Políticas migratorias, el derecho a la igualdad y el principio de no discriminación. Una aproximación desde la jurisprudencia del Sistema Interamericano de Derechos Humanos. In: Ceriani P, Fava R, Eds. Políticas migratorias y derechos humanos. Buenos Aires 2009.

[40] Novick S. Migraciones. Políticas e Integración regional. Avances y retrocesos, In: Novick S, Dir. Migraciones y Mercosur: una relación inconclusa. Buenos Aires 2010; pp. 9-28.

[41] Seventh South-American Conference on Migrations, Los estándares internacionales en materia de Derechos Humanos y políticas migratorias, Bolivarian Republic of Venezuela, 2 and 3 July 2007.

[42] The Rapporteurship on Migrant Workers of the IACHR established a series of standards applicable to the detention conditions of migrans and their families (IACHR, *Fourth Progress Report of the Rapporteurship on Migrant Workers and their Families*, paragraph 92).

[43] *Resolution 03/08. Human Rights of Migrants, International Standards, and the Return Directive of the EU.* IACHR, July 2008.

[44] IACHR, Advisory Opinion OC-18/03, op. cit., paragraphs 123 and 124. The Inter-American Commission of Human Rights has progressively specified what could be considered minimum standards of due process applicable to status determinations, exclusions and deportations. These include, *e.g.*: having a responsible and impartial surveyor; right to be heard; to availability of information, translation and interpreting; legal representation; judicial review; possibility of access to consular authorities; and appropriate conditions of detention. IACHR, *Fourth Progress Report of the Rapporteurship on Migrant Workers and their Families* (oea/ser./l/v/i111 doc. 20 rev.), 16 April 2001, par. 99.

[45] The IACHR has pointed out that "migrants are generally in a vulnerable situation as subjects of human rights; they are in an individual situation of absence or difference of power with regard to non-migrants (nationals or residents). This situation of vulnerability has an ideological dimension and occurs in a historical context that is distinct for each State and is maintained by *de jure* (inequalities between nationals and aliens in the laws) and de facto (structural inequalities) situations. This leads to the establishment of differences in their access to the public resources administered by the State", IACHR, Advisory Opinion OC-18/03, op. cit., paragraph 112. An identical position can be read in the Concurring Opinion of AA Cançado Trindade (paragraph 15) and the Concurring Reasoned Opinion of S Ramirez (paragraphs 9 and 11).

[46] IACHR, Advisory Opinion OC-18/03, Juridical Condition and Rights of the Undocumented Migrants, par. 133.

[47] IACHR, Advisory Opinion OC-18/03, Juridical Condition and Rights of the Undocumented Migrants, par. 157 and 158.

[48] As stated by Abramovich about of the Inter-American system, although applicable to the European system too, for a long time, migration policies were kept outside the sphere of human rights. However, there are currently compelling reasons to start bridging the gap between the world of public polices and rights at the regional level. Such policies should gradually conform to the provisions of the international law of human rights, considering among other sources, the body of principles, standards and case law of the Inter-American and European systems of human rights. This would encourage the harmonisation of policies at the regional level, so strategies respecting the multilateral normative agreements on human rights could be reach, thus facilitating greater legitimacy and greater support of the civil society. Abramovich V. Los Estándares Interamericanos de Derechos Humanos como Marco para la Formulación y el Control de las Políticas Sociales, Anuario de Derechos Humanos, 2006.

[49] De Lucas J. Sobre los fundamentos de la igualdad y del reconocimiento. Un análisis crítico de las condiciones de las políticas europeas de integración ante la inmigración. In: VVAA. Inmigración e integración en la UE. Dos retos para el siglo XXI. Bilbao 2012; pp. 11-91.

[50] IACHR, Advisory Opinion OC-18/03, Juridical Condition and Rights of the Undocumented Migrants, *par. 88.*

[51] The case law of the ECHR is determinant in the European Union's secondary law on the matter of immigration and asylum. In the international dimension, the so-called "subsidiary protection" was critical in cases such as family reunification. Nevertheless, the merely "subsidiary" nature of such control has been questioned, on the grounds of its practical dimension and after considering that, more than one decade after the Treaty of Amsterdam and from the beginning of the legislative production in the European Union, there are still questions on the gaps in production. Furthermore, the current position of "legal subsidiarity" of the ECHR must be, logically, prudent and restrained, taking into account that in matters of subsidiarity it does not protect at the national level. The magnitude of the difficulties encountered in the courts when managing disputes on immigration and asylum should encourage European courts (including the Court of Justice of the European Union) to participate more actively on the sphere of the legal protection of persons. European Parliament, Impact de la jurisprudence de la CEJ et de la CEDH en matiere d'asile et d'immigration,... *cit.*

[52] IACHR, Advisory Opinion OC-18/03, Juridical Condition and Rights of the Undocumented Migrants, *par. 173.*

Current and Future Developments in Law, 2017, *Vol. 2*, 113-130

CHAPTER 5

The Human Rights of the Migrants

Juan Antonio Gómez García*

Department of Legal Philosophy, Faculty of Law, UNED, Madrid, Spain

Abstract: This work raises and develops the fundamental questions about the phenomenon of the migration in the current world, from the theory of the human rights and its contrast with the praxis. After stating the big vulnerability that characterizes the migrants, the author tries to offer proposals and possible solutions to this problem in the context of the national and international politics.

Keywords: Human rights, Migration, National and international politics, Vulnerability.

1. INTRODUCTION

The migrations of people between diverse places of the world is an essential fact to his condition partner-cultural like such people from the most remote times. Already from the training of the first political units to one some scale and with one some continuity in the Antiquity (remember the Roman *ius gentium*), and especially, from the origins of the States in modern sense, the phenomenon of the migrations has been central object of consideration by part of the political authorities and of the distinct juridical rules, so much national like international.

However, in the current times, this phenomenon has adopted some outlines and some special characteristics, that show his deep importance, so much quantitative like qualitative, until the point that today the world cannot comprise properly if it does not consider the migratory phenomenon in all his complexity, like a systemic, structural, phenomenon, of the same. For example, the Report of International Migration of United Nations, published in 2002, signaled that, already then, the people that resided out of his country of birth reached the unusual figure of 175 million, more than the double that the number of people of the generation precedent.

* **Corresponding author Juan Antonio Gómez García:** Department of Legal Philosophy, Faculty of Law, UNED, Madrid, Spain; Tel: 0034 913988059; Fax : 0034 913986154; E-mail: jagomez@der.uned.es

J. Alberto del Real Alcalà (Ed.)

In effect, it is in the frame of the contemporary globalization (especially, in the context of the dialectics North-South) where the migratory movements have increased extraordinarily and have become qualitatively more complex if they are compared with last times, due to the enlargement of the current migratory networks to more territories, to the diversification of the migratory types, to the sharp socio-economic inequality and to the existing cultural differences between the persons of the different places of the planet. In the question of the migration there are involved so important and thorny topics as the processes of decolonization in the Third World, the problem of the massive and uncontrolled migrations of persons towards the First World (for example, the question of the mafias and of the economic development of the migrants), the problem of the multiculturalism and of the interculturalism expressed in the contrast (even, often, in the shock) between the different sociocultural conditions of the nationals of different countries that have to coexist under the sovereignty of the State, the questions of genre in different cultural ambiences, *etc.* ...For that reason the subject today is so controverted and so difficult to approach in all aspects, by the multiplicity, wealth and diversity of dimensions that it owns, considering the pressing necessity to reformulate and to re-update permanently, as much the concepts and the implied political-legal categories, like the positive norms and the political actions around such phenomenon.

In my opinion, the best way to contemplate the migratory phenomenon, facing understanding it and pointing satisfactory answers well on the matter, is that one that approaches it in the light of the philosophy and of the praxis of the human rights [1], since under these coordinates the tension is perceived by major depth and comprehensive capacity between the universality that is proper of any human right with the peculiarity that is proper of its achievement, exercise and protection in practice. The observation of which the migratory phenomenon is not today, not much less, solved is demonstrated by the permanent need, for the States, of implementing new politics that attack this phenomenon from new perspectives, without breaking the classic categories of the human rights (specially, as I say, the demand of its universality, while rights of all the human beings), which, otherwise, constitute historical products that have its origin and development in the own modern western culture. In effect, what characterizes politically and legally to the migrants, is its subjects condition with a peculiar status, generally with less and more limited fundamental rights than the nationals of the country to which they migrate, which, in principle, it can turn out to be contradictory with the universal entitlement of the human rights.

For example, Spain is not foreign to this tendency at present, with added of that such a phenomenon has supposed a substantial change with regard to the migratory tendencies of the persons in the last times, opposite to not very distant others: of being an emigrants' country, Spain has happened to be an immigrants' country, although in the last years this tendency is adjusted due to the serious economic crisis that he is living through our country and that, as everyone knows, it is provoking a situation of the highest unemployment in all the sectors of the working population, especially between the young people, the most sensitive, more flexible sector and, in principle, better predisposed to move back and forth to look for better opportunities. Anyway, in general terms, it is true that, practically during the whole XXth century, our country was registering a number greatly major of emigrations than of immigrations, for reasons of diverse nature (political, economic, social, cultural), too well-known, related principally to the convulsed Spanish history of last century (Civil War, diverse crises and economic depressions, sociocultural delay of the population, *etc.* ...). With the socio-economic explosion produced at the end of the nineties, Spain had happened to turn into a destination longed by many foreigners who were trying to find a few better material conditions that in its fatherlands, coming untied an immigration wave (especially, of Latin Americans, East Europeans,...) that changed substantially the existing perspective in our country on the migratory phenomenon (the paradigmatic legal product was the called *Ley de Extranjería-Ley Orgánica 8/2000, de 22 de diciembre-*). It is necessary to add an element of big importance to it, talking each other of Spain, as it is that of the illegal entry of immigrants proceeding from Africa in boats that cross the Strait of Gibraltar, that arrive to Canaries or that try to gain access for Ceuta and Melilla avoiding the frontier line with Morocco. This migratory phenomenon, singularly humiliating for the integrity and the dignity of the persons, accentuates moreover, if it fits, all the complex problems that he accompanies to the phenomenon of the migration.

2. SOME PREVIOUS CONCEPTUAL EXPLANATIONS: *MIGRANTS, EMIGRANTS, IMMIGRANTS, REFUGEES* AND *TOURISTS*

Within dependence of its current profiles and its historical phenomenology, the migration has always been considered the exercise of a faculty of the persons, or of groups of persons, while condition inherent in its freedom of movement, displacement and transit for the world [2]. The majority of the times (by all means, the casuistry offers numerous exceptions and shades) has been seen like a conduct that responds there to a voluntary decision of the migrant who tries to look for better circumstances, contexts, opportunities and living conditions, from here his consideration like human right (soon we will deepen on the theoretical idiosyncrasy of this right).

Anyway, in front of the existent confusion around the terminology (that it is used to confuse, especially, *migrant* with *emigrant* and *immigrant*), suits to clear, in the first place, what understands by *migrant*, in order to require conceptually such right. The subject of the human rights related with the migration is the person in his condition of migrant. This generic condition can have two concrete dimensions: on the one hand, it can treat of a person migrant that goes out of his country to install in another, in whose case would be speaking specifically of an *emigrant*; whereas, on the other hand, from the point of view of the country that receives to this person, would treat of an *immigrant*. It is a question of terms that must not make a mistake, of entry, to locate properly all the political-juridical problems that accompanies the person who moves from its original State to other with the intention of settling (this is to the *migrant*).

Also, to locate the topic in its just terms, it is important here to realize another two important conceptual distinctions: the first distinction between *migrant* and *tourist*, and other one between *migrant* and *refugee*, since it is a question of two very specific types of migrants who must be differentiated with regard to the generic category, and because both phenomena, the tourism and the refugees' flows, it constitutes also distinctive information of the current encompassed world.

The *tourist* is a *migrant* who moves another State, in use of its freedom of movement. Certainly, a tourist who travels from its country towards other or others, is a migrant who emigrates from its country and who immigrates in the destination country. In this distinction is where stress even more the contextual factors that determine the differences between the people that migrate in general, conditioning decisively the special and complex problematic that accompanies to the human rights of the migrants. Obviously, the tourist is a simple visitor, with an idea formed previously on the country of destination that provokes especially interest and curiosity, which attitude is dyed of a certain economic and cultural superiority, and whose purpose is merely a dawdler, enjoying itself in what the destination point can offer him; while the immigrant aspires to integrate in the country of destination moved by the state of material need that is thinking about satisfying if he travels and settles there, being based on the initial image that it takes of the destination country as an opportunities place, and with a constructive attitude and a purpose; to sum up, with an initial disposition to offer itself.

The intention of entailment and the commitment with the destiny place is, then, much more deep in the case of the immigrant who in the one of the tourist, and it determines the different legal treatment that it receives, on the part of the receiving country in front of the simple tourist, generally in a limiting, restrictive sense, getting it to even consider, in many cases, outside the law, an *illegal one*. They are, then, two figures that only can be understood in this way within the framework of the globalized society present, where the facilities to move from a place to another one are considerably majors that in times (not so) last.

Finally, in spite of being typically a migrant, the figure of the refugee differs for the political nature of the reasons that push to the refugee to go out of its country, be already for wars, political repression or revolutions, in order to look for protection on the part of another State. The economic and cultural motives remain here very blurred in favor of the politicians and, therefore, the refugee (as the International Law shows it) possesses a particular legal system that distinguishes it and grants him a very specific condition, as regards the migrants in general.

3. FROM THE THEORY TO THE PRAXIS OF THE MIGRATION: THE MIGRANTS AS VULNERABLE GROUP

If it is descended from the theoretical plane to the praxis of the human rights of the migrants, especially in the relative thing to its protection and effective guarantees on the part of the States, it is comprised better than the proclaimed is still very far of realize in practice. Certainly, advances have taken place during the last years on the subject of human rights, but in case of the migrants the situation is singularly deficient, there being still stated regulations, practices and state institutional ambiences that do not give the minimums demanded in the theoretical plane (normative and doctrinal), going so far as even to ignore, in many cases, any type of protection of the human rights of the migrants: it is symptomatic that the figure of the migrant is not still protected by any specific international institution, as it happens with the case of the refugee on the part of the UNHCR, even if also it must be indicated that the last one does not enjoy of the protection that, in principle, the States of origin can bring him the migrants..

Therefore, the migrants constitute a category of people in especially vulnerable situation, in which to his human rights it talks about; vulnerability that responds to diverse causes and that occurs in different situations: in its origin, since, the emigration responds to the necessity to look for an improvement in the existential conditions of a person (also with regard to its rights) before a conjuncture of uncertainty in its country of origin; in its transit towards the destiny country, very frequently due to the great ties and difficulties that are to save the migrants to arrive, to enter legally and to be welcomed by the State of destiny; and, finally, in its final goal, when being like immigrants, generally and supposing that they are admitted legally, under political, social, economic and legal a status more unfavorable than the citizens of that State. Hence one has affirmed that the first human right that we must bear in mind in this topic should be *the right not to migrating*, if the phenomenon of the migration is contemplated in view of right to development of the peoples.

The main problems that they have come reviewing, as regards the human rights of the migrants, can be synthesized in the following types:

1. *Smuggling* and *trafficking*. These practices happen when there exist threats, coercions, tricks, abuse of authority, abduction … (in sum, physical or psychic violence) to catch, to receive, to move, to transport, to receive people in a State, in order to exploit them in all of the referent to his personal and laboral dignity [3].
2. The detention and deportation of the irregular migrants. It is very frequent that the detentions and migrants' deportations realize under conditions of serious risk for the human rights of these, especially when there are important differences between the national regulations of the States and the international regulation. In the border zones these problems acquire a much more pressing appearance, since, often, they are intimately tied to situations of big violence that finish with the proper life of the migrants (for example, the called *coyotaje* practices). Also, a phenomenon especially serious the massive deportations of undocumented immigrants constitute it, especially when they take a wide time living in the destination countries, generating consequences, sometimes very traumatic, for these persons who are very integrated to the country.
3. Partial integration of the immigrants. The irregular situation of many immigrants in large number of countries of reception, is a cause of frequent violations of its human rights, especially as for its economic and social rights. Even, in the assumptions of legal immigration, the entire integration is not usually habitual for giving him situations of clear discrimination on the part of the state legislations, before the social depreciation that many immigrants endure in the country for the simple fact of it being.
4. Social discrimination and exclusion for racial and xenophobic motives. Intimately linked to the previous phenomenon, such situations acquire a very sharp profile when it is a question of undocumented immigrants.
5. The feminine and infantile migration as ambiences especially vulnerable. All the previous problems is extremely difficult when it is contemplated as regards the feminine and infantile migration, which vulnerability is accentuated moreover with regard to the migrants males, for the incidence of other factors like the sexual violence and the development (forced prostitution, sexual commerce,…), treats her as persons, its low level of education, the biggest instability of its wages, the neglect of the children…

All this casuistry of the migratory phenomenon constitutes a factor of big relevancy to understand all the relevant problematic to the human rights of the migrants and, consequently, it has to be born very in mind at the time of making compatible them with the theoretical-normative plane of the rights, facing which the praxis does not distance too much of the theory.

4. PREVIOUS REFLECTION: SOME NOTES ABOUT THE CONCEPT OF HUMAN RIGHTS

Anyway, when we talk about human rights, it should be also clarify, prior to, that we understand under this notion so problematic. The famous French philosopher Jacques Maritain (as we know, one of the main impellers of the Universal Declaration of the Human rights of United Nations) described therefore to the situation and the mood of the participants in one of the discussions of such Commission in which he struggled on the concept and foundation of the human rights that were tried to proclaim: "Somebody indicated its surprise when seeing that certain defenders of ideologies violently opposed had agreed themselves to write up a list of rights. 'Clearly - they talked back we agree in those rights on condition that she does not wonder herself to us why'. He is with `why' and so the discussion begins".

All the present (of very diverse origin and with very different religious, ethical, morals, political, legal conceptions) showed of agreement in the need to establish a concrete relation of human rights, but without going in to define them neither to give account of the reasons of such enumeration, giving, then, a to a large extent paradoxical situation: "the rational justifications –continues Maritain- are indispensable and, at the same time, are unable to create an agreement between the men. They are indispensable because each one of us believes instinctively in the truth and does not want to give his consent more than to what has recognized like true and like rationally valid. But they are unable to create an agreement between the men because they are fundamentally different or, even, contrary" [4].

Really, I believe that in this description there is one of the fundamental keys today to tackle the difficult and thorny question of the human rights: its paradoxical nature. This is very important to bear it in mind at the time of conceptualizing and defining the human rights, since the innumerable quantity of concepts, terms, characters, ... that they have come offering from its historical origins in the Modernity, denote reliably that such a notion depends on the question of its foundation. Obviously, for clear reasons of time and space, I am not going to enter here to tackle in detail this thorny question; simply, I would like stating, to effects purely operative, that such a paradoxical condition is proved today of a pragmatic foundation, of such rights, which one considers the mere formal agreement to be a sufficient reason between the deliberatives parts on what sound and what are such human rights. This is philosophically very functional, but barely realistic when we descend to the daily praxis, as much at normative level as existential, of such rights.

In any case, this conception, could say, ideological of the human rights -whereas expression of a *consensus omnium gentium*-, like means of legitimation, like ethical political and legal referents that have a fundamental paper in the context of the transformative political action of a *statu quo* valid whereas right subjective that make possible to preach of them his existence and efficiency (without going in to tackle of entrance, in reason of ethical, politicians and legal arguments, questions such as the need of his recognition or proclamation in a concrete juridical legislation, or in any another problematic relative to his violation), constitutes the starting point and the conceptual frame that allows to develop at present the speech on the human rights and, therefore, the one that we must have to have present here when I refer me to this category of rights and, especially, in relation with the human right to migrating. The ontological findings are, then, relegated today to background, forgetting (in my opinion, unjustly) that the rights have to be based on the things [5].

5. ABOUT THE HUMAN RIGHT TO MIGRATE: CONCEPT AND CHARACTERS

Nobody discusses today that the right to migrate is a human right, thus recognized specifically by most important international declarative texts (for example, art. 13 of the *Universal Declaration of the Human Rights* -December 10, 1948-; arts. 12,1° y 13 of *International Covenant on Civil and Political Rights*; art. 45 of *EU Charter of Fundamental Rights* -December, 2000-; art. 22 of *American Convention on Human Rights,...*): it is a right of freedom of the persons, specially of free circulation, which entitlement the nationals of any country show, and which it authorizes to them to move and to be established in another State for economic, political, social and/or cultural reasons. Consequently, the emigrant's condition is a substantial condition of every person who decides to go out of its country for these reasons.

Nevertheless, what does not seem so clear is the existence of a right to immigrate in so absolute terms, since here there enters scene the receiving State of the migrant, who, in reason of his own sovereignty, is who establishes it as such, and in its case, it fixes its requisites and scope, according to diverse particular criteria (political, economic, of public order, social, cultural,...). This is the reason that it justifies and explains, infact that this right of free access to settle in the receiving State (right to immigrate), has so legally different treatments on the part of the different States. In any case, the value that sublies to this supposed human right to immigrate is, principally, the solidarity, since the particular legal condition of the immigrants in the receiving country is determined by the engagement grade in its politics towards them in such countries, specified in the level of legal equality as regards the nationals.

All this makes much more complex the problem than in case of the emigrants, since it would be necessary to contemplate it in view of the called rights of cooperation and solidarity, a category of difficult technical joint (in fact they usually consider in the doctrine like rights of third generation, with all the conceptual problems that such a type of rights endures from the theoretical point of view [6]); up to a point a hybrid category between purely the individual and the social ones, although predominating over the social aspect, to the being the public condition of the subject (the immigrant is defined by the fact of its nationality) the one that provides of specificity this group of persons, in addition to whom its practical achievement takes place, of a way or other one, in the frame of the international cooperation between the States, the international organizations and the civil society.

Setting off from here, the politics that can be applied as regards the migratory phenomenon from the perspective of the human rights, they are linked basically to three aspects:

1. The control of the migratory flows on the part of the country that receives immigrants.
2. The relations of the receiving State with the States from which they come immigrants' major quantity.
3. The problem of the integration of the immigrants in the receiving country.

All these aspects have to do, especially, with the general question of the rights of the immigrants inside such a State. Let's see in a more detailed way.

6. THE FUNDAMENTAL TENSION IN THE MIGRATION POLICIES: STATE SOVEREIGNTY *VS.* HUMAN RIGHT TO MIGRATE

The general frame of this question is determined by the debate on the liberalization grade in the politics of the countries opposite to the phenomenon of the migration. Therefore, the beginning of sovereignty is the central element to think in the design and execution of the migration policies of the States, given that that the sovereignty is one of its essentials shots from its emergence in the beginnings of the Modernity. Hence one derives that, as a rule, the States show an almost absolute aptitude to fix the conditions of admission and immigrants' stay inside the borders of its territory, which act like frame of the identity of its people, like expression of its own sense of nationality and like physical condition of the exercise of its citizenship [7].

Now then, the solution is not so simple as it seems, since it can collide with questions as important as the following ones: Until point the sovereignty of the States can ignore human rights of the immigrants? To what extent can the proclamation of these rights, how dedicated in the Universal Declaration of United Nations, subordinate itself to the beginning and particular interests of the States? Is it possible to justify differences (when not discriminations) between the emigrants and the nationals as for its fundamental rights? In the fund, all this is only the demonstration of the classic dialectics between the universality of the human rights of the persons and the peculiarity of the sovereignty of every State to establish identical politics to its condition, conjunctures and interests.

In this sense, different and numerous positions and arguments fit, according to the diversity of criteria that also can be adduced on this matter. Synthetically, it is necessary to use fundamentally reasons of religious, moral, economic and cultural nature:

1. The opening, enclosing, positions, from an economic optics, they understand that, in a world encompassed like the current one where a capital free circulation exists, it turns out to be coherent that free circulation of labour exists. The opening of the borders and the liberalization of the flows of population would facilitate the development of those places where there was manpower need, that of the emigrants' own countries, since they would see its wealth increased thanks to the entry of capital and remittances derived from the activity there of its national emigrants.
   On the other hand, from a moral perspective, the liberalization is sustained in reasons of distributive justice, over criteria like the nationality, the race, the culture or the economy. Undoubtedly, the opening of borders and freedom of movements to international scale would allow those who have been born in poor countries to improve its position and its vital opportunities.
   Finally, there are adduced cultural reasons based, especially, on the idea of cultural merger and crossbreeding as expression of a mutual cultural enrichment.
2. On the contrary, the most closed or exclusive positions depart from the difficulties that the making of unilateral decisions raises on the part of the receiving States, before the material inability to adopt common and simultaneous politics between all the countries of the world. In this sense, to adopt too open positions can endure big problems for the States that this way were doing it, for diverse reasons: first of all, for economic reasons, since it can be a cause of conflicts for the citizens of the receiving country, since, to the universalising indiscriminately the public services (as for example, the health, the education, the use of the infrastructures,…) damages might be caused to such services by the massive immigrants arrival, turning out to be harmed the nationals on having had to share them on equal terms with those; secondly, social and cultural reasons are adduced, as the uncontrolled immigrants arrival could be a danger for the identity of the receiving country (language,

fundamental values, traditions, social behavior standards,...) [8].
Admitting the possibility of gradations between these two positions, we might say that the prevailing tendency today in practice inclines towards the second one, between other reasons, because no institution exists on a global scale with sufficiently effective influence as to encourage the politics implementation on a global scale, in favour of a major liberalization in the immigrants' reception, on the part of the principally receiving countries. And so, there is each of these countries the one that he designs and implants its own politics on this matter, depending on its own needs, especially of material character.

In conclusion, the context of the debates on migration and human rights is synthesized in the search of a balance between the sovereign prerogatives of the States and its duties towards the migrants in the frame of the international law and of the current encompassed world, in accordance with its particular national political, economic, social and cultural circumstances. This is an expression of the permanent tension between the sovereign power of the States to control and to regulate the admission, permanence and transit of migrants and immigrants in its territories, and the needs for migration that increasing groups of population have, due to the painful existing conditions in the fatherlands and to the demand of the receiving countries.

7. THE INTERNATIONAL REGULATION ON HUMAN RIGHTS OF THE MIGRANTS

An important factor to be borne in mind also is the international regulation of the human rights concerning the phenomenon of the migration, since it constitutes a fundamental modality in the existing general consideration on this phenomenon. In addition to the reviewed proclamations of the right to migrate like human right in the main international declarative texts of human rights, the International Law offers regulations based on beginning, recommendations, institutions and procedures based in turn on the fundamental beginning of the agreement of the sovereign States. And so, it is the self-regulation sustained on the principle of autonomy of its will and the bona fide principle, the fundamental criterion for its normative joint on a global scale, specified in agreements, treaties, pacts, protocols,... celebrated between the States signatories.

The hierarchy relations between the International Law and the internal Law of every State are variable depending on the country that we consider; nevertheless, the general principle is that the State has the power to define them in its own arranging, although the agreements and adopted commitments cannot be avoided in the assumption of which the State that is a part in one of them decides that its internal Law prevails over the international Law from a certain moment, unless such instruments violate its internal norms of clear and self-evident form (Vienna Convention on the Law of Treaties, May 23, 1969).

In the concrete field of the international regulation on human rights, the international agreements of the United Nations are the main modality, imposing juridical duties for all the countries that ratify them and that adhere to them, in the sense of recognizing them, of respecting them, of protecting them and of guaranteeing them, proclaiming them in its internal arranging with the status of *fundamental*, without interfering in the capacity and the action of the persons to exercise them, arbitrating measurements against possible violations of the same ones and tackling legislative, executive and judicial actions for its suitable exercise. Due to the exemplary function that fulfil the international norms of United Nations on human rights, the States that have not adhered to them they provoke, of entry, certain mistrust, suspicion and alertness on the part of the international community.

The main normative instruments of United Nations on human rights of the migrants are the following ones: the *International Convention on the Protection of the Rights of All Migrant Workers and Members of Their Families* (December 18, 1990, although its coming into effect was in 2003), that it is the most important, and that it has served as base of most of specific and sectorial regulations on human rights of the migrants (of looking over its fulfilment one entrusts the Committee of the United Nations for the Protection of the Immigrant Workpeople and of its Families);the *Declaration on the human rights of the individuals who are not nationals of the country in which they live* (December 13, 1985) and the regulation that establishes the figure of the *Special Rapporteur on the human rights of the migrants* (created in 1999 by the Commission of Human rights, in accordance with the resolution 1999/44), like organ of inspection and protection of these human rights in practice across its Reports, as well as the normative activity developed by the General Assembly, the Commission of Human rights and of the Council of Human rights on the protection of the human rights of the migrants in numerous normative instruments, from the due thing typically in the International *Covenant on Civil and Political Rights, International Covenant on Economic, Social and Cultural Rights,* the *Convention against Torture and Other Cruel, Inhuman or Degrading Treatment or Punishment* (commonly known as the *United Nations Convention against Torture*), the *Convention on the Elimination of All Forms of Discrimination against Women*, the *Convention on the Rights of the Child*, the *International Convention on the Elimination of all the Forms of Racial Discrimination*, the *Vienna Convention on Consular Relations*, and, finally, the *Convention on the Rights of the Persons with Disability* [9].

At inter-regional level numerous specific normative instruments exist also on human rights of the migrants, inspired by general terms in those of United Nations, although adapted to the proper peculiarities of its spaces of regional validity. The most important are, in the European space, the *Community Charter of the Fundamental Social Rights of Workers* (December 9, 1989), the Directive 2008/115/CEf the European Parliament and of the Council of 16 December 2008 on common standards and procedures in Member States for returning illegally staying third-country nationals, and the Regulation (EC) No 562/2006 of the European Parliament and of the Council of 15 March 2006 establishing a Community Code on the rules governing the movement of persons across borders (Schengen Borders Code) - the main institutional organs of control and protection of the Human Rights of the migrants in Europe are: the European Court of Human Rights, the Court of Justice of the European Union and the European Commission-; in the inter-American space, it emphasizes, within the framework of the activities of the Organization of American states, the *Inter-American Program for the Promotion and Protection of the Human Rights of Migrants, Including Migrant Workers and their Families* (May 25, 2005) -at inter-American level, the main institutions that look over the fulfilment and the protection of the Human Rights of the migrants are the Inter-American Court of the Human Rights and the Inter-American Commission of Human Rights-; and in the African space it is the *African Charter on Human and Peoples' Rights*, in its art. 12, the fundamental normative referent, as well as -specially for the refugees- *Convention Governing the Specific Aspects of Refugee Problems in Africa* ("OAU Convention", 1969) -in the African ambience the most important institutions of inspection and protection of the human rights of the migrants are the African Court of Human Rights and the African Commission of Human Rights-.

8. SOME FINAL REFLECTIONS ABOUT THE THEORY AND THE PRACTICE OF THE HUMAN RIGHTS OF THE MIGRANTS

I have aiming at it along all my exhibition: since it usually happens with the human rights, what is formulated in the theory is far from be fulfilling in practice. In effect, the traditional one and appellant arises here, again, critical speech with regard to the efficacy and the protection of the human rights: what steadies itself in abstract, in the theory, in the declarations and in the norms, does not happen necessarily in particular, in practice socially of the human rights of the persons. The human rights of the migrants are not foreign to this axiom luck; it is more, he is one of the specific groups of persons whose routine character, with regard to its human rights, is more distant than the proclaimed theoretically, and that there is more needed from protection, both at normative level (needed still from more specific and realistic normative instruments), and of protection and concrete political and legal guarantees, which makes it an extremely vulnerable group.

Against this, it is possible to adopt an ethical position: as what it serves to speak about human rights when do not occur, neither the material conditions, nor the disposition to promote its accomplishment and its respect in the life of the people, in this case the migrants?

This is a fundamental problem as regards the human rights in general, more pressing, as I say, as regards the migrants. This way numerous reports testify it on this matter, on the part of the main international institutions [10], which affect constantly in the frequent and indiscriminate violations of many human rights of the migrants, due especially to racist and xenophobic conducts, to the traffic and to it treats about persons, to detentions and massive deportations of irregular migrants without any legal guarantee, to the violence in the frontier regions between the States and to the absence of full integration of the immigrants in the receiving countries (the irregular immigrants).

Certainly, the most important migratory flows owe to reasons of fundamentally economic character. The scarcity and the instability of the material conditions of life obligate the persons to migrate to other more prosperous countries economically in search of better existential horizons. Generally, the poverty and the underdevelopment usually happen in countries where an accented political and social dismantling exists (in the frustrated or not democratic States), so that the protection and the effective guarantees of the fundamental rights of the persons who emigrate from them (and that migrate for them, with the target to arrive at its final destination) they are, little less, than fictions, when not vain well-intentioned illusions. To speak here about human rights is almost a sarcasm and, therefore, any reflection on this matter is absolutely determined by the extreme real vulnerability of these persons.

In a globalized world like the present one, it turns out to be necessary, then, to understand the right to migrate under the most generic right to development of the peoples. Such right shows a collective dimension that comes out the borders of the simple States, individually considered, being an expression of goods, values and interests of general and common character. And so, one must be understood with the frame of a criterion that allows to agglutinate the members who compose a certain community of interests and responsibilities: this is, under the beginning of solidarity, that the foundation has constituting of recently so called *human rights of third generation*.

The principle of solidarity allows to integrate the diversity of particular interests in a common interest, in the light of a spirit of cooperation and altruistic sacrifice, for the sake of the attainment of the needs and objectives that the communitarian, collective nature imposes, of such goods and I interest declared by this new category of human rights. Solidarity is the criterion for the interrelation between the different people and communities from the idea of dignity, that is to say, its reciprocal recognition like equals in the amplest sense of this term. Consequently, its practical accomplishment must estimate a global identity of preoccupations and decisions in the international scope, since tries to be a form of protection of supranational legally protected interests that they concern directly to the universality of the human rights in as much expression of a universal equal dignity for all man. And so, the division that there introduce the traditional criteria of distinction of political and legal status (social class, ethnic group, religion, nationality, *etc.*), own of a statalist conception of the rights, they lack here sense, and there any consideration will have to appear from a wider and open perspective and any exercise try will have to be realized from a proportion that exceeds the scale (in this order, excessively small) proper of the national States: from the unit of the world in its set.

Therefore, it is by the vindication of an equal dignity for all the people, reason why the human rights of the migrants must, at heart, articulate. This is translated, actually, in the vindication of the possibility, for the poor countries, of an economic development that makes possible a greater justice and equality to them, in relation to the richest States, in the property and distribution of the fundamental goods, appealing for it to its dignity. This need articulated like right to development, has turned out to be gathered institutionally in an implicit way by the route, especially, from the right to the equality; explicitly, in such normative instruments like the paragraph 1 of the Preamble of the Declaration on the Granting of Independence to Colonial Countries and Peoples (December 14, 1960), the art. 22 of the African Charter on Human and Peoples' Rightsand, especially, the Declaration of the United Nations on the Right to development (December 4, 1986).

It is understood, then, how the right that there possess all the peoples and its members to be informed in the development process and to obtain a report jousts of the benefits derived from this one. This development must be understood with a wide sense: as biological development (better health, better nutrition,…), economic (economic growth, aptitude to have the proper natural resources,…), socio-political (political autonomy, promotion of the human rights,…) and cultural (enrichment and diffusion of the education and the culture). Finally, it talks each other to obtain an integral development of the most disadvantaged countries and of the peoples and persons who inhabit them, from all the institutional instances (the States, international organizations, social institutions,…). From a conceptual point of view, the right to development is intimately tied to another human right of third generation: the self determination of the peoples (for many authors it is the same right in its economic, social and cultural dimension).

In view of these general considerations, it is interesting to bear in mind at the time of articulating concrete politics, the differences between the migrants' diverse typology, especially between the refugees and the rest of types, after those to be the group of migrants on which it has existed and a major worry and normative development exists. The International ex-Repporteur Gabriela Rodríguez, in its first management Report presented to the Commission of Human rights of the United Nations, proposed, after any generic legal *migrant* concept did not exist in the International Law, as regards that of *refugee* (concept, this one yes, declared explicitly at international normative level), to be considered to be migrants the persons who are out of the territory of the State of its nationality or citizenship and who are out of its legal protection (a special category, for its big vulnerability, they are the undocumented migrants or in irregular situation out of its country, which are exposed to discriminations and violations of all kinds, or to the refusal of its rights and its fundamental freedoms). They differ this way from the refugees in whom the above mentioned show a specific legal recognition of its rights, while permanent residents, naturalized or other similar forms, and in which there are subjects of the general legal protection by virtue of diplomatic agreements, visas or others [11].

Consequently, the protection politics of the migrants need a wider and integral perspective than that of the refugees, for the complexity of its situation (problems derived from the differences of language, customs, cultures –that usually derive in a negative perception of the immigrant- the economic, social pressures that they have to confront, as well as the obstacles to return to its respective fatherlands); in sum, for its unequal social, economic, cultural and legal status as regards the nationals.

The politics of bilateral and multilateral cooperation between the States, and of solidarity for with the least developed countries, constitutes essential aspects for the effective guarantee of the human rights of the migrants. In this sense, the progressive adherence and ratification of the instruments of international Law for the protection of the rights of the migrants (condition much related here is the immediate rehabilitation of the internal legislations of the States to make the fulfilment of its commitments possible on this matter) and the struggle from treats about persons it must be fundamental modality.

At intra-state level, such politics has to materialize in measurements that attenuate, as far as possible, the problems at present existing to gain access to judicial guarantees and protection on the part of the immigrants, of discrimination, racism and xenophobia, of restrictions to the personal freedom and to the labour law, from a transverse approach that bears in mind the differences of age and genre of the migrants, and implying jointly, both to the international organizations and to the civil society, by means of the joint of instruments of information to the migrants, (both in the fatherlands, and in those of transit and destination), and the promotion of the alertness and the denunciation of the violations of its human rights in coordination with the States.

In conclusion, it is necessary to think the migration a structural phenomenon of our current world globalized (and therefore, that demands politics and structural answers), that has to be a dear from a positive, united and cooperative perspective, recognizing the valuable contribution of the migrants so much to its own country as after that of reception, when they manage to integrate into him.

CONFLICT OF INTEREST

The author declares no conflict of interest, financial or otherwise.

ACKNOWLEDGEMENTS

Declared none.

REFERENCES

[1] Bhabha J. Trafficking, Smuggling, and Human Rights. Migration Policy Institute 2002. Available from: www.migrationinformation.org; and Grant S. Migrant´s human rights: from the margin to the mainstream. Migration Policy Institute 2002. Available from: www.migrationinformation.org [cited: 10th Oct 2014]

[2] This way it is contemplated in art. "(1) Everyone has the right to freedom of movement and residence within the borders of each state. (2) Everyone has the right to leave any country, including his own, and to return to his country", Universal Declaration of the Human Rights of United Nation Dec 1948; Article 13.

[3] These practices are typified in two specific, complementary normative instruments to the Convention of the United Nations against the Transnational Organized crime: Protocol to Prevent, Suppress and Punish Trafficking in Persons Especially Women and Children, supplementing the United Nations Convention against Transnational Organized Crime (Protocol of Palermo, 2000) and the protocol against the Smuggling of Migrants by Land, Air and Sea (European Union, July 24, 2006). However, it is important to indicate here that the difference enters tries and traffic of people not always is clear, and nevertheless the qualification that becomes of a situation, in a sense or another one, can mean an effective negation of the rights of the involved people: this distinction implies practical and very important consequences, since to distinguish between an undocumented migrant and a victim of treat or, even, a refugee, can suppose committing an outrage against the same rights of the migrant. This way for example, often, the hard-working migrant prefers the development conditions in a rich country to the scarcity of its situation in its fatherland, in such a way that the denunciation of its conditions of development can be supposed by them its immediate deportation, and, therefore, turn in the paradox of which its *rescue* means really its *capture*

[4] Maritain J. El hombre y el Estado. Madrid: Encuentro 1983: 94

[5] About an ontological foundation of the human rights, in view of analogical logic, my work: El problema de la fundamentación de los derechos humanos desde una hermenéutica analógica, in Conde Gaxiola N. Contornos de hermenéutica y analogía. México DF: Torres Asociados 2014; pp. 297-328

[6] For example, my work Gómez García, JA. Los llamados derechos humanos de tercera generación. In: Filosofía del Derecho. Lecciones de Hermenéutica jurídica. Madrid: Universidad Nacional de

Educación a Distancia 2006; pp. 259-274

[7] Barbalet JM. Citizenship. Rights, Struggle and Class Inequality. Minneapolis-Minnesota: University of Minnesota Press 1988

[8] As extreme example of these positions, serve the judgment dictated at the end of last century, on the part of the Supreme Court of the United States of America, which concluded the following thing: "It is a recognized international law maxim that any sovereign nation has the power inherent in its sovereignty and essential for its self-preservation, to prohibit the foreigners' entry inside its domains or to admit them only into certain cases and under some conditions that can be prescriptible" (Goodwin-Gill G. International Law and Human Rights: Trends Concerning International Migrants and Refugees. International Migration Review 1989; 23(3): 526

[9] This regulation can be consulted on the web page of the Office of the United Nations High Commissioner for Human Rights (Available from: www.ohchr.org [cited November 12, 2014]

[10] As example, in the official webpage of ACNUDH, there are the reports of the first Special Repporteur on the human rights of the migrants of the United Nations, Gabriela Rodríguez, realized between January, 2000 and March, 2005 (available from: http://www.ohchr.org/spanish/issues/migration/rapporteur/)

[11] Rodríguez Pizarro G. Grupos e Individuos específicos: trabajadores migrantes. Informe presentado por la Relatora Especial sobre los derechos humanos de los migrantes (E/CN.4/2005/85/Add.4, January 13, 2005)

CHAPTER 6

Gender Discrimination, Immigration and Multiculturalism

Catalina Ruiz-Rico Ruiz* and **Luis Francisco Sánchez Cáceres**

Faculty of Law, University of Jaén, Jaén, Spain

Abstract: The fusion of immigration and multiculturalism problems generates new legal challenges and a constitutional quandary focused on the Equality as a fundamental right. Discriminatory practices by gender such as anthropological practices, cults and traditions have been imported obstructing any legal relativism in the framework of an alliance between different civilizations. The Equality as a constitutional principle and as a multiculturalism limit involves a constitutional answer in relation to discriminatory practices that emerges from religious freedom, forced marriages and other coercive behaviors suffered by immigrant women.

Keywords: Gender discrimination, Multiculturalism, Religious freedom, Violence against women.

1. LEGAL APPROACH

The legal and social debate about multiculturalism reveals one of the unfinished business of the national legislature in response to the phenomenon of immigration. The clash between civilizations' practices, traditions and religions necessarily requires a legal solution within the constitutional framework. With the aim of incorporating the legality in the space of religious freedom and multicultural practices, the predicament is addressed from a gender perspective.

The resource to the equality right provides a parameter of legal legitimacy of multicultural practices that, in spite of being primarily religious, they are not so exclusively.

* **Corresponding author Catalina Ruiz-Rico Ruiz:** Faculty of Law, University of Jaén, Jaén, Spain; Tel: 0034 953212995; Fax: 0034 953212222; E-mail: crrico@ujaen.es

J. Alberto del Real Alcalà (Ed.)

2. RELIGIOUS FREEDOM FROM A GENDER PERSPECTIVE

2.1. About the Religious Symbolism

Among the issues that fuel the debate over religious symbols from a gender perspective, exists, the use of the veil, especially in public spaces.

In principal, the Organic Law 7/1980 about Religious Freedom does not specify the content of this Fundamental Right in Article 2 OLRF, although the use of religious veil could be integrated into the right to freely express their own beliefs.

In this respect, Article 10 of the Charter of Fundamental Rights of the European Union, adopted by the Lisbon Treaty, recognizes the right to manifest one's religion in public or in private through practice and observance [1]. This European legal source designed for freedom of religious expression constitutes the legal basis of the right to religious symbols. While, however, the rights of the European Charter, their values and European freedoms can counter the absolute nature of religious freedom [2].

Although the Lisbon Treaty has not achieved a uniform treatment of the religious veil in the different European countries based on the uneven level of multiculturalism and secularism various criteria such as state or non-denominational.

In this regard, several divergent stances have been adopted such as the banning of the Islamic veil in France or others more permissive in Belgium and in the United Kingdom, though the absent Spanish position only altered by several City Ordinances, especially in Catalonia [3].

It is therefore paradoxical that a common European law relating to religious freedom has covered various legal responses in a sociopolitical context with identical values of dignity, safety and equality [4].

The dilemma between acceptance and rejection of religious symbols in Europe must be regulated about equality for compromising the dignity of women and equal treatment of immigrants in the European area [5]. Against this background of legal inequality in the religious veil, would adopt a unified strategy regardless of the religious model, secular or secular force in each European country to avoid religious freedom present a different legal effect within EU level, otherwise the spirit of the Charter of Fundamental Rights.

2.2. Conflict of Rights

Among the most controversial aspects, religious symbolism highlights the multiplicity of conflicts of rights that converge on this issue from religious freedom, personal rights and equality. In this regard, the right to religious freedom cannot prevail over personal freedom of women and their autonomy to carry the veil. In parallel, religious discrimination cannot overlap the sex discrimination derivable from the use of the veil by women.

Nevertheless, the battle between these rights must be examined in a wider context of religious symbology at the danger of unequal treatment between religious symbols and decorative details.

From the legal consistency, it cannot be justified that crucifixes should be removed from the classroom while simultaneously permissiveness of heads carves in schools is supported. Although the process of secularization of religious symbols and ornamental veil is not parallel is hard to justify unequal treatment of each other. Likewise, various factors involved in the admission of religious symbols such as their use in the public or private space, major or minor, and the traditional or exogenous origin.

However, this heterogeneity of symbols and their unequal legal effectiveness should determine a unifying criterion applicable legal response. Equality as courage and right can help inform the common thread in religious symbolism, in its general aspect and gender.

First, the implementation of the right to equality in general contributes to the high approval of religious symbolism to avoid unequal treatment of symbols. However, the Non-denominational Clause of the Spanish State interferes with the legal equalization of religious symbols. Indeed, religious symbols intrinsic of tradition, history and Spanish culture logically have a higher level of legal consolidation and standardization with respect to those of other religions and cultures as the religious veil. In addition, there has been a process of secularization of most of the traditional religious symbols in our country, institutionalized and shedding its original character. This phenomenon prevents precise delimitation between the cultural, popular, historical or artistic and religious, and has gradually gained more and more symbols. As indeed it is with symbols, practices and traditions of the multicultural character of the difficult delimitation of its religious component.

Meanwhile, migratory phenomena have contributed to the importation of religious symbols without roots in our rural area, making difficult an equalization with those who have undergone a process of secularization. Now it is foreseeable that a state theoretically neutral religiously supports the implementation of a purely religious symbol through the creation “ex novo” of new religious traditions. Thus, this distancing between religious symbols tends to consolidate the detriment of the newly introduced symbols for cultural and traditional reasons.

Not even in the field of the same religion, religious symbols ornamental have an equal treatment like garments with a religious, because the process of secularization has not been parallel and like it has been referred (JSCS [6] December 14, 2009). Indeed, the status of religious symbols in public places away from the habit of religious clothing, causing different legal responses. The exclusion of religious symbols in classrooms or public institutions seem to be freed on the same right to religious freedom that is put forth for the admission of religious clothing in the same places.

It has gradually verified an unquestioned legal segregation of religious symbols depending on whether ornaments or clothing inside the space in which they pretend to be introduced (Public schools, Private school or Public Private Partnership), or depending on the public or private nature of the subject (the State or a private person). Moreover, The Supreme Court Jurisprudence addresses the protection of subject and places, particularly vulnerable in the presence of religious symbols, showing a tighter stance in education due to the risk of proselytism.

Thus, the need to protect minors in a particular training area such as school classrooms, tends to justify the strict judicial control on religious symbols. At the heart of this, underlies the idea that the presence of religious symbols in the training phase of minors may involve an impermissible indoctrination. Certainly, the educational setting is an area prone to conflict converging the right to religious freedom of the parents, the right to education and others rules and discipline in schools where certain clothes are banned.

The aspiration to unify a legal response towards religious symbols is complicated by the need to weigh the circumstances that shaped each case, not being indifferent the conflict that occurs in a school, a public institution or even outside the institutional space [7]. Moreover, it appears that uniform treatment of religious symbolism in all its variations and in different environments is complex because the state imposition is not legally valued in the same way that the voluntary and private use of religious symbols, although in both cases conflicts can be reduced to the collision of religious freedoms. So, while an extra of religious neutrality is required for the state and public institutions, individuals hold, however, a right to ostensible practice of religious symbols, even those ostensibly discrimination of women [8].

The equality right can and must offer a legal and constitutional solution to legal inconsistencies derived from real inequality between religious symbols. Specifically, the gender perspective can address the legal treatment of those symbols that merges two aspects, sexual and religious. As the Islamic headscarf, which has a religious dimension, but also sexual, because it regulates predominantly sexual relations between sexes, and suggests the preferential protection of the equality right over religious freedom.

Gender equality represents a legal solution to the conflicts around religious symbolism, due to its role as a constitutional limit to the right to religious freedom and the use of not exclusively religious symbols. From a legal perspective, the potential discriminatory religious symbols should not find coverage in the Law even under the protection of religious freedom.

2.3. Limits of the Right to Religious Symbols

2.3.1. Sex Discrimination from Gender Equality

Among the glaring deficiencies of the Organic Law of Religious Freedom, highlights the lack of foresight about the equality right as an explicit limit to the exercise of rights under the religious freedom. The equality right of rights holders to use religious symbols has not been regulated from a gender perspective. The Lawmaker has ignored one of the main problems that affects to religious symbols such as the violation of the constitutional equality right and the prohibition about sex discrimination.

Indeed, religious symbols with a sexual dimension can incorporate the limit of the equality right for the exclusion of those that involve discriminatory practices. The legal tolerance of religious symbolism has the limit in the dignity of women and the prohibition of sex discrimination.

Specifically, the use of certain religious symbols such as the burqa [9] or niqab [10] is obviously discriminatory to women, unlike other kinds of veil which are less shocking to the Western world. Among the parameters to determine the legal admission of certain religious veils would have to determine whether they are a cause of persecution in their countries of origin. The exercise of violence to compel women to wear sexual- spiritual symbols in certain nations, cannot substantiate that these same women are free to take in our country. The risk of coercion extends our geographic space which requires public authorities to be especially wary of these type of symbols.

However, whatever symbols, religious practices or traditions based on the inferiority of women and their submission or subordination, regardless of their mode of externalization, must be excluded from legal protection unambiguously. If geographic variants or the diverse modalities of a same religious symbol are based on restricting women's freedom, in their sexual submission or garments that undermine the dignity of women, is unsustainable from a constitutional perspective the legal protection of the fundamental right to religious freedom.

The unsuccessful attempt to ban certain religious symbols in public spaces through City Ordinances while is not disputed that the municipalities prohibit the use of bathing suit or go shirtless outside, also suffers from legal consistency [11]. About this inconsistency is possible to talk if the decorum and decency are supporting restrictions on the right to personal liberty without the constitutional right of equality permits the banning of religious symbols contrary to the women's dignity and other discriminatory symbols.

2.3.2. Based on its Coercive Imposition

The legal acceptance of questionable religious symbols from a gender perspective is based on its voluntary use in the private sphere and public space.

However, the pressure that traditions, cultures and minorities can exercise in women hinders the distinction between voluntary and coercive uses of religious veil.

Having said that, the existence of wills weakened by ancestral or cultural practices that find shelter in individual and religious freedom, justifies the intervention of the Law. In spite of objecting the inalienability of the gender equality right by their owners and their individual liberty for religious reasons from a constitutional perspective, the legal argument about the voluntary use of discriminatory religious symbols collides with the constitutional rejection of a resignation to Fundamental Rights, such as gender equality.

In this perspective,it is necessary to address the rising problem of religious harassment and pressure from religious communities or minorities on Westernized immigrant women who dispense with religious symbols, constituting a gender harassment based on religious grounds liable to prosecution even under the Criminal Law.

2.4. Duty of Integration for Gender Equality Purposes

The legal issues surrounding religious symbols that enforce the necessary use of the immigration rules for foreigners regarding to the applicable solutions. In this regard, the Organic Law 2/2009, of 11 December in reform of the Organic Law 4/2000 of 11 January on the rights and freedoms of foreigners in Spain and their social integration provides the foreigners integration in a framework of coexistence between different cultures and identities without limits with the exception of the respect to the Constitution and law, reaffirming the effective equality between men and women (Article 2 ter). Training activities are planned in order to obtain the knowledge and respect of constitutional and statutory values of Spain, European Unión, and Human Rights, Public Freedoms, democracy, tolerance and equality between men and women.

As a limit to religious symbols, the Article 3 of the Immigration Law in its last reform, establishes that is impossible to allege the profession of religious beliefs or diverse ideological convictions in order to justify acts and conducts contrary to the same beliefs, and must be interpreted in according to the Universal Declaration of Human Rights, International Treaties and Agreements over the same topics in force in Spain.

In parallel, the Spanish Asylum Law provides regulates the asylum concession including persecution cases due to non-use of any religion (Article 6), considering that in the valuation of persecution reasons is obliged to take into account a religion concept that includes, in particular, the profession of theistic, non-theistic and atheistic beliefs, the personal participation or abstention in public or private ceremonies, either individually or communally, as well as in others acts or expressions that include a religious character opinion, or personal and communal conducts based on any religious belief or commanded by this belief.

According to this normative, the legal admissibility of religious symbols imported is held to its coercive imposition in their countries of origin. The introduction in our country of religious practices contrary to the Spanish Constitution and other laws, suggests the need of a duty of integration in relation to the gender equality.

The religious freedom and the right of wearing religious symbols, like any other constitutional right, include limits in order to prevent discriminatory practices. The legal intolerance on discriminatory religious symbols because of the gender is based on the constitutional right of equality.

2.5. The Banning of Islamic Veils in Public Spaces by the Ordinances of Coexistence According to the Judgement of the Supreme Court on the 14th of February of 2013

In principal, the constitutional component of the City Ordinances lies in the classification of all individual or collective practices that violate the dignity and equality, such as those practices with a xenophobic, racist or sexist nature (Article 15 of the City Ordinance of Barcelona) [12]. The multicultural phenomenon transcends to the plane of citizenship, even though its regulation by the municipalities can affect to fundamental rights as has been said recently by the Judgement of the Supreme Court of the 14th of February 2013 about the prohibition of burqa by the City Ordinance of Lleida.

The assumption of legitimate and municipal powers in order to protect the social harmony and public spaces is projected on goods protected constitutionally and fundamental rights (Judgment of the Court of Justice of Catalonia 1156/2009 of the 23th of November).

The legitimacy of Local Governments in the maintenance of security, the social peace and respect of the rights of others, although its origin is based on the commitment with these pillars of the constitutional system, however, can be questioned due to its restrictive effects in the field of fundamental rights. The constitutional development of social harmony by Local Governments with legal powers interferes in a banned field to Municipalities from a constitutional perspective such as the fundamental rights ambit.

From this perspective, the City Ordinances is breaking into the sphere reserved to the fundamental rights regulating the use of the religious veil by its banning in public spaces. The restriction of the burqa in the access to buildings and municipal facilities is based on security reasons such as any other garment that is hindering the identification and without thinking in its condition as a fundamental right [13].

However, the Judgement of the 14th of February of 2013, has recently declared the nullity the banning of the religious veil in according to the City Ordinance of Lleida and has argued its dimension as a fundamental right. Even without declaring whether the veil "is in all cases a compliance of a religious duty", the Spanish Supreme Court confirms its external dimension "*agere licere*" [14] that empowers to the citizens to act in accordance with their convictions and keep them facing others (JSC 19/1985, P. 2; JSC 120/1990, P. 10; and JSC 137/1990, P. 8).

Without ruling about the religious character of burqa, the Spanish Supreme Court argues the incompetence of Local Governments in matters of fundamental rights and, in particular, to rule their essential meaning. For this reason, the Judgement in question considers that "in what is not an essential content an open space must be open to be regulated by other authorities different from the Lawmaker ant through normative instruments different from the Law."

The Spanish Supreme Court has decided that "the alleged attribution to the Local Governments to regulate accessory aspects on fundamental rights is against with the Spanish Constitution in its Article 53" [15]. The Supreme Court advises that is necessary to distinguish between what is the regulation of "accessory, accidental or circumstantial aspects" in a fundamental right, and whatever regulation in specific areas of Local Governments in their competencies that, in this case, may affect in the exercise of a fundamental right, though they do not aim a direct regulation of fundamental right's aspects.

The constitutional problem arises from the competency of Local Governments to regulate the public space where fundamental rights are exercised and the right of others when it is limiting those. In this sense, the Judgement of The Spanish Supreme Court of the 14 of February admits that "*the fundamental rights may give in, of course, in front of legal rights, and even other interests constitutionally relevant protected, but only if the limit that they are undergoing is necessary in order to achieve a planned legitimate aim, proportioned to reach and, in any case, be respectful with the essential content of the restricted fundamental right*" (JCC 57/1994 of the 28 of February, P. 6; and JCC 18/1999 of the 22 of February, P. 2).

From this Case-Law, the Local Governments seem legitimated in the implementation of the Equality Principle whose cross-sectional nature allows its implementation on civic relations and in public space. However, the Judgement of the Supreme Court of the 14th of February of 2013 even recognizing that the Local Governments must apply the Article 9.2 of the Spanish Constitution [16], admits that is not their competency the resolution of conflicts as a consequence of this disturbance, and so the Supreme Court is inhibited about the competency of Local Governments in relation with the equality principle and dignity as limits of fundamental rights and, specifically, as limit of the religious freedom, and without any legal argument, determines that it is not their competency the resolving of problems derivatives from Multiculturalism.

In relation to the religious veil, the Supreme Court addresses an aspect of the equality that shows a constitutional point of view noting that "the possibility of creating new regulations that, circumscribed to the ambit of Local Governments, do not have the same coextensive character facing of law ambit, so that the right might be limited in a part of the country but not in others. The risk of inequalities because of a new local regulation about fundamental rights is also worrying in according to the legal basis of the Judgement of the Supreme Court of the 14th of February of 2013, though it does not exist any legal or constitutional impediment for an interpretation and an unequal application of the equality principle.

In relation to the impossibility of a City Ordinance to regulate certain aspects about fundamental rights in order to penalize some behaviors against to the Public Security, the Case Law uses the legal reserve as a guarantee of the same fundamental rights [17]. In this regard, the Judgement of the 14th of February of 2013, admitting the absent of a prohibitive law for the religious veil, recognizes that this question was proposed in the Spanish Senate by a motion urging the

Government "to carry out the necessary legal reforms to prohibit the use of religious veil in public events and in public spaces that do not have a strictly religious purpose, garments and accessories in the attire that, as a result, hide completely the visage and complicate the identification and visual communication, supposing these practices a real discrimination against the dignity of people and lesive to the real and effective equality between men and women" [18].

2.6. Legal Prospective

A future reform of the current Organic Law of Religious Freedom should address the controversial aspects of the right to religious symbols and its boundaries, including the constitutional right to equality.

The introduction of the gender perspective as a limit of the religious freedom is unpostponable and would avoid that Local Governments and Education Centers to assume competencies in matter of fundamental rights.

The Multiculturalism cannot justify the ambiguity and the relativism facing discriminatory religious manifestations that relax the application of equality right infringing the Constitution. The coexistence between civilizations in the European and Spanish space cannot serve as an excuse for a lack of legal protection facing discriminatory religious symbols. In the same way, the subsidies to religions based on discriminatory practices against women should be object reconsideration by the Authorities.

In particular, the risk of religious harassment claims the legislative attention in order to prevent any pressure on the collective of immigrant women and prevent that a future right of living in accordance with religious beliefs, involves a setback in the right of gender equality.

3. MULTICULTURALISM AND DISCRIMINATORY PRACTICES BASED ON GENDER

The legal impact of multiculturalism demands a balance from the perspective of equality gender in relation with the current quandary that is expressed in reality. The multiculturalism as a political concept, and not as a legal concept, expresses serious weaknesses in the protection of immigrant women.

The Spanish Law has debated between the regulation of multiculturalism practices and its legal invisibility based on the risk to avoid legal ghettos. Nowadays, saving exceptions, the Multiculturalism remains in a legal limbo with just a few applicable rules beyond police protocols that detect risk situations.

For this reason, the multicultural phenomenon requires a control of constitutionality because of the permissiveness regarding to discriminatory conducts from gender equality.

From the initial indifference of the lawmaker and the legal relativism toward Multiculturalism, a process of classification of certain serious practices imported from migratory movements and contrary to the human rights of women has begun.

In relation to the problem of gender violence, the numbers show a greater impact among immigrant women one in four were foreigners to a greater extent, especially from Latin America, and their attackers were also predominantly foreigners.

The human rights of immigrant women victims of gender violence have a special lack of legal protection in the assumption of regrouped women in Spain by their attacker and also in the assumption those women who are undocumented immigrants.

The current legislation in gender violence presents profiles of indirect discrimination due to its neutrality in relation of the collective of immigrants. Is argued that neither the resident permit, which are independent for women regrouped by their attacker, nor any other residence permit by exceptional circumstances for victims of gender violence when they have the category undocumented immigrants, entail a work permit. Due to this reason, immigrant women have serious difficulties to escape from the spiral of gender violence, because a job offer is required to obtain a work permit, or to report the suffered aggressions.

The Lawmaker does not assume a legal commitment with immigrant women victims of gender violence nor victims of sexual slavery that appeared invisible at present. Only is providing a framework protocol to protect victims of human trafficking among State Departments. In parallel, it has been detected in some mosques an apology of gender violence, where some imams have been teaching how to mistreat women "without leaving traces" and this kind of apology has forced the intervention of the Public Prosecutor's Office.

Also, the City Ordinances are banning prostitution near to residential areas and public schools, but only as a civic problem and not like a human rights of gender. The legal tolerance for violence against prostitutes is a reflection of its acceptance by society. In addition, is omitted multiple discrimination forms against immigrant women by reasons gender, age, illness and risk of social exclusion.

Regarding marriages or forced marriages, the Spanish lawmaker has not protected women, nor young girls sufficiently as victims of a sexual and cultural practice based on coercions, threats, and even kidnappings contrary to the human rights and fundamental rights. For this reason, a legislative initiative has been proposed in the Spanish Congress of Deputies in order to regulate this problem. In the meantime, only in Catalonia some "extra legem" protocols have appeared as risk indicators on forced marriages.

The protection of children's interest in Spain has also revealed a big absence of regulation in relation with female genital mutilation in young girls, because according to police data, ten thousand young girls are in a serious risk, and in 2011 the number of genital mutilations in young girls increased in a 14 percent. In parallel, the incest in some cultures requires in Spain prevention measures and legal prosecution in accordance to the Resolution Adopted by The General Assemble of the United Nation on Traffic in women and girls in the 94th plenary meeting dated on the 23th of December of 1994 [19], which includes the concept of sexual abuse of young girls in the household inside of the concept of gender violence.

Neither polygamy has been addressed by the Spanish lawmaker thus ignoring discriminatory consequences suffered by immigrant women in Spain. The family regrouping has as an only impediment to regroup more than one spouse, admitting a simple affidavit act in which the man just have to declare that there is not another spouse living with him to avoid polygamy. In this case, the submission of women and the violation of their dignity is already evident in countries with a multicultural long tradition, such as France, although the dimension of this problem as a precondition for a legal intervention is still unknown.

Finally, the passivity of the lawmaker, the absence of positive actions, and ultimately, the failure of the intrinsic equality mainstreaming in the multicultural space allow doubts about compliance with international treaties in Spain. In particular, the assumption by the Spanish Government of the Declaration of the United Nations of 1995 [20] admitting that the violence against women throughout the life cycle arises from cultural norms and customary traditions, acts of extremism in related to gender, race or religion to perpetuate the inferior social status assigned to women in the family.

In short, the legal protection of women cannot be stopped by political alliances of civilizations, nor the protection of minorities that discriminate them, not even because of reasons of Multiculturalism.

CONFLICT OF INTEREST

The authors declare no conflict of interest, financial or otherwise.

ACKNOWLEDGEMENTS

Declared none.

REFERENCES

[1] Charter of Fundamental Rights of the European Union. Article 10. Freedom of thought, conscience and religion; 1. Everyone has the right to freedom of thought, conscience and religion. This right includes freedom to change religion or belief and freedom, either alone or in community with others and in public or in private, to manifest religion or belief, in worship, teaching, practice and observance. // 2. The right to conscientious objection is recognized, in accordance with the national laws governing the exercise of this right.

[2] Because of this, the prohibition of sex discrimination under Article 21 of the Charter of Fundamental Rights, is fully extrapolated to counteract the adverse effects of religious freedom, even if there was an implied waiver of the right to equality for its own headlines.

[3] In the Nordic countries, especially Denmark, Greece, Great Britain, Ireland, but Italy, Portugal, Germany, Spain, and among the new Community countries, Cyprus and Malta the predominant model is closer to a secular country. Facing them France maintains within the European Union a model of secularism of public authorities.

[4] However, even from the perspective of equality, there is a consensus, because while the French Council of State declared legal misgivings about the total ban on burqa by colliding with the autonomy of women in this country is available to an legislation protecting the rights of women to religious symbols, regardless of its coercive or voluntary use.

[5] The European Court of Human Rights has addressed this issue in its judgment of 4 December 2008, the case Dogru *vs.* France, the ECHR dismisses the plaintiff's claims regarding the use of the headscarf in French classrooms (in the same direction was the case KERVANCI *vs.* AIR FRANCE).

[6] Judgement of the Supreme Court of Spain.

[7] The Jurisprudence rejects the equalization of the presence of religious symbols in a public schoolhouse a more symbology in other acts of public life situations such as the takeover of public office (for the limited duration of the already said presence and adulthood of people), Christmas events, religious assistance in barracks and hospitals, etc.

[8] The Spanish Constitution establishes a principle, an idea about non-denominational or positive secularism "ban any confusion between religious and state purposes." Our legal system based on political pluralism, ideological and religious freedom of individuals and the Non-denominational Clause of the State, so all public institutions and, especially, teaching centers have to be ideologically neutral (JTC Plenary session, 13.021981, no. 5/1981, rec. 189/1980). However, the Spanish Constitution establishes a mandate in order to take into an account all the religious beliefs of Spanish society.

[9] Burqa; A loose garment covering the entire body and having a veiled opening for the eyes, worn by Muslim women.

[10] Niqab: A type of veil worn by some Muslin women that is made of light weight opaque fabric and leaves only the eyes uncovered.

[11] It should be pointed out that the position of the City of Coin, which will be the first Andalusian township to ban the burqa without penalties and adopting this initiative in a logical way with gender equality policies supported by public administrations. In our opinion, the Mayor recognizes that burqas

and niqabs cannot be justified on any religious or cultural tradition and these garments are vexatious for women, so the Public Institutions cannot stay passive. Also, the Mayor recognizes that a radicalizatión of Muslim people has been detected in their customs and even they have stopped to attend to the Spanish Language courses taught by the local government.

[12] Academic resource: Gracia Retortillo. Convivencia ciudadana, prostitución y potestad sancionadora municipal. El caso de Barcelona. Estudios Fundación Democracia y Gobierno Local 2008. Referring to an area over which it extends the notion of coexistence is what we might call generically the protection of the dignity of individuals, which frequently is translated into programmatical statements about the ban of discrimination or rejection of violence by the respective Local Government.

[13] Legal resource: Recommendation 1927 (2010) of the Council of Europe on Islam, Islamism and Islamophobia in Europe. In this text, the Council of Europe urges to all Member States to not to establish a general banning of burqa or any other special or religious garment with the exception of this banning is useful in order to protect women of all physical and psychological coercions. However, all Member States are requested to protect the free decision of these women to use religious or special garments and to warrant the same opportunities for Muslim women to participate in public life and carry out their professional and educational activities.

[14] Lawful act.

[15] In this sense the Judgement of the High Court of Justice of Catalonia, denies that the City Ordinance of Barcelona impugned infringes the legal reservation about organic Laws in matters of fundamental rights, because "a City Ordinance may effect on municipal regulation of fundamental rights and public liberties, considering that the general criterion is that is possible to regulate accessory matters of those fundamental rights [...]".

[16] Spanish Constitution. Article 9. P.2; It is incumbent upon the public authorities to promote conditions which ensure that the freedom and equality of individuals and of the groups to which they belong may be real and effective, to remove the obstacles which prevent or hinder their full enjoyment, and to facilitate the participation of all citizens in political, economic, cultural and social life.

[17] Academic resource: Pemàn Gavín I. La política de civismo en los Ayuntamientos españoles. Entre policía, acción social y educación cívica. Estudios 2010. In this regard, is noteworthy the flexibility in legal reserve principle to impose penalties carried out by the Constitutional Court, especially under the doctrine contained in the Judgement of the Constitutional Court 132/2001, on the 8th of June. In this Judgement, the Constitutional Court has softened the limiting effect on local autonomy derived from this principle. Therefore, the Constitutional Court has recognized the possibility of the City Ordinances to categorize infractions and administrative penalties on the framework of legal broad authorizations.

[18] Official Bulletin of the General Courts. Senate. Series 8. Number 484. (The 21th of June, 2010).

[19] Legal resource: (A/RES/49/166) Resolution Adopted by The General Assemble of the United Nation on Traffic in women and girls. P.5; " Condemning the illicit and clandestine movement of persons across national and international borders, largely from developing countries and some countries with economies in transition, with the end goal of forcing women and girl children into sexually or economically oppressive and exploitative situations, for the profit of recruiters, traffickers and crime syndicates, as well as other illegal activities related to trafficking, such as forced domestic labour, false marriages, clandestine employment and false adoption [...]".

[20] Legal resource: Report of the Fourth World Conference on Women. Beijing Declaration and Platform for Action. Beijing, 4-15 September 1995.

CHAPTER 7

Internally Displaced Persons: A Vulnerable Group in Need of Protection

Cristina Churruca Muguruza* and **Patricia García Amado***

Pedro Arrupe Human Rights Institute, University of Deusto, Bilbao, Spain

Abstract: The chapter highlights the situation of IDPs as a vulnerable group and the limits of humanitarian action in preventing and resolving displacement. Given the increasing number of IDPs in the world and the protracted nature of displacement there is a need to address the gaps that continue to limit their protection. In this context the search for durable solutions to internal displacement is understood as a complex process addressing human rights, humanitarian, development, reconstruction, and peacebuilding challenges. In this context, when the state is unable or unwilling to fulfill its responsibility to protect, the role of the international community is critical. Moreover, durable solutions require a human security approach that builds on the efforts and capabilities of IDPs. In order to put an end to internal displacement, it is necessary for professionals and academics to better understand the precise impact of the idea of sovereignty as responsibility and the rights-based protection approach on current international politics.

Keywords: Durable solutions, Internally displaced persons, Peacebuilding, Protection, Vulnerable group.

1. INTRODUCTION

The increasing and alarming number of internally displaced persons (IDPs) has made this issue a matter of international concern so that their situation, assistance and protection is not only a humanitarian imperative, but a question of regional and international security and sustainable development [1]. According to the Internal Displacement Monitoring Centre (IDMC) 38 million were affected by conflict-induced internal displacement by the end of 2014. This means a 15 per cent increase in comparison to 2013, including 11 million newly displaced persons during the year. In other words approximately 30,000 people being forced

* **Corresponding authors Cristina Churruca Muguruza:** Professor of International Relations and Humanitarian Action and Peace Building at Pedro Arrupe Human Rights Institute of, University of Deusto, Bilbao, Spain; Tel: 0034 94 413 90 03 Ext. 2749; Fax: 0034 944 139 282; E-mail: cristina.churruca@deusto.es

Patricia García Amado, Researcher at Pedro Arrupe Human Rights Institute, University of Deusto, Bilbao, Spain; Tel: 0034 94 413 90 03 Ext. 2916; Fax: 0034 944 139 282; E-mail: patriciagarciaamado@deusto.es.

J. Alberto del Real Alcalà (Ed.)

to migrate a day [2]. The fact that in 2014 90% of the 60 countries monitored by the IDMC had people living in protracted displacement for over 10 years gives an indication of the difficulties in finding sustainable solutions to displacement [3].

Despite the prominence of internally displaced persons in international political discourse and the recognition of their existence in almost all transition or post-conflict situations, IDPs are largely marginalized in peacebuilding processes. It is not only that the plight of IDPs is being considered mainly as a humanitarian problem. The critique to the containment policies of forced migration [4] and the misuse of humanitarian and development aid for international security purposes [5] have relegated the real protection problem of IDPs to the background. In spite of that, the achievement of a sustainable peace and the end of internal displacement are interlinked. In this sense, supporting durable solutions to internal displacement cannot only address the root causes of conflicts but help preventing further displacement [6].

Although IDPs should be an integral part of peacebuilding processes it is clearly not the case. Recognizing the intrinsic difficulties of finding durable solutions to IDPs our argument is that the failure to solve the plight of internally displaced people also lies in the conceptual approach that is being used to address this issue. We claim that there is a need to adopt a human security approach to address the problem of finding durable solutions to IDPs. Indeed human security should be the first priority of peacebuilding in the period immediately following a conflict. Human security, understood not only as an objective but as a policy framework, offers a perspective from which to address the plight on internally displaced people [7]. It is a rights-based approach which should be ensured through protection and empowerment strategies. If human security becomes the main priority of peacebuilding the people in general —not only IDPs— would be the focus. Ultimately peace building is about "building human security".

With this aim we will first address how the protection of IDPs has become an international issue, although still not a priority (section II). In this context, we will explain the case of IDPs, their particular needs and vulnerabilities, and the problem of finding durable solutions (section III). Then, we will evidence how the practice of peacebuilding and the liberal peace project have relegated human security and in particular the problem of IDPs to the background. While critical approaches to liberal peace claim that the most marginalized sectors have been forgotten, some critics neglect the importance of promoting human rights as a form of empowerment. In the conclusion we will suggest some pending issues for research.

2. INTERNALLY DISPLACED PERSONS AS AN INTERNATIONAL ISSUE

Internal displacement related to conflict and persecution is certainly not a new phenomenon. Yet it was in the 1990s when the increasing incidence of gross human rights violations and resulting massive human displacement, caused mainly by internal armed conflicts, linked international and national security with the protection of internally displaced persons [8]. Internal displacement was placed on the international agenda as a result of the convergence of pressing humanitarian, regional and international security concerns, broader debates in the field of security and development studies and trends in international law and relations. These trends were giving precedence to the protection of human rights over the sovereignty and integrity of states and challenging traditional conceptions of sovereignty [9].

The concern for internal displacement is related to the development of the international humanitarian system and the growing involvement of humanitarian agencies with IDPs [10]. The increase of internally displaced people due to internal conflict and the accompanying humanitarian engagement led to greater international awareness of the protection crisis produced by these conflicts. According to Roberta Cohen, "*estimates of the global population of IDPs increased exponentially, from 1.2 million in 11 countries in 1982 to 25 million in 40 countries by the end of the 1990s*" [11]. Indeed the plight for IDPs was born out of the recognition that in a number of situations of uprooted persons of an exceptional magnitude (Afghanistan, Liberia, Iraq), "*in the absence of clear mandates and an international body with special responsibility for the protection of internally displaced persons, the international response had been 'ad hoc, limited and unsatisfactory'*" [12].

The raising awareness of the crisis of internal displacement caused by conflict in countries like Iraq, the former Yugoslavia and Rwanda in the early 1990s, led to the view that forced displacement was a matter of international peace and security. Collison highlights how the containment policies over refugee movements, together with the 'humanitarian' military interventions and a heightened humanitarian presence led to "*a growing interest in protecting people within their own countries as reflected in the (disastrous) creation of so-called 'safe havens' for displaced and other civilian populations in the midst of ongoing conflicts*" [13]. From 1991 the United Nations Security Council resolutions started to demand access to internally displaced people and other vulnerable populations affected by conflict and massive human rights violations, even authorizing the use of force to ensure the delivery of assistance [14]. As a response to violent conflicts involving gross violations of human rights that threatened to generate wider instability or unacceptable human suffering, the requirements of security had begun to include the protection of communities and individuals from internal violence. State security could no longer be narrowly interpreted in terms of protecting territory against external threats but should also include the protection of citizens. The focus should therefore be on ensuring the safety of people, that is to say, human security. Ultimately the state, as the main provider of security, should be an instrument for the security of its people. Advocates of human security will claim that international actors have a responsibility to come to aid populations at risk [15]. This development opened the way to see state sovereignty as a matter of responsibility.

The issue of the internally displaced from the perspective of the international community was and still is that they fall within the domestic jurisdiction and are therefore not covered by the protection normally awarded to those who cross international borders and become refugees [16]. In this regard, the work done by of Francis M. Deng, at the time the Special Representative of the Secretary-General on internally displaced persons, and Roberta Cohen, to help address the problem of IDPs was influential in building a broader understanding of the concept of state sovereignty to introduce the possibility of international intervention for human protection purposes [17]. They refined a conceptually distinct approach centered on the notion of "sovereignty as responsibility" underscoring that state sovereignty entails enduring obligations towards two constituencies: one's own people and to the community of states complying with human rights and humanitarian obligations [18]. This broader understanding means that sovereignty is not absolute but contingent. If a state fulfills fundamental protection obligations and respects core human rights, it would not have a reason to be concerned about unwelcome intervention from abroad. As a result, increasingly emphasis was placed on the primary responsibility of states to protect their nationals as the fundamental and ultimate function of sovereignty.

Since the 1990s the case of IDPs became a regular item on the international agenda and created new opportunities for international action. However in spite of the work done in the last twenty years to increase awareness of IDP rights issues, the recent rise of violent extremism and terrorism worldwide and the unprecedented migration crisis is decreasing instead of increasing international attention on the plight of internally displaced people. Moreover although durable solutions for IDPs are described as a humanitarian, development and peacebuilding challenge, the issues of displaced persons are still considered as requiring primarily humanitarian rather than development and peacebuilding solutions [19].

3. INTERNALLY DISPLACED PEOPLE AS A VULNERABLE GROUP

There are many reasons why people remain internally displaced within their country, varying from situation to situation and from person to person. In conflict situations uprooted people may be unable to reach the borders safely. Sometimes IDPs cannot leave their country because they lack transportation or resources. Geographical barriers, like mountains or rivers, or factors such as age, disability and health can prevent their transit. On the other hand, external displacement may not be an option. The IDPs may be denied freedom of movement by their own government or face restrictions on their right to seek asylum by foreign governments. This was the case of Turkey where Kurds fled Iraqi repression in Iraq in 1991; and the case of Afghanistan in the aftermath of the terrorist attacks against the United States on September 11, 2001, because, while the Taliban restricted the possibility of Afghans to move freely within their country, neighboring countries closed their borders. As a result, the masses of refugees that were anticipated in both cases did not materialize [20].

The discussion about who can be considered internally displaced persons has been intense in recent years. Erin Mooney in a seminal article on the concept of internal displacement and the case IDPs as a category of concern notes that "*for some, the term 'internally displaced persons' refers only to people uprooted by conflict, violence and persecution, that is, people who would be considered refugees if they crossed a border.[...]Others, however, consider internal displacement to be a much broader concept and to encompass the millions more persons uprooted by natural disasters and development projects. Still others question whether it is useful to single out internally displaced persons, who commonly are referred to as 'IDPs', as a category at all*" [21].

The more widely used definition today is the one put forth in the Introduction to the Guiding Principles on Internal Displacement. These principles identify rights and guarantees relevant to prevent displacement and to IDPs' protection and assistance during displacement and its aftermath. For this purpose internally displaced persons are defined as:

"Persons or groups of persons who have been forced or obliged to flee or to leave their homes or places of habitual residence, in particular as a result of or in order to avoid the effects of armed conflict, situations of generalized violence, violations of human rights or natural or human-made disasters, and who have not crossed an internationally recognized State border" [22].

This definition is meant to be descriptive rather than normative, drawing attention to the characteristics of IDPs that make them inherently vulnerable. It highlights following Erin Mooney two core elements of the concept: one, the coercive or involuntary character of the movement and two, the fact that the latter takes place within national borders [23]. The main purpose of this definition is not to create a new category of persons with special rights but to ensure protection to persons in similar situations and thus "*promote a more harmonious and coherent approach to human rights*" [24].

Questions arise on the need to consider the internally displaced as a category concern. The Representative of the Secretary-General on the human rights of internally displaced persons, Walter Kälin, pointed out in his 2010 report to the Human Rights Council the arguments brought up by some analysts against the delivery of special protection and assistance to IDPs, mainly that "*this tends to detract attention from the true causes of vulnerability such as poverty, gender or ethnic minority status or that they disregard the needs of other affected populations unable to reach a safer part of the country*" [25]. While IDPs may not always be worse off than non-displaced populations, the opposite argument is that IDPs require special protection and assistance because displacement creates specific needs and vulnerabilities not experienced by others. In support of this opinion the current Special Rapporteur on the human rights of internally displaced persons, Chaloka Beyani states [26]:

"*Displacement, whether caused by conflict, violence or disaster, usually leads to extreme poverty and renders IDPs highly vulnerable. It typically results in loss of land, homes and property, loss of employment or livelihood, food insecurity, lack of access to basic services, including water and sanitation and health care, and poor access to education. Displacement may cause IDPs to be more at risk of violence, including sexual and gender-based violence, trafficking and other forms of abuse, either in the context of ongoing conflicts or due to the perilous and poor conditions in which IDPs find themselves. Displacement causes disintegration of community and family cohesion, and of socioeconomic networks and support mechanisms.*"

Moreover as his predecessor Walter Kälin stressed that "*unlike those remaining in their homes, the displaced leave their property behind, risking its occupation by others and creating the challenge of how to have it restored. They may not be able to replace lost documentation or participate freely in elections*" [27]. Many studies corroborate that IDPs have specific needs [28]. In summary, as Erin Mooney has pointed out, "*it is difficult to deny that IDPs have certain needs that are distinct from the general population and which require special attention. What distinguishes the internally displaced are the unique needs and heightened vulnerabilities that arise as a result of forced displacement, including their need for a durable solution*" [29].

4. DURABLE SOLUTIONS TO INTERNAL DISPLACEMENT

Ever since the Guiding Principles on Internal Displacement were elaborated aid practitioners and academics have struggled to establish an identifiable stage to determine the end of displacement [30]. The term internally displaced person does not confer an internationally recognised legal status, and therefore there is no cessation clause applicable to their situation, as is the case of refugees under the 1951 Convention. Therefore, aid institutions and national governments were in need of indicators to inform their programmes and policies and show progress, while international donors were pushing for some kind of benchmarks to determine when internal displacement is over and funding was no longer necessary [31].

The complexity of determining when internal displacement ends, and the aim to differentiate IDPs specific needs from those that are common to their host/return community led to the elaboration of the Framework on Durable Solutions [32]. This instrument is a guide to governments and international development and humanitarian organization to identify and address IDPs protection needs. It establishes that a durable solution is achieved when IDPs no longer require assistance or have any protection needs associated to forced displacement, and can enjoy human rights without discrimination. The state is the main guarantor of IDPs' rights and primarily responsible for the achievement of durable solutions, and may be supported by humanitarian and development organizations to meet this goal. The Framework defines durable solutions as a long-term process, requiring from the coordinated intervention of national and international institutions to address humanitarian, development, peacebuilding and human rights challenges.

The Framework highlights several key principles that should lead the provision of durable solutions. The first is the primary responsibility of the state to assist and protect IDP. In order to do so the state must secure the rapid and unimpeded access to humanitarian and development actors if needed. Second, the policies on durable solutions must be based on the rights, needs and interests of IDPs and no person should be forced or encouraged to return when the conditions for a safe reintegration are not present. Third, IDPs have the right to make a free and informed choice about durable solutions, but their decision should not affect their right to return. Fourth, a community-based approach should be adopted in order to support IDPs (re)integration, taking into consideration the needs and vulnerabilities of the community. In this sense, measures should be adopted to avoid discrimination against IDPs that may hinder their options of (re)integration.

Finally, it is reminded that IDPs continue to be protected and assisted by national and international human rights law, and international humanitarian law when applicable, after they have achieved a durable solution.

IDPs participation, capacities and decisions are regarded as central to end displacement. The framework reminds their right to a free and informed choice over settlement options, to participate in the design and definition of policies destined to their assistance and to be part of the peacebuilding process. Human rights are at the core of the framework but its recommendations need to be tailored to the specific context of displacement in order to be effective.

Bearing in mind the great contribution of the IASC Framework to the characterisation of the multiple factors which contribute to the achievement of durable solutions; and to the operationalization of protection policies as guidance to governments, humanitarian, development and peacebuilding actors, there are several aspects that limit its scope:

In the first place, the definition of durable solution as absence of displacement-based discrimination is blurred. Sources of discrimination in societies are multiple and it is often not discernible when prejudices are based on conditions of displacement, race, gender, age or other. Another deficit of the concept is the limited interpretation of what could constitute a durable solution. Several scholars have argued against what they perceive as a primacy of permanent settlement over mobile livelihoods options. Long, Stepputat and Sørensen have described how some IDPs are able to attain socio-economic sustainability through the maintenance of a permanent transit between their acquired urban livelihood and their past rural source of income [33].

Nevertheless, what is really challenging the operationalization of this framework is the absence of data and record on IDPs and the insufficient follow up of their situation once the emergency situation is over. Current monitoring mechanisms, like the IDMC [34], seldom follow the evolution of IDPs after return and do not provide information about processes of local integration or resettlement. Indeed, the figures of those who choose to stay in their area of refuge or resettle elsewhere in the country are lacking [35]. The Framework clearly states that simply making an election between return, integration or resettlement do not entail the achievement of a durable solution. Nevertheless, many governments erase the names of IDPs from national records once they receive initial support for definitive settlement. Profiling exercises are insufficient especially in urban areas, where IDPs are difficult to locate and register [36]. This hinders the measurement of progress according to IASC Framework benchmarks, the provision of assistance and information on durable solutions to IDPs, and the meaningful participation of displacement-affected people in the design of policies and the construction of peace.

In spite of the rights of IDPs being highlighted once again by the IASC Framework, meaningful choice is put into question when settlement options receive unequal financial and political support of national governments and international institutions. Return, local integration and resettlement of IDPs do have an impact over peacebuilding processes, and return and restitution of properties are progressively being included in peace agreements. Thus, IDPs would receive assistance if their option for a sustainable settlement matches with the interest and goals of elite negotiators. Return is often conceived as an indicator of peace taking hold [37]. As a result, people usually receive multiple incentives to go back to their areas of origin while their protection needs in areas of displacement are left unattended if they exceed humanitarian mandates. This strategy intends to reduce the chances of permanent settlement in areas of displacement, a fact that is perceived as problematic by local governments and often host communities [38]. At the same time, international agencies, donors and governments involved in peace processes see return as a tool to undo the wrongs of war [39].

Return could be the most desired option to many IDPs and maybe the most suitable solution to short-term displacement. Nevertheless, over 16 million people have been displaced for more than two decades [40], and protracted displacement requires from a comprehensive response to address the progressive deterioration of IDPs condition with no prospect of sustainable settlement. By the end of the 1990s, the increasing debate over the inadequacy of encampment solutions to protracted displacement and the search for alternatives through local integration and self-reliance opened a space for dissent from the mainly return-oriented policies [41]. Although integration alternatives met resistance on the side of host governments, which tend to benefit segregation, control and perceived temporariness of settlement in camps, the transformation of camps into permanent structures had also become an unresolved problem. A common conclusion was that the inadequacy of basic humanitarian shelter provisions to prolonged dislocation and the absence of policies addressing housing needs of IDPs during displacement, on a permanent or transitional basis, undermine their possibilities to achieve a durable solution [42].

Another common limitation to the participation of IDPs in policies and strategies on durable solutions is the deficient communication between donors, national, local and grassroots. Foreign countries assume the monetary costs of (re)integration and negotiate with national governments about priorities and ways forward [43]. These decisions usually do not consider the limited capacity of local authorities to manage return or integration of IDPs [44], neither the wishes, interests nor the needs of IDPs and other displacement-affected people (like hosts communities or people living in areas of return).

Solutions to long-term displacement are to be inserted within development and peacebuilding strategies taking into consideration IDPs specific protection needs together with those of their host/return community [45]. Coordination with local government and community representatives are central in transitional periods and early recovery stages when the gap between humanitarian and development responses threatens the sustainability of IDPs livelihoods. It is often difficult to establish the appropriate timing to introduce programmes supporting mid to long-term settlement options due to the unpredictable nature of conflicts. The virtual absence of development actors and programmes during conflict adds to the difficulties of humanitarian organisations to provide responses outside of lifesaving priorities and to the fluctuations in donors' financial support [46].

The plight in internal displacement requires a comprehensive policy of assistance and protection. From a human security perspective a comprehensive policy is not the sum of the different strategies for displaced people, but an integrated approach: from those dealing with human rights and humanitarian concerns, those with security and those with development [47]. Ultimately, the protection of IDPs means ensuring that IDPs can resume a normal life by achieving a lasting solution. The search for any of these durable solutions is as a gradual and often lengthy process [48] which must be inclusive and, in pursuit of full equality, comprise the entire displaced population, particularly women, children and people with special disabilities that may become marginalized [49].

Nevertheless, the limited success of responses to internal displacement and the scant progress in protecting people from displacement have been further evidenced by the growing numbers of IDPs and protracted internal displacement situations [50]. This failure highlights the challenges of a coordinated response between entities with multiple and conflicting goals in relation to durable solutions and the difficult harmonisation of their strategies [51]. It is the outcome of so-called solutions that puts IDPs needs and interests on the fringes of decision-making processes.

5. INTERNALLY DISPLACED PERSONS AND PEACEBUILDING

Building peace in conflict-prone countries and in transition or post-conflict contexts is aimed at preventing the resumption or escalation of violent conflict and support the establishment of a lasting and self-sustainable peace. The focus of international conflict management has increasingly evolved from peacekeeping —aimed at just maintaining the status quo— to peacebuilding which strives "*with a far more ambitious approach of managing change*" [52]. Peacebuilding comprises overlapping agendas for peace and development in support of conflict prevention, conflict management and post-conflict reconstruction [53].

In this context it is understood that assistance to the return, resettlement and integration of IDPs can simultaneously help to address the root causes of conflict and prevent further displacement. Otherwise, unresolved displacement problems could feed instability and threaten the peace efforts. Durable solutions, in particular return, cannot be reached while there is a lack of security, property rights are not restored and conditions like reconciliation, post-conflict reconstruction, and restoration of the rule of law and a legitimate government are not in place [54]. Thus, the search for dignified and durable solutions for displaced persons is recognized as a fundamental element for peacebuilding and the achievement of a sustainable peace. However, although there have been normative and conceptual developments regarding the process of finding durable solutions, the fact that there are at least 54 countries with people in protracted displacement means that no progress has been made in the process and that these people live in conditions of marginalization. The continued marginalization of IDPs without a prospect of a lasting solution can become an obstacle to long-term stability, recovery and reconstruction in post-conflict countries.

It is assumed that peacebuilding is aimed at meeting the needs of societies emerging from conflict. However, the attention of the liberal peace has not been the local stakeholders and communities, neither the most vulnerable groups, such as IDPs [55]. Critical peace studies have shown that liberal peace has been directed toward the states, elites, and international actors; with a focus on security, liberal institutions, and norms [56]. People have become the "means" for political stability rather than the "end" of peacebuilding [57]. Human security has been relegated to a secondary position. Yet, as emphasized by Jonathan Goodhand, based on his experience in Afghanistan and other conflicts, the ultimate peacebuilding refers to "*the construction of human security*" within the meaning of democratic governance, human rights, rule of law, sustainable development and equitable access to resources [58].

Policy makers and peacebuilding practitioners have begun to recognize the limitations and challenges of peacebuilding, in particular in the period immediately after the conflict. The Report of the Secretary-General on peacebuilding in the immediate aftermath of conflict states that "*the immediate aftermath of the conflict provides an opportunity to create basic security conditions, make explicit the benefits of peace, strengthen and build confidence in the political process and strengthening the national core capacity to take the lead in the activities of peacebuilding, thereby laying the foundations for sustainable development*" [59]. The report acknowledges that, in too many cases, the international community has failed to catalyze a response that offers immediate and tangible results. Capabilities and resources have been insufficient to meet the demands on the ground, in particular in the priority areas such as "*support to the safe and sustainable return and reintegration of internally displaced persons and refugees*" [60].

In addition the few studies on the IDPs participation in peace processes and peacebuilding find that they are often not consulted. Their individual circumstances are usually overlooked in the language of peace agreements, and peacebuilding initiatives often forget or marginalize them [61]. This undermines the possibilities to build peace from below, with IDPs as key stakeholders, and hinders their ownership of the process during the negotiations and the later implementation of agreements. Notwithstanding the growing incorporation of IDPs rights in the wording of peace agreements, which often promote the creation of new monitoring and dispute-solving institutions, the absence of tangible and sustainable results is appalling. To bring this to the fore, Patricia Weiss Fagen analysed the implementation of IDP-related provision in Bosnia and Herzegovina, Burundi, Guatemala and Liberia [62]. The conclusions of her research put into question the real participation of IDPs and showed how they play a marginal role in peace negotiations, while many IDP organisations disband after a peace agreement is reached, diminishing their options to advocate for the full implementation of its provisions.

Building peace and in particular post-conflict reconstruction is currently understood by the United Nations and other international organizations and actors as a comprehensive and integrated complex system, which covers a wide range of programs and mechanisms in the areas of peace, security, development and humanitarian action in the short, medium and long term. Issues such as the need for consistency in strategic planning and funding mechanisms, coordination between different actors, and local ownership, among others, are normally discussed in the reports of United Nations and other organizations on peacebuilding [63]. In relation to IDPs, it is explicitly recognized that the prolonged displacement is often the result of "*political indifference of the authorities, development actors and donors*" [64]. In many cases, the internally displaced, having received generous humanitarian assistance in the worst part of the crisis, are forgotten in the ending of gun violence. Without assistance to rebuild their lives IDPs fall into a vicious cycle of aid dependency and prolonged displacement [65]. In addition, IDPs are often encouraged or forced to return to their places of origin before it is safe or sustainable for them to do so. The lack of support for transition and recovery activities, which should be focused on supporting local ownership, is also a matter of particular concern [66].

Transitional justice measures have also performed as a mechanism for a pretended return to a situation of *status quo ante*. IDPs rights to housing, land and property restitution and the primacy of restoration over compensation or alternative solutions to dispossession –enshrined by the Pinheiro Principles– were design to support return process [67]. However, these initiatives have fallen short from addressing the multiple issues associated to land use, access and control which often are part of the root causes of violence [68]. In fact, restitution processes have contributed to sanction previously existing tenure systems disregarding their possible exclusive nature [69]. Moreover, restitution is not a solution to IDPs without previous property rights or those unable to demonstrate their claims over land. Land reform and the fulfillment of social, cultural and economic rights, including the right to adequate housing, are left out of the peace agenda.

The privilege by governments and international agencies of immediate return instead of other solutions is an example of how peacebuilding can be seen as part of international assistance through social engineering. Return without the minimum conditions for sustainability poses a minimalist rehabilitation that aims to return to pre-conflict situation without taking into account the complexity of transition processes or the needs, interests and rights of displaced persons. In this regard Michael Pugh denounces how "*humanitarian assistance has been geared towards social engineering rather than towards civil development based on local ownership of the peacebuilding process*" [70].

6. CONCLUSIONS

Protection policies that focus on internally displaced persons are not intended to grant preferential treatment compared to other populations at risk but to improve the quality of the response developed for forcibly displaced persons whose needs are still inadequately addressed. Indeed one of the main challenges facing the global protection system nowadays is to change their focus from status to needs.

The case of internal displacement requires a comprehensive policy of assistance and protection. Ultimately, the protection of IDPs, means ensuring that IDPs can resume a normal life by achieving a lasting solution. The search for any durable solutions for IDPs should be understood as a complex process that addresses difficulties related to human rights issues, humanitarian, development, reconstruction and peacebuilding. In other words it requires an integrated human security approach that builds on the efforts and capabilities of IDPs.

The search for dignified and durable solutions for displaced persons is recognized as a fundamental element for peacebuilding and the achievement of a sustainable and lasting peace. However the practice of peacebuilding and the liberal peace project have put human security and the plight of IDPs in the periphery of politics.

Liberal peacebuilding has promoted a minimalist rehabilitation, an act of *social engineering* that focuses on the situation back to pre-conflict society and favors the immediate return of IDPs without taking into account the complexity of transition processes or the needs, interests and rights of displaced persons.

When the state is unable or unwilling to fulfill its responsibility the role of the international community to support the protection of internally displaced persons and assisting in their return or resettlement and integration is critical. It is necessary to study the changes in political and legal discourse on IDPs, together with a study of decision making and institutional commitments adopted by governments, intergovernmental organizations and NGOs. Professionals and academics should better understand the precise impact of the idea of sovereignty as responsibility and a rights-based protection approach on current international politics.

CONFLICT OF INTEREST

The author declares no conflict of interest, financial or otherwise.

ACKNOWLEDGEMENTS

Declared none.

REFERENCES

[1] Newman E, Van Selm J, Eds. Refugees and forced displacement. International security, human vulnerability, and the state. Hong-Kong, United Nations University 2003; United Nations General Assembly (UNGA). Report of the Representative of the Secretary General on human rights of internally displaced, Walter Kälin, UN doc. *A/HRC/13/21*, 5 January 2010; Commission on Human Security. Human security now: Protecting and empowering people. In: United Nations. Report of the Commission on Human Security. New York: The Commission 2003, pp. 44-45.

[2] IDMC. Global Overview 2015. People internally displaced by conflict and violence. Geneva: IDMC 2015: 7.

[3] IDMC. Global Overview 2015. People internally displaced by conflict and violence. Geneva: IDMC (2015):11.

[4] Castles S. The international politics of forced migration. Development 2003; 46 (3):11-20.

[5] Duffield M. Security, development and unending wars. London: Polity 2007; Duffield M. Global governance and the new wars: the merging of development and security. Zed Books 2001.

[6] Koser, K, Addressing Internal Displacement in Peace Processes, Peace Agreements and Peace-Building, Washington D.C: University of Bern Project on Internal Displacement-Brookings Institution 2007.

[7] By doing so we would like to vindicate a pragmatist approach that without renouncing being critical and questioning prevailing structures of power and power relations, tries to be policy relevant and address an issue that has been dismissed and neglected in most critical perspectives to peacebuilding. On the discussion about the usefulness of human security arguments and the difficulties in attempting to be critical and policy relevant. Newman E. Critical human security studies. Review of International Studies 2010; 36: 77-94.

[8] Newman and Van Selm Eds. (2003). p. 14. *Op Cit. (see ref. 1).*

[9] Churruca C. Human Security as the Link Between Humanitarian Action and Peacebuilding in Heintze, H-J. and Gibbons, P, The Humanitarian Challenge. The Humanitarian Challenge. 20 Years European Network on Humanitarian Action (NOHA), Berlin: Springer 2015; 31-46.

[10] For example, in Sudan in the early 1970s, the UNHCR extended its refugee resettlement assistance to returning IDPs. ECOSOC. Report on refugees, displaced persons and returnees prepared by Mr. Jacques Cuénod, consultant. UN doc. E/1991/109/Add.1: para.117, 27 June 1991.

[11] Cohen R. Developing an international system for internally displaced persons. International Studies Perspectives 2006; 7: 89.

[12] ECOSOC. Comprehensive study of the Representative of the Secretary-General on the human rights issues related to internally displaced persons. UN doc. E/CN.4/1993/35: para. 3, 21 January 1993.

[13] Collinson, S., Darcy, J., Waddell, N. y Schmidt, A. (eds.). Realising protection. The uncertain benefits of civilian, refugee and IDP status, HPG Report 28, London: Overseas Development Institute 2009; 8.

[14] Ibid. 46.

[15] Churruca C. Human security as a policy framework: critics and challenges. In: Yearbook on humanitarian action and human rights 2007. Bilbao: Universidad de Deusto 2007:15-35.

[16] Woodhouse T. Humanitarian intervention in contemporary conflict. Cambridge: Polity Press 1998; pp 70-85.

[17] Weiss TG. Internal exiles: what next for internally displaced persons? Third World Quarterly 2003; 24(3): 429-430.

[18] Deng FM. Frontiers of sovereignty: a framework of protection, assistance, and development for the internally displaced. Leiden Journal of International Law (8): 249-286; Deng FM, Kimaro S, Lyons T *et al.* Sovereignty as responsibility: conflict management in Africa. Washington DC: Brookings Institution Press 1996: 27-33.

[19] UNGA. Report of the Special Rapporteur on the human rights of internally displaced persons, Chaloka Beyani. A/HRC/29/34, 2015.

[20] Churruca C. (2015).Op.cit. (see ref.9); 36.

[21] Mooney, E. The Concept of Internal Displacement and the Case for Internally Displaced Persons as a Category of Concern, Refugee Survey Quarterly 2005 (24:3); 9.

[22] UNCHR. Report of the Representative of the Secretary-General on Internally Displaced Persons: Guiding Principles on Internal Displacement. UN doc. E/CN.4/1998/53/Add.2: 1998.

[23] Mooney (2005). *Op. cit.* (see ref. 21); 10.

[24] ECOSOC (1993). *Op. cit.* (see ref. 10): para 54.

[25] UNGA (2010). *Op. cit.* (see ref. 1): para 52-53.

[26] UNGA. Report of the Special Rapporteur on the human rights of internally displaced persons, Chaloka Beyani. A/HRC/29/34, 2015: para.19.

[27] UNGA (2010). *Op. cit.* (see ref. 1): para.13.

[28] Kälin W. Introduction: scope and purpose. In Kälin W. Guiding Principles on Internal Displacement. Annotations. Washington DC: The American Society of International Law and the Brookings Institution 2000: para: 2.

[29] Mooney (2005). Op. cit. (see ref. 21); 18.

[30] This has led to adoption of specific handbooks see, Brookings Institution-University of Bern Project on Internal Displacement. Protecting internally displaced persons: a manual for law and policymakers, October 2008. UNHCR, Handbook for the protection of internally displaced persons. Geneva:

UNHCR 2010; Brookings Institution-University of Bern Project on Internal Displacement. Addressing internal displacement: framework for national responsibility. Washington DC: 2004.

[31] Mooney E. An IDP no more? Exploring the issue of when displacement ends. Discussion paper for the brainstorming session on "When Internal Displacement Ends". Brookings-CUNY Project on Internal Displacement and Institute for the Study of Forced Migration, Georgetown University, Washington DC: 22 April 2002.

[32] UNHRC. "Framework on Durable Solutions for Internally Displaced Persons." *Report of the Representative of the Secretary-General on the human rights of internally displaced persons, Walter Kälin. Addendum 4.* UN doc. A/HRC/13/21/Add.4. 29 December 2009.

[33] Long, K. Permanent crises? Unlocking the protracted displacement of refugees and internally displaced persons. Oxford: Refugee Studies Centre, October 2011; Stepputat F, Sørensen N. The rise and fall of 'Internally Displaced People' in the Central Peruvian Andes. Development and Change 2001, 32: 769-791.

[34] The IDMC was established by the Norwegian Refugee Council in 1998, upon the request of the United Nations, to set up a global database on internal displacement. IDMC remains the leading source of information and analysis on internal displacement worldwide http://www.internal-displacement.org/about-us/.

[35] Ferris E. Ed. Resolving internal displacement. Prospects for local integration. Washington DC: Brookings-LSE Project on Internal Displacement, 2011: 7-23.

[36] Davies A, Jacobsen K. Profiling urban IDPs. Forced Migrations Review 2010; (34): 13-15.

[37] UNGA. Durable solutions for internally displaced persons: advancing the agenda. In: Report of the Special Rapporteur on the human rights of internally displaced persons. UN doc. A/68/225. 31 July 2013:17.

[38] Crisp J, Morris T, Refstie H. Displacement in urban areas: new challenges, new partnerships. Disasters 2012, 36 (S_I): 26-28.

[39] Smit A. Restitution and Return Home. In: Smit A. The Property Rights of Refugees and Internally Displaced Persons. New York: Routledge 2012: 101.

[40] Long K, (2011). Op. cit p. 1. (see ref. 33).

[41] SmithM. Warehousing refugees: a denial of rights, a waste of humanity. World Refugee Survey 2004. Washington DC: US Committee for Refugees; Black R. Putting refugees in camps. Forced Migrations Review 1998; (2); Jacobsen K. The forgotten solution: local integration for refugees in developing countries. New Issues in Refugee Research 2001; 45.

[42] Ferris E, Ed. (2011). Op. cit p. 9. (see ref. 35).

[43] Fagen, PW. Peace Processes and IDP Solutions. Refugee Survey Quarterly 2009, 28 (1): 56.

[44] Ibid.: 39-40.

[45] UNGA (2013). Op. cit. (see ref. 37): para. 40, 44-47.

[46] UNHRC. Report of the Representative of the Secretary-General on the human rights of internally displaced persons, Walter Kälin. UN doc. A/HRC/13/21, 5 January 2010: para. 62.

[47] UNCHR. Balance de la política pública para la atención integral al desplazamiento forzado en Colombia. Bogota: ACNUR 2007: p.24.

[48] UNHRC (2009). *Op Cit.* (see ref. 32): 5.

[49] UNGA. Report of the Representative of the Secretary-General on the human rights of internally displaced persons, Walter Kälin. Addendum Framework on Durable Solutions for Internally Displaced Persons. UN doc. A/HRC/13/21/Add.4, 9th Feb 2010: para. 16, 22 and 23.

[50] Long K (2011). *Op. cit.* (see ref. 33): 8.

[51] There have been several initiatives trying to address this problematic relation, like the UNDP, UNHCR and World Bank, Transitional Solutions Initiative. Concept Note, October 2010; the UNSG Preliminary Framework for Supporting a more Coherent, Predictable and Effective Response to the Durable Solutions of Refugee Returnees and Internally Displaced Persons. Decision no. 2011/20, 4 October 2011; and the one developed by Chaloka Beyani, special rapporteur on the human rights of IDPs, Durable solutions for internally displaced persons: advancing the agenda (UNGA 2013).

[52] Eide, B.A. From Peacekeeping to Peacebuilding. Ojanen, H., Peacekeeping. Peacebuilding. Preparing for the future. UPI/FIIA Report (14): 2006; 46.

[53] Tschirgi N. Peacebuilding and the link between security and development: is the window of opportunity closing? New York: International Peace Academy 2003. For a critical approach to this discourse see: Duffield M (2007). *Op. cit.* (see ref. 5).

[54] UNGA (2010), *Op. cit.* (see ref. 49): para. 48-52.

[55] The consensus of the liberal peace is characterized by the widespread belief among policy makers and "peacemakers", reflected and applied in peacekeeping operations and conflict zones in general after the end of the Cold War that the promotion of democracy, market economy and all institutions associated with the modern state are the engine of peace building. It refers to a theoretical and political concurrence. The theoretical underpinning of liberal peacebuilding is the liberal peace. The idea that certain types of societies, those with a liberal constitution with liberal democracy and market economy tend to be more peaceful. See, Newman E, Paris R, Richmond O, Eds. New perspectives on liberal peacebuilding. New York. United Nations University 2010: p.11.

[56] See, for example: Chandler D. Empire in denial: the politics of state-building. London: Pluto Press, 2006; Duffield (2007), *Op. cit.* (see ref. 5); Duffield (2001), *Op. cit.* (see ref. 5); Heathershaw J. Unpacking the liberal peace: the dividing and merging of peacebuilding discourses. Millennium – Journal of International Studies 2008; 36 (3): 597-621; Newman *et al.* (2010). Op. cit. (see ref. 55); Paris R. International peacebuilding and the 'Mission Civilisatrice'. Review of International Studies 2002; 28 (4): 637□656; Pugh M. The political economy of peacebuilding: a critical theory perspective. International Journal of Peace Studies 2005; 10 (2): pp. 23-42; Richmond O, Ed. Palgrave advances in peacebuilding. Critical developments and approaches. New York: Palgrave Macmillan, 2010.

[57] Conteh-Morgan E. Peacebuilding and human security: a constructivist perspective. International Journal of Peace Studies 2005, 10 (1): 70.

[58] Goodhand J. Aiding peace? The role of NGOs in armed conflict. Rugby: Intermediate Technology Publications 2006, p. 12.

[59] UNSG. Report of the Secretary-General on peacebuilding in the immediate aftermath of conflict. UN doc. A/63/881–S/2009/304, 11 June 2009: para. 3.

[60] *Ibid.* para: 17.

[61] Khalid K, Addressing internal displacement in peace processes, peace agreements and peace-building. Washington DC: Brookings Institution-University of Bern Project on Internal Displacement, 2007.

[62] Fagen (2009). *Op. cit.* (see ref. 43): 58.

[63] Paris R and Sisk TD. Understanding the contradictions of post-war state-building. In Paris R, Sisk TD Eds. The dilemmas of state-building: confronting the contradictions of postwar peace operations. London and New York: Routledge Security and Governance Series 2009: pp. 3-4.

[64] UNGA (2010). *Op. cit.* (see ref. 49): para. 48-52.

[65] *Ibid.* para. 78.

[66] *Ibid.* para.19.

[67] The UN Principles of Housing and Property Restitution are also known as the Pinheiro Principle in reference to its main architect, the Special Rapporteur on housing and property restitution for refugees and internally displaced persons, Paulo S. Pinheiro. In an effort to provide a guideline to restitution

policies and a legal base for its implementation, this soft law instrument is based in a compendium of laws (international human rights law, refugee and humanitarian law) and a systematic review of previous restitution processes with the aim to provide minimum standards to address the '*legal and technical*' aspects of restitution and establish good practices. ECOSOC, *Principles on housing and property restitution for refugees and displaced persons*, UN doc. E/CN.4/Sub.2/ 2005/17, 27 June 2005.

[68] For a critical analysis over restitution processes see Ballard M. Post-conflict Property Restitution. Flawed Legal and Theoretical Foundations. Berkeley Journal of International Law 2010, 28 (2): 462-496; Heimerl D. The return of refugees and internally displaced persons: From coercion to sustainability? International Peacekeeping 2005, 12 (3): 377-390.

[69] Wily LA. Tackling land tenure in the emergency to development transition in post-conflict states: From restitution to reform. In: Pantuliano S. Ed. Uncharted Territory. Land, Conflict and Humanitarian Action. Warwickshire: Practical Action Publishing, 2009: 27-50.

[70] Pugh M. Post-Conflict Rehabilitation: Social and Civil Dimensions. Journal of Humanitarian Studies.2000: 3. http://www.jha.ac/articles/a034.htm. Document posted June 3, 2000.

CHAPTER 8

Human Rights Violations of Vulnerable Groups in Conflict Situations

Ana María Jara Gómez[*]

Criminal Law, Criminology Human Rights and Democracy. University of Jaen, Jaen, Spain

Abstract: Analysing the situation of human rights in areas of conflict requires, especially when we want to speak about vulnerable groups, constant confrontation with the past. In this chapter, we address briefly the relationship between women and war in the former Yugoslavia. Our aim will be to understand the itinerary of women's human rights in society from the times previous to the war until the moment when law and justice seem to be ready to act, in times of peace. One important element to understand where human rights stay for women in the post conflict processes of transitional justice is to see how law builds which acts are actually crimes.

Keywords: Armed conflict, Ethnic violence, Former Yugoslavia, Transitional justice, Women's rights.

1. INTRODUCTION

It seems to be an obligation to start this chapter with a warning for readers. It is a warning about the obvious: the title of the chapter is too generic and requires clarification from the start in order to be useful and escape from vagueness. The analysis will be mainly focused on human rights violations affecting women in the former Yugoslavia during the nineties. Deliberately I will try not to address again issues concerning the relationship between human rights violations and conflict or the concept of vulnerability in conflict settings. This chapter will try to illustrate what happens to a certain group of people in a given scenario and which are the main answers that justice can offer to them today.

I am not an expert in gender. I write here with the intention of sharing my experience and direct knowledge of the Balkan societies. Working in Kosovo as Human Dimension Officer for the OSCE for some years gave me a privileged position to observe and understand the situation of human rights after an armed conflict.

[*] **Corresponding author Ana María Jara Gómez:** Criminal Law, Criminology Human Rights and Democracy. University of Jaen, Jaen, Spain; Tel 0034 958 135566; E-mail: ajara6@ugr.es

J. Alberto del Real Alcalà (Ed.)

The individual perspective is particularly useful when we speak about women who have been through war. War, by its nature, has effects both in the political sphere and in the private sphere, where it mobilises and traumatizes ordinary individual subjects. The issue of wars and conflicts is usually an androcentric discussion. A discussion that leaves aside the experiences of women and their memory [1].

Memory, as opposed to history, is informal, created, manipulated, changed, undermined, *etc.*, but it always exists in the social world and is significant for what it chooses to remember as well as for what it chooses to forget. Memory is what still exists when people cannot raise their voices anymore and it becomes, therefore, important in marginalized groups.

The topics related to women's rights in the Balkans are different depending on which country we speak about and which social group we are referring to. It is possible, however, to draw some common lines for the region that once was Yugoslavia. During the aftermath of WWII the Balkans enjoyed relative improvements in gender matters. This was mainly due to the governmental efforts dedicated to promote women's political participation, access to health and education and the emphasis on employment as a right and a duty for men and women. This was in the public field. At home women were still playing their womanly roles and therefore their position was far away from emancipation.

When it appears, ethnic nationalism plays a great role not just in perpetuating wars but also in the patriarchalisation of society and gender relations in general [2]. The rise of nationalism and the massive militarization lead Yugoslavia to rekindle traditional, authoritarian and patriarchal relations and ways.

2. THROWN BACK TO THE PAST

The massive call to arms had a major consequence, it joined groups of men who, in formal and informal processes formed ethnic armies and paramilitary groups. In this environment, what was transmitted both on and off the battlefield were norms and values celebrating the power and control of men [3]. As a result, the gender differences that already existed were strengthened and institutionalized primarily through nationalist propaganda. Nationalism has the power to provide visibility to politicians lacking an established electorate and to eliminate other differential considerations. This is to say that ethnic identity comes at the expense of gender identity, class identity, professional identity, *etc.* [4].

A social archaization took place in Yugoslavia. The main features of such process were the glorification of the past, the revival of religious traditions, and a general increase in right-winged conservative ideology [5]. When stability is broken, governments and churches try to mobilize popular devotion, their ideological speeches and propaganda celebrate the warrior who defends the future of the nation and the mother who ensures the survival of the national biological generator. Myths on the war hero expand in literature and society. This mythology is characterized by the desire of the devotees to sacrifice their lives on the battlefield, and many did [6].

Those who were non-nationalists, pacifists and feminists, those who challenged the new archaic order were labelled as enemies. Feminists and women's associations were portrayed as subversive groups and demonized by the State controlled media. This is still happening in Serbia nowadays. An extremely aggressive campaign was orchestrated in Croatia against the so called “five witches”. These were five writers, political activists and critics that were considered traitors to their homeland and threatened publicly in the pages of newspapers accused of crimes against ethnicity. Those five women were writing about the social attempts to return to the traditional gender roles or simply against the war. They, and many others, spoke out against family relationships that were becoming brutal and condemned the increasing level of domestic violence since the advent of nationalism [7].

One of these activists, who had been attacked in Belgrade, was described as a traitor when he questioned the violence of the soldiers with their own wives. Many people thought she had no right to question the actions of their war heroes, who risked or sacrificed their lives for the nation. When she tried to protect the women of her country against her countrymen, she was challenging the authority of men, of warriors, and questioning a war hero is to question what gave him power in the first place, the nation he is fighting for [8].

In Serbia today these situations are not unrealistic. Serbian “Women in Black” stand out among non-governmental organisations for the courage of their demands and their struggle. This Organisation requires constant confrontation with the past and the application of models of transitional justice which include all forms of accountability: individual, collective, moral and political, punishment of all crimes, extradition of criminals to The Hague, domestic trials and creation of new forms of justice from a feminist point of view. Fighting for these values in Serbia is extremely difficult because state institutions and the government are politically placed at the opposite end, and do not allow for other positions. The support of other women's history and the resistance to war is not only difficult in Serbia, it involves physical risk for those who do it.

In this sense, we must necessarily pay particular attention to the Kosova Women's Network. A network of women associations and groups that promotes the rights and interests of women and girls throughout the territory of the Republic of Kosovo, regardless of their political choices, religion, age, education, sexual orientation and ability. Serbian Women in Black and the Kosova Women's Network together form the Women's Peace Coalition. This alliance focuses on giving visibility to nonviolent resistance to war, nationalism, religious fascism, ethnic homogenization, homophobia and any other form of discrimination. An unprecedented union of crucial importance in the region that achieves practical results. This sort of solidarity also promotes a constant demand for the punishment of war criminals. Women do something no one else in their countries has been able to do so far: they work together.

3. WOMEN'S RIGHTS TODAY

After the wars, we can identify certain areas where the situation of women's rights is most problematic: Although women's rights have been assumed by human rights legislation throughout the region, the real situation is that equality is present *de jure* but not *de facto*. Discrimination persists, it is present everywhere and is reflected both in the private sphere and in the public. The laws that protect women from violence or discrimination are neither applied, nor are they imposed or obeyed. Efforts in order to rectify inequalities at schools, at work and at home are not a priority for any government.

Domestic violence goes usually unanswered, very few places or safe houses are available to host women at risk and there are no other available resources to turn to. The disruption of law and order and instability in post-war have been capitalized by organized crime to increase the number of human beings trafficked. It is estimated that 200,000 women and girls transit to and from the Balkans every year, all of them are battered, raped and forced into prostitution [9].

Women who belong to national minorities experience greater discrimination in general. Despite legislative protection, they have additional difficulties to get to the labour market, also they find it very hard to have access to health care and they are the latest in line when it comes to reconstruction priorities. Roma women find themselves in a worse situation worse than any other ethnic group in all areas of life and routinely lack basic rights, they are hardly ever given any jobs and have high chances of being denied police protection if attacked [10].

Unemployment, poor infrastructure and lack of institutions that provide assistance to women and care to children deteriorate even more the economic situation of women. As an example we can mention that in some areas of Kosovo female unemployment is close to 80%, with an official figure of total female unemployment up to 60% [11]. Older women in rural areas are particularly affected by the poor economic situation, as they often do not receive any pension or have no income at all [12].

In Kosovo and Bosnia Herzegovina, men are still the traditional owners. Regardless of equality before the law, men are the owners of private property, women do not inherit and the real estate properties are registered under the name of man [13]. Since they have no *de facto* property rights on any goods, it becomes also very difficult for women to be were granted loans for starting private businesses. All this suffocates the economic independence of women.

4. THE CONSEQUENCES OF A WAR TO WOMEN

Virtually all reports that speak about rights in the region identify one negative impact factor which is always present to diminish human rights' efficiency in the Balkans: the lack of analysis of the consequences of armed conflict from the point of view of sexual affiliation [14]. Those consequences are an important part of the current scene:

The public nature of terrorism against women in Yugoslavia is unique and the punishment for crimes of sexual violence is also unique. Only Yugoslavia and Rwanda have specific international criminal tribunals for crimes committed in their territories during the wars. This gives us the opportunity to examine their proportions and their consequences. To comprehend what women have endured, what has been done to them, it is imperative that the entire history of sexual terrorism in all its manifestations is revealed and to identify how law fails to assimilate the gender nature of the crimes, keeping its patriarchal structure, in times of war and also in peace, internationally, nationally and in the field of human rights.

The victimization of women in the former Yugoslavia begins with rape, we are not talking about isolated incidents of errant soldiers. We are speaking about a carefully planned strategy, with a standard, effective pattern involving the systematic rape of tens of thousands of women and girls aged between 6 and 81 years. The rapes occurred in the eyes of up to 200 witnesses, including children. As a result, women became reminders of Serb repression and domination for the whole community, their families and themselves.

Almost all media focused on rapes but many gender crimes happened at the time and still are happening today. Those include forced pregnancy, forced maternity, forced prostitution, sterilization and all kinds of abuses within the family.

To understand the meaning, the purpose and the effect of such acts, we must understand the meaning of rape in the cultures of the former Yugoslavia. In these cultures honour is paramount, and its loss means shame [15]. Although both men and women are to be honourable, women are the objects through which the honour of men is determined. If a woman has sex outside of marriage, men related to her (her husband, her father, her brother) will temporarily lose their honour. She is going to lose it permanently. The conditions in which it is lost are irrelevant, loss of honour is no less real if it is the result of a rape, and the consequences are the same. Husbands kill or abandon their wives, young unmarried women are rejected by their families, and women of all ages are kept on sedatives to avoid suicide. Many others have gone crazy because of the tortures experienced and the pressure to maintain silence over them. They have been kicked out even from refugee camps.

Therefore, in the Balkans, if a raped woman was lucky enough not to get pregnant, she will bury the story within herself to save her family from dishonour. If she is forced to make it public this will constitute an added tragedy. Silence helps save the honour of men. Women's honour reflects men's honour, which will be reflecting, as well, that of the nation [16].

The significance of the rapes was such that it turned a very successful strategy to consolidate territorial gains of the Serbian soldiers. The rapes were approved and sometimes ordered by superiors, the soldiers had unrestricted access to constant sex, which kept booming their feelings of superiority and domination. This access was guaranteed by the establishment of rape camps, where brutal and systematic rapes took place all along the years of war. It is still unknown how many women were imprisoned in these camps and raped, raped and raped again, usually by large groups of soldiers and paramilitaries. A 19 year old girl declared she had been raped 5-6 times a day during the four and a half months he was a prisoner in one of the Serb camps, which means she was raped 750 times [17].

Figures are only an estimation, it is estimated that from 30,000 to 50,000 women were raped in Bosnia, while in Kosovo the number moves from 15,000 to 40,000. The Croatian government has not even made an estimation. Out of these numbers, around 40 cases have been seen in a court, whether this is the International Criminal Court for the former Yugoslavia, the International Criminal Court and the national courts of all these countries [18].

In 2003, the local Bosnian women's organization, VIVE Žene gathered the testimonies of 35 women from a village near Zvornik. The women told that in the village, in the year 1992, paramilitary groups from Serbia and the Serb inhabitants arrested them, along with four hundred other people and locked them inside some houses. Inside these houses 120 women and girls were raped and tortured repeatedly and denied food. After two weeks they were released by village men who had been hiding in a nearby forest. Survivors made official statements on what happened to investigators from the Tribunal for the Former Yugoslavia in 1995. Those statements were sent to the court of Tuzla and Tuzla prosecutor admits to have done no further inquiries. This prosecutor was required, in 2007, to send the case to the War Crimes Chamber in Sarajevo for being a 'highly sensitive' case with multiple victims and multiple perpetrators. In 2009, many of the survivors had to repeat their statements at the state attorney's office of Bosnia Herzegovina and have not yet received any information about the case. In many cases prosecutions have helped to increase the suffering of the victims rather than to provide justice, often those women involved in criminal proceedings had to face very serious consequences because most victims who have served as witnesses had to testify again and again and their identity has been revealed in one way or another [19].

Forced pregnancy and motherhood are other facets of Serbian sexual terrorism in the Balkan wars. Although pregnancy is a result that can be expected from the massive rapes, the Serb aggressors tried to impregnate women purposely and kept them prisoners until it was too late for a voluntary termination. Forced pregnancy pollutes the Bosnian, Croatian or Albanian blood with Serbian blood. Making women expect Serb babies reveals the patriarchal nature of cultures in which sperm determines ethnicity [20]. After the delivery, the presence of a baby who is the product of uncountable rapes is the constant reminder for a woman, her family and her community of the sexual torture he went through and the domination held by the Serbs. No one should be surprised by the fact that many of these women experienced feelings of disgust and revulsion toward their pregnancies and toward the babies they were expecting. These feelings led in many cases to the rejection of the babies once they were born. The women and girls that did not reject their children are caring for a child that they were forced to have, and in any case they are dishonoured forever. This is a shame that neither they nor their families can ignore.

A well-known Croatian writer and journalist, Jasmina Kuzmanovic, tells the story of a seventeen year old girl called Marijana, whose experience illustrates the way many female victims of ethnic cleansing suffered simultaneously different types of attacks specific to their gender: “I met Marijana in a hospital in Zagreb. Her doctor told me she had arrived from Bosnia three days earlier. Though our interview was difficult, seventeen year old Marijana was beyond tears: dry, tense little face, child’s body. She didn’t exactly tell me what had happened; I had to coax the words out of her, one by one. One day in April, Serb irregulars came to the village near Tesanj, in Central Bosnia, where Marijana, a Muslim-Croat, lived with her family. Marijana, her mother and her seven-year-old sister were tending their vegetable garden. The soldiers raped Marijana and her mother there, then loaded Marijana on a truck, along with twenty-three other women from the village. This was the last time she saw her mother or her sister. Raping continued on the truck. The soldiers took the women to an improvised camp in the woods that operated as a military brothel. Women between the ages of twelve and twenty-five were kept in one room and raped daily. Marijana became pregnant in the first month. After four months, the soldiers let her and seven other visibly pregnant women go. Marijana says, 'They told us to go and have our Serbian babies'. Marijana's face was empty and she had trouble speaking. The only time she became agitated was when asked about the delivery. 'I will not give birth', she said with hard determination. That conviction seemed to be the only thing keeping her on this side of the precarious line of mental health. But her doctor told me they would not be able to perform an abortion, since Marijana had long since passed into the second trimester of pregnancy. Nobody in the hospital had dared to tell that to Marijana" [21].

This is not all, we must take into consideration three objective factors that make women extremely vulnerable to be prostituted. Once we apply them to our analysis of the life circumstances of women in the former Yugoslavia, -and this brings us to the present, - we can conclude that some probably many who were raped during the war are prostituted once it is over [22].

The first factor is social isolation, virtually guaranteed by the code of honour. A woman who survives the rapes and returns home during or after the war will not be accepted in the community, or in her family, nor by her husband. The second factor is a story of incest and sexual victimization, which can be applied to almost all female survivors of the Serbian sexual terrorism, vulnerable to traffickers and pimps just for what they went through. The third factor is poverty. After the war women are subjected to severe economic hardship, not only because the situation of nations after years of war is usually wretched, but because in their case there is no further possible social integration [23]. We could add a fourth factor here, which unfortunately we can't develop appropriately in this chapter: the deployment of peacekeepers [24].

5. WHICH RIGHTS CAN BE ADDRESSED BY JUSTICE

After all we have explained so far, the only crime of sexual violence specified in the Statute of the International Criminal Tribunal for the former Yugoslavia is rape, something that can happen to men and women equally. Other crimes that happen exclusively to women as forced pregnancy and forced prostitution are missing.

The Statute does not establish the elements of the offense. A mechanical definition was developed by the Tribunal in the case Kunarac, Kovac and Vokovic "[T]he actus reus of the crime of rape in international law is constituted by: the sexual penetration, however slight: (a) of the vagina or anus of the victim by the penis of the perpetrator or any other object used by the perpetrator; or (b) the mouth of the victim by the penis of the perpetrator; where such sexual penetration occurs without the consent of the victim. Consent for this purpose must be consent given voluntarily, as a result of the victim's free will, assessed in the context of the surrounding circumstances. The mens rea is the intention to effect this sexual penetration, and the knowledge that it occurs without the consent of the victim" [25].

This concept has been criticized because it reflects male models of sexuality, defining the damage by the intention of the aggressor and not the victim's experience. It also understands the act in terms of an active male body penetrating a passive female victim. Furthermore it is unclear whether consent is an element of the crime, an affirmative defence or a probationary matter. The victim's consent does not seem to be an appropriate mean of determining sexual violence in the context of armed conflict. In our view, it is hard to understand why rape cannot be considered like other violations of international criminal law as torture or slavery, where there is no need to establish a lack of consent for the existence of damage [26].

How the law itself builds the crime is essential to understand the relationship between gender and the international ban on sexual violence in war. The Rome Statute does include all crimes but so far no international tribunal has pronounced itself about the crimes of forced prostitution, forced pregnancy or forced sterilization [27]. In the words of Mackinnon, "women's absence shapes human rights in substance and in form" [28].

CONFLICT OF INTEREST

The author declares no conflict of interest, financial or otherwise.

ACKNOWLEDGEMENTS

Declared none.

REFERENCES

[1] "The history of war has preoccupied itself with the decisions of elite men to declare war, with mythic generals who command with charismatic virility, and with non-elite war heroes who have done 'the noblest of deeds', given or risked their lives for their country. War and militarism, that is, the encroachment of military institutions and ends into politics and society, are normalized by 'rites', such as war veterans' parades and 'sites', such as monuments to war heroes and the military war dead. Few have noted that the greatest casualties of modern war are non-combatant civilians not soldiers. Fewer still have acknowledged that, among civilian casualties, women and girls are deliberately targeted and disproportionately harmed by war and its aftermath" Hynes PH. On the Battlefield of Women's Bodies: An Overview of the Harm of War to Women. Women's Studies International Forum 2004;

(27): 431-445.

[2] Batinić J. Feminism, Nationalism and War: The 'Yugoslav Case'. In: Feminist Texts. Journal of International Women's Studies 2001; 3(1): 3-11.

[3] See Kirby KM, d'Estrée C. Peacekeepers, the Military and Human Trafficking: Protecting Whom? University of St. Thomas Law Journal 2008; 6(1): 240-241. The concept of an "other" is essential for identifying the group and for the creation of a strong warrior spirit based on a sense of brotherhood and fraternalism which obviously excludes women. When you call a certain military organization to war, the mission is to kill and dominate the opposing force. And dominance is usually associated with male things and leaves no space for remorse. Defining an "other", different and separate, has been an essential part of military life. It serves the purpose of creating a boundary between the group and outsiders, anyone who finds his or herself out, and that because of this will be found in an unfavourable condition. Soldiers are often trained to separate automatically those who are non-comrades, creating instant enemies. The enemies usually lack martial qualities, are often sexualized (*i.e.* being "queers") or hated (*i.e.* "mistreat women"). Consequently, to go to war and kill other human beings can be rationalized as the fulfilment of the duty to protect the group against a common foe. Masculinity, in its militant form, reflects the following principles: a) armed forces constitute the ultimate conflict solver; b) human nature is prone to conflict; c) having enemies is a natural condition; d) hierarchical relationships produce effective actions; e) a state without an army is naive, outdated and hardly legitimate; f) in time of crisis the womanly ones need armed protection; g) in times of crisis the man who rejects armed action is jeopardizing his own status as masculine man. In addition, masculinity works as rationale for military separatism, it creates a division between loyalty to the military unit and responsibility with other members of society.

[4] Woodward SL. Balkan Tragedy: Chaos and Dissolution after the Cold War. Washington DC: Brookings Institution 1995; p. 124.

[5] Albanese P. Nationalism, War and Archaization of Gender Relations in the Balkans. Violence against Women 2001; 7(9): 1010.

[6] Lepa Mladjenovič describes how during the twelve years prior to the breakup of Yugoslavia there was a network of feminist organizations from Zagreb, Belgrade and Ljubljana that met annually. Mladjenovič laments the current position of women stating: "everything that we had fought for and that was part of the rights of women during Communism was somehow deleted the minute the war began". See Mladjenovič, L. Serbian Women Unite against the War. Madre Newsletter 1993 August; p. 6.

[7] Batinić J. *cit.* (see reference no. 2), pp. 9 and ff.

[8] Albanese P, *cit.* (see reference no. 5), p. 1016.

[9] See Limanowska B. Trafficking in Human Beings in South Eastern Europe. United Nations Development Program. UNICEF/UNOHCHR/OSCE-ODIHR 2005; Sarrica F. Trafficking in Persons. Analysis of Europe. United Nations Office on Drugs and Crime. Vienna 2009; Almodovar NJ. For Their Own Good: The Results of the Prostitution Laws as Enforced by Cops, Politicians, and Judges. Hastings Women's Law Journal 1999; (10): 119-133; Demleitner NV. Forced Prostitution: Naming an International Offense. Fordham International Law Journal 1994; (18): 163-197; Agathangelou AM, Ling LHM. Desire Industries: Sex Trafficking, UN Peacekeeping, and the Neo-Liberal World Order. Brown Journal of World Affairs 2003; 10: 133-148; Murray J. Who Will Police the Peace-Builders? The Failure to Establish Accountability for the Participation of United Nations Civilian Police in the Trafficking of Women in Postconflict Bosnia and Herzegovina. Columbia Human Rights Law Review 2003; (34): 475-527; and Reynolds S. Deterring and Preventing Rape and Sexual Slavery during Periods of Armed Conflict. Law and Inequality 1998; (16): 601-631.

[10] About this particular matter see, for example, Janević T, Sripad P, Bradley E, Dimitrievska V. There's no Kind of Respect Here. A Qualitative Study of Racism and Access to Maternal Health Care among Romani Women in the Balkans. International Journal for Equity in Health. Nov 2011; Janević T, Janković J, Bradley E. Socioeconomic Position, Gender, and Inequalities in Self-rated Health between Roma and non-Roma in Serbia. International Journal for Public Health. Summer issue 2011; Ravnbøl

CI. The Human Rights of Minority Women: Romani Women's Rights from a Perspective on International Human Rights Law and Politics. International Journal on Minority and Group Rights 2010; (17): 1-45; and Human Rights Watch. Rights Displaced. Forced Returns of Roma, Ashkali and Egyptians from Western Europe to Kosovo. Oct 2010. Available from http://www.hrw.org/node/93832.

[11] World Bank: Kosovo Youth in Jeopardy. Being Young, Unemployed, and Poor in Kosovo. A Report on Youth Employment in Kosovo. Report nº 43596-XK September 2008; and World Bank: Program Information Document (PID). Concept Stage. Report nº 63238. January 2012.

[12] Kusari Purrini M. Economic Empowerment of Rural Women through Enterprise Development in Post-Conflict Settings. Expert Group Meeting Enabling Rural Women's Economic Empowerment: Institutions, Opportunities and Participation. Accra, Ghana: UN WOMEN 2011 Sept 20-23.

[13] See Stanley V, Di Martino S. Assessing Land Administration Project's Gender Impacts in the Western Balkans. Country Case Studies: Albania, Bosnia-Herzegovina and Montenegro. World Bank 2009. Available from http://siteresources.worldbank.org/INTECA/Resources/landgenderassessment.pdf.

[14] Committee on the Elimination of all forms of Discrimination against Women. Concluding Observations for Bosnia Herzegovina. CEDAW/C/BIH/3, June 2006. As references we would point the following documents: United Nations General Assembly Resolution. Rape and abuse of women in the areas of armed conflict in the former Yugoslavia. 1997, A/RES/51/115; Report of the Secretary-General. Rape and abuse of women in the territory of the former Yugoslavia. United Nations Commission for Human Rights; Rehn E, Johnson Sirleaf E. Women, War and Peace: The Independent Experts' Assessment on the Impact of Armed Conflict on Women and Women's Role in Peace-building, UNIFEM 2002; Bunch C. Transforming Human Rights from a Feminist Perspective. In: Peters J, Wolpe A, Eds. Women's Rights Human Rights: International Feminist Perspectives. New York: Routledge 1995; Mudrovčić Ž. Sexual and Gender-based Violence in Post-Conflict Regions: The Bosnia and Herzegovina Case. In: United Nations Population Fund. The Impact of Armed Conflict on Women and Girls. A Consultative Meeting on Mainstreaming Gender in Areas of Conflict and Reconstruction. Bratislava 2001 Nov. 13-15.

[15] To know more about culture from a gender perspective in the Western Balkans see, among others, Olujić MB. Embodiment of Terror: Gendered Violence in Peacetime and Wartime in Croatia and Bosnia Herzegovina. Medical Anthropology Quarterly 1998; 12 (1): 31-50; and Iorčanova D. Women in New Balkan Cinema: Surviving in the Margins. Film Criticism 1997; 21 (2): 24-39.

[16] Ray AE. The Shame of It: Gender-Based Terrorism in the Former Yugoslavia and the Failure of International Human Rights Law to Comprehend the Injuries. American University Law Review 1997; 46 (3): 804.

[17] Women in the Law Project of the International Human Rights Law Group. No Justice, No Peace: Accountability for Rape and Gender Based Violence in the Former Yugoslavia. Hastings Women's Law Journal 1994; 58 (1): 109.

[18] Amnesty International. Old Crimes, Same Suffering. No Justice for Survivors of Wartime Rape in North-east Bosnia and Herzegovina. EUR63/002/2012 2012; p. 4.

[19] *Ibídem*, p. 6.

[20] MacKinnon CA. Crimes of War Crimes of Peace. UCLA Women's Law Journal 1994; (59): 67.

[21] Kuzmanovic J. Legacies of Invisibility: Past Silence, Present Violence Against Women in the Former Yugoslavia. In: Peters J, Wolpe A, Eds. *cit.*, p. 57.

[22] Ray AE. *cit.* (see reference no. 16), pp. 810-850.

[23] Amnesty International, *cit.*, pp. 8-13. See also Reilly N- Seeking Gender Justice in Post-Conflict Transitions: Towards a Transformative Women's Human Rights Approach, International Journal of Law in Context 2007; 3 (2): 165. Not only the nation's economies are destroyed as a result of years of war, it is already clear that many of the women victims of war will be ostracized by their families and communities as a result of their 'sexual disgrace'. Taking all factors together, the social isolation that

survivors experience, the repeated rapes, the economic hardship they will have to face, and the fact that prostitution increases much after the sexual abuse of women during a military conflict, there is no doubt that tens of thousands of women from the former Yugoslavia became particularly vulnerable to being prostituted in the nineties. In fact, organized crime flourished in this context of war and trafficking of human beings makes, still today, one of its most lucrative businesses. In addition to these risk factors, many women are 'pushed' also by pimps or traffickers who approach or kidnap them. Kathleen Barry refers to this process as seasoning. It is a process aiming to break the victim's will, reduce or eliminate her ego, and separate her completely from her former life. All procurement strategies include some form of seasoning, consisting of different practices for different victims. Some women, for example, are subject to the requirement of prostitution relatively quickly when offered affection and promises of love. If the victim resists, her pimp can beat her, rape her, sodomize her, drug her, torture her, starve her or use other ways to force her to submit to prostitution. For women who are routinely raped, brutalized, starved and tortured in military brothels the process of seasoning has already taken place when released from the brothel or the concentration camp. Barry K. The Prostitution of Sexuality. New York University Press 1995; pp. 207-213.

[24] One work focused exclusively on giving evidence of this connection between peacekeeping operations and the increase of human trafficking is the article of SmithCA, SmithHM. Human Trafficking: The Unintended Effects of United Nations Intervention. International Political Science Review 2010; 20(10): 1-21. Smithand Smithtake four case studies where the UN intervened: Kosovo, Haiti and Sierra Leona, and one case study, Nepal, where it didn't intervene. They show that the deployment of peacekeeping forces in a crisis area produces the increase of human trafficking and that the magnitude of the forces deployed determines the magnitude of the increase.

[25] International Criminal Tribunal for the Former Yugoslavia. Appeals Chamber, June 12 2002, para. 127-132. See also Campbell K. The Gender of Transitional Justice: Law, Sexual Violence and the International Criminal Tribunal for the former Yugoslavia. The International Journal of Transitional Justice 2007; (1): 415-416.

[26] *Ibídem*, pp. 418-419.

[27] Bou Franch V. Los Crímenes Sexuales en la Jurisprudencia Internacional. Revista Electrónica de Estudios Internacionales 2012; (24): 13.

[28] MacKinnon CA. *cit.* (see reference no. 20), p. 60.

CHAPTER 9

Conceptual Approach and Proposals for the Assertion of Lesbian, Gay, Bisexual and Transgender Community Rights

Cristina Monereo Atienza*

Department of Legal Philosophy, University of Málaga, Spain

Abstract: The interest in equality and rights of the lesbians, gays, bisexuals and transsexuals group (referred to as LGBT herein) has aroused intense debate concerning the individual and social status of people belonging to this vulnerable group, which has furthermore taken on board a set of complex concepts that are also examined and discussed by other groups, such as the feminist community. The heterogeneity of the members of this group and the organization of the social system makes it difficult to define the implicated concepts, which implies an obstacle for achieving equality. Therefore, it is essential to clarify the concept map regarding sexual orientation and gender identity: firstly, to come to an understanding of who the members of this group are; secondly, to understand what their differences are and indicate whether they are relevant in order to make any distinction in terms of equality; and, thirdly, to identify new strategies for equality and the recognition of rights. All this is condensed into the possibility of discussing a unique subject with equal rights that respects the individual differences of everyone else. This equal subject would be based on the concept of human dignity, which in turn falls back on the fundamental values of freedom, equality and solidarity, established under law. Moreover, this struggle for equality requires complex measures that go beyond the customary assertion of equality and non-discrimination. As for the concerns for women, a profound social transformation is required to break with the traditional mind-sets defining the sexes and the patriarchal system. At this point, international as well as regional legislation, despite positive advances, is still sparse and inadequate, in addition to being focused on mere formal equality and non-discrimination, which does not actually promote any profound change in society.

Keywords: Bisexuals, Dignity, Equal subject of rights, Gays, Gender identity, Lesbians, Sexual orientation, Transsexuals, Vulnerable group.

* **Corresponding author Cristina Monereo Atienza:** University of Málaga, Spain; Tel: 0034 952137606; Fax 0034 952132338; E-mail: cmonereo@uma.es

J. Alberto del Real Alcalà (Ed.)

1. CONCEPTS OF SEXUAL ORIENTATION AND GENDER IDENTITY

The concepts of sexual orientation and gender identity are diffuse and often confused with each other and with other associated notions. On the one hand, *sexual orientation* has been defined as the attraction to another person on an emotional, romantic, sexual or emotional level, which may be heterosexual (that is when the object of attraction is a person of the opposite sex) or homosexual (when feelings arise for people of the same sex). It is also talked about bisexuality, when there is an attraction that is indifferent towards either sex (Principles of Yogyakarta, principles on the application of international human rights law in relation to sexual orientation and gender identity, 2007).

This definition of sexual orientation appears to be transparent. However, this issue is more complex since, undoubtedly, sexual desire is a biological mechanism (like hunger or thirst), but at the same time it carries a social element. In fact, studies on homosexuality in ancient Greece have found that during this period sexual appetite was divided into the active party and the passive party [1]. For the active party, the sex of the passive party was of irrelevance. Therefore, homosexuality did not exist as such, that is, there was no person who had a sexual preference for others of the same sex. Thus, sexual orientation is a cultural construct (of course that is not to imply that culture is monolithic and fixed). Desire is something human, but the means in which human beings respond to sexual desire are socially constructed. Society divides people from childhood according to their genitals, however, organs cannot be interpreted on their own and two people with the same genitalia may have one or another sexual orientation.

In any case, the problem stems from, above all, in its desire to classify unjustly, society dividing what is normal (heterosexuality) and what is not (homosexuality), while excluding a third possibility, bisexuality (a position widely misunderstood by both heterosexuals and homosexuals).

And not without reason, it is argued that the origin of this consideration is found in many countries in the Christian religion and, specifically, in a certain conservative interpretation of biblical texts [2], which has been transmitted though schooling and *via* "religious media*"*. This tendency argues the existence of certain predetermined identities and roles assigned to the sexes, and the specific concept of the Christian family, supported in marriage and sexual differentiation. The most dangerous of these positions is that homosexual relationships are seen as a threat to heterosexual order. Thus, from this point of view, allowing homosexual unions would devalue the importance of family and even trigger social upheaval.

This explains why the community of homosexuals (gays and lesbians) and bisexuals are a vulnerable group, which has historically suffered social rejection and discrimination.

Oh the other hand, the concept of *gender identity* has been defined in the psychological sense of being either a man or a woman, which implies adherence to social norms (gender) that are either masculine or feminine. In this context, the issue corresponds to people whose gender does not correspond to their biological sex. This is defined as transgender (Yogyakarta Principles, 2007). Here the inconvenience is that, once again, society has taken the responsibility to divide human beings into two absolute categories: man or woman, and it has assigned to them behaviours, values and certain social functions.

Transgender has been viewed as breaking the binary condition of man/woman, but at the same time it may actually strengthen it, since transgender people are forced to choose and emphasize one sexual identity in order to find themselves [3]. Yet, it is essential to understand that the identification with either of these fixed identities is artificial and also, within a political-legal and social context, it may be counterproductive in achieving equality, as it promotes the preservation of a hierarchical system of the sexes.

Otherwise, as defined, the conceptual difference between sexual orientation and gender identity is obvious. Those with a determined sexual orientation do not tend to have issues with gender identity. While a person considered as transgender may have different sexual orientations [4].

Another distinct concept is a person considered as being intersexual (hermaphrodite) or being asexual. These are people with genetic modifications that cause them to have both sexes at the same time or, in fact, not have one at all. In principle, this group is not included within the LGBT community, although certainly alliances on certain issues can be positive. Intersexuality is usually welcomed by the LGBT group, because the legal challenges are largely in line with those regarding the condition of being transgender, that is, that the law is capable of determining their sex. But, the transgender-intersexuality association is significantly rejected by many intersex people who believe their condition goes beyond the boundaries marked by sexual orientation and gender identity. Moreover, for many the confusion between transgender and intersexuality may encourage, among other things, surgical interventions on the physical body, which are the main subject of complaint in the case for intersexuality (Intersexual people strive to put an end to the medical term "defective" when applied to their genitals, which has justified the surgery on babies to provide them with genitalia that is more similar to one sex or the other. These interventions have been the source of many psychological and physical problems later on in life). For this reason, we must distinguish and in principle exclude them from the group discussed here.

In summary, sexual orientation and gender identity are two blurry concepts, especially since they imply two notions with complex definitions: sex and gender. Below, a brief conceptual approach to these two terms will be made in order to identify the issues and assertions of these groups.

2. CONCEPTUAL APPROACH TO SEX AND GENDER: REFERENCE TO THE PROPOSALS OF QUEER THEORY

Commonly, the term *sex* is defined in relation to an immutable and ahistorical level of the biological state, meanwhile *gender* is considered as being a product of cultural construction which, therefore, undergoes changes [5]. Male and female individuals are presented as being opposites, different biologically (male/female) and socially (masculine/feminine), since biological differences are translated socially, in such a manner that it creates a system that distinguishes stereotypes and unequally distributes roles. The masculine/feminine polarity exists on a biological level and it is also found in the social sphere where the patriarchal ideology has been responsible for subordinating "the feminine" under "the masculine", not only creating differentiation but also inequality.

Nonetheless, this broad vision on the concepts of sex and gender is questionable. For example, since *postmodern difference feminism*, it has been critically noted that sex is also socially constructed and, therefore, it does not make sense to define gender as a cultural interpretation of sex, if sex itself is considered as a category of gender. Effectively, it appears that society moulds both personalities and behaviours, as well as the forms in which the body is presented.

In this sense, the idea that sex is constructed appears reasonable. Nevertheless, we must be cautious with postmodernist positions, as it is difficult to accept the entirety of their arguments. Thus, many of the proponents for difference feminism tend to argue that social construction of sexual identity follows a single universal pattern in all cultures, based on male and female bodies, in other words, that there is some *biological foundationalism* for the definition of sex [6]. In this regard, it creates a false identity uniformity concerning sex and sexuality, which entails a genuine obstacle in order to understanding authentic differences of all human beings (not only between women and men, but also among women themselves and among men). For example, we no longer speak of "the women", but rather "women", which is defined essentially as a mother (in this line of thought is Luce Irigaray) [7].

This is the reason why we do not just think that sex is socially constructed [8]. We must influence the idea that male and female genders have been socially constructed identitary and collectively. The reality is that individuals are not divided into men and women, and we all are human beings with individual differences.

Therefore, within postmodern feminism, the proposals for *queer* theory appear to be more interesting. For example, Donna Haraway creates a new unique individual that she calls a *cyborg* [9]. The term *queer* is the place of paradoxical identity, which is the only identity that seems possible [10]. This is an individual and a unique identity, and this identity includes sexual orientation without labels. Any gender essentialism is impossible, since differences are found everywhere.

There is also, Judith Butler, who caused herself problems with the notion of both gender and sex as being cultural constructions. According to her views, gender cannot be separated under any case in the political and cultural intersections of class, race, ethnicity or other power relationships that are continuously and incoherently created and reconstructed [11]. In response, the practical solution consisted in the proliferation of incoherent genders. The concept of gender is presented as one that is open, which is continuously being redefined [12]. From this emerges the critical and reflexive attitude of political struggle.

So then, the term *queer* is established beyond the political assertion of the diversity of sexual options on the discourse concerning identity/gender/sex/desire, and heeds attention to visual mechanisms (body representation, *etc.*) and invisible mechanisms (power, norms, policy, *etc.*) [13]. All these attributes affect everyone, because a mandatory political and social order has been imposed, this is to say, a labelling system that provokes the illusion of a predetermined identity. Identity and gender appear as elements inserted into the very nature of human beings, but certainly this nature can also be constructed. The body is something that is culturally constructed, and from birth human beings are artificially classified as either man or woman, pertaining to a certain gender on the basis of the interpretation of sexual genitalia.

It is true that the consideration of collective identities may be (and has been) useful at certain moments in the fight against discrimination (for women and LGBT), however, in the long-term it is identities that segregate humans artificially [14]. Thus, the consideration of a "third sex" may be problematic.

In short, the concept of gender (male/female polarity) may be a useful tool in order to question the biological basis of sexual difference, the cultural/natural dichotomy and associated framework for domination/subordination, but their opposition to sex is questionable as sex is also a cultural construction.

Additionally, neither gender nor sex can be utilised in order to categorize human beings, as they are all different. If the concept of gender has meant that an individual has been wrongfully incorporated into a single common collective identity, sexuality can fall into the same mistake. Sex is individual and multiple, and cannot be explained through any duality or triality.

3. THE DEFINITION OF THE SUBJECT OF RIGHTS: IDENTITY, EQUALITY AND DIFFERENCE

Once people within the LGBT community are delimited, it is necessary to justify that LGBT are subjects entitled to equal rights regardless of their many differences compared with heterosexuals, essentially because people belonging to the "heterosexual" group are also very different amongst themselves.

Undoubtedly, the postmodern proposals of *queer* theory are very interesting for the deconstruction of the concepts of sex and gender. However, the individual disappears within these proposals, which is no less controversial. The absence of an "initiated" individual that could reflect upon his or her existence and his or her rights, being free and autonomous does not seem to assist human emancipation. For this reason, the task should be the reconstruction (and not the destruction) of the subject of rights.

In view of the criticism of the notions of sex and gender, as mentioned in the previous section, it is considered dangerous to base the definition of the subject of rights on the basis of *identity*. Identity entails absolute equality of all characteristics that define individual members of a group. But in reality, the *difference* is somewhat intrinsic to every individual human being, and identity is no longer a mere artificial fabrication, with potential negative consequences. Therefore, it is more convenient to define the subject on the basis of *equality*. Equality recognizes or equates the qualities of different individuals, in such a way that it determines what is relevant to form the group without disregarding the differences of each and every member.

In this regard, it is paramount to distinguish between different ideas on the subject of rights. The proposals by postmodern equality feminism in the difference have already been mentioned above. Difference feminism tends to define the sexes in an identitarian manner, and labels them with a number of qualities based on their biology. Women would have a few attributes based on love and nurturing, especially for the idea of being a "mother". The problem with this viewpoint is not that love and nurturing should be revalued (of course they should). However, if women do not change anything and simply take on these activities that are considered superior, they would be paralyzed by a strategy that would amount to nothing in changing the power structure of the sexes. The tactic is doomed to failure, furthermore, upon considering the importance of the values traditionally assigned to the feminine sex, it would conclude in the defence of a matriarchal organization just as unjust (although this matriarchal system is expressed only in a utopian manner [15]. And, first and foremost, there is no understanding of why these values must be exclusively feminine.

The identitary definition for men also holds the same problems. From the standpoint of radical feminism, the masculine group is considered more rational, and also stronger and more violent. In this sense, Rachel Osborne explains that American cultural feminism considers violence attributable to the group of men, which can easily be transformed into sexual violence against women [16]. However, to think that male violence against women has a biological origin is to ignore macro-powers of the patriarchal social system.

Therefore, the plasticity of identities in the face of a deterministic conception highlighting the rigidity of the biological state must be made apparent. No one denies the existence of differences between male and female, but it must not neglect the ideological manipulation of these biological differences.

Specifically, this variability also occurs for sexual desires. Since its inception, the issue of sexual freedom and freedom of sexual orientation have been diversely dealt with from various stances. Radical feminism reacted against the sexual revolution of the sixties to be interpreted as male stratagem to obtain more sex without offering anything in return [17]. Moreover, at the same time, some feminists attacked the heterosexual institution itself as they considered it as another imposing element and male violence against women. For example, in 1980 Adrienne Rich argued that heterosexuality is not necessarily a natural institution, but is socially constructed and imposed on women through the structural forces controlled by men. Indeed, heterosexuality has been considered (and still considered today) unjustly as "normal" sexual behaviour, compared with the "deviant" behaviour of LGBT. Additionally, although we cannot ignore that most women do not understand their heterosexuality as an exploitative element, it is very interesting and revealing to analyse these criticisms supporting heterosexuality, especially since some conservative arguments against sexual freedom are resurfacing today.

Confronted with these ideas like those of Rich, certain conservatives attacked sexual freedom with very distinct arguments. Germaine Greer argued that sexual freedom and sexual orientation were a demonstration of irresponsibility and selfishness by both sexes in place of family responsibilities. And stemming from here was their fight against feminism, abortion and gay rights. The new Right was termed "Pro-life", "Pro morality", "Anti-Homosexuality", "Anti-feminism",

"Anti-abortion" and "Anti-divorce", all falling under the motto of "PRO-FAMILY" [18]. Furthermore, this anti-feminist movement joined forces against the services provided by the Welfare State that intervened, according to their defence, unjustly in private life (which is paradoxical in itself as they considered the existence of laws as necessary in order to strengthen the family institution or punish abortion). Conservative arguments viewed, among other things, the dangerous creation of a moral hierarchy of women on the basis of what was considered sexually appropriate (the division between good and bad girls). Such positions were defended not only by men but also by women. It is no wonder that men are conservative and endeavour to retain their privileges and social power. What is odd and curious is that women do also. However, no blame can be placed upon them. The gender system generates a set of processes that mitigate the need to employ the power over resources that men possess, causing women to make choices that inadvertently reinforce the system itself, which places them at a disadvantage and also devalues them [19].

It is noteworthy to stress that difference feminism can be approached by its consequences to conservative positions, as it defends established identities about what is feminine and what is masculine. By coming to an understanding that women are more sensitive and more suitable for love and nurturing, this fatally leads to the preservation of the patriarchal *status quo*, and that power is held by men and value little what women have to say or think. Another paradigmatic example of a fatal approach is the feminist anti-pornography cultural movement. Pornography was considered as a cultural translation of male domination and sexual violence against women and, therefore, had to be censored (this was also the stance of conservatives) [20].

It can be deduced, therefore, that the issue of sexual freedom and sexual orientation has been a source of discussion within feminism itself. But sexual orientation is also a matter for men, attacked even more so than women. There is the mistaken social belief that relationships between men (not among women) are usually promiscuous and superficial. This has been highly negative for the achievement of certain rights, such as the adoption of children. The fact that homosexual men are treated even more harshly than homosexual woman is a consequence of the same patriarchal system where masculinity is held in higher esteem [21]. For a long time, lesbians and lesbian behaviours were always ignored as long as women adapted to the remaining social behaviours.

Therefore, it is certain that issues regarding sexual orientation are relevant for maintaining the gender system, however, mandatory and exclusive hetero-sexuality is not the only fundamental pillar of this system. Thus, mere sexual consciousness cannot serve as a mechanism for a large-scale change in the system

[22]. This is because it also runs the danger of creating new fixed identities, among other issues.

At any rate, as already stated, identities may be convenient on certain occasions, this is to say, the use of "strategic essentialism" that unites groups of individuals to strive in defence of their interests [23]. In this sense, one may come to understand social identities as being complex and continuously evolving. Nancy Fraser insists that the cultural separatism of women is inadequate [24]. She claims it was a short-term need, but ultimately become counterproductive for the goals of equality. However, at the same time, she believes that a historiography of gender based on female identity may help to determine patterns of behaviours and also to provide solutions to the feminist struggle. This author is a critic of female gender identity, however, she understands that there may be a common experience for women that leads to generalized conclusions on the basis of gender, without this erasing the real differences such as for race, sexual behaviour or social class [25]. Identities are constructed and deconstructed, although not in the sense of postmodern feminism, but rather in the sense that the general discourse on women must be subject to review. The same may happen with other groups, such as the LGBT community.

Identities (such as sex) pursue emancipatory ends, but suppose several pure identities may be counterproductive and go against the individual differences of each one [26]. For this reason, the definition of the subject proposed by *Equality in the difference feminism* appears to be more appealing. From this stance, the essential point here is what makes us equals, in other words, that we are all equally free to choose and be different.

This model of gender equality re-forges a universal concept of subject that is compatible with the idea that gender is something constructed, and most likely so is sex (coincides well with the assertions of LGBT communities).

The purpose of this trend is to show that all individuals are different because they are subjects constructed through individual and contextual choice, but at the same time they also have something in common due to the fact that they are all human beings. This common element is human dignity.

Accepting the difference of all individuals (either men or women), this model attempts to highlight any common ground, which would be the basis for defining a universal subject as a dignified subject. In this manner, for this model is possible to reconstruct the universal subject identifiable to all human beings, without the sexual distinction between men and women and, at the same time, being sensitive to all individual differences.

This position is not, as it might appear, "essentialist". On the contrary, it may be considered as moderate nominalism in vision or, at any case, non-metaphysical realism (This stance is interesting, as maintained by Amorós in the controversy between realism and nominalism [27]). In other words, it defines human beings on the basis of a common aspect, which refers to several basic constituents. These constituents are not defined as being rigid but are always open to debate. Human dignity must be conceived as a complex and broad concept, whereby moral values can be redirected. These moral values have achieved consensus between countries of differing political views and also between differing religious denominations and lines of thought. Peces-Barba defines dignity as "a precedent, a starting point and an outcome, an endpoint (...) a *prius* of Public Ethic with the compulsion of becoming legalised morality, or what is the same to be Positive Law (…) the basis of political and legal order (...) It has relevant and pre-legal standing (...) It is the motivation for decisions based on values, principles and rights (...) But it is not contained under Law (...) It is not a trait or a quality of a person that gives rise to only principles and rights, but rather a task to be carried out and accomplished. It has occurred throughout history (...) a reflection on the means to be achieved and from this reflection will stand the basis of Public Ethic" [28].

4. A REVIEW ON THE RECOGNITION OF EQUALITY AND NON-DISCRIMINATION IN REGARDS TO SEXUAL ORIENTATION AND SEXUAL IDENTITY UNDER POLITICAL-LEGAL INSTRUMENTS: ACHIEVEMENTS AND LIMITATIONS

The LGBT social movements (all of them "strategically" considered as belonging to the same group) have been and are essential for the clarification of many of the discussed concepts and also for the progress to establish rights for the group, especially since the instruments and political, legal and social measures are still insufficient and dispersed.

If the approach to regulation is conducted, it can be seen that despite the achievements, regulations on equality and non-discrimination on the grounds of sexual orientation and gender identity are sparse and also there are few specific instruments of protection.

On an international level, both the Universal Declaration of Human Rights (UDHR, December 10, 1948), including the International Covenant on Civil and Political Rights (ICCPR, December 16, 1966) and the International Covenant on Economic, Social and Cultural Rights (ICESCR, December 16, 1966) generically regulate equality and the principle of non-discrimination in several precepts (preamble and Articles 1, 2 and 7 of the UDHR; Articles 2, 24, 25 and 26 of the ICCPR, Articles. 2, 7. a and c and 10 of the ICESCR). But, orientation and sexual identity are not specifically named as direct causes of discrimination and remain encompassed in the open clause establishing discrimination on the grounds of various reasons. This entails that any issue or topic constantly requires the justification for their inclusion, citing equal dignity and rights of all people as a whole and, therefore, also the LGBT group members in particular.

In the sphere of the United Nations (UN), the Human Rights Council (HCR), the Human Rights Committee (CCPR) and the Committee on Economic, Social and Cultural Rights (CESCR) safeguard the equal rights for all [29].

While the principle of non-discrimination in specific situations, such as those suffered by women, children or immigrants, was covered early on and extensively under various provisions and declarations, the assertion of the principle of non-discrimination on the grounds of sexual orientation and gender identity and recognition of the rights of LGBT people was included and addressed by the United Nations much later [30].

For several years there have been various attempts to put the social issue of this group onto the political agenda. A Resolution was intended to be drafted, the failed Resolution on human rights and sexual orientation in the Commission on Human Rights, in 2003, known as the "Brazilian Resolution". Various Declarations were also presented: the Declaration of Jelena Postic in 2004, the Declaration of New Zealand in 2005, and the Declaration of Norway in 2006, supplemented by the Declaration of Non-Governmental Organizations on sexual orientation, gender identity and Human Rights. All of these declarations were submitted to the Commission on Human Rights but, despite the fact that the number of countries signing was increasing for each one, they did not acquire the expected number. Also in 2006, Non-Governmental Organizations presented a Joint Written Statement to the Secretariat entitled: "The Promise of Human Rights Council: Marginalised Groups, Sexual Orientation and Gender Identity". But it was not until 2007 that these efforts bore fruit. During this year, the Yogyakarta Principles were presented, adopted by the Human Rights Council. These principles were understood as being a breakthrough in the application of international law on human rights in relation to sexual orientation and gender identity. In parallel, this Commission addressed the issue of sexual orientation and gender identity in relation to extrajudicial, summary or arbitrary executions, as well as Working Groups on Arbitrary Detention and Rapporteur Reports on the subject, which have resulted in the drafting of several Resolutions. Similarly, the Economic and Social Council has prepared Reports on the situation of this group. In addition, several organizations have achieved the status of being an advisory body, for example, the International Lesbian and Gay Association (ILGA in Europe). Yet, any specific Resolution on the matter has been very difficult. The reason for this is that some countries that are part of the UN still consider homosexuality a crime (sometimes even punishable with the death penalty). Ultimately, the following Resolution was accepted: the Resolution of 28 September 2011, on Human Rights, Sexual Orientation and Gender Identity.

Other international organisations, such as the International Labour Organization (ILO) and the World Health Organization (WHO) also pronounced to be in favour of these groups (it must be noted, however, that the WHO had not declassified homosexuality as a disease until 1992).

In a European context, it is worth mentioning the progress in this matter. The Treaty Establishing the European Community adopts the principle of non-discrimination in Article 13 (amended by the Treaty of Amsterdam, in 1997, and the Treaty of Nice, in 2001), making explicit reference to sexual orientation. This is another step towards an international framework. Similarly, the Charter of Fundamental Rights of the European Union (CFREU, Strasbourg, of 12 December 2007) refers to equality of all people before the law (Article 20) and prohibits any discrimination on the basis of sexual orientation (Article 21). However, not all instruments directly mention the matter. The Convention for the Protection of Human Rights and Fundamental Freedoms (ECHR, Council of Europe, Rome, 4 November 1950) contains Article 14 and Protocol No. 12, which makes generic references to equality and the principle of non-discrimination, but unfortunately only in regard to the rights mentioned within the text, without any general reference. Furthermore, Article 14 of the ECHR states that the enjoyment of the rights of the Convention be ensured "without distinction", and specifically identifies some causes which it would consider as the basis of discrimination. These do not contain any text regarding sexual orientation or gender identity, although, once again, it is treated not as a set list but left open to "other reasons".

In Europe at any rate, the European Court of Human Rights (ECHR), the Court of Justice of the European Union (CJEU) and the European Commission are fundamental mechanisms of control. There is ample jurisprudence in regard to equality and non-discrimination of LGBT community [31]. Likewise, the Council of Europe has made several notable recommendations [32].

Also important are the Directives [33], the diverse Resolutions of the European Parliament [34] and the reports on the situation of the fundamental rights in the European Union drafted by the Parliamentary Assembly and the Committee on Citizens' Freedoms and Rights, Justice and Home Affairs [35].

In Spain, there are many fundamental rights and constitutional values that could be understood as being infringed upon, should the rights of homosexuals be restricted and treated as a minority bastion within a heterosexual majority. In a

Social and Democratic State, laws such as that advocated under Article 1.1 of the Spanish Constitution, whose highest values are freedom, justice, equality and political pluralism, do not square up with the inequalities concerning this group, which could lead to the violation of rights such as freedom, the free development of personality, personal and family privacy and, above all, equality.

Article 14 of the Spanish Constitution (CE) does not make any reference to sexual orientation or gender identity, but these are understood as falling under "other condition or social or personal circumstance". The Spanish Constitutional Court (TC) may make differentiations in terms of treatment but only on the basis of a relevance and reasonableness test (purpose, congruence and proportionality) [36]. Additionally, there is Article 9.2 of the Spanish Constitution that mentions substantive equality.

At a legislative level, Law 3/2007, 22 March, on effective equality of women and men, mentions sexual orientation and gender identity on various occasions, and amends the labour legislation, including, among other reasons, the prohibition of discrimination based on sexual orientation. The various laws of the Spanish Autonomous Communities on equality between women and men also mention sexual orientation [37]. They have also begun to create laws that are specific to this matter [38]. Apart from the legislation, sexual orientation and gender identity have been included to a greater or lesser extent and with varying success on a national and Autonomous Community level.

In general, the central assertions of the LGBT community have been the marriage of same-sex couples and the renaming of transgender persons [39]. In regards to marriage, Law 13/2005 on same-sex marriage was approved. This law maintains the term "marriage", however, has amended the terms "husband" and "wife" for spouse. It includes rights to inheritance, tax, nationality, divorce, housing, adoption, *etc*., however, it is a law attributed with a number of defects. For example, it has not incorporated the gender perspective nor has it modified other laws such as Law 45/2003 on Assisted Reproduction (in this sense, it is significant that lesbians are forced to use anonymous donor eggs and not of their partner). On the issue of name changing of transgender people, Law 3/2007 on the registration of name changes was approved. This law makes it possible to amend the registry without any surgery being performed, however, as long as certain requirements are fulfilled: the diagnosis of gender identity disorder (GID), having spent two years under treatment, be of legal age and be of Spanish nationality. Despite being a very forward-thinking law, it does not address the comprehensive treatment of transgender people. This being that the law introduces relevant changes of not requiring sterility or the compulsory need of not being joined in marriage, as is the case in other countries. But, for example, it ignores the need to cover hormonal, psychological, medical, treatments, *etc.*, of transgender people throughout the country.

In conclusion, the progress and achievements on equality and rights of the LGBT community, on an international, European and national level, are not entirely negligible. There is progress towards social equality for this group, using the concepts of formal equality and non-discrimination, which has become an absolute necessity. However, it is also true that equality for this group cannot be achieved solely through measures based on this formal sphere of equality. What is required are other instruments and policies that seek real or substantial equality for LGBT people and that, additionally, are not too generalized or tunnel-visioned, since the ultimate goal should be the profound transformation of the social system.

5. A STRATEGY TO ACHIEVE EQUALITY OF THE LGBT COMMUNITY: COMPLEX EQUALITY AND THE SET OF RIGHTS FOR THE CONCRETION OF HUMAN DIGNITY

National and international political-legal instruments usually regulate equality and the principle of non-discrimination in a generalised manner, and in some circumstances they more aptly express reference towards the specific circumstance of sexual orientation and gender identity. Yet, the question is not only about whether the legislation is inadequate but also, as previously indicated, whether the strategy for equality and non-discrimination is restricted in order to achieve real equality.

If the first of the Yogyakarta Principles is examined, it states that "All human beings are born free and equal in dignity and rights. Human beings of all sexual orientations and gender identities are entitled to the full enjoyment of all human rights", and following this there is a series of listed obligations by the States: to embody the principles of universality, interrelatedness, interdependence and indivisibility of all human rights, ensure the protection of all rights, amend any legislation to ensure the enjoyment of the rights of all, to undertake education and awareness programmes and integrate policies with a pluralistic approach that recognizes the interrelatedness of all aspects of the human identity.

Of these declared obligations, it is noteworthy to mention the indivisibility and interrelatedness of all rights. This has been an arduous issue debated under *jusphilosophical* doctrine [40]. Indeed, one of the great aspirations of LGBT rights and movements in particular, is that rights are actually dealt together since they are the realisation of the values of freedom, equality and solidarity, which in turn fall under the broader sole concept of human dignity. All people are worthy and, therefore, are equal and free, and they should enjoy all rights without exception. The Vienna Declaration of 1993, already reaffirmed the principles of indivisibility and interdependence of all human rights. For this reason, we must correct the imbalance in the treatment of different rights implemented by International Human Rights Law, as it contradicts the Declaration itself and other texts [41].

At the same time, this has to do with the idea that values possess a dual formal-material dimension that are intimately connected. It is questionable that, at an international and regional level, equality continues to be principally interpreted in a formal manner as equality before the law. This is to say, it essentially pursues equality on the basis of a formal and non-material dimension under this concept, however, there is an undeniable connection between them. In fact, the second principle of the Yogyakarta Principles establishes that "everyone is entitled to enjoy all human rights without discrimination on the basis of sexual orientation or gender identity. Everyone is entitled to equality before the law and the equal protection of the law without any such discrimination whether or not the enjoyment of another human right is also affected. The law shall prohibit any such discrimination and guarantee to all persons equal and effective protection against any such discrimination (...) ". Then continues by naming a series of state obligations: to include (if it has not already been done) the principle of equality and non-discrimination in its legislation, repeal all criminal provisions prohibiting any kind of sexual activity of people of the same sex, establishing the same age of consent for sexual relations for all, adopt legislative and other measures to eliminate discrimination based on sexual orientation and gender identity in public and private spheres, take measures to ensure advancement and the equal enjoyment of all human rights, and adopt measures for education and training in this area.

All this is, of course, absolutely indispensable. But the concept of equality must be more profoundly stressed. Firstly, while speaking of formal equality, it is necessary to determine what it is that makes human beings equal in order to identify and apply such with the same legal effects. At the same time, this equality cannot be static and must establish the differences that are relevant in comparative terms, since only those that are accepted may lead to the consideration of cases as being different and involving distinct legal treatment. Indeed, after the consideration of any relevant differences, formal equality connects with another fundamental dimension: the material, real or substantive. Substantive equality is an equality of results not to be confused with absolute egalitarianism (all are equals in all). Rather, it is the result of a continuous set of measures applied by the authorities in order to achieve a similar quality of life. Among these, it includes the possibility of unequal legal treatment in the case of factual inequality, winding back and reconnecting the substantive dimension of equality to the formal one.

Another of the aspirations of the movement for equality and recognition of LGBT community rights is that this double dimension of equality be taken into account, above all, since the achievement of equal dignity cannot only be a struggle against formal discrimination, but rather, as with discrimination against women, a structural reform of the sex-gender system is required. Unfortunately, this social system artificially and unfairly *categorises* human beings. In fact, the strategy of comprehending the LGBT community, as a group is useful, but undoubtedly it does not mean taking into consideration fixed identities that eliminate any innate differences of any individual.

Here the need to influence the material dimension of equality has been discussed. But, additionally, it would be pertinent to examine other possible strategies for the reform of the system, which has an impact on the reformulation of other classical liberal concepts [42]. Freedom, equality and solidarity cannot be discussed without going further. In regard to freedom, we must speak of its material dimension and, above all, of a new concept of autonomy separated from self-sufficiency (this has been given the term relational autonomy). In regard to solidarity, a new concept is born: vulnerability. Vulnerability is a condition of every human being, and this places the ethical and political-legal obligations onto Justice. At the same time, vulnerability is not a passive concept and is related to freedom and relational autonomy.

The lack of the reworking of the current system has often made the rights acquired by the LGBT community insufficient. Many times these rights still demonstrate and further reinforce the dominant values of the sex-gender system, such as monogamy, the alleged irreversibility of identity and desire, to name a few. Many of the policies that have sought to redress discrimination are lacking a gender perspective, and they do not concurrently observe nationality, age, place of residence, social class and access to resources, *etc*. The greatest assertion must be the recognition of a right to be different, since difference is really what makes human beings equal. All human beings are different, and precisely, in order to safeguard this difference, equal rights of lifestyle choice and the right to our own personal concept of what is right and what is wrong have been granted.

In summary, a more robust strategy must be developed in order to encourage structural reform of the patriarchal system, which breaks away from the classification and hierarchy of human beings according to sex, and that pursues the recognition and satisfaction of the individual right to a different sexual orientation and to gender identity, and in general, any fundamental and basic aspect of being human, among others, with the purpose of safeguarding human dignity.

CONFLICT OF INTEREST

The author declares no conflict of interest, financial or otherwise.

ACKNOWLEDGEMENTS

Declared none.

REFERENCES

[1] Nussbaum M. Sex and Social Justice, Oxford: Oxford University Press 1999.

[2] Caramagno TC. Irreconciable Differences? Intellectual Stalemate in the Gay Rights Debate. London: Praeger 2002; pp. 24 ff.

[3] MacCredie J. Making Girls and Boys. Inside the Cience of Sex. New South-Australia: University of New South Wales Press Ltd 2011; pp.180 ff.

[4] Alventosa del Río J. Discriminación por orientación sexual e identidad de género en el Derecho español. Madrid: Ministerio de Trabajo y Asuntos Sociales 2008.

[5] Tubert S. Introducción. La crisis del concepto de género. In: Tubert S, Ed. Del sexo al género. Los equívocos de un concepto, Madrid: Cátedra 2003; pp. 7-37, 8; Accati L. La diversidad original y la diversidad histórica: sexo y género entre poder y autoridad. In: Tubert S, Ed. Del sexo al género. Los equívocos de un concepto, Madrid: Cátedra 2003; pp. 215-252, 220, 260. For a more complete understanding of the origin of the concept of gender and the sex-gender system, see Oliva Portolés A. Debates sobre el género. In: Amorós C, De Miguel A. Teoría feminista: de la Ilustración a la globalización. De los debates sobre el género al multiculturalismo. Madrid: Minerva Ediciones 2005; pp. 15-60.

[6] Nicholson L. La interpretación del concepto de género. In: Tubert S, Ed. Del sexo al género. Los equívocos de un concepto, Madrid: Cátedra 2003; pp. 47-81, 51.

[7] Irigaray L. Espéculo de la otra mujer. Trans. by Sánchez Cedillo R. Madrid: Akal 2007.

[8] Nicholson L. La interpretación del concepto de género. In: Tubert S, Ed. Del sexo al género. Los equívocos de un concepto, Madrid: Cátedra 2003; pp. 47-81, 53.

[9] Haraway DJ. Ciencia, cyborgs y mujeres. La reinvención de la naturaleza. Trans. by Talens M. Madrid: Cátedra 1995.

[10] Acebrón J, Mérida RM. Diálogos gays, lesbianos, queer, Lleida: Universidad de Lleida 2007; p. 99.

[11] Butler J. El género en disputa. Trans. by Muñoz MA. Barcelona: Paidós 2007; pp. 49 ff.

[12] Butler J. El género en disputa. Trans. by Muñoz MA. Barcelona: Paidós 2007; p. 282.

[13] Acebrón J, Mérida RM. Diálogos gays, lesbianos, queer, Lleida: Universidad de Lleida 2007; p. 102.

[14] Bourdieu P. La dominación masculina. Transl. by Jordá J. Barcelona: Anagrama 2000; pp. 143 ff.

[15] Irigaray L. Espéculo de la otra mujer. Transl. by Sánchez Cedillo R. Madrid: Akal 2007.

[16] Osborne R. La construcción sexual de la realidad: un debate en la sociología contemporánea de la mujer, Madrid: Cátedra 1993; p. 48.

[17] Osborne R. La construcción sexual de la realidad: un debate en la sociología contemporánea de la mujer, Madrid: Cátedra 1993; p. 25.

[18] Osborne R. La construcción sexual de la realidad: un debate en la sociología contemporánea de la mujer, Madrid: Cátedra 1993; p. 213.

[19] Saltzman J. Equidad y género. Una teoría integrada de estabilidad y cambio. Transl. by Coy M.

Madrid: Cátedra 1992; p. 102.

[20] Osborne R. La construcción sexual de la realidad: un debate en la sociología contemporánea de la mujer, Madrid: Cátedra 1993; p. 48.

[21] Saltzman J. Equidad y género. Una teoría integrada de estabilidad y cambio. Transl. by Coy M. Madrid: Cátedra 1992; p. 111.

[22] Saltzman J. Equidad y género. Una teoría integrada de estabilidad y cambio. Trans. by Coy M. Madrid: Cátedra 1992; pp. 113, 130 131.

[23] Oliva Portolés A. Debates sobre el género. In: Amorós C, De Miguel A. Teoría feminista: de la Ilustración a la globalización. De los debates sobre el género al multiculturalismo. Madrid: Minerva Ediciones 2005; pp.15-60 and 49-50.

[24] Fraser N. Iustitia Interrupta. Reflexiones críticas desde la posición "postsocialista". Transl. by Holguín M and Jaramillo IC. Columbia: Siglo del Hombre Editores-Universidad de los Andes 1997.

[25] Del Castillo R. El feminismo de Nancy Fraser: crítica cultural y género en el capitalismo tardío. In: Amorós C, De Miguel A. Teoría feminista: de la Ilustración a la globalización. De los debates sobre el género al multiculturalismo. Madrid: Minerva Ediciones 2005; pp. 63-120 and 119.

[26] Amorós C. Feminismo y multiculturalismo. In: Amorós C, De Miguel A. Teoría feminista: de la Ilustración a la globalización. De los debates sobre el género al multiculturalismo. Madrid: Minerva Ediciones 2005; pp. 217-264, 223.

[27] Amorós C. La gran diferencia y sus pequeñas consecuencias...para las luchas de las mujeres. 2ª ed. Madrid: Cátedra 2006; p. 60.

[28] Peces-Barba Martínez G. La dignidad humana de la persona desde la filosofía del Derecho, Madrid: Dykinson 2002; pp. 64-65.

[29] Among the jurisprudential cases there is, for example, the case of Toonen v. Australia, Communication No. 488/1992, U.N. Doc CCPR/C/50/D/488/1992 (1994) in which it was considered that the criminalization of homosexuality cannot be a measure for the prevention of AIDS, and it was even considered as counterproductive since it prevents the public health programmes from reaching marginalized groups. It also rejects that public morality is merely a domestic matter. The Edward Young v Australia, Communication No. 941/2000, U.N. Doc. CCPR/C/78/D/941/2000 (2003), it is understood while speaking of "sex" under the ICCPR, it includes issues of sexual orientation, which considerably broadens protection in this area.

[30] Alventosa del Río J. Discriminación por orientación sexual e identidad de género en el Derecho español. Madrid: Ministerio de Trabajo y Asuntos Sociales 2008; p. 55.

[31] Matters relating to the prohibition of homosexual relations: the legendary case of Dudgeon v United Kingdom, 22 October 1981; the case of Norris v Ireland, 30 November 1987; the case of Modinos V Cyrpus, 22 April 1993; the case of A.D.T. v United Kingdom, 31 October 2000; the case of B.B. v United Kingdom, 10 February 2004; the cases of Lustig-Prean and Beckett v United Kingdom and Smithand Grady v United Kingdom, 27 December 1999. Matters relating to the age of consent for homosexual relations: The cases of L. and V. and S.L. v Austria, in separate decisions of 9 January 2003. Matters pertaining to the marriage of persons of the same sex: the case of Karner v Austria, 24 July 2003; the case of Kozak V Poland, 2 March 2010; the case of Schalk and Kopf. v Austria, 24 June 2010; the case of P. B. and J. S. v Austria, 22 July 2010; the case of J.M. v United Kingdom, 28 September 2010; the case of Vallianatos and others v Greece, 7 November 2013. Matters concerning parentage: the case of Salgueiro da Silva Mouta v Portugal, 21 December 1999; the case of Frette v France, 26 February 2002; the case of E. B. v France, 22 January 2008; the case of Gas and Dubois v France, 15 March 2012; the case of X. and others v Austria, 19 February 2013. Regarding matters of transgender, cases such as the case of Van Oostrwijck v Belgum, 6 November 1980; the case of Rees v United Kingdom, 17 October 1986; the case of Coosey v United Kingdom, 27 September 1990; the case of Norbert B. v France, 25 March 1992; the case of Botella v France, 25 May 1992; the case of X., Y. and Z. v United Kingdom, 22 April 1997; the case of Frette v France, 26 February 2002; the

case of E.B. v France, 22 January 2008; the case of I. V United Kingdom, 11 July 2002; the case of Pretty v United Kingdom, 29 April 2002; the case of Mikulic v Croatia, 7 February 2002; the case of Goodwin v United Kingdom, 11 July 2002; the case of Grant v United Kingdom, 26 May 2006; the case of Schalk and Kopf v Austria 26 June 2010; Gas and Dubois v Francia, 15 March 2012; the case of X. and others v Austria, 19 February 2013; the case of Y. Y. v Turkey, 10 March 2015. The CJEU also has extensive jurisprudence. To cite an example, the case of P. v S. and Cornwall County Council, 1996; the case of Lisa Jacqueline Grant v South-West Trains Ltd, 1998; K. B. v National Health Service Pensions Agency and Secretary of State of Health, 2004; Tado Maruko v Versorgunganstalt der deutschen Bühnen, 2008; the case of Jürgen Römer v Freie und Hansestadt Hamburg, 2011.

[32] Recommendation 924 of the Parliamentary Assembly of the Council of Europe, October 1981, (that, among other issues, urged the WHO to eliminate homosexuality as a disease); Recommendation 1470, 30 June 2000, on immigration and asylum of gays and lesbians and their partners; the Recommendation 1474, 26 September 2000, on the situation of gays and lesbians in Europe; la Council Decision 2000/750/EC, 27 November 2000, on the establishment of a community programme to combat discrimination (2001-2006); Recommendation 1635, November 2003, on gays and lesbians in Sport, *etc.*

[33] Among these, Directive 2000/78/EC, 27 November 2000, concerning the establishment of a general framework for equal treatment in employment and occupation. This provision makes mention of sexual orientation in its preamble (points 29, 31), and also in Article 2. 2. a), in regards to the prohibition of indirect discrimination. In the same manner, Directive 2002/73/EC, 27 November 2002, amending Directive 76/207/EEC concerning the implementation of the principle of equal treatment between men and women in regard to access to employment, vocational training and promotion, and working conditions. This Council Directive considers the discrimination against transgender people as a form of discrimination on the basis of sex. Also, Directive 2004/58/EC 10 on the right of citizens of the Union and their family members to move and reside freely within the territory of the Member States, alludes to the member of the family as being a "registered person". Directive 2004/83/EC, 29 April 2004, on minimum standards for the qualification and status of third country nationals or stateless persons as refugees or as persons who otherwise need international protection and the content of the protection granted, which defines the term "refugee" as any persecuted national on the grounds of "membership of a particular social group". Lastly, we must name Directive 2012/29/EU, 25 October 2012, on the establishment of minimum standards on the rights, support and protection of victims of crime, which mentions sexual orientation in two occasions (Preamble, Points 9 and 56). Directive 2013/32/EU, 26 June 26 2013, on common procedures for granting and withdrawing international protection (recast), which expressly refers to this group.

[34] European Parliament Resolution, 13 March 1984, on sexual discrimination in the workplace; European Parliament Resolution, 12 September 1989, on discrimination against transsexuals; Resolution, 8 February 1994, on equal rights for homosexuals and lesbians in the European Community; Resolution, 8 June 2005, on the protection of minorities and anti-discrimination policies in an enlarged Europe; and Resolution, 18 January 2006, on Homophobia in Europa, which lead to the drafting of Resolution, 24 May 2012, on the fight against homophobia in Europe; on the EU Roadmap against homophobia and discrimination on grounds of sexual orientation and gender identity.

[35] The first Report of the Assembly, 6 June 2000, presented by the Committee on Legal Affairs and Human Rights, on the situation of gays and lesbians in Council of Europe member states.

[36] In the opinion of some authors, the relevance test has been removed from the application of equality proceedings by the Constitutional Court. Martínez Tapia, R. Igualdad y razonabilidad en la justicia constitucional española, Almería: Universidad de Almería-Servicio de Publicaciones, 2000; p.117.

[37] Law 1/2003 of Castile and León, amended by Law 7/2007; Valencian Law 9/2003; Galician Law 7/2004; Basque Law 4/2005; Balearic Islands Law 12/2006; Andalusian Law 12/2007; and Murcia Law 7/2007.

[38] For example, Law 2/2014, of 14 April, on equal treatment and non-discrimination of lesbians, gays, transsexuals, bisexuals and intersexuals in Galicia. Or comprehensive Law 2/2014, of 8 July, on non-discrimination on grounds of gender identity and the recognition of the rights of transgender people of

Andalusia.

[39] Platero R. Discriminación por orientación sexual e identidad de género. In: Álvarez E, Figueruelo A, Nuño L. Estudios interdisciplinares sobre igualdad. Madrid: Iustel 2009; pp. 169-182.

[40] Monereo Atienza C. Herramientas para una teoría de los derechos sociales. Anuario de Filosofía del Derecho 2005; 22: 265-290; Monereo Atienza C. Ideologías jurídicas y cuestión social. Los orígenes de los derechos sociales en España, Granada: Comares 2007; Monereo Atienza C. Desigualdades de género y capacidades humanas. Granada: Comares 2010; Monereo Atienza C. Hacía un concepto complejo de igualdad. La igualdad formal en la Carta de Derechos Fundamentales de la Unión Europea. Madrid: Dykinson 2012.

[41] Villán Durán C. La Declaración Universal de Derechos Humanos en la práctica desarrollada por los órganos de derechos humanos de las Naciones Unidas. In: Asociación para las Naciones Unidas en España: La Declaración Universal de los Derechos Humanos. Comentario artículo por artículo, Barcelona: Icaria 1998; pp. 73-89 and 75-76; Pigrau Solé A. Preámbulo. In: Asociación para las Naciones Unidas en España: La Declaración Universal de los Derechos Humanos. Comentario artículo por artículo, Barcelona: Icaria 1998; pp. 93-103 and 95.

[42] This has been analysed in other papers, Monereo Atienza C. Diversidad de género, minorías sexuales y teorías feministas, Dykinson, Madrid, 2015.

CHAPTER 10

Exploring the Intersections of Disadvantaged Groups Protection: In Pursuit of Development

Maria Isabel Garrido Gómez*

University of Alcalá, Alcalá de Henares (Madrid), Madrid, Spain

Abstract: Increasingly, there is a new relationship in the borders between public and private law. Public authorities are progressively turning to private law when selling their assets and use contracting to fulfil the missions entrusted to them, providing services indirectly through licences to private companies, extrapolating to the public ones formulas which are used in private law or resorting to the forming of foundations. In short, to be able to overcome these serious problems, the objective that we have to set ourselves is to find a model of law which is able to carry out an alternative project which we are seeing today. And that can only be achieved through the discussion of human rights.

Keywords: Disadvantaged groups, Equality, Intersections, Legal protection, Private law, Public law, Non-discrimination.

1. INTRODUCTION: SOME PECULIARITIES OF THE LAW

The idea of peculiarities of the law refers to a State of reason or State of understanding which governs according to the general rational will and only seeks the best in a general way. It is based on the idea of a free and autonomous individual. The actions of the State have to be directed towards ensuring individual freedom and protecting the autonomous development of subjects. The State organization and its regulation have to be governed on rational principles, which can be transferred to the law as a basic element. As a result, this system tries to ensure that the State and its organs can only act in accordance with a faculty granted them by the legal system, by which they are thus limited. In this way, legislation applies to all on an equal basis and arbitrariness in public powers is proscribed [1].

* **Corresponding author María Isabel Garrido Gómez:** University of Alcalá, Alcalá de Henares (Madrid), Spain; Tel: 0034 629074098; E-mail: misabel.garrido@uah.es

This article has been made in the framework of Project Diversidad y convivencia. Los derechos humanos como guía de acción" (DER 2015-65840-R), Spanish Ministry of Economy and Competitiveness.

But at the present the Law has two basic types of regulations: the domestic and the international; the nation-States, societies and legal systems are largely isolated areas that can be analyzed separately; the Law and the theory of modern law are secular, apart from its historical and cultural roots in the Judeo-Christian tradition; the Law of the modern State is rational-bureaucratic and instrumental, has a means to achieve social purposes and has sharp features; the Law is more understandable if you look up and down. From this point of view, the view held by users or customers becomes secondary; the issues that form the core of a legal discipline are first ideas and norms, placing the empirical study of social facts in a secondary role; the Law of the modern State is almost entirely a creation of the North, *i.e.*, of European and Anglo-American, which spans almost the entire world with phenomena such as colonialism, imperialism, trade and the postcolonial influences; the study of non-Western legal traditions is a secondary side and not entirely relevant; the fundamental values that are under the modern law are universal, even if the philosophical foundations are very diverse [2].

In short, we have seen a dissolving of the nexus between democracy and the people, and between the decision-making powers and the Rule of Law, traditionally affected by the representation and by the primacy of the law and the policy which produces the legal norm. So, the question is whether there can be a democracy without a State, leading to a subsequent question, of whether it is feasible to talk, as we have done up till now, of a link between the State and Law, or between the State and the Rule of Law. Consequently, the crisis of the national State and the deficit of democracy and of the Rule of Law which characterises the new powers mean that we have to reconsider the functionality of the Law and its different manifestations in the face of an absence of rules, limits and links which serve as guarantees for peace and human rights faced with new trans-national orders [3].

The birth of the new paradigms of Law arises from the awareness that a monistic and monolithic context is not possible, when it is seen that new forms of Law have emerged which are above and below the State. But one has to go further still, because the regulatory complexity of the systems in force transcends mere complication, and develops the notion of resourcefulness and criss-crossing of relations from one institutional level to another [4]. One of the new paradigms which should be mentioned is that of the logic of the flexibility which intends to generalise flexible logics. These flexible logics have different origins: the origin of some is strict traditionalism, which is the case of the objectives of the Law, of the general principles, of the standards or of the democratic legitimacy.

And also, in an environment like the current one in which transformations synthesise an historic process of structural change, having a direct effect on the forms of organization and exercise of political power in the world, with sovereign States surviving with less actual autonomy and with legal powers in a functional crisis, the question we should ask ourselves is: what remains of the positive Law constructed in accordance with the very rationality of modernity, systematised and arranged into legal structures whose principal characteristics are unity, plenitude and coherence? The State is seeing an ever greater reduction in its unitary authority as an active agent of production of Law, acting as just one more framework together with many others [5].

In contrast, we also made a reference to nationalisms, which tend to independence and self-determination, the most radical ones; or that desire some political autonomy and the respect to their cultural environment, the most moderate ones. The idea of the former nationalism is the defence of the theory of minority rights which is identified with the justification of the given demands. For instance, Kymlicka criticises the liberal conceptions because they do not respect groups, and he states that equality requires to value the national groups' membership. Hence, individual rights and the right to citizenship do not solve questions derived from multiculturalism, and cannot prevent the rights of minorities from remaining unheeded [6].

The idea of the latter nationalism, tries to justify the existence of devices so as to satisfy nationalism's requirements different from State recognition. For instance, MacCormick shared this opinion in which, the more important nationalism becomes for individuals, the more important nationalism becomes. Nationalism would be in this dimension, an option of the individuals required as an element of their identity. Arguments are made at the level of equal treatment deserved by individuals, taking into account that the majority must act respecting the minorities [7].

In particular, globalization presents a reference to a social, economic, cultural and demographic process from which Law cannot escape. From this perspective, and starting from the new relationship between the public and private spheres, what stand out are the relevance of deregulation as a reality and the need for the State to continue maintaining its functions, albeit renewed in accordance with the demands of the new scenario in which it operates. But the reality of Law demonstrates a number of problems which need to be overcome through a new understanding of globalization and the implementation of new legal techniques and formulations [8].

More in particular, the absence of the complete delimitation of a concept's extension and the semantic indecisiveness seems, within these limits, unyielding, discerning that a text's clarity or darkness is not just relative to its expository context, but also to what we call application context, or nature of the situations to which they are intended to be applied. In a material way, we are moving in the debate between imperativist thesis of the legal rules which envisage Law from the angle of power, and the anti-imperativist ones, which envisage Law from freedom. Formally, the legal norm shows a meaning with linguistic signals which must be interpreted in accordance with a logic structure. However, we cannot forget that Law is a cultural fact, deriving from human life, taking into account that human acts are integrated, as far as rules are concerned, in relation with certain values [9].

The Law, as a complex institution, is made up of regulations and techniques, of practices and ideologies. They all have to do with those functions of the Law which have to be developed if society wants to survive and attempt to achieve justice. If society, or any type of association, wants to survive and carry out its functions, it has to perform those listed below: a) problem-solving; b) preventive channelling of conducts and expectations; c) preventive re-channelling of conduct; d) the determination of authority and the establishment of procedures which designate the action as one which has authority; e) the organisation of society as a whole, to guarantee integration, management and incentives; and f) the *juristic method* as a manifestation which synthesises the task of handling the legal instruments so that they contribute to achieving the objectives of Law [10].

2. THE NEW LEGAL CODES

Meanwhile, we should not overlook the part of the doctrine that advocates the unification of private Law, or in some cases harmonization, through the commercialization and generalization of commercial Law, claiming that its autonomy, which arose spontaneously when trade was carried out exclusively by traders belonging to the corporations, is anachronistic in a period in which acts of commerce are performed freely by all kinds of citizens. In addition, the growing uniformity of the economic environment in the globalized society means that contractual demands are today for all producers. The duality of Codes of private Law has numerous drawbacks because it brings repetitions which are useless, and complicates the application of the Law by stirring controversies with regard to the way in which its provisions have to be combined and, above all, regarding the delimitation of the acts and business which must come under civil or commercial jurisdiction. That, even scientifically, the division is negative because it damages the commercial Law, insofar as it isolates its institutions from the general theory of obligations; and it damages civil Law, by depriving it of the elements which might renew it, adapting it to the new circumstances [11].

Nevertheless, what is true is that there are areas of civil Law which are and always have been inaccessible to commercial Law, such as the rights of personality, family relations and successions. Similarly, there are sectors such as bills of exchange, payment orders, cheques, societies with commercial form, insurance, banking, bearer industries and, in general, all those which require a company organization, which claims an autonomous treatment whether or not it is included in the commercial Code [12].

To solve the problems, a proposal expressed with a generalist sense which I consider of great interest is the one made by Günther, who estimates from an internal point of view that communications within the transnational network of pluralist interlegality have a reference in Law. This happens in relation to a formal and material legality oriented at human rights, containing elements of procedural legality in their democratic self-determination aspect. But the current legality does not correspond to that of modernity, becoming transformed into a sort of universal Code of free circulation.

In answer to the question of whether we are faced with fiction, what is true is that transnational legal communication displays some common fields, even despite the differences given by the different cultures. As far as the previously mentioned Code is concerned, in it there are other legal concepts, principles, rules and institutions. For example, Günther quotes the concept of rights assigned to the individual and exercised autonomously, duties complementary to these rights, secondary rules such as authorizations for the decision on primary rules, the concepts of culpable and objective responsibility, the elementary rules which are attached to them for the charge of conducts and their consequences for the physical and/or collective subjects, the principle of forecasting responsibilities and sanctions, the rules for distribution of the test between the actor and the respondent, the presumption of non-culpability, the institutionalization of the role of an impartial third party including the right to present resources against the decisions or the principle of the *audiatur et alter pars*, amongst others.

From the coordinate of internal Law, Günther talks of a universal Code of legality in transnational networks of experts of state and non-state actors, which require concretization in legitimate procedures of creation and application of the Law. But those mentioned previously are concepts, rules or principles of a formal nature. The programme materials are basically human rights which, in turn, are linked to the formal concepts of subjective right, which is attributed to the individual to be exercised individually, as happens with the link in relation to ordinary positive Law and the supreme Law of the person [13].

However, even despite appearances, it must be clear that the existence of this procedural and material Code does not produce a generalization or a universal homogeneity of a transnational Law which arises. Its principal feature is that of non-determination. Concrete determinations are established on the basis of a negotiation of the participants, and are valid both for the programme principles and for the material rules. The Code of legality always refers to this Code [14]. In this line, the horizontal regulatory spaces have an effect on making the Law uniform and coincide with centralizing processes of policy or redistribution of power and the authority between different forces.

This harmonization must be carried out at the same time as the proliferation of the various regulatory orders and of the legal cultures dealt with previously. As intervening factors, there is evidence that the legal cultures have a historical resignation and, when it comes to taking on the global Law by means of the replacement of the national legal order, this does not mean the complete disappearance of the previous legal culture. Other factors are the resurgence or recognition of autonomous legal orders inside and outside national borders. Similarly, we need to point out the emergence of new international institutions and governmental and non-governmental bodies, courts, committees, etc, which contribute treaties, judgments, recommendations and opinions to the world legal panorama [15].

However, I think that this should be understood from a context in which we understand the existence of a principle of constant change in the legal forms, and a minimum and essential unit must be used. From the comparison between the different models it is possible to extract the idea that a lack of regulation integrated by the relevance of a model from another cultural sphere is reconstructed on the basis of the displacement of the interest it might awaken, moving on to study sociologically the social constitution and the strategies of assimilation which belong to the context. From this perspective, at the bottom of the reception it can be seen that there is no dialogue or exchange. What was first seen as the reproduction of a legal model which was imported, is now taken as the original production reforming a legal form which is not its own. Nevertheless, the reception has to be contrasted with a new form which adopts the opposite solution consisting of determining above all else the historical originality of certain legal utterances [16]. So, the aspects which should be taken into account would be the differences in levels between the players involved, the type of objectives pursued, the instrumental variants and the degree of rationalization [17].

I believe should start from the fact that, increasingly, there is a new relationship in the borders between public and private Law. Public authorities are progressively turning to private Law when selling their assets and use contracting to fulfil the missions entrusted to them, providing services indirectly through licences to private companies, extrapolating to the public ones formulas which are used in private Law or resorting to the forming of foundations [18].

Now, another good assumption is that of the trend towards Americanization of the Law, explained because globalization is given impetus by the needs of the global economy and by the unequal distribution of power. There is dissemination of concepts, figures and practices coming from the United States of America [19]. Although also from this viewpoint, it is worth underlining that it comes from a restructuring of the international legal field, which has its origin basically in the practice of Law carried out by the large American legal firms and by the influence of American legal education on the elites of the Latin American States. But, if we go deeper into the matter in question, this idea of unification which is present in the legal dimension of globalization poses some questions: Do all countries have the political, social and cultural prerequisites to bring this harmonization to a successful conclusion? Can we talk of a genuine harmonization of Law, or rather that there is uniformity of the rules, but not the practice of application? And, in all the fields of Law, are all these tendencies carried out in the same manner [20]?

3. THE SPECIFIC NATURE OF CERTAIN RIGHTS

As we know, it was Bobbio who referred to a particular reality that led to a person no longer being seen as an abstract entity but as a person according to their position in society and age [21]. The manner in which the model being studied in the XXI century actually came about is symbolic of the insufficiencies both of the previous classification and of equality at law as a means to render the sexes equal.

The correction currently taking place in the field of women's rights is occurring due to a new awareness that certain social groups exist in conditions of inequality and are not able to stand up for themselves. This has brought about economic and social rights, subsequently generalised and implying equality of civil and political rights. The specific characteristics are therefore addressed, from a technical point of view, of women who find themselves in situations of inferiority in social relationships for cultural reasons.

What occurs in the cases we are concerned with here is that equality as demanded up until now, without having dealt judicially with a series of factors, has effectively been sought with regard to differences involved in the right to be treated differently. Such differences should be used to make a judicial-political evaluation which would permit identifying human beings as existing in contexts where they are not equal to each other. Common principles and values that draw those differences together are however necessary if we are to render those contexts compatible with equality. Problems arise when one attempts to reconcile integration and differentiation in States which have differentiated minority groups that are growing in size. An example of this in our own case would be that we need to ask ourselves how best to protect polygamous families [22].

Equality at law does not take the circumstances of individuals into account. The initial objective sought was to start to erode privilege and inequalities, establishing both a general and abstracted relationship with legislation and seeking equal judicial status both at law and in the application of legal standards in that all persons are deemed to have and to exercise rights equally [23]. One should not forget, however, as Prieto Sanchís has said, that if one takes equality and differentiation then a certain degree of priority is afforded to the former and a general rule emerges to be followed: "there are always motives for equality and one should therefore seek equality as long as true inequality – which will always exist – doesn't provide a reason to either permit or, after having evaluated the motives being challenged, impose differentiated regulation" [24].

The criteria of relevance which should prevail when adopting any type of measure specifically rendering fundamental rights must consist in respect for individual autonomy and meeting basic needs in so far as morality is concerned. There is a third aspect to consider alongside those two and which De Asís describes as the insistence on considering rights as the outcome of bringing together different demands having to do with realising lifetime achievements [25]. Determining which criteria are relevant when it comes to establishing equality and differentiation is in essence axiological in that it implies making value judgments with legal regulations serving as the vehicle for and expression of those judgments. Differentiation is arbitrary if there are insufficient grounds to justify it and determining what comprises sufficient grounds is essentially an issue of evaluation. "Different treatment brought to bear on situations of fact that are in themselves unequal, with the purpose of re-establishing true equality by means of a different judicial regime" is supported by article 9.2 Spanish Constitution. Ruiz Miguel distinguishes between discrimination *for* equality and discrimination *as* equality. Equality as a criterion for apportioning rights is double sided: there is equality in the form of *negative* discrimination, which treats different circumstances or situations which are to be held irrelevant equally, in order to use or to exercise certain rights or to apply legislation; and then there is equality as *positive* discrimination, which involves treating circumstances and situations held to be relevant differently [26].

The rights serve to limit the official authority in order to add to its definition and to obtain the support and help it offers in the form of benefits and services. In relation to civil society they serve to defend its members from the official authority and from themselves, to be effective and surpass the natural state, to communicate and establish links between the official authority and the civil society, instead of having the official authority separated from society or a civil society that does not consider the official authority. In short, the purpose of the entire public service must be to ensure the enjoyment of rights and promote them [27]. We draw the conclusion that the actions of the State which we have set out should be modernized and improved constantly, because, given the growing scarcity of many goods and having achieved universal social rights, in many cases the demands are excessive and impossible to meet; and, given the problems that arise when determining the individual who is entitled to State's action, the decision-making becomes increasingly more complicated [28].

The contemporary concept of equality has its origin in the creation of a legal and social order in which the independence of the individual could only be obtained by positioning him under the auspices of the legal power of the State, with the concept of independence being linked to a formal system and economic autonomy. As Rosenfeld highlights, the history of constitutional equality is the result of a long and difficult struggle against feudal status and privileges. This is a dialectical struggle divided into three stages. In the first, difference is a correlate of inequality: "Those who are characterized as different are treated as inferiors or superiors depending on their position in the hierarchy". In the second phase, identity is a correlate of equality: "If certain criteria are met, everyone has the right to be treated equally". Finally, difference is the correlate: "Any person shall be treated in proportion to their needs and aspirations" [29].

4. SOME EXAMPLES

4.1. Immigration and Collective Rights. The Migration Movement

One of the key features of the literature on multiculturalism is its emphasis on the need of according collective rights, as human rights, to minority groups. A theory that integrates individual and collective rights can eventually provide a better account for many of the policies and institutions [30].

On the other hand, one of the most important current questions to be tackled in the field of collective rights is that referring to immigration. This phenomenon gives rise to problems in terms of recognizing and guaranteeing the rights of immigrants, as collective rights, to freedom of thought and expression, freedom to pursue different ways of life, and freedom to create, maintain and develop their own culture. To these we could add the right to autonomy, and the right to cultural differentiation and freedom, as in addition to a framework of freedom, action by the state is needed to remedy marginalization [31].

The reference to migration movements is becoming more interesting, the Host Countries are divided into two big areas which vary concerning the existence of more or less tradition. In order to solve the current conflicts, the acceptance of the other by means of tolerance and non-exclusion, recognising the diversity within the unit, is urgently needed. This means that we should not succumb to the risk of a mere juxtaposition, creating a legal systems conglomerate, nor elude the diversity trying to result in a standardization process [32].

The problems become manifest in the area of reconciling integration and differentiation within states where immigration is rising. In this context groups arise which have distinguishing features and exist as independent entities with relationships of interdependence among their members. The search for a new answer also leads us to support the idea that there are two meanings to universal citizenship: universality as generality, *i.e.* what citizens have in common and what makes them different; and universality in the sense of the rules and standards that ensure equal treatment for all, applied across the board without considering individual or group differences. In all, the model should aim to achieve certain objectives synthesized as follows: fundamental rights for all citizens, by way of a policy of universalization that allows integration whilst respecting certain inalienable minimum elements; differential rights for all through a policy of recognition that does not clash with the previous point; and minimum conditions of equality for dialogue through a policy that includes actions to create equality and incentives for cultural exchange, preventing homogenization or assimilation by the more powerful majority or minority [33].

There are more and more political communities that act as interpreters; there is a new perception of reality. In the same way, there is a contrast with manipulation and marginalization, and the use of new domains of emancipation is pursued. Radical needs are a result of daily emancipatory practice, which is why the method itself is based on radical subjectivity. We need a new theory of subjectivity that shows that we are before a complex network of growing subjectivities. The growth of the market makes the role of altruistic actions less important, and may make it become the setting for capitalist production [34].

Finally, there is an underlying problem in ensuring that the management of immigrants' rights should be satisfactory from a cultural perspective, as there are situations in which people belonging to a particular group suffer inequalities through marginalization and consequent poverty. To overcome this problem, difference should be treated *via* the recognition of rights, or through provisions within the framework of affirmative actions that transform the root causes of these disadvantages, which lead to a situation of weakness, oppression, and lack of opportunities for a decent life [35].

4.2. The Women´s Rights

Pursuant to what has already been stated, feminism implies two categories of theory. On one level, feminism represents a theory for equality; at another level it symbolises a theory that turns on the objectivity of Law. In both of these cases, however, feminism has served to challenge both political and judicial traditions. The legal thought process has meant that male domination has simply been seen as an aspect of life rather than as a construction imposed by force in a unilateral fashion to benefit the dominant group. Law, from the masculine perspective, combines obligation with authority and extends the social power of men over women as part of the community while failing to perceive the interest of women's survival in such matters. By contrast, feminism as a method considers that women and men are not equal given that a substantive, rather than an abstract, understanding of equality is defined as being truly feminist and is stated in terms of women's specific experience, being what women have the greatest need of in social terms [36].

In this sense, Rawls, Ackerman and Kymlicka define the political aspect of developing feminism, whereas Minow and Young combine the principle of equality and existing differences between social groups with the intention of lessening or eliminating oppression. All in all, E. Bodelón summed up the problems brought to light by these issues under the following points: The possibility that policies can in fact serve to increase exclusion and reinforce certain stereotypes which, from the beginning, underpinned the very existence of the groups concerned. Also, the desire to make up for differences and to demand specific rights also originated in community oriented principles [37].

There is an anthropological dimension to the differential evaluation of the sexes and this comes down through parenting models and the universal reality of the sexual/ritual/family co-division of partners. Division of labour according to the sexes brought about a reciprocal state of dependency, in line with the principle of maternity and lesser physical strength of women. Judicial inequality of men and women in marriage was maintained throughout the 19th century and the wife remained subordinate to the husband. Under Common Law the male was to provide for his wife and family. She was subject to the *ius maritale* and her job was to look after her husband and children, run the house and educate her children. Marriage meant the woman was no longer allowed to have her own property nor to enter into contracts on her own accord without the consent of her husband. The Codifications deemed that the husband was the head of the family; he directed matrimonial matters and ruled on family affairs. It was only certain European Legal Regimes, particularly the German circle of Codifications, which attributed certain rights to women [38].

The situation described above has a great deal to do with the traditional notion that one of the basic functions of the family unit is the union between the genders as complementing each other and as a means to ensure procreation of the race. In this sense, if the family can be said to be the biological link to conservation, propagation and development of the species, then children are the outcome of that union between the parents and are the expression of the human being's desire to perpetuate mankind. Aristotle referred to the family by saying that it is the first union between people which arises out of need, between beings that are incapable of living without each other, *i.e.* union between the male and the female in order to perpetuate the race. That it does not occur as the result of a deliberate proposition but rather because a natural instinct exists in man, just as it does in other animals and plants, one's desire to leave behind one another being of the same race [39].

Having remained subordinate for a long period of time, women were soon to begin an intensive socio-political battle and sought to be acknowledged as equal to man in dignity. That example of feminism was based on equality of the sexes and then, later on, there was the 20th century feminism of French origin, which was the product of post-structuralism and Italian feminism that considered that "being a woman" was neither comparable nor subordinate to "being a man". A distinction has been made from that point of view which of itself serves as a root cause of exclusion. For its part, radical feminism sets the two sexes against each other as enemies and looks on all things male as being somehow inferior. It effectively forgets the complementary aspect of sexual duality that comes from the ontological dimension of the person. Neo-feminism promotes male-female equality by equating their rights, given the changed roles and involvement of the female sex in the workforce, while still taking their differences into account.

5. CONCLUSIONS

The globalization of Law has two main regulatory dimensions: the degree to which the world is subject to a set of legal rules, and reference to the certainty that human relationships are governed by Law everywhere in the world. Legal rules undergo conversion into obsessive-compulsive rules and become a system that legitimates itself based on its inherently self-generating nature. In addition, the initial concept of legal relations and their components are transformed into a techno-legal order under the influence of a new technical focus. Thus, a new order emerges, characterized by the formation of networks that imply that the globalization of law must center around commercial and Contract Law, Public Law, protecting human rights and also the growing importance of lawyers, together with the dissemination of contents and legal procedures. All three of these mean that the regulatory authority of the State with respect to these areas is unlimited, although States can decide whether to participate or else to withdraw. In this state of affairs, linear systematicity is forgotten in order to implement a circular system, surpassed by the specification of new concepts [40].

In this work, there is an interdisciplinary and plural concept of what the term globalization means. In particular, globalization presents a reference to a social, economic, cultural and demographic process from which Law cannot escape. From this perspective, and starting from the new relationship between the public and private spheres, what stand out are the relevance of deregulation as a reality and the need for the State to continue maintaining its functions, albeit renewed in accordance with the demands of the new scenario in which it operates. But the reality of Law demonstrates a number of problems which need to be overcome through a new understanding of globalization and the implementation of new legal techniques and formulations [41].

Consequently, we should attempt to establish the bases for the creation of a legal project based on a democracy on the international plane. From this perspective, the key is to be found in the extendible nature of the value of solidarity, exceeding certain social expectations and considering the need to totally modify the estimation of man in relation to his rights. With this new consideration of globalization, man would no longer see himself as a holder of rights, but as a direct participant in the determination of which rights correspond to him. At the same time, all the rest of us individuals would be obliged by solidarity to put into practice all the means possible to overcome the obstacles and the conditioning factors which might be presented in this free participation [42].

Progress in the analysis of human rights is what will make it possible to go deeper into a fairer Law in the era of globalization. In this area, then, a preferential place must be given to legal Science which up till now has preserved a conceptual apparatus of a paleo-liberal type, and there has been no concern to draw up a theory of the guarantees and a Science of the Constitutions which meets the standard of the instances of tutelage expressed by the new and old rights. Legal Science has had no impact on the creation of a constitutionalism of private Law which imposes limits and guarantees against the abuse of power by economic authorities. And, if we place ourselves in the public sphere, it can be seen that neither has legal Science drawn up, outside the criminal and procedural guarantees which protect our rights of freedom, appropriate guarantees for political and social rights [43]. Nevertheless, this is not contradicted by the fact that legal Science must be independent and take on spaces which are clearly of non-Law, together with informal dimensions within the current legal dynamics. All of this brings with it the requirement or the opportunity to carry out research goes deeper into the real structure of the new forms and dynamics of Law [44].

At the present time increasing attention is being given by legal theorists and practitioners to the whole area covering equality and social rights. Despite this growing volume of work, we consider that any contribution to the subject which adds a new vision and perspective may be of interest. Our study deals with the subject of substantive equality in the sphere of social rights. First, we investigate the semantic and practical complexity of these concepts, together with the obligations which correspond to the public authorities in terms of putting them into practice. Secondly, we discuss the role of substantive equality in the discourse of social rights, explaining the points at which the two concepts interact, and the ways that formal equality can be improved. Lastly, we reach the conclusion that there are two distinct senses in the concept of discrimination, one which is equivalent to any infringement of the general principal of equality, and another stricter one, which is the infringement of equality when any of the proscribed differentiating factors are present (race, sex, *etc.*). The legal aspect of the mandate to exercise and guarantee social rights is manifested in the programmed objective, as well as in the fact that the measures aimed at these objectives are protected from the possibility of their not being complied with, or of their being complied with in such a way that they have no real effect.

One of the most innovative perspectives in the comprehension of rationality, for example, is the one offered by critical theory, which is a materialistic theory that sees the object of Law as a production process and not so much as a finished product. The matters dealing with ideology and power are dealt with in its Constitution [45]. The starting point is complexity and growing legal opaqueness. Complexity causes contradictions and conflicts, and the rationalist legalism of the enlightenment is attacked. Pérez Lledó describes the general characteristics of these currents: 1) Before natural Law and positivism, the historical and social dimension of Law stands out, even though its relative autonomy is recognized; 2) before the autonomy of legal dogmas, interdisciplinarity is defended, at the same time as legal regulation and its formal structure is internally criticised; 3) the political dimension of Law and of legal speech is emphasized; 4) the indeterminate character of Law and the subjectivity of legal reasoning are defended; 5) the ideological character of Law is reaffirmed, paying special attention to the production and reproduction of legal conscience; and 6) the ambivalence with regards to Law is presented and criticised as a conservation factor, developing in a setting of a counter-culture that tries to escape what is usually taken as right. In conclusion, the criticism of Law is directed against legal positivism, however, we must say that they both originate from positivist epistemology, if this reality is not taken into account; we come across much ambiguity and many contradictions [46].

Legal criticism develops along with a reflection about the fact that legal Sociology has no political consideration, which is why they are described as ideological and somewhat subjectivist. In this sense, for post-modern critics, modern paradigms are no longer valid. They have disappeared for two reasons: abandon and obsolescence. Currently, we can perceive a crisis, but what is really taking place is a transition [47]. The modern idea of global rationality of a social and personal life breaks down into micro-rationalities that depend on a *global, incontrollable* and *unexplainable* rationality. What post-modern criticism should do, as B. de Sousa Santos puts it, is vindicate the micro-rationalities in such a way that they stop being parts of a whole and become realities present in different places [48]. Two of fundamental ideas are being worked on; they refer to hyper-politization and that the larger the political sphere is, the more freedom there will be.

There are more and more political communities that act as interpreters; there is a new perception of reality. In the same way, there is a contrast with manipulation and marginalization, and the use of new domains of emancipation is pursued. Radical needs are a result of daily emancipatory practice, which is why the method itself is based on radical subjectivity. We need a new theory of subjectivity that shows that we are before a complex network of growing subjectivities. The end of the legalist myth marks a legal minimum that is characterized by revolutionary practice. The growth of the market makes the role of altruistic actions less important, and may make it become the setting for capitalist production. There are new spaces where there are innovating socio-pos--materialistic programmes and policies to promote peace, the well-being of the environment, gender and racial equality, that are led by new groups and social movements. B. de Sousa Santos describes contemporary capitalist societies as having four structural contexts and hence four structural subjectivities: home is the responsibility of the subjectivity of the family, production or work is the responsibility of the class, citizenship is the responsibility of the individual and the world is the responsibility of the nation [49].

CONFLICT OF INTEREST

The author declares no conflict of interest, financial or otherwise.

ACKNOWLEDGEMENTS

Declared none.

REFERENCES

[1] Böckenförde E-W. Escritos sobre derechos fundamentales. Translated by JL Requejo, I Villaverde. Baden-Baden: Nomos Verlagsgesellschaft 1993.

[2] Twining W. Derecho y globalización. Translated by O Guardiola-Rivera, C Sandoval, De López Medina. Bogotá: University of Los Andes-Faculty of Law 2005; Nelken D, Feest J, Eds. Adapting Legal Theories. Oxford: Hart 2001.

[3] Ferrajoli L. Razones jurídicas del pacifismo. Edited and translated by Pisarello G. Madrid: Trotta 2004.

[4] Arnaud A-J, Fariñas MJ. Sistemas jurídicos: Elementos para un análisis sociológico. Translated the second part by Escudero R. Madrid: Carlos III University of Madrid-BOE 2006; Jenson J, Sousa Santos, B de. Globalizing Institutions, Case Studies in Regulation and Innovation. Aldershot: Ashgate 2000.

[5] Sousa Santos B de. El milenio huérfano. Ensayos para una nueva cultura política. Translated by Barreto A, Salazar G, Ceceña AE, Herrera J, Cammaert F, Palacio D, Eras J. Madrid: Trotta 2005; Tulchin JS, Bland G, Eds. Getting Globalization Right. The Dilemmas of Inequality. Boulder-Colorado: Lynne Rienner Publishers 2005.

[6] Kymlicka W. Ciudadanía multicultural: una teoría liberal de los derechos de las minorías. Translated by Castells C. Barcelona: Paidós 2010.

[7] MacCormick N. Institutions of Law: an Essay in Legal Theory. Oxford: Oxford Univerity Press 2008.

[8] Appadurai A. Globalization. Durham-North Carolina: Duke University Press 2001; Reich S. What is Globalization? Four Possible Answers. Notre Dame: The Helen Kellog Institute for International Studies, University of Notre Dame 1998.

[9] Soriano R. Compendio de Teoría general del Derecho. Barcelona: Ariel 1993.

[10] Llewellyn K. The normative, the legal and the law-jobs: The problem of juristic method. The Yale Law Journal 1940; 49(8): 1355-1400.

[11] Flood J. Megalawyering in the Global Order: The Cultural, Social and Economic Transformation of Global Legal Practice. International Journal of the Legal Profession 1996; 3, 169-214.

[12] Wiener J. Globalization and the Harmonization of Laws. London: Pinter 1999.

[13] Günther K. Pluralismo jurídico y Código Universal de la Legalidad: La globalización como Teoría del Derecho. Translated by Brage J. Anuario de Derechos Humanos-Complutense University of Madrid 2003; 4: 229.

[14] Günther K. Pluralismo jurídico y Código Universal de la Legalidad: La globalización como Teoría del Derecho, translated by J. Brage. Anuario de Derechos Humanos-Complutense University of Madrid 2003; 4: 247-248.

[15] Furger F. Global Markets, New Games, New Rules: The Challenge of International Private Governance. In: Appelbaum R, Felstiner W, Gessner V, Eds. Rules and Networks. The Legal Culture of Global Business Transactions. Oxford: Hart 2001; pp. 201-245; Hirst P, Thompson G. Globalization in Question: the International Economy and the Possibilities of Governance. Cambridge-Oxford: Polity Press-Blackwell 1997; López Ayllón S. Globalización, Estado de Derecho y seguridad juridical. Mexico: National Supreme Court of Justice 2004.

[16] Serrano A. Dogmática jurídica y análisis sociológico: El Derecho. Doxa 1991; 10: 180 ff; and Wiener J. Globalization and the Harmonization of Laws. London: Pinter 1999.

[17] Serrano A. Dogmática jurídica y análisis sociológico: El Derecho. Doxa 1991; 10: 198-199.

[18] Chevalier J. Vers un droit post-moderne? Les transformations de la régulation juridique. Revue du Droit Public et de la Science Politique 1998; 3: 659-690; Zapatero V. El arte de legislar. Navarra: Thomson-Aranzadi 2009.

[19] Shapiro M. The Globalization of Law. Indiana Journal of Global Legal Studies 1993; 1(1): 37 ff.

[20] López Ayllón S. Globalización, Estado de Derecho y seguridad juridical. Mexico: National Supreme Court of Justice 2004; Mittelman JH. The Globalization Sindrome. Transformation and Resistance.

Princeton-New Jersey: Princeton University Press 2000.

[21] Peña AM. La garantía en el Estado constitucional de Derecho. Madrid: Trotta 1997.

[22] McGlynn C. Families and the European Union. Law, Politics and Pluralism. New York: Cambridge University Press 2006; Peces-Barba G. Curso de derechos fundamentales. Teoría general. Madrid: Carlos III University of Madrid-BOE 1999.

[23] Asís R de. La igualdad en el discurso de los derechos. In: López García JA, Del Real Alcalá JA, Eds. Los derechos: entre la ética, el poder y el Derecho. Madrid: Dykinson 2000; pp. 150-168.

[24] Prieto L. Igualdad y minorías. Derechos y Libertades 1995; 5: 119.

[25] Asís R de. Sobre el concepto y el fundamento de los derechos: Una aproximación dualista. Madrid: Dykinson 2006..

[26] Asís R de. Sobre el concepto y el fundamento de los derechos: Una aproximación dualista. Madrid: Dykinson 2006; Ruiz Miguel A. La igualdad como diferenciación. In: Derechos de las minorías y de los grupos diferenciados. Madrid: Escuela Libre 1994; pp. 286-290.

[27] Peces-Barba G. Derechos sociales y positivismo jurídico (Escritos de Filosofía Jurídica y Social). Madrid: Dykinson 2006.

[28] Donati P. I diritti-doveri dei mondi vitali: l'Europa delle famiglie. Rivista Internazionale di Filosofia del Diritto 1990; 1: 51-81; Eekelaar J. Uncovering Social Obligations: Family Law and the Responsible Citizen. In: Maclean M, Ed. Making Law for Families. Oxford: The Oñati International Institute for the Sociology of Law-Hart Publishing 2000; pp. 9-28.

[29] Rosenfeld M. Hacia una reconstrucción de la igualdad constitucional. Translated by Dorado Porras J. Derechos y Libertades 1998; 6: 415.

[30] Torbisco N. Group Rights as Human Rights. A Liberal Approach to Multiculturalism. Dordrecht: Springer 2006; and the references to Kymlicka W. Multicultural Citizenship: A Liberal Theory of Minority Rights. Oxford: Oxford University Press 1995; Kymlicka W. Liberal Individualism and Liberal Neutrality. Ethics 1989; 99: 883-905; Taylor C. The Politics of Recognition. In: Gutmann A, Ed. Multiculturalism and "the Politics of Recognition". An Esssay by C Taylor. Princeton-New Jersey: Princeton University Press 1992; pp. 25 ff; Young IM. Polity and Group Difference: A Critique of the Ideal of Universal Citizenship. In: Phillips A, Ed. Feminism and Politics. Oxford: Oxford University Press 1998; pp. 250-274.

[31] Lucas J de. Algunas propuestas para comenzar a hablar en serio de política de inmigración. In: Lucas J de, Torres F, Eds. Inmigrantes ¿cómo los tenemos? Algunos desafíos y (malas respuestas). Madrid: Talasa 2002; pp. 23-48.

[32] Fariñas MJ. Globalización, ciudadanía y derechos humanos. Madrid: Dykinson 2000.

[33] Young IM. Polity and Group Difference: A Critique of the Ideal of Universal Citizenship. In: Philips A, Ed. Feminism and Politics. Oxford: Oxford University Press 1998: pp. 401-429.

[34] Sousa Santos B de. Beyond Neoliberal Governance: The World Social Forum as Subalterm Cosmopolitan Politics and Legality. In: Sousa Santos B de, Rodríguez Garavito C, Eds. Law and Globalization from Bellow: Towards a Cosmopolitan Legality. Cambridge: Cambridge University Press 2005; pp. 58 f.

[35] Rosenfeld M. Affirmative Action and Justice. A Philosophical and Constitutional Inquiry. New Haven: Yale University Press 1991.

[36] Mackinnon CA. Toward a Feminist Theory of the State, Cambridge (Mass.): Harvard University Press 1991.

[37] Bodelón E. Pluralismo, derechos y desigualdades: una reflexión desde el género. Derechos y Libertades 1995; 5: 205-209; Minow M. Making All the Difference. Ithaca-New York: Cornell University Press 1990; Young IM. Justice and the Politics of Difference. Princeton-New Jersey: Princeton University Press 1990.

[38] Coing H. Derecho privado europeo. Vol. I. Translated by Pérez Martín A. Madrid: Spanish Cultural Foundation of the Notary 1996.

[39] Aristotle. La Política. Translated by Araujo M, Marías J. Madrid: Center of Political and Constitutional Studies 2005.

[40] Garrido MI. Las transformaciones del Derecho en la sociedad global. Pamplona: Thomson-Aranzadi 2010, pp. 59 f..

[41] Garrido MI. Las transformaciones del Derecho en la sociedad global. Pamplona: Thomson-Aranzadi 2010., p. 17 f..

[42] Ara I. Las transformaciones de los derechos. Madrid: Tecnos 1990, pp. 35 f..

[43] Twining, W. Derecho y globalización, translated by O. Guardiola-Rivera, C. Sandoval Villalba and D.E. López Medina. Bogota, University of Los Andes-Faculty of Law, 2005, p. 220.

[44] Calvo M. Transformaciones del Estado y del Derecho. Bogotá: Externado University of Colombia 2007; Harris RL, Melinda JS. Critical perspectives on globalisation and liberalism in the developing countries. Leiden: Brill 2000.

[45] Aseff LM. La teoría crítica en Argentina. Doxa 1998; 21: 24-25.

[46] Pérez Lledó JA. Las teorías críticas del Derecho. In: Garzón E, Laporta FJ, Eds. El Derecho y la justicia. Madrid: Trotta-Spanish National Research Council 2000; pp. 99-100.

[47] Arnaud AJ, Fariñas MJ. Sistemas jurídicos: Elementos para un análisis sociológico. Translated the second part by Escudero R. Madrid: Carlos III University of Madrid-BOE 2006; pp. 52-53 and 79.

[48] Sousa Santos B de. La transición postmoderna: Derecho y política. Doxa 1989; 6: 224-225.

[49] Sousa Santos B de. La transición postmoderna: Derecho y política. Doxa 1989; 6: 237 ff.

CHAPTER 11

Rationality and Discrimination in the Political Integration of Minorities

José Antonio López García*

Department of Legal Philosophy, University of Jaén, Jaén, Spain

Abstract: The first conceptualisation of equal rights in the modern sense, understood to mean equality of ownership of the same individual freedoms, was offered by the theorists of the social contract, from Hobbes to Rousseau, but equal rights still appeared as an immaterialisation hypothetical in a Civil Society (State) that was yet to be constructed. Starting from the same enlightened principles, legal positivism takes on the task of redirecting all disputes about material equality, that were specific to the Enlightenment period, towards the more accessible proposal of formal legal equality regarding the respect of individual rights, essential for a liberal social order that holds up the written Constitution as a materialisation of popular Sovereignty. Leaving aside the complex preoccupation with the material equality of individual rights, all of jurists' efforts centre upon developing the aspect of the concept of equality that can be interpreted as universally valid (the formal-legal aspect). And also, the modern conception of democracy, *i.e.* the clearest and most conscious system for determining collective social institutions was built on the basis of opting for multi-ethnic and multi-national States for the purpose of political integration of minorities. The consensus and relativism of values considered as the basic criteria for the functioning of democracy discouraged the possibility of mono-ethnic States, thereby favouring a situation where several communities live side by side and get along within the same State.

Keywords: Civil society, Democracy, Discrimination, Material equality, Minorities, Political integration, Rationality, Rights.

1. THE MODERN STATE AS A UNIVERSAL MODEL

One of the classic authors in the study of nationalism, Benedict Anderson, noted in the revised version of his work, *Imagined Communities*, that such simple elements of the European States as *census, map and museum*, had, in the 19th and 20th centuries, turned the whole world into a world of States. The *census* of the inhabitants of the colonies conducted by the Europeans had used the category of

* **Corresponding author José Antonio López Garcia:** Department of Legal Philosophy, University of Jaén, Jaén, Spain; Tel: 0034 953 212483;, Fax: 0034 953 211905; E-mail: jalopez@ujaen.es

This work forms part of the activities of the research group of the Andalusian Government (Spain) at University of Jaén: "Criminal law, Criminology, Democracy and Fundamental Rights"(SEJ-428).

J. Alberto del Real Alcalà (Ed.)

"nationals" of a territory, which did not correspond at all to the pre-colonial tribal or ethnic reality: "This is why the colonial State imagined a Chinese series before any Chinese, and a nationalist series before the appearance of any nationalists [1]. With the *map*, which used a ruling pen to mark out the territory of the new states, an imagined space was organised, in which realities - in themselves heterogeneous - were gathered and "naturalised": "In London's imperial maps, British colonies were usually pink-red, French purple-blue, Dutch yellow-brown, and so on. Dyed in this way, each colony appeared like a detachable piece of a jigsaw puzzle. As this 'jigsaw" effect became normal, each "piece" could be wholly detached from its geographic context. In its final form, all explanatory glosses could be summarily removed: lines of longitude and latitude, place names, signs for rivers, seas, and mountains, neighbours" [2]. Lastly, the *museum* recreated, in another imaginary space, a historical pre-colonial past at the height of the new State reality. Primarily, archaeological remains, along with the expert technical reconstructions of the finds, were reorganised, to be displayed in museums as emblems that the new States had managed to rescue from time. Only the large machinery of the State was capable of reorganising history in a great museum, and all of this would contribute to legitimising the new State.

With these three basic elements, along with the imposition of a common language for the new State, which was almost always, either exclusively or in conjunction with codified native languages, the language of the metropolis itself (English, French, Spanish, *etc.*), a clearly fragmented world had been ordered and made into States. The world *was now fully accessible in accordance with the abstract forms of European thought*, incapable of stopping at the infinite and unexpected aspects of historical and concrete concepts without demarcating and classifying them [3]. If any sort of feeling of national belonging was developed in these former colonies, whether in the form of identification with the State or fight against it, this is down to the previous work of the colonial State.

But the creation of the Nation States and consequent national spirit in the former European colonies has been fairly fast, particularly if we compare it with the long historical process that determined the formation of the European States. Therefore, when Ernest Gellner invented an imaginary country in the centre of Europe, Ruritania, in which a group of peasants and craftspeople led by intellectuals and local politicians came together to form the first modern Nation State, he was simply applying internally to Europe the same explanation that had previously been exported to the colonies: in other words, the idea of the supremacy of general abstraction over pre-modern particularisms: According to Gellner, "The general emergence of modernity hinged on the erosion of the multiple petty binding local organisations and their replacement by mobile, anonymous, literate, identity-conferring cultures" [4]. It was not that Gellner was unaware of the controversial historical process that stretched from the Absolute State to the Europe of nations of the 19th century, but that, with hindsight, the whole historical process can be summed up in the image of Ruritania. From Machiavelli and Bodin to the liberal theories of the social contract, history of political ideas confirms a slow but irresistible transformation of the modern Universalist identity and the collapse of a substantialist, localist pre-modern past. Meanwhile, the rise of this "universal reason" that did not respect the old communitarian political ways, had its justification in the spread of such important objectives as *economic and social progress, equal rights and democracy.*

The modern notion of *progress*, in particular its *economic aspect,* was only made possible by eliminating all of the local economic obstacles and creating the first national markets [5]. The concurrence in the market of free subjects to exchange goods, and exchange themselves as a *work-merchandise force*, required the standardisation of the structure of productive occupations and the homogenisation of cultural working habits. In Gellner's commentary on Adam Smith's work, *The Wealth of Nations*, he gives an economic explanation for the birth of Nationalism in Europe, demonstrating the symmetry between the appearance of nationalism and modern industry: "In simpler words, agrarian civilisations do not engender nationalism, but industrial societies do" [6]. As for the idea of *social progress*, Auguste Comte defined it as the quantitative accumulation of social experiences, which were discernible thanks to the new "positive spirit" that was being consolidated in the sciences in the 20th century, doing away with "the obstacles arising from prejudice, ignorance and mythology" [7] of the theological and metaphysical states of Humanity.

Equal rights did not appear all of a sudden in the modern age. The first steps towards them were laid down by the elimination of feudal jurisdictions *via* the power of the Absolute Monarchy. The will of the Prince (autoritas non veritas facit legem) is imposed on the political principles of theological natural law [8], meaning that the exercise of its power is only limited by the prudential ethos, essential for managing the State [9]. The first conceptualisation of "equal rights" in the modern sense, understood to mean equality of ownership of the same individual freedoms, was offered by the theorists of the social contract, from Hobbes to Rousseau, but equal rights still appeared as an unmaterialised hypothetical in a Civil Society (State) that was yet to be constructed [10]. Starting from the same enlightened principles, legal positivism takes on the task of redirecting all disputes about material equality, that were specific to the Enlightenment period, towards the more accessible proposal of formal legal equality regarding the respect of individual rights, essential for a liberal social order that holds up the written Constitution as a materialisation of popular Sovereignty. Leaving aside the complex preoccupation with the material equality of individual rights, all of jurists' efforts centre upon developing the aspect of the concept of equality that can be interpreted as universally valid – the formal-legal aspect. This use of legal Dogma, defined in the latter part of the 19th century by Paul Laband as "a practice of purely logical thought, leaving aside any historical, political or philosophical consideration" [11], culminated in the 20th century with the Kelsenian identification of the Rule of Law: "There is only one legal concept of State: the State as a centralised legal order" [12]. So the defence of the democratic legitimacy of the Rule of Law is another of the basic elements.

In effect, the modern conception of *democracy,i.e.* the clearest and most conscious system for determining collective social institutions, as Cornelius Castoriadis recently described it [13], was built on the basis of opting for multi-ethnic and multi-national States. The consensus and relativism of values considered as the basic criteria for the functioning of democracy discouraged the possibility of "mono-ethnic States" [14], thereby favouring a situation where several communities live side by side and get along within the same State. As Walker Connor pointed out, in the 19th century, Lord Acton was the great defender of the idea that: "The coexistence of several nations under the same State is a test, as well as the best security of its freedom" [15]. The opposite of this, consisting of encouraging the proliferation of States founded upon one original and incommunicable "living community", went against trade and legal equality, but above all, it despised the democratic idea that held that the individual, and not the community, was the fundamental element of legitimation. It is from this that the more intuitive suggestion from Jürgen Habemas, on the*Gleichursprunglichkeit* (equiprimordiality) of the subjective rights and democratic popular sovereignty takes on the meaning of a "twin birth", as, in Habermas' rejection of a prepolitical vision of subjective rights, we can see Hegel's criticism of the theorists of the Social Contract. Thus, if the subjective side of modernity is represented by individual or private subjective rights, the objective side anchors these rights in their necessary democratic legislative production: According to Habermas, "*At a conceptual level,* subjective rights do not immediately refer to atomistic and estranged individuals who are possessively set against one another. Rather, as elements of the legal order they presuppose collaboration among subjects who recognise one another, in their reciprocally related rights and duties, as free and equal consociates under law. This mutual recognition is constitutive for a legal order from which actionable rights are derived. In this sense "subjective rights" emerge equiprimordially with "objective" law... Certainly, the source of all legitimacy resides in the democratic process of law production, and this process in turn calls upon the principal of popular sovereignty" [16].

2. CRISIS OF THE NATION STATE AND NATIONALIST MINORITIES

The question mark that arose from the universal implementation of these social and political principles (progress, equality and democratic rights), came about because their global spread in the 20th century coincided with the political experiences which determined their most painful crisis. In the heart of Europe, in the same movement caused by the triumph of Fascism, equal rights and democracy came to be deeply questioned. In 1935, controversial author Carl Schmitt questioned the normativity of the universal principals of the Rule of Law: "Today we can talk about Christian, Anti-Christian, liberal, national or anti-national Rule of Law, given that the Rule of Law is not presented as a conceptual body against other conceptions of the State, religious or moral, but as a mere means and method" [17]. We are well aware of the consequences of this questioning of the Rule of Law: the European Fascist States also proclaimed themselves as States that upheld the Rule of Law (Legal States) and "democracies" (organic democracies, such as in the case of Spain) [18]. In as much as what it did for the project of *social and economic progress*, as an integrating socio-economic element for equal rights and democracy, the crisis of the "Welfare State" in the 1970s definitively shut down what Jürgen Habermas called " the utopia of the working society" [19], in other words, the idealisation that supported a material situation in which class, social and economic differences would start to disappear. The Social State, conceived as a State that integrated rights and democracy with distributive economic progress, has not been able to meet all of the social expectations and has been forced to choose between *systemic collapse* or withdrawal from its role as socio-economic programmer [20].

As a result of the crisis of these universal concepts being evaluated, from the 1970s onwards current legal and political theory has been inundated with new explanatory concepts: complex societies, multicultural societies, ungovernability and globalisation. All of these point in the same direction: the irreparable loss of sovereignty of the modern Nation State [21]. From the *theory of systems*, Niklas Luhmann maintains that, in order to understand *modern complex societies,* the old European idea that placed too much value on the State as the main pillar of society is inadequate. The two basic structures that make up the State - Law (and rights) and (democratic) Political Power - must be re-theorised. Regarding *Law*, Luhmann considers that: "the question is not whether the Law can take on the functions of social programmer and guide of social behaviour; rather, the question is the following: how can the Law adapt to the fact that these functions must increasingly be developed in other areas of society" [22]. In terms of *Political Power*, Luhmann argues that power as a *symbolically generated medium of communication* is widespread throughout society, vastly reducing: "the limits on power becoming politicised within the State" [23]. Political vocabulary no longer talks about universalities, but rather differences, inequalities, the complexity and absence of a centre of sovereignty. The "particularist" movements (nationalist, ethnic, cultural, *etc.*,) as well as "trans-state" movements (transnational businesses, supra-state policies, *etc.*,) can find a good opportunity in this to increase their legitimisation. When the "great universalist network" that the State hung over all of these movements is weakened, new formulas acquire the capacity to explain the new reality: differentiality *versus* equality; unequal development *versus* progress; self-government *versus* (formal) democracy.

The historic success of this classic triad linked to the modern Nation State - equal rights, progress (social and economic) and democracy - is called into question by current nationalist movements. In effect, two fundamental theoretical positions in the study of nationalism can be discerned; one being what is called*modernist* (or instrumentalist) position; the other being the *ethnonationalist* (or primordialist) [24]. The difference between the two theoretical positions consists of the decidedly political or cultural nature that they give to the idea of nation. The modernist position is based on the idea of a political nation. The idea of a *cultural nation*, on the other hand, is the basis for ethnonationalist theories [25].

According to *modernist theory*, both the old nationalism of the 18th and 19th centuries and the nationalisms of the 20th century are solely phenomena that accompanied the evolution of the State and modern industrial society. Regardless of any characteristic that may be put forward as an agglutinate for national collectivity, be it race, culture, language or anything else, according to modernist theory the determiner is the consideration of nationalism as an *instrumental element*of the modern State. John Breuilly expresses this clearly: "Nationalism must be understood as a form of politics and that that form of politics makes sense only in terms of the political context and the particular objectives of nationalism. Central to an understanding of that context and those objectives is the modern State. The modern State both shapes national politics and provides that politics with its major objective, namely possession of the State" [26]. From this modernist perspective, the link between nationalism and the formation and political development of the modern State is conclusive: "Thus, the problem of nationalism does not arise when there is no State" [27]. According to modernists, the *national identification* model is by definition anonymous, requiring a high level of homogeneity and collective literacy of the masses, requirements that only became possible with the arrival of the State and the industrial society. For authors such as Gellner or Breuilly, the modern borders of nationalism are clearly demarcated, eliminating the possibility of the pre-modern basis for cultural or ethnic nationalism supported by ethnonationalism.

In contrary to the modernist theory, the *ethnonationalist theory*, at first glance, is presented as an answer to the modernist thesis on the state dependency of the nationalist phenomenon. According to Jáuregui Bereciartu: "The statist conception of the nation linked to a process of unification and centralisation, that has not taken into account the existence of other nations, and other national sentiments outside the one officially accepted by the State, has generated enormous injustices and, as a consequence, led to the appearance and spread - in Europe at least - of large restoration movements, if not resistance and liberation movements, of the mis-named ethnic minorities" [28]. In this view, the construction process of the State, a process that is eminently rationalist and abstract, avoided, if not disregarded, other historical and cultural forms of collective identification.

Ethnonationalism argues that the pendulum that determines the moment a nation is founded has to swing from politics to culture, from unity from above to unity from below, from the legal-political "form" as a social reference to the "substance" of traditional culture. The "primordial fact", that structures collective conscience, distances itself from politics in order to lay its roots in a collective and unique history and culture. A moderate representative of ethnonationalism, Neil MacCormick, argues that nationalist principles were present before the modern era: "I cannot consider it reasonable or appropriate to accept current orthodoxy on the meaning of "nationalism" or its temporal placement exclusively from 1789 onwards. The principle according to which those who belong to different nations should have different governments based on their own laws and customs is much older than all of that; and there is no possible way of describing such a principle other than calling it 'nationalist'" [29]. The ethnonationalist position, formulated in this way, has encountered two main problems that contradict the logic of its arguments:

The first problem, consists of justifying why, if culture is the fundamental aspect for forming a collective link, is it the aim of practically all nationalisms to form a political State, after having positioned the whole ethnonationalist strategy precisely as being critical of the State. This attempt to establish congruence between culture and government, as Benjamin Akzin called it, a "monoethnic State", reintroduced ethnonationalism to the modernist problematic.

On the other hand, the *second problem* hanging over ethnonationalism is the accusation that it has "invented tradition" through an "ad hoc" reconstruction process (an *anamnesis* made from pieces of tradition that are connected through a fully modern discourse which is what grants it an explanatory and narrative continuity), in order to justify its political aspirations. Once again, the author who has been most accusatory of falsehood in tradition is Ernest Gellner, for whom modernity is only intelligible to us because it has produced in modern man a *cultural amnesia regarding everything in the past* (as opposed to any *traditional anamnesis*) [30]. In the same vein, although more tentatively than Gellner, Eric J. Hobsbawm has pointed out that the reasoning that ethnonationalism is based on is not pre-modern, as Gellner argues, rather they belong to the historical context of the late 19th and early 20th centuries. Thus, in order for linguistics, race or genetics to enter into the political discourse of ethnonationalism, first the linguistic standardisations and research of the 19th century had to happen; the appearance of Darwinian evolutionism; the explosion in the field of biological genetics in the late 19th century; and, most importantly, the industrialism and mass migrations from the countryside to the cities that lead to the growth of business and salaried work. Until then, racial and linguistic differences had not arisen as signs of identity, contempt, or localist defence [31].

The arguments justifying *ethnic nationalism*, however, may still be defended from a point of view of "statist abstinence"; that is to say, focusing on the potentiality of ethnonationalism as an "alternative way of life" to the Nation State. This interpretation of nationalism denies the possibility of *the ethnic nation becoming a State*, but it considers it appropriate to express ethnic and cultural differences through nationalism [32]. Finally, the criticism of the modernists can also be contradicted by looking at the historical existence of *diaspora populations* [33], whose origins lay in religious motivations and who have never had any interest in forming a State, as could be said for the "Jewish People", at least until the appearance of the Zionist movement pushing for the State of Israel [34].

As tends to happen in academic debate, there are authors who assert that there is a *third way* that softens the edges of the positions taken by modernists and ethnonationalists. In Spain, Andrés de Blas Guerrero favours introducing elements of political and ethnic studies, for a more unified understanding of nationalism [35]. The famous nationalism scholar, A. D. Smith, expresses this third way clearly: "We have to draw from a more eclectic perspective if we want to understand the complex relationships that occur between, on the one hand, the interests and strategies of the current elites and, on the other hand, the echoes of continuity of ethnic links and sentiments" [36].

It is precisely this political, social and cultural complexity brought about by nationalisms that brings us to a first provisional conclusion: *they are an expression of the exhaustion of the Nation State as a universal model.* From here arises the "suspicion" that what had been established since the Enlightenment with connotations of impartiality and universality had resulted in a strategy of establishing domination and exclusion. The right to subscribe to this "suspicion" has been clearly expressed by Javier de Lucas: "It is the abstract universalism... a universalism that hides the reality of the domination, of the asymmetry, of the inequality of the individuals and the marginalised or even excluded groups. This blindness is revealed precisely at the moment in which maximum dignity for the individual is proclaimed, because this refers to individuals stripped of any attribute, and within this requirement for universality is hidden the Sophism of the universalist argument that we inherited from the Enlightenment: one is worthy because we share common values, that rise above our differences - which in reality means on condition that differences are forgotten about" [37]. But if it is the case that the "abstract universalism" of the Nation State has excluded and submitted to any serious proposal of "differences as attributes of life", then, as Javier Lucas puts it, the number of aggrieved people and the reasons for their grievances is greater than the nationalist minorities have expressed. At the very least, immigrants and religious and ethnocultural minorities must be included [38].

3. THE POLITICAL INTEGRATION OF MINORITIES: TRADITION AND REASON

If there are more than serious doubts about the validity and prospects of the liberal, enlightened Universalist project, the pressing issue is finding new forms of *social integration* that are more interested and respectful towards non-liberal traditions. Following the position of Will Kymlicka's *Multicultural Citizenship* [39], a *prima facie* characterisation of the *integration formulas* of the minorities identified previously offers us the following panorama for each of the different minorities: a)*ethnonationalist minorities* should have their traditional rights (tradition), that have been excluded by the majorities, recognised, up to a point where a negotiated form of self-government is reached (reason); b)*religious minorities,* settled within the State, should have the right to their "traditional practices" (tradition), without self-government being a clear ambition, due to their reduced community arrangements or any other deficiency for full self-government (non-reason); c)*minorities made up of immigrants (and refugees),* given their heterogeneity and the fact of having waived – voluntarily in the case of immigrants – their traditional place of origin, do not have a right to follow their traditions (non-tradition), at least if they are *different* from the majority in the host country, and, of course, they also do not have access to formulas for self-government within the host society (non-reason).

In this characterization of the *forms of integration* proposed by Kymlicka - on the one hand rich in subtleties compared with the tradition brandished by the *communitarians*, and on the other hand with large doses of reflection on the old, standardising liberal theories, I nevertheless find an acute short-sightedness regarding immigration and refugees as products of globalisation: Kymlicka points out that, "the best that refugees can realistically expect is to be treated as immigrants, with the corresponding polyethnic rights, and hope to return to their homeland as quickly as possible. This means that, in the long run, refugees are victims of an injustice, as they did not reject their national rights voluntarily. But this injustice was committed by the government of their country, and it is not clear whether we can ask, on a realistic basis, redress from the hosting governments" [40]. With this I would like to demonstrate the current *Tendenz* towards traditional arguments, even in Kymlicka's moderated proposal.

This tendency towards respecting the *tradition* of minority religious and ethnonational communities requires individualist liberalism to reflect upon its own constitution as a *comprehensive doctrine*. This reflection is a warning that liberalism also views itself with distinct, deep seated "illiberal" tones, which are accepted by its supporters as elements of deep-rooted cultural identity that do not need to be rationalised. "To talk as if the world was divided into completely liberal societies on the one hand, and completely illiberal societies on the other, inhibits a constructive dialogue between cultures" [41]. In this way, *liberal tolerance* towards non-liberal (illiberal) minorities extends as far as accepting "restrictions to individual autonomy within the group", as long as these restrictions to not cross certain limits: "This is not to say that federal intervention to protect liberal rights is never justified" advises Kymlicka. Obviously, intervention is justified in the case of gross and systematic violation of human rights, such as slavery or genocide or mass torture and expulsions, just as these are grounds for intervening in foreign countries. The exact point at which intervention in the internal affairs of a national minority is warranted is unclear, as it is in the international context" [42]. The challenge for contemporary liberalism must be to maintain its doctrine within the limits of "attractive ethics", as a better explanation of the "good life". From this Dworkinian position, the insistence on negotiation and respect of *other comprehensive non-liberal doctrines,* must be the key to the "collective life" within multicultural societies in which minority groups have their "societal culture", *Weltanschauung*, jointly with the liberal majority group.

As for the "wandering groups", *i.e. the immigrants and refugees*, it must be a political possibility for the Host State to take them on. Therefore, particularly for *immigrants*, due to the fact that they *voluntarily* abandoned "their culture of origin" [43], meaning that their situation is the product of a *liberal choice*, they have the Universalist status of recognition that comes from modern liberal individualism. This means that, in a certain sense, they are the *ultimate fully liberal individuals*, given that, on the one hand, liberalism has become "illiberal" in terms of understanding its own citizens living within the State and that, as has been shown, this "illiberal turn" has compromised contemporary liberalism (advocated by Rawls, Dworkin and Kymlicka) with non-liberal traditions situated within its territory.

I therefore consider the *instrumental treatment* given to the issue of immigration to be an irony of this*Tendenz*towards tradition. Turning all eyes back onto *tradition*, the patterns in current political and moral discourse seem to have been drawn up in order to exorcise *communitarianists* (Sandel, Taylor or MacIntyre [44]); one of the effects of this is the creation of an "illiberal national atmosphere", that is surely a form of justification for current restrictive and conservative immigration policies. Due to the demands entailed by this cultural gaze towards tradition, States have necessarily become more *essentialist*, meaning that the loss of the Nation State's Sovereignty does not seem to relate to its policies on minorities - there the State still has "power of action" - but it relates to its own doubts about *tout court* liberalism; its accepted inability to solve problems not located within *its own* Sovereign territory. Thus it seems that, for all of those "wandering groups" that are a product of globalisation, the only policy it is possible to apply is that of the old *"Laissez-faire, Laissez-passer"* [45].

The "illiberal turn" that liberalism offers with theories such as those of Rawls, Dworkin, right up to Kymlicka, however, and with nuances of a "family feeling", it is not exactly the "linguistic turn" with which Jürgen Habermas confronts the problem of multiculturalism. Regarding the disputes in the US between *communitarianism, republicanism* and *liberalism,* Habermas has spoken of an "ethical overload" [46], in which they fall into a scale from largest to smallest - first communitarianism, then republicanism and, in John Rawls' version, lastly, "political liberalism". The coincidences between Habermas and Rawls are well known, as are their divergences in terms of the true value of "political autonomy" (democracy). For Rawls, it has a reasonable neutral value, with true value being reserved for "private autonomy" (rights). For Habermas, on the other hand, this basic intuition of "true cooriginal value" is given both to "private autonomy" and "public autonomy" [47]. From this same position of distance from Rawls (notwithstanding the "family feeling"), Habermas is even more critical of the positions of particularist and group "privative ethical overload", in the case of communitarianists, and of republicanism's "political autonomy" overload [48]. Through these criticisms of the different most influential positions today, Habermas presents his *deliberative political theory* as the only one capable of providing a coherent and universal response to the problems of complex multicultural societies.

In other words, according to Habermas' theory, there are no spaces reserved for *ethical tradition* that would be present, to a greater or lesser degree, in the other positions: Habermas states: "As soon as we take this*internal* connection between the Rule of Law and democracy seriously, it can clearly be seen that not only is the system of rights not blind to the social inequalities of life, but neither is it blind to cultural differences. The "colour-blindness" of selective reading disappears when it is supposed that we attribute an intersubjectively conceived identity to the bearers of subjective rights. People, including legal persons, are only individualised through a process of socialisation. Under this premise, a correctly understood theory of rights demands precisely a policy of recognition that protects the individuality of the individual, including in areas of life that shape their identity. For this to happen, no alternative model is needed to correct the individualist bias in the system of rights through other regulatory points, just its consequent realisation" [49].

So for Habermas, the universal criteria for solving the problem of multi-culturalism is democratic public debate of the ethical starting points, that are accessible in terms of an open discussion, because of the fact that the content of these ethical issues *necessarily* tie in with their implementation in terms of equal subjective rights for all parties. The practice of this *deliberative democracy* includes all "private autonomy", regardless of whether this has "its own origin" - liberal or traditional - giving it the same opportunities in terms of rights to shape collective political decisions. This Universalist character put forward by Habermas makes it more conducive to obtaining global solutions. In this respect, the aspirations of traditional minorities can be said to tie in with those of immigrants whose situation is the result of globalisation. The starting premise is not family, community or the ethnic group, but rather the rights that should also extend to those who do not come from a traditional background. When pondering the different aspirations, for Habermas the democratic Nation State is still the public-political space that must be counted on. For Habermas, the project of a *Weltstaat,* with the strength to project deliberative decisions on a worldwide scale, poses as many ideal hopes as it does real risks [50].

A more decisive position, in the realistic search for a "democratic prince" who is up to the challenge of economic globalisation is Ulrich Beck's proposal [51]. For Beck, while it is appropriate to rescue the notion of the *democratic State*, because it is necessary to organise democratically the economic and social structure of globalisation (kosmopolitische Form der Staatlichkeit), what can no longer be rescued is the *democratic national State*. This, and the large transnational businesses, are without any doubt the agents of globalization, selfish international subjects whose economic, accounting and political strategies Beck describes in detail. What Ulrich Beck calls "the second great transformation", alluding to Polyani, places the *counterweights* of a new "global policy" (Weltpolitik) - that has *irremissibly* refused to frame the debate in any other setting apart from "cosmopolitan politics" - in a cosmopolitan orientation of the State that is *no* *longer*national or nationalist, and in a cosmopolitan mobilisation of civil society. All the forces have to point in that direction, in the exact same direction, but the current dominant acting forces of globalisation - the national States and transnational companies - direct their forces in a selfish and non-democratic direction.

In Beck's proposal, which he takes as serious and real "als ob", the notion of state Sovereignty remains intact, and so it is the self-interested management of a type of Sovereignty, the Sovereignty of the national State, that we want to be rid of. Paradoxically, in a "neoliberal" world, the notion of State is rescued. Within this Kantian-based "Cosmopolitan State", cultural differences have to be taken into account *in the same way*, meaning that there should not be room for the "wandering groups". It seems like a fair solution to both problems. Perhaps it is worth taking the "as if" attitude seriously.

CONFLICT OF INTEREST

The author declares no conflict of interest, financial or otherwise.

ACKNOWLEDGEMENTS

Declared none.

REFERENCES

[1] Anderson B. Imagined Communities. Reflections on the Origins and Spread of Nationalism. México DF: FCE 1993; p. 258.

[2] Anderson B. Imagined Communities. Reflections on the Origins and Spread of Nationalism. México DF: FCE 1993; p.244.

[3] M. Foucault, throughout his works, has been critical of rationalist thought and its love of abstraction. But the expressiveness of the following text in which Foucault summarises the writing of his work, The Order of Things, is invaluable for clarifying the point that we want to highlight here: "This book first arose out of a passage in Borges. Out of the laughter that shattered, as I read the passage, all the familiar landmarks of my thought - our thought, the thought that bears the stamp of our age and our geography - breaking up all the ordered surfaces and all the planes with which we are accustomed to tame the wild profusion of existing things, and continuing long afterwards to disturb and threaten with collapse our age-old distinction between the Same and the Other. This passage quotes a certain Chinese encyclopaedia in which it is written that "animals are divided into: a) belonging to the Emperor, b) embalmed, c) tame, d) sucking pigs, e) sirens, f) fabulous, g) stray dogs, h) included in the present classification, i) frenzied, j) innumerable, k) drawn with a very fine camelhair brush, l) et cetera, m) having just broken the water pitcher, n) that from a long way off look like flies". In the wonderment of this taxonomy, the thing we apprehend in one great leap, the thing that, by means of the fable, is demonstrated as the exotic charm of another system of thought, is the limitation of our own, the stark impossibility of thinking that" (Foucault M. Las palabras y las cosas. México DF: Siglo XXI 1988; p.1.).

[4] Gellner E. Nations and Nationalism. Madrid: Alianza Universidad 1988; p.116.

[5] On the formation of the national markets, seeHobsbawm E, MARX K. Pre-Capitalist Economic Formations. Barcelona: Crítica 1979; SWEEZY-DOBB-HILTON *et al.* The Transition from

Feudalism to Capitalism. Barcelona: Crítica 1977.

[6] Gellner E. Culture, Identity and Politics. Nationalism and new social changes. Barcelona: Gedisa 1993. On this identification that Gellner makes between INDUSTRIALISM AND NATIONALISM, now related to Eastern Europe, see: Gellner E. Nationalism and politics in Eastern Europe. Viento Sur 1992; 3(May-June).

[7] Kolakowski L. Filosofía positivista. Madrid: Cátedra 1981; p. 84.

[8] On the controversy between the new political principles of the Absolute State and medieval natural law, see: *Actes du College Interdisciplinaire D'Angers,* Angers, Presses de l'Université d'Angers, 1995 (in this volume there are some very important studies by: BARRET-KRIGEL B, BODIN J: De l'empire a la souverainete; and the text by BELLUSSI G. L'Absolutisme politique et la tolerance religieuse dans l'ouvre de Jean Bodin et Thomas Hobbes. On the other hand, we have these excellent studies: PRODI P. Il sacrameno del potere: Il giuramento político nella storia costituzionales dell'occidente. Bologna: Il Mulino 1992; and KANTOROWICZ E. The King's Two Bodies. Madrid: Alianza Universidad 1985.

[9] Here is Friedrich Meinecke's reading of the modern national interest: "Through a series of imperceptible transitions, the reason of state becomes noble and a forms a unifying bond between *Kratos* and *Ethos*" (Meinecke F. La idea de la razón de Estado en la edad moderna. Madrid: Centro de Estudios Políticos 1959; p.12.

[10] Decimononic positivism's criticism of Rousseau centres precisely on the Genevan thinker's refusal to accept bourgeois civil society: "Rousseau reasons and constructs, a priori, wherever it is necessary to observe and incite" (HUBERT R. Rousseau et l'école positiviste. Archives de Philosophie du Droit 1932; 3-4: 507).

[11] Friedrich M. Paul Laband und die Staatsrechtswissenschaft seiner Zeit. Archiv des Öffenliches Rechts 1986; 111(2): 200.

[12] Kelsen H. Teoría General del Derecho y del Estado. México DF: UNAM 1969; p. 224.

[13] The article by CASTORIADIS. La democracia como procedimiento y como régimen. Leviatán 1995; 62, seems to me to be an essential contribution for understanding modern democracy. Castoriadis' full definition of "democracy" is as follows: "We can therefore define politics as an explicit and lucid activity that concerns the implementation of the desired institutions, and democracy as the explicit and lucid system of self-institution – as far as possible – of the social institutions that depend on an explicit collective activity" (*cit.,* p. 69).

[14] This expression forms part of the terminology use by AKZIN B. State and Nation. México DF: FCE 1968; pp. 44-52, especially: "The simplest model of a nation is that of a politically organised ethnic group - whether sedentary of nomadic - living in relative isolation from other ethnic groups... The political organisation formed by such a group will be, accordingly, a monoethnic state" (p. 44).

[15] Connor W. Ethnonationalism. The quest for understanding, Princeton University Press 1994; p. 6.

[16] Habermas J. Facticidad y validez. Madrid: Trotta 1998; pp.154-155.

[17] Schmitt C. Was bedeutet der Streit um den Rechtsstaat? Zeitschrift für die gesamte Staatswissenschaft 1935; 95: 193.

[18] On the Spanish experience of rupture from legal equality and democracy, see López Garía JA. Estado y Derecho en el franquismo. Madrid: CEC 1996.

[19] Habermas J. La crisis del Estado de bienestar y el agotamiento de las energías utópicas. In: Escritos políticos. Barcelona: Península 1988; p.129.

[20] See Luhmann N. Teoría política en el Estado del bienestar. Madrid: Alianza Universidad 1993.

[21] Luhmann N. Klasisische Theorie der Macht. Kritik ihrer Prämessen. Zeitschrift für Politik 1969; 16 (Heft 2).

[22] Luhmann N. Ausdifferenzierung des Rechts 1981, citation from the Italian edition De Giorgi R, Ed. La

differenziazione del diritto. Bologna: Il Mulino 1990; p. 96.

[23] Luhmann N. Poder. Barcelona: Anthropos 1995; p.130.

[24] Blas Guerrero, A de. Nacionalismos y naciones en Europa. Madrid: Alianza Editorial 1995; pp. 34-37.

[25] Blas Guerrero A de. Nacionalismo e ideologías políticas contemporáneas. Madrid: Espasa Calpe 1984; pp.20-25.

[26] Breuilly J. Nationalism and the State. Barcelona: Pomares-Corredor 1990; p.370.

[27] Gellner E. Nations and Nationalism, *cit.*, p.18.

[28] JÁuregui Bereciartu G. Contra el Estado-nación. En torno al hecho y la cuestión nacional. Madrid: Siglo XXI 1986; p. 60.

[29] MacCormick N. Nation and Nationalism. In: Legal Right and Social Democracy. Madrid: Tecnos 1990; p. 206.

[30] Gellner E. Culture, Identity and Politics. Nationalism and new social changes, *cit.*, pp. 25-39.

[31] See Hobsbawm EJ. Nations and Nationalism since 1780. Barcelona: Crítica 1995; pp.111-140. In the Spanish field of theoretical thought, Juan Pablo FUSI AIZPRÚA holds a similar position to Hobsbawm in "La aparición de los nacionalismos", *Revista del Centro de Estudios Constitucionales,* n°11, 1992. Fusi argues that Catalan, Basque and Galician *nationalist sentiment* was only achieved in the latter part of the 19th century and early 20th century. Before this, we can speak of "regional, local or provincial sentiment", but never nationalism.

[32] See González de Molina M, Garrido Peña F. La cuestión nacional: una propuesta desde la ecología política. Anales de la Cátedra Francisco Suárez 1994; 101-110.

[33] See Juaristi J. Identidad en la intemperie: comunidad, asociación y errancia. Historia contemporánea 1990; 4: 355-370. For a more detailed typology of the nationalisms, made from the point of view of a sociological analysis of the issue, see: Herranz de Rafael G. La vigencia del nacionalismo. Madrid: Centro de Investigaciones Sociológicas 1992; pp. 86-100.

[34] On the rise of the Zionist movement among Jews before Nazism, as well as its negative evaluation as an indicator of intolerance in Europe, see EHRLICH EL. Max Horkheimer et le judaïsme. Archives de Philosophie 1986; 49: 239-248.

[35] Blas Guerrero A de. Nacionalismo y naciones en Europa, *cit.*, p. 37.

[36] Smith AD. Ethnic Myths and Ethnic Revivals. Archives Européennes de Sociologie 1984; 24(3): 289.

[37] Lucas J de. El vínculo social, entre ciudadanía y cosmopolitismo. In: Lucas J de, *et al.* El vínculo social: ciudadanía y cosmopolitismo. Valencia: Tirant lo Blanch 2002; p.14.

[38] Clearly all of this is only true as long as we are referring to the outlines of the notion of "minorities" within the space of the Nation State. By that I mean that the "historical exclusion" of the working class and women, who are not by any means a minority, is an issue that is yet to be concluded. I have dealt with some of the problems that arise in the "collective differences" of the working class and the feminist movements in "Derecho, democracia y diferencias colectivas", in: Ansuátegui Roig FJ. Ed. Una discusión sobre derechos colectivos. Madrid: Dykinson 2001.

[39] Kymlicka W. Multicultural Citizenship. Barcelona: Paidós 1996.

[40] Kymlicka W. *cit.*, p.140. This "realistic" quote from Kymlicka is not the only one. The ambiguity in the treatment of immigrants and refugees can be seen throughout the whole book (especially pp.111-150). On immigrants who voluntarily waive their "national rights", Kymlicka states: "Cases regarding recently-arrived immigrants are very different. In these cases, it is more legitimate to compel them to respect liberal principles, for the reasons discussed" (p. 234). Kymlicka refers to "recently-arrived immigrants" to differentiate them from the "colonisers of North America", who obviously did not have a liberal society to receive them in the 17th and 18th centuries. At that time, there were only the "non-liberal societies" of the "Indian" tribes.

[41] Kymlicka W. *cit.,* p. 236.

[42] Kymlicka W. *cit.,* p. 233.

[43] On immigrants' "voluntary choice", Kymlicka says: "The expectation of integration is not unjust, I believe, so long as immigrants had the option to stay in their original culture. Given the connection between choice and culture that I have previously alluded to, people should be able to live and work in their own culture. But like any other right, this right can be waived, and immigration is one way of waiving one's right. In deciding to uproot themselves, immigrants voluntarily relinquish some of the rights that go along with their national membership" (Kymlicka W. *cit.,* p. 136).

[44] Within moral philosophy, there is a very widespread idea that the success of Alasdair MACINTYRE's work: After Virtue. Barcelona: Crítica 2001, is due to its "acute criticism of the failings and errors of modern morality" (Victoria Camps, preface, p. 8). However, considering MacIntyre's great knowledge of sociology and moral philosophy, there is an issue that cannot be forgotten. I am referring to MacIntyre's use of Nietzsche's criticism of Modernity. This is a self-interested use of "irrationalism" as point of arrival for the whole of the Enlightenment, thereby rescuing "pre-modern Aristotelian tradition" as the only alternative to "irrationalism". Hence we can deduce that the only benefit gained from Nietzsche's "irrationalism" is "frightening the Enlightenment", leaving aside Aristotle, the Tradition and Saint Benedict. This is, in my opinion, an overly biased reading.

[45] For an examination of the current situation and offensive against "social rights", as rights that attempt to achieve social integration in the face of the "laissez-faire, laissez-passer" of the market, and within the perspective of loss of "social Sovereignty" of the State, see AÑÓN ROIG MJ. La contribución de los derechos sociales al vínculo social. In: Lucas J de, *et al.* El vínculo social: ciudadanía y cosmopolitismo. *cit.*, pp. 277-307.

[46] Habermas J. The Inclusion of the Other. Barcelona: Paidós 1999; p.231.

[47] On the coincidences y differences between Habermas y RAWLS, see Habermas J – RAWLS J. Debate on Political Liberalism. Barcelona: Paidós 1998.

[48] Regarding Habermas: "theoretical distance" between "communitarianism" and "republicanism", see: Habermas J. The Inclusion of the Other, *cit.*, pp. 189-258.

[49] Habermas J. The inclusion of the other. *cit.*, pp. 194-5.

[50] This is the opinion of Habermas, who considers that overdoing "post-national" criticism of the Nation State would leave the international framework open to those States who, de facto, would be able to impose themselves on the international stage. See Habermas J. Die interkulturelle Diskurs über Menschenrechte. In: KÖHLER WR, LUTZ-BACHMANN M, Eds. Recht auf Menschenrechte, Frankfurt am Main: Suhrkamp 1999; pp. 216-227.

[51] Beck U. Macht und Gegenmacht im globalen Zeitalter. Frankfurt am Main: Suhrkamp 2002.

CHAPTER 12

National Minorities and Secession Today: Surpassing the Right to Self-Determination

Joan Ridao Martín*

Department of Constitution Law, University of Barcelona, Catalonia, Spain

Abstract: The recent decades have broken various secessionist movements related to national minorities existing within liberal-democratic multinational states like Belgium, Canada, United Kingdom and Spain, which, once assimilated by force or free, have maintained throughout History territory, language and cultural traits. They are nations like flemish, quebecois, catalans or scots. In this context, International Law neither authorizes nor prohibits secession, leaving this type of processes in the political sphere. Only in response to the case of colonized peoples through the right to self-determination recognized by the United Nations. However, the holding of referendums as Quebec and Scotland have stressed that they have begun to operate other principles of international law like the democratic principle or the effectiveness principle. The same International Court of Justice stated that the secession of Kosovo could sustain in another kind of legitimacy: the existence of a *de facto* state in the absence of violence after intense negotiations prior well-conducted and good faith, but failed.

Keywords: National minorities, Secession, Self-determination, Unilateral declaration of independence.

1. INTRODUCTION

It is known that the International Law does not consider secession as a right [1]. On the contrary, it establishes the principle of territorial integrity of the States on the basis that the international community is made up by the States, which, logically, are not only the source but also the direct target of the International Law [2]. However, as it is also broadly known, it acknowledges the right to self-determination (external or the right to secession), linked, as has been said, to «oppressed and colonized communities», although it is not specified either in the Charter of the United Nations from 1945 (art. 1.2, 55 and 76) [3], nor in the International Covenants of civil and political Rights and economic, social and cultural Rights (New York Agreements from 1966) [4], or in each of the

* **Corresponding author Joan Ridao Martín:** Department of Constitution Law, University of Barcelona, Catalonia, Spain, Parliament of Catalonia's Legal Adviser; Tel: 0034 933046500; Fax: 0034 932213989; E-mail: jridao@ub.edu

Resolutions of the General Assembly (GAUN) which deal with the issue: 1514 (XV Assembly) and 2625 (XXV Assembly) [5].

The breakup of the Central European empires, the implosion of the old USSR and the beginning of the processes of decolonization, especially in the African continent, lead International Law to accept the creation of new States, already in the first half of last century, with their own identity or national signs. In this way, it legitimized the breakup of the territorial integrity of the original States. However, this right has been progressively more closely associated to the rights of colonized or oppressed peoples. So, the secessionist claims of communities within liberal-democratic States with Constitutions that respect their internal self-determination (cultural rights, language and minimal forms of self-government, *etc.*) can hardly be justified in front of this classical right.

This explains why many states have been generally reluctant to accept the secession of other States, even if they have sporadically accepted them in front of the eventuality of some of the breakup processes such as the one in the USSR or Yugoslavia, or because of internal agreements such as the case of the Czech Republic or Slovakia [6]. Besides, it is obvious that one of the most renowned cases, the independence of Kosovo (2008) does not make a traditional assumption of self-determination, as it took place outside a context of decolonization.

The right to self-determination and the right to decide are not, in fact, equivalent terms. They were linked to one another originally, but this does not imply that they are conceptually the same thing. On the contrary, as has been seen, the right to self-determination in its external aspect is exercised by those communities which are internationally accepted, with equally acknowledged conflicts [7]. On the other hand, the right to decide, that could imply a territory's secession, is not acknowledged by public international law, or by the internal legal system of most States. However, it is known that the *Primary Right Theories* understand that secession is an inalienable right in liberal democracy [8], independent of the treatment of the parent State towards the secessionist sub-state entity [9].

Plebiscite and democratic theories, based on the individual right for association, specifically confirm this possibility from a democratic principle point of view. This, together with the principle of federalism was decisive in the decision of the Canadian Supreme Court regarding Quebec [10], and that, effectively, is leading the traditional constitutional repudiation of any attempt of secession to give way to at least a mutual obligation for all federated parties or those united by constitutional ties to negotiate the needed changes to grant those wishes. This has been reinforced by the fact that referendums or other types of popular consultations are common practice in liberal democracies.

It is also good to remember that, on an international scale, the democratic principle is incorporated in various relevant instruments, like the Universal Declaration of Human Rights from 1948, which establishes «The will of the people shall be the basis of the authority of government» (art. 21.3) [11]. At a European level, there have also been different reformations of founding treaties that reinforce the commitment of respect for human rights and basic freedoms (Charter of Fundamental Rights, EU) [12]. Even at an internal State level, in most cases, once a community's democratic will to peacefully become a State in its own right has been established, this will is given the same importance as the provisions of the constitutional order of the parent State, even if it does not allow secession or simply does not provide for it, as in the case of Quebec or Scotland, that we will analyse in the following pages.

It is undeniable that the Ruling of the Canadian Supreme Court regarding the secession of Quebec in August 1998; the Ruling of the International Court of Justice regarding Kosovo; the agreements between the British and Scottish governments regarding the Scottish referendum; or the Ruling of the Commission of Venice from the Council of Europe regarding the Montenegro referendum, represent an emerging set of guidelines or rules that control the exercise of the right to decide everything, although not legislated by International Law or the internal law of each state, putting to one side the motives behind the secession, seeing as these are understood to be fruit of «the complexity of different political realities» [13], covering the democratic principle, the still well-known doctrine of effectiveness, as is seen in the fact that 69 members of the United Nations acknowledged Kosovo as an independent State, even if Serbia did not accept its existence and keeps claiming its territorial integrity [14].

Therefore, for the infra-state groups that aim at their independence or at a given political status, the question is either in the need to reach, and democratically express a wide majority for the separation (or the intended status) by means of the instruments of a negotiation which allows the corresponding reforms in the internal constitutional order, or else, in some extreme cases, a unilateral but legal decision, provided it gathers the support of a critical mass of States in the international community which is enough to make the declaration viable.

2. THE PROBLEMS THAT ARISE IN THE PRESENT NATIONAL MINORITIES IN THE FRAMEWORK OF LIBERAL DEMOCRACIES

2.1. The Recent Case of Catalonia (Spain)

As has been stated, the Spanish Constitution (SC) claims the indissoluble unity of the Spanish nation and, consequently, it does not acknowledge the right to secession. The Sentence 42/2014 from the Spanish Constitutional Court (CC)

[15], regarding the «Resolution 5/X from the Parliament of Catalonia, whereby the Declaration of sovereignty and the right to decide of the Catalan people is passed» declared that the acknowledgement that such a declaration made of the Catalan people as a «legal and political sovereign subject» is contrary to articles 1.2 and 2 SC and articles 1 and 2.4 of the Catalan Statute of Autonomy, and connected to these, contrary to articles 9.1 and 168 SC as well.

In fact, on 21 January 2013 the Catalan Parliament passed the Resolution 5/X [16], previously known as «Sovereignty Declaration», which invoked the «Democratic Principle» and abandoned the classical invocation of sovereignty of the right to self-determination (Resolutions 1514-XV from 1960 and 2625-XXV from 1970 of the United Nations), since they considered that this new right was only applicable in the case of the making up of an independent State *ex novo*, or in the case of secession of colonially-subjugated communities, military-occupied nations or those communities which belong to a repressive State which violates human rights (art. 1.2 of the 1945 Charter and art. 1.1 of the International Agreements on Civil and Political Rights, or New York Agreements, from 1966).

What is relevant is that, even though the «Sovereignty Declaration» of the Catalan Parliament has been declared to be unconstitutional, sentence 42/2014 issued by the Spanish Constitutional Court warned that there is no normative nucleus which is inaccessible to the procedures of a reform of the Spanish Constitution. Besides, it acknowledges the right to decide as a political aspiration protected by the freedom of expression and by the right to participation in political issues established in the Magna Carta. For the Spanish High Court, this right to decide is not the right to self-determination and it has its own nominalization: it is not a conferring of sovereignty but the right of the citizens of Catalonia to decide on their political future. For this, as preparation measures, it would be even possible to call a consultation or a referendum before the opening of a process of constitutional reform which could not lead to a reconsideration of the identity or the unity of the sovereign subject from the start or, even less, a reconsideration of the relationship which only the sovereign subject can establish between the State and the Autonomous Communities (nationalities or regions of Spain).

From this point, on the basis of the democratic principle of article 1 SC, and with a lack of limits to the constitutional reform, several directions can be found in the Spanish legal system by means of which, apart from the constitutional revision *via*[17] article 168 SC [19], a declaration may be allowed with a consultative nature regarding the beginning of this process, and especially the consultative referendums of article 92 SC [18], which have a state scope, but which could be applied to the autonomous communities; the delegation of the state competencies to allow referendums of article 149.1.32 SC, in line with the events in Scotland with the Order of Council [19] which allowed a Scottish referendum on 18 September 2014 by the Edinburgh authorities; and the referendums and the non referendary consultations of an autonomous or regional scope. Doubtlessly, these examples represent an appeal to the possibility that the members of a political community could define their own legal and political framework on the basis of clear and freely formed majorities, in accordance with the doctrine emanated from the Canadian Supreme Court in the case of Quebec.

So, while the Sentence asserts that «in the constitutional framework, an autonomous community cannot unilaterally call a referendum of self-determination to decide on their integration in Spain», it also explicitly states the possibility of a «constitutional interpretation» of the so-called right to decide, understood as «a political aspiration which is reached by means of a process which comes to terms with the constitutional legality», respectful to the principles of «democratic legitimacy», «pluralism» and «legality», and explicitly put forward in the Declaration of sovereignty of the Catalan Parliament, closely connected to the right to decide.

This is, without a doubt, the most innovating and important aspect of the Sentence, since the Court acknowledges the right to decide as a right which can protect the execution of activities focused on «preparing» and «defending» the separation of Catalonia, and to urge the «effective consecution» of this objective in the framework of the process of the reform of the Constitution. Regarding this point, the Sentence takes the premise, which is already stated in many other resolutions, that the Spanish constitutional legislation does not meet a model of «activist democracy» and that, consequently, there is room for any kind of conception «which aims at modifying the foundations of the constitutional order» such as «the will to change the legal status» of an Autonomous Community. Therefore, according to the Court, the right to decide is not a right to self-determination, since it has its own character. It represents a legitimate political aspiration protected by the freedom of expression and, in broader terms, by the right to participate in political issues. It is worth noting that, furthermore, the Sentence does not restrict or limit the right to decide just to the possibility to motivate a process of constitutional reform but, for the first time, it explicitly states that the public powers of an Autonomous Community can legitimately carry out activities aimed at «preparing and defending» the political objective which they consider convenient.

Notwithstanding what has already been stated, the Spanish government keeps an unyielding attitude in front of all these possibilities and it puts forward that the subject matter of the Catalan consultation clashes with the fact that the Constitution claims the unity of the Spanish nation, and that the only sovereign subject is the whole of the Spanish people (art. 1.2 and 2 SC).

This means that, in Catalonia, the scenario of the future relationship with the Spanish State has changed in a very short period of time. And even more so if you also take into account that, before the Catalan institutions openly contemplated holding a consultation, there was an attempt to agree a new Statute of Autonomy, passed by the Catalan Parliament in 2005 with a wide political and citizen support, aimed at institutionalizing a status of bilateralism between Catalonia and the State. However, it was frustrated during its development, first by the Spanish Parliament and later, and with final consequences, with Sentence 31/2010 of the Constitutional Court [20], from the 28th of June, that had already been operationally deactivated by a declaration of unconstitutionality or the reinterpretation of a large part of its precepts, regarding key aspects such as financing, competencies or considering Catalonia as a nation.

This Sentence led most of the Catalan society to draw two conclusions: the evidence of the successful actions to politically deactivate the Statute by the powers of the State and, at the same time, a great disappointment –politically speaking- towards the Spanish State in terms of coming to a joint agreement. This second conclusion, of great importance, forced a change in the positions of traditional political catalanism which, from mid-nineteenth century, had accepted an autonomous fitting of Catalonia within Spain which respected its national, linguistic and cultural singularity to a bet by the citizens, which until then was minority-but growing-, to become a singular State [21].

Precisely, the governability agreement subscribed by Convergència i Unió (CiU) (the party of President Artur Mas) and Esquerra Republicana de Catalunya (ERC) (the center-left party, historically for independence) after the last autonomic election, on December 19, 2012 «Agreement for the national transition and to guarantee the Parliamentary stability of the Catalan Government» explicitly added the commitment of the two parties to support every kind of executive an parliamentary actions with the aim of calling for a consultation to the Catalan citizens (finally the 9th of November 2014) with a clear double question: «Do you want Catalonia to be a state?», and if so, «Do you want this state to be independent?». It is, without a doubt a broad political agreement as, apart from the two parties mentioned above, it also included Iniciativa per Catalunya-Esquerra Unida i Alternativa (ICV. EUiA) and the Candidatures d'Unitat Popular (CUP), covering Catalonia's whole political spectrum, from Christian democrats to the alternative left.

The consultation to be held on November 9, 2014, accepted by the majority of the Catalan Parliamentary forces and with a wide support of the public opinion [22], would be regulated by a Catalan law on consultations [23], which will be presumably passed by the Catalan Parliament after the summer. Law 10/2014 from the 26th of September, on popular non-referendum consultations and other forms of citizen participation, anticipated the organization by the *Generalitat de Catalunya* of popular consultations for political questions of special importance. But, as the Spanish Government has repeatedly announced, both this law and the Decree to call the consultation itself, which will be signed by the President of the *Generalitat of Catalunya*, would be appealed in front of the Court, with the intention to declare them unconstitutional after having stopped them. The predetermination which would claim that the Spanish Constitution democratically consecrates the united nature of the Spanish Nation, as well as the united sovereignty of the Spanish people regarding a process based on popular will, would be a positioning which would deny the chance to know the real will of a nation, in this case the Catalan nation, to initiate a political process from a popular consultation, a democratic process that has been indeed considered in Canada or the United Kingdom, with the referendum on the independence of Scotland formally called on September 18, 2014.

On the 30th of September, the Constitutional Court accepted an appeal of unconstitutionality presented by the Spanish government against the law and the decree for a summons to the consultation on the 9th of November. Which is why the summons was automatically suspended, as a precaution, in agreement with article 161, 2 SC. In spite of this, both the Catalan Government and the parties that were supporting the consultation held preparatory meetings, and even selected in Parliament the members who would make up the controlling Commission that should exercise electoral authority over the process, according to the previsions under the suspended law. As a token of support for the Catalan institutional world for the consultation, on the 3rd of October some 800 mayors delivered to the headquarters of the Catalan Government the agreements from their municipal plenary sessions supporting the summons to the consultation.

With the argument that, in the end, the consultation would not be held, even though no secondary legal measures had been made for the provisional suspension by the Constitutional Court, the president of the *Generalitat de Catalunya*, decided on the 14th of October to cancel it and substitute it with a so-called «participative process», that would take place under the protection of the statutory powers of the *Generalitat*, keeping the same date and the double question of the consultation that had been dismissed. Specifically, this act was based, to start with, on article 122 of the Statute of Autonomy, even though the legality had to be judged according to the doctrine of the CC, regarding autonomic and local referendums, upon which it has had the chance to pass sentence in various occasions, and was collected in the successive appeals of unconstitutionality made by the Catalan Government. Therefore, the «process» is protected, according to the Catalan government, by the provisions of title III of the same Catalan law 10/2014. These precepts that regulate surveys, public audiences, participative forums, and other processes with citizen participation, are currently in force, they have not been impugned by the Govern nor has the State Council reported in favour of doing so (sentence 964/2014 from the 28th of September). The CC has not made even a provisional ruling regarding said «processes».

Once again, the Spanish Government impugned the «actions of the *Generalitat*» related to the participative process and both the impugnation and the previous sentence of the State Council 1092/2014 from the 30th of October 2014, were based on the fact that these actions were legal formal acts, liable to impugnation under title V of the CC's organic law, understating that it was actually a «masked and covered» consultation. Unlike the appeal against law 4/2010, the decision was not immediate; it took two weeks, during which the Spanish government initially chose to congratulate itself for cancelling the consultation, and then went on to discredit the new summons and directly oppose it, presenting it as a mere re-edition of the cancelled summons. Subsequently, the Constitutional Court also provisionally suspended this «process».

However, both the Catalan government and the group of political and citizen forces in favour of the consultation on the 9th of November, carried on with the preparations, having understood, that the CC had once again suspended a consultation, but had said nothing regarding the «participative process.» Supported by the *Generalitat*, the process went ahead with the collaboration of 40.930 volunteers. The voting took place in 1.317 participation points all over Catalonia, using many local venues as well as those belonging to the *Generalitat*. The day went ahead with no remarkable incident and with the participation of 2.305.290 people, as well as the 14.000 Catalan citizens living abroad that placed their ballots in one of the 19 participation points set up in the international headquarters of the *Generalitat* [24]. In light of this, the State's General Attorney, after listening to the Board of Prosecutors and with the opposition of the Attorney for the Superior Court of Justice of Catalonia, presented a lawsuit against the president of the *Generalitat,* Artur Mas, the vice president of the Catalan Government, Joana Ortega and the Catalan Minister of Education, Irene Rigau, who were accused of various crimes such as disobedience, perversion of justice, misuse of public resources and misappropriation of roles.

2.2. The European Union when Facing a Unilateral Declaration of Independence: A Legal and Political Interpretation of the Treaties

At this point, we must briefly revise the position stated by the EU regarding both primary and derived Law on the secession and independence of territories of its member States. In fact, as it has been explicitly stated, the only precept which has any connection to this question is article 4.2 TEU, which states that the EU should respect the essential functions of its member States, amongst which is the one to guarantee their territorial integrity. But essentially, this precept proclaims the non-interference of the European Union in a range of affairs. Nothing is said about the secession or independence of territories of a State, or about the consequences that this secession could have for the residual State or for the new States which emerged from the separation, or about the consequences of a phenomenon of this nature for the Union itself. We must conclude, therefore, that if the consequences of these facts are not contemplated in Treaties, the criteria used in order to establish whether dissident territories from a member State should remain outside the EU have been simply criteria of authority. What is more, after having seen some precedents, what happened at one point with the fusion of the two Germanys is an indicator of the solutions that the European Union can assume beyond what is contemplated in Treaties. Recent mutations of the European Union Law are a good example of «the imaginative solutions that could be given to the new challenges beyond the Union Law» [25].

Apart from this, it is needless to say that, in the case of isolated secessions, it would not only be necessary to consider how the new State would be, but also the consequent situation for the parent state. If we conclude that the secessions of territories of a member state are indeed a rupture from the original state, which results in the creation of two new states (or several ones), the States resulting from this process could be considered heirs of the original State. This would necessarily imply that the two States should ask for their attachment to the EU, as well as to the hundreds of international organizations to which they previously belonged. All of this without forgetting the fact that it seems plausible that the two States could reach a previous agreement, with the unanimous acceptance of its terms by the rest of the States, especially in the case of the EU, which would consist in asking for the continuity of both political units in the international organizations of which they were part originally, although they would have to adjust the conditions of their membership and participation to their new reality. This procedure seems complex, but it is not impossible.

This way, after the secession of a territory of a member state, the Predecessor State would still be the owner of the rights acquired by the original State in the international community, that is, within the European Union and the International

Organizations. According to the mainstream position of the doctrine and the international praxis, the State resulting from the secession would be, to all effects, a new State that should ask for its incorporation or continuity in the European Union and the rest of international organizations, unless we were talking about a State that chooses to remain absolutely isolated.

Nonetheless, the problems that emerge for the parent State in this case do not have an easy solution. Apart from the hardly comparable precedents of Greenland and Algeria, which will be later examined, in the Spanish case, for example, there would be a remarkable decrease of its population, of its internal gross product and its territory. If we were, for example, in front of a supposed secession of Catalonia, we would be talking about the decrease of 16.5% of the Spanish population (7.5 million inhabitants), 18.5% of IGP (around 200,000 million Euros) and 6.3% of its territory (around 32,000 square km), with a tax contribution far beyond its percentage of population, since Catalonia represents 24% of the total tax income in Spain [26]. In terms of the EU, it would be beyond complicated for Spain to keep the same number of representatives in the European Parliament, votes in the Council, or the same contribution to communal expenses or to the European Central Bank. Actually, and this is what is relevant, this casuistry is not contemplated and it would result in an essential reform of the Union Treaties and the derived law, in order to make the necessary adjustments or to adopt political agreements, this time unanimously, to reproduce familiar patterns, such as the one regarding the above-mentioned German reunification, or even the cases of Greenland-Denmark or France-Algeria. In this sense, it is necessary to highlight that the Lisbon Treaty, with effects on 1 December 2009, contemplates the voluntary withdrawal of a member state from the Union for the first time. But previous to the Lisbon treaties there were not any legal procedures that regulated this eventuality [27].

However, in that case, the non-contemplation of a legal procedure of withdrawal in the Treaties was not considered important enough to avoid that a State could decide on its continuity in the European Union. That was the case of Greenland, which left in 1985 due to a dispute regarding fishing rights. As a Denmark territory, this island joined the Economic European Union (EEU) in 1973, although a referendum showed they were against it. Consequently, in a referendum held in 1982, the option to abandon the EU won, with a slight difference of 52% of the votes [28]. Nevertheless, it is still regulated by the EU Treaties through the Association of the Overseas Countries and Territories.

On the other hand, when Algeria stopped being a French colony in 1962, it also abandoned the EU. Precisely, as an answer to a question asked in 2004 by the Welsh socialist representative Eluned Morgan to the College of European

Commissioners regarding the usefulness of the Algerian precedent in the event of independence of a European region, Romano Prodi, president of the College of Commissioners at that time, answered: «A new independent region, because of its independence, would become a third state in connection to the European Union and, from the day of its independence, [Treaties] wouldn't be of application in its territory» [29]. What is relevant, nevertheless, is that the independence of Algeria and its withdrawal from the EEU in 1962 did not have consequences for France, one of the six founding States.

Therefore, we can conclude that, in the event of the rupture of a member state resulting in two states (either if one has split from another or because of the emergence of two new states from an original one), the reform of the EU Treaties is not essential to accommodate them to a new reality if there exists a political agreement, as shown by the Algerian precedent. Regarding the case of Greenland, it must be highlighted that in the adaptation of the EU Treaties, from 13 March 1984, where the withdrawal is articulated, there is no modification of the parent State, Denmark. Besides, Greenland currently keeps an Overseas Territory status associated to the EU. Indeed, from an institutional point of view, there were no changes either in the number of commissioners (two for France, one for Denmark, with or without those territories) or in the assignation of seats in the European Parliament (or Parliamentary Assembly, until 1979), which was not affected until the German reunification took place, when the parity of seats held by the five great States of the Community/European Union was broken.

As additional considerations, and regarding the current situation (with the current TEU and the EUFT, modified in Lisbon), the European Parliament cannot exceed 750 members and the president, and this is nowadays fixed, even if there were other incorporations (nevertheless, due to the recent incorporation of Croatia, this has needed to be temporarily adjusted, but with no effects on the European Election of May 2014). Last, with the present system of each state's own resources (Customs rights, 0.3% tax of the harmonized VAT basis and resources based on a uniform percentage of the gross national income) there is not a direct dependence on fees or contributions by the States depending on their size in terms of territory or population.

Apart from the legal speculations, a different scenario would take place when a unanimous position, or even a majority one among the Union States, was not reached to achieve this political agreement or to reform the Treaties, in particular if most of the States were unwilling to confirm the pulling effect that this process could have within their respective states. In any case, all these precedents show that the Union has always solved these issues politically, regardless of the strict content of the Treaties. In addition, it must be taken into account that, as it has already been explained, article 49 TEU contemplates that any European State which respects the values mentioned in article 2 of the same Treaty and commits itself to promote them, could apply for membership to the Union.

3. SURPASSING THE RIGHT TO SELF-DETERMINATION: THE INTERNATIONAL LAW IN THE CASE OF THE UNILATERAL DECLARATION OF INDEPENDENCE

Sometimes, regulations go beyond the legislator's initial intentions. This would be the case of the provisions of International Law in connection to the self-determination of the nations, which have occasionally found themselves in contexts which are very different from the decolonization phenomena to which they are associated. As we have already analyzed, Kosovo's UDI, on 7 February 2008, is perhaps the most recent and clearest example of a presumably ultra-active normative if we consider what the ruling of the International Court of Justice, from 22 July 2010 [30], states (see sect. 3). In fact, in this Advisory Opinion, the ICJ concluded that the UDI proclaimed by the Kosovan Assembly was neither opposed to general International Law nor to Resolution 1244 (1999) of the Security Council. For this reason, this is a precedent of unquestionable importance, despite the critical attitude of the *ius-internationalist* doctrine and that of some States towards the position of the ICJ.

This can be explained because, as we have also seen, the position of the ICJ, which would declare the independence of Kosovo as non-opposed to International Law, dismisses the most orthodox thesis regarding the principle of self-determination (see section 1) which distinguishes between the assumptions of external and internal self-determination. Thus, it keeps the cases of external self-determination for classical colonial situations or for sudden similar situations, and relates internal self-determination to the cases in which the citizens of a nation exercise their right by means of their pronouncement in elections and internal consultations. If we consider this thesis, the modality of external self-determination could not be based on the same grounds as those cases of colonial situations inside a formal democracy.

A totally different case is the UDI proclaimed by the institutions of Crimea, because of its later annexation to Russia. The secession of this peninsula on the shore of the Black Sea started on February 27, 2014, when Russian soldiers, who initially tried to hide their nationality, occupied the airports and buildings of the capital city, Simferopol, with the support of the pro-Russian militia. In this situation, a few days later, on March 16, a referendum took place which did not meet the minimum acceptable requirements for electoral processes in Europe, since its aim was to legitimate a decision taken by the Russian authorities and exercised under conditions of forced subjugation. The «yes» obtained 96.77% of the votes. After the proclamation of the results, on March 17, the authorities of Crimea gave Moscow the formal petition to integrate their territory in the Russian Federation and the Duma voted the annexation project on March 21. In spite of the undeniable historical, cultural and geostrategic bonds that this territory had with Russia (with nearly 57% of Russian speakers), the International Community did not accept the results of the referendum, as they violated the Constitution of Ukraine and Crimea, as well as International Law. Despite the differences, the Russian Authorities argued that the case was presumably analogous to the case of Kosovo, and that the International Community had reacted in an inequitable way in this case. Nonetheless, the subsequent conflicts in the eastern area of Ukraine have led to new international summits which, within diplomatic tensions, have translated into a tacit recognition of the annexation of Crimea to Russia [31].

Thus, if we observe any of the current member states of the EU, it is impossible to appreciate any situation of subjugation, exploitation or violation of the fundamental human rights regarding the sub-state entities that conform them or their citizens. This has a special significance because it means that, with higher or lower intensity, all the states in the EU guarantee the rights and freedom of their citizens with their internal laws, the EU law and International Law. As we know, in general International Law, it is also impossible to find any kind of explicit prevision that normatively allows the passing of a UDI.

Which one is then the basis of secession or independence of those nations that are not entitled to the right of external self-determination? Under which circumstances would International Law allow a UDI to be passed?

3.1. The Precedent of Kosovo

The International Court of Justice, in the above-mentioned Advisory Opinion of 22 July, 2010 (under the title «Accordance with International Law of the Unilateral Declaration of Independence In Respect of Kosovo» sections 79, 81 and 84) set a doctrine of general interest: No UDI, whether proclaimed by the Parliament or in a popular way, can count on the protection of International Law, but it is not opposed to it [in the same way, Resolution 1244 (1999) of the Security Council, was not opposed to any applicable regulation of International Law]. Moreover, the ICJ states that in order for any UDI to be legitimate, it must be followed (or preceded, for that matter) by a '*de facto* situation', in which the effective presence of the proper elements of a State and, in particular, the exercise of the sovereignty through concluding acts, can be proved.

Consequently, the global High Court states that a UDI which is proclaimed in territories in which the self-determination principle (external) is not applicable is not opposed to the basis of the principle of state territoriality [32]. These UDIs, added the Court, are not forbidden if they do not entail any serious fault to general International Law, especially to those issues of imperative nature (*ius cogens*), such as an illegal use of force (par.84). In other words, a UDI cannot be considered opposed to International law if it is the result of a democratic pronouncement (par.79), carried out in a peaceful context, without the use of force or violence. In this sense, The High Court specified that, in those cases where a UDI had been declared in breach of international law (*e.g.* South Rhodesia, North Cyprus or the Srpska Republic), the precise contravention of the international law order had dealt with the illegal use of force (par. 81) [33]. The guarantee of the territorial integrity of the State is a guarantee that corresponds to the States, which cannot violate it. But the prohibition of the use of force, or the threat alone of using it, constitutes an imperative obligation of general nature and, for this reason, it becomes applicable to sub-state entities [34].

Therefore, it can be seen that the Court disregarded the internal constitutional order of Serbia in that particular case. It is not in vain that art. 8 of the Serbian Charter explicitly banned that possibility: «The Serbian territory is inseparable and indivisible». However, the internal constitution had already been partially replaced by an interim regime of self-government set by the United Nations according to resolution 1244 of the Security Council (1999) [35]. For this reason, the ICJ assumed that the authors of the UDI (the stunning majority of the members of the Kosovan Parliament and its president) had not violated the Serbian constitutional frame given the fact that, when they formally declared their independence, they were not acting as bodies of entities of provisional self-government, but as a real constitutive powers, according to the capacity conferred by their condition of legitimate representatives of the Kosovo nation. After all, the procedure adopted by the Kosovan representatives resulted fully democratically legitimated as it had been their own «decision», making the democratic principle prevail over the principle of constitutionality.

The independence of Kosovo, province of Serbia under international administration since 1999, was unilaterally declared by its Assembly on 17 February 2008 [36], on the basis of a report and a Program made by the Special envoy of the United Nations, Matti Ahtisaari. At the same time as the parliamentary UDI, the same Assembly passed a Constitution which replaced the constitutional framework based on the Resolution 1244 of the Security Council of the United Nations, which the administration of the UN had regulated. However, it did not become effective until 15 June of the same year [37]. The Declaration was supported by the United States and a majority of the member States of the European Union, which did not assume a common position at the Security Council of the UN. Russia and China opposed the proposal. It was in July 2010 when, as it has been repeatedly said, the ICJ issued the Advisory Opinion stating that the UDI neither violated general International law nor resolution 1244 of the Security Council.

Regarding the internal institutionalization process of the new Republic and given the particular concurrent circumstances, the Civil International Office responsible for the supervision of the process was created. On 10 September 2012, the International Steering Group for Kosovo (ISG) considered that its duty in the country had officially concluded, which was interpreted by the Pristina Parliament as the first concluding manifestation of full sovereignty. Progressively, 106 out of the 193 countries of the United Nations recognized the independence of Kosovo. Amongst them, there were 23 out of the 28 States of the European Union [38], 22 out of 27 NATO members and 7 of the 8 members of the G-8, remarkably, the USA [39]. In addition, the Republic of China (Taiwan) has offered its recognition, although Kosovo has not accepted it. Nevertheless, several countries (amongst them Algeria, Argentina, Azerbaijan Belarus, Spain, Slovakia, Georgia, Kazakhstan, Moldavia, Romania, Russia, Sri Lanka, Venezuela, Vietnam and Cyprus) keep their rejection to the Declaration of Independence of Kosovo, and their respect to the territorial integrity of Serbia. On their behalf, Brazil, Chile, Jordan, Mexico, Thailand and Uruguay are waiting for a pronouncement by the Security Council of the United Nations to adopt a final decision.

Concerning the membership to international organizations, it must be noted that the Republic of Kosovo has never formalized an application of membership to the United Nations, due to the announced veto from Russia at the Security Council. In the case of the EU, although it does not formally recognize new states, unanimity would be necessary regardless of the position of its members. This unanimity does not exist nowadays, in spite of the political recognition reached at the European Parliament [40]. The International Monetary Fund started the process of integration of Kosovo as a permanent member in June 2008, and on 5 May 2009, it was accepted with 96 favorable votes. Later on, this fostered its application of entry to the World Bank, which was passed on 4 June 2009 and was made official on 29 June, obtaining, therefore, its first adhesion to a specialized body of the United Nations.

Kosovo is living a strong process of integration into Europe from the negotiation of an Agreement of Stability and Association with the EU initiated by its Council on 16 October 2013. Therefore, it is overcoming the initial refusal of some of the member states to its future integration. It is a negotiation that is coming to a final point in 2014 [41], and which has a direct bond to the application of the case of Serbia, to follow the steps of Croatia and become a new member state of the EU.

4. BEYOND KOSOVO: CASUISTRY OF THE UNILATERAL DECLARATION OF INDEPENDENCE PROCESSES

Next, we will study ten recent cases in which a UDI has been part of the successful process of secession or independence of a territory within the European continent. We will leave out, for now, the processes that have not yet received rulings (Abkhazia, South Ossetia, or Transnistria), or those that have taken place within the African continent (Eritrea or South Sudan).

4.1. The Case of the Baltic Republics and Ukraine

In August 1989 around two million of Estonians, Latvians and Lithuanians formed a human chain of more than 560 kilometers, from Tallinn to Vilnius, to ask for the independence of the Baltic States. Next, the independence of Lithuania was unilaterally declared by its Parliament, on 11 March 1990, after the pro-independence leader Vytautas Landsbergis, was elected president in the elections held in February 1990 (still as part of the USSR) in which the Communist Party was defeated by the Reformation Movement of Lithuania, Sajudis, who obtained 101 out of the 141 seats. After a failed soviet intervention (on 10 January 1991) a referendum was held, on 9 February 1991, in which the support to independence reached 90%, with a turnout of 84.43% of the census. The question, asked in Lithuanian, Russian and Polish was: «Do you want Lithuania to be a new independent republic?». Later, in August 1991, this new republic was recognized at an international level and, on 17 September of the same year it entered the United Nations. Once the constituent process had begun, the Constitution was passed more than a year and a half after the UDI proclamation (on 25 October 1992 to be precise) and it became effective on 11 November 1992.

In Estonia, it was initially a convention of representatives who proclaimed a unilateral declaration of independence in February 1990, on the basis of the Tractu Treaty which was signed on 2 February 1920 with the Bolshevik Russia. According to this Treaty, the Republic of Estonia obtained international recognition and became a member of the League of Nations on 1921. Later, on the election of 8 May 1990, the PFE (Popular Front of Estonia) and other pro-sovereignty groups conquered the Parliament, and the nationalist leader, Edgar Savisaar, was elected president of the first government which had emerged from an election since 1940. Nonetheless, it was not until August 1990 that the Parliament formally proclaimed their independence, although Moscow did not consider it valid.

This UDI was later ratified in a referendum on 3 March 1991. The turnout was 83% and the question was «Do you want the restoration of sovereignty and the independence of the State of the Republic of Estonia?». The supporters of the «yes» obtained 78.6% of the votes, equivalent to 64.6% of the inhabitants with the right to vote, although no quorum of participation or minimum percentage to validate the «yes» had been previously defined. On 20 June 1992, a referendum ratified the Fundamental Law or Constitution (based on the one from 1983) and a new Parliament was elected (Riigikogu). On 5 October, Lennart Meri, from the National Coalition Party Pro-Patria (NCPP) was elected president. Two days later, the new Constitution became effective. The Constitution was passed on 28 June 1992, a year and a half after the referendum, and it became effective on 3 July of the same year.

In Latvia, on the election of March 1990, the Popular Front obtained 131 seats in the Supreme Soviet (8 together with 55 of the PCUS and 15 independents) which led to a UDI on 4 May 1990, formally proclaimed as a «Declaration of Independence Restoration». At the same time, it was decided to make the Constitution of 1922 effective, as it had been abolished with the Soviet invasion in 1940. On 3 March 1991, a public consultation took place. It had the nature of a referendum in order not to contravene the Soviet legality, but to legitimate it at the same time. The formulation of the question was: «Are you for the democratic and independent constitution of the State of the Republic of Latvia?». While there was a minimum turnout set on 50%, it reached 80%. The supporters of the «yes» were 73.7% (64.47% of the electoral census) and the supporters of the «no», 24.7%. The new Constitution was passed on 15 February 1992, almost a year after the referendum, and became effective on 7 November, a year and five months after the UDI.

In Ukraine, within the framework of the reforms started in 1985 by President Mikhail Gorbachov in the USSR, communists and nationalists Ukrainians started the Popular Movement for Perestroika in Ukraine (RUKH), which claimed a wider political and economic autonomy. In the legislative election of March 1990, the Supreme Soviet (Parliament) unilaterally proclaimed the independence of the Republic and, on 24 August 1991, the Act or Law of Independence was passed, for which a referendum of ratification was called, held on 11 December 1992. In this referendum, the question was «Are you for the Act of proclamation of Independence of Ukraine?». The turnout was 84.18% and the supporters of the «yes» reached 90.2% [42]. At the same ceremony, Leonid Kravchuk, ex-first secretary of the KPU (Communist Party of Ukraine) was elected president. At dawn on 28 June 1996, the Parliament adopted a Constitution which, according to the interpretation of the Constitutional Court, became effective at the same time as the result of the parliamentary election was made public (five years and eleven months after the UDI). Previously, on 8 June 1995, President Leonid Kuchman and spokesman Oleksandr Moroz, in the name of the Parliament, had subscribed a provisional Constitutional Agreement whose validity was extended until the moment of the passing of the Constitution. Law num. 254/96-BP ratified the Constitution, leaving the above-mentioned provisional Constitutional Agreement without effect.

4.2. Slovenia and Macedonia

On 23 December 1990 a referendum on the independence of Slovenia took place. In this referendum, both the government and the opposition forces unanimously supported the secession. The Parliament set a minimum turnout of 51% and the question was «[S]hould the Slovenia Republic become a sovereign and independent State?». The supporters of the «yes» reached 88.6% of votes and those for the «no» reached 4%. The Independence was formally proclaimed on 25 June 1991 at the same time as the one in Croatia, and on 5 October of the same year, the Parliament approved the end of its official commitment with Yugoslavia. From that moment on, Slovenia set its own currency, the *Tolar*, its own national institutions and applied several measures to make its sovereignty stronger. The National Assembly adopted the Constitutional text on 23 December 1991, and it became effective on the same day. In January 1992, the EEC recognized Slovenia and Croatia as independent States, although there still was a civil war in Croatia. The homogeneity of its population made its secession one of the less bloody ones in the breakdown process in ex-Yugoslavia, and its international recognition was one of the clearest, because the country dominated its borders, kept its own army and issued its national currency.

In Macedonia, on 16 April 1991, the Parliament passed an amendment to the Constitution in which the word «Socialist» was removed from the official name of the State. On 7 June, the new name, Republic of Macedonia, was officially accepted. After the beginning of the breakdown process in Yugoslavia, the Republic of Macedonia proclaimed their independence, after calling a popular consultation on 8 September of that year. The question was: «Are you for an independent Macedonia, with the right to enter in a future union of the sovereign countries of Yugoslavia?». With a turnout of 72%, the supporters of the «yes» were 95.1% and the ones for the «no» 4.8%. There were no minimum turnout requirements to validate the agreements. The Constitution was passed and became effective two months later, on 17 November 1991. Afterwards, a second referendum was held, this time for ratification, on 12 January 1992. This time, the Albanian minority voted for the creation of their own State. In the next month, the Social Democrat Branko Crvenkovski was elected Prime Minister and got the recognition of Macedonia by Russia, Albania, Bulgaria and Turkey. In April 1993, the country obtained its recognition as a member of the United Nations under the provisional name of «Ex-Yugoslavian Republic of Macedonia».

4.3. Montenegro and Bosnia and Herzegovina

The case of Montenegro presents some remarkable singularities, such as the fact that in this republic there was a referendum on independence under constitutional coverage. Indeed, the Serbia and Montenegro Union Constitution of 2003, was one of the few constitutional texts of a federal-confederate nature that explicitly contained a clause on secession. It also contemplated political, institutional, economic and social structures practically divided from Serbia.

But before this, a first referendum (1992) was held, in which those for remaining within the Yugoslavian Federation obtained 95.96% of the votes. The magnitude of this result is explained by the fact that Muslims, Albanians, and Catholic minorities boycotted the consultation, in the same way as the supporters of independence did. All these sectors alleged that the referendum had been organized under non-democratic conditions. As soon as the pro-independence forces, led by Milo Dukanovic, came to power (with a narrow margin of votes, in 1996) the relationships between the two confederated republics got worse. The leadership of Montenegro asked for the celebration of a referendum for independence and decided to set an economic policy aside from Serbia. Among other measures, this policy contemplated the establishment of the German Mark as official currency (which would be replaced by the Euro later on, despite of them not being part of the Eurozone). Nevertheless, both of them reached a new cooperation agreement in 2012, according to which the Yugoslavian Federation allowed the so-called Federation of Serbia and Montenegro, which became constitutionalized, as said before, in 2003, contemplating the possibility of secession and postponing the celebration of a referendum with this purpose to 30 April 2006 (which was postponed once again to May 21).

However, Europe did not support this independence process at first. What most concerned the international community, especially the European diplomacy, led by Javier Solana, was that the case of Montenegro could open, once again, a door to solve other conflicts in European regions (*i.e.* the Srpska Republic, Abkhazia or Nagorno-Karabaj). It must be taken into account that even Transnítria and South Ossetia, called for referendums to be held on 17 September and 12 November 2006, respectively. Finally, however, the EU and the NATO accepted the referendum, and they even fixed the regulations and sent international observers to the process: a minimum turnout of 50% and favorable result of 55%, in addition to other conditions like respect to fundamental rights (especially freedom of speech and demonstration), neutrality in the campaign by the authorities and the media, and clarity in the question. These requirements were outlined by the Venice Commission, which issued a *dictum* requested by the Parliamentary Assembly of the European Council, which was assumed by the Ministry Council and the High Representative of Foreign Affairs and Security Policy of the European Union [43]. The requirements of the referendum were negotiated with the Montenegrin political representatives and were reflected on the Montenegrin Law on the referendum of the State, from 1 March 2006. From here, the referendum of 21 May 2006 was organized. The consultation was held on 21 May 2006, with a turnout of 86.5% and a question that said: «Do you want the Republic of Montenegro to be an independent State with full legal and international personality?». The «yes» option obtained 55.5% of the votes, five tenths more than what had been stipulated as the minimum percentage, and the «no» obtained 44.5%. The parliamentary UDI was delayed until 17 February 2008. The new Constitution was adopted on 19 October 2007 and replaced the previous one, from 1992, when the country was part of the Yugoslavian federation.

Bosnia and Herzegovina held a referendum on 28 and 29 February 1992. It had a binding nature and participation and results were established on 50% to be valid. The question was: «Are you for a sovereign, indivisible and independent Bosnia and Herzegovina?». The opposition to the referendum by the main Serbian party went beyond the threat of a violent answer and it led to war. However, the Washington Agreement, signed on 18 March 1994 led to the creation of a Constitutive Assembly (Ustavotvorna skupstina/Ustavotvorbeni Sabor), which was kept until 1996. On 21 November 1995, this Assembly adopted the text of a Constitution, enacted on 14 December, which reproduced the fourth annex of the Dayton Peace Agreement, from 21 November 1995. It was formally signed in Paris on 14 December 1995 and the war ceased with it. For this reason, The Constitution of Bosnia and Herzegovina has the nature of an International Treaty.

CONFLICT OF INTEREST

The author declares no conflict of interest, financial or otherwise.

ACKNOWLEDGEMENTS

Declared none.

REFERENCES

[1] According to T. Musgrave, «[s]ecession is a domestic question and, therefore, a completely neutral act in terms of International Law. Besides, since it is not considered within the jurisdiction of international laws, not just any attempt of secession entails an act of self-determination in juridical terms. Even when consequences for International Law are derived, with the emergence of a new State, the act of secession itself has a rather political and not juridical nature». Musgrave, T. Self-Determination and National Minorities. Oxford. 1997: p. 210.

[2] For the most unyielding doctrine, even «in its legal dimension it is evident that self-determination does not subsume today, and probably will not subsume in the future, a general right of secession for the

infra-state groups. On the contrary, what can be concluded from the experience of these last years is that the International Law is still hostile to secession, even in the colonial context [...] unless the very exceptional theory of "remedy-secession" can be objectively applicable». (Cristakis, T. Le droit à l'autodetermination en dehors de situations de décolonisation. La Documentation française 1999: 617). For Dieter Murswiek, «the states with a longer history typically have greater stability, but this does not mean that they are not also the object of secession demands. Many states, especially in the East, fear that the concession of autonomy to certain ethnic minorities might be the first step towards secession and the breaking up of the State. However, I am convinced of the opposite. Autonomy is the best prevention against the demands of secession». (Murswiek D. The issue of a right of secession reconsidered. In: Tomuschat C, Ed. Modern Law of Self-Determination. Kluewer Academic Publishers 1993; p. 39).

[3] Art. 1.2 of the Charter from 26 June 1945 establishes that «[t]he Purposes of the United Nations are to maintain international peace and security, and to that end: to take effective collective measures for the prevention and removal of threats to the peace, and for the suppression of acts of aggression or other breaches of the peace». Articles 55 and 76 are expressed in very similar terms.

[4] International Covenant on Civil and Political Rights of the GAUN, New York, 23 March 1976. Resolution 2200A (XXI) of 16 December 1966.

[5] Resolution 1514 of the GAUN about the Independence to the countries and colonial communities, New York, 14 December 1960. In these lines, see Margiotta, C. L'ultimo dirito. Profil Storici e teorico della secessione, Il Mulino. 2005: 89-209.

[6] Many events are closely related to the disappearance of great empires such as the Austro-Hungarian Empire or the Ottoman Empire, after the Great War, or the Soviet Empire at the end of 1980s. Some States also had their origins in unusual national protests against the colonial authorities, such as the English, the French or the Portuguese in the case of Indochina or Africa, after the Second World War and until mid 1960s. In the context of liberal and pluralist democracies, the new States emerged as a result of social and ethnic conflicts. More remotely, we could mention the case of Norway (1904) and Ireland (1921) as well as some insular regions: Cyprus and the Isle of Malta. Finally, there were bursts of several movements of identity assertion of great intensity in plurinational states with a complex structure such as Belgium, Canada, the UK or Spain. In all cases, it is a matter of States drawn together as a result of unions of crowns, religious wars or, as in the case of Quebec, the great colonizing campaigns of the British.

[7] As warned by Milano, E.: «the practices of the States and the international community in the Post Cold War era seem to have remodeled the nature and the effects of such a principle, from which one can mainly derive a right of the peoples to become independent from the authority of a foreign, enemy or merely illegitimate government, as a way to reassert the requirement of respect to the principle of territorial integrity of the States» (Milano E. Autodeterminazione dei popoli, Treccani.it, L'enciclopedia giuridicca italiana. 2013; p. 8). No federal Constitution, except for the case of art. 39 of the Constitution of Ethiopia from 1995 or article 60 of the federal Constitution of Serbia-Montenegro from 2003 acknowledge the right to secession and they impose respect to the adopted agreements. See Constitution of Ethiopia (Constitution of the Federal Democratic Republic of Ethiopia, 1995).

[8] No federal Constitution, except for the case of art. 39 of the Constitution of Ethiopia from 1995 or article 60 of the federal Constitution of Serbia-Montenegro from 2003 acknowledge the right to secession and they impose respect to the adopted agreements. See Constitution of Ethiopia (Constitution of the Federal Democratic Republic of Ethiopia, 1995).

[9] In this regard see Roepstorff K. The Politics of Self-Determination. Beyond the Decolonisation Process. Routledge 2013.

[10] The opinion of the Supreme Court of Canada [Reference by the Governor-General Concerning Certain Questions Relating to the Secession of Quebec from Canada (Reference re Secession of Quebec, (1998) 2 SCR 217] came to solve a double question raised by the government Canadian federal: «Behold international law the right to unilaterally declare independence of Quebec from Canada by the National Assembly, Parliament or the Government of Quebec»; and in the same sense, There is one

right to self-determination under international law that grants to the National Assembly, Parliament or the Government of Quebec the right to unilaterally declare independence of Quebec from Canada?.

[11] Universal Declaration of Human Rights 207 A (III) by the General Assembly of the United Nations. Paris, the 10th of December 1948 http://www.un.org/es/documents/udhr/ [visited: 25th of October 2014].

[12] Charter of Fundamental Rights of the European Union, Nice, 7th of December 2000. Available from http://www.europarl. europa.eu/charter/pdf_es.pdf [visited: 25th of October 2014].

[13] For a general overview of the case of Kosovo, see Arcari M, Balmond L. Questions de droit international autour de l'avis consultative de la Cour Internationale de Justice – International law issues arising from the International Court of Justice advisory opinion on Kosovo. In: Balmond L, Arcari M, Milano E, Pertile M, Martin J, Palchetti P, Czaplinski W, Vitucci M, Tancredi, A: Declarations of independence and territorial integrity in general international law: some reflections in light of the Court's advisory opinion. Giuffré 2011; pp. 59-90; Thürer D, Burri T. Self-Determination. In: Max Planck Encyclopedia of Public International Law. Oxford Public International Law. Oxford University Press 2013; and Milano E. Formazione dello Stato e processi di State-building nel diritto internazionale. Kosovo 1999-2013. Editoriale Scientifica 2013.

[14] In fact, even though we will discuss the case of Kosovo further on, we will state now that when this old Serbian province made a unilateral declaration of independence, the EU immediately adopted a joint resolution in which it qualified it as a «unique case», leaving it up to each State whether they accepted it or not. Most states, with Germany, France and the United Kingdom at the forefront, did so. This wide international support was decisive as that same year, the General Assembly of the United Nations, agreed, as proposed by Serbia, to transfer the matter to the International Court of Justice, if the declaration violated international law. Presently the European Commission itself is directly negotiating with the Kosovar authorities regarding their future entry into the EU, after the European Council decided in June 2013, to open negotiations to establish an Agreement for Stabilization and Association.

[15] STC 42/2014, 25th March 2014 BOE (Spanish Official Bulletin) number. 87, 10th of April 2014, pp. 77-99.

[16] See for further information, Vintró, J. La declaració de sobirania i el dret a decidir del poble de Catalunya: un apunt jurídic. Blog of the Catalan Review on Public Law 2013.

[17] The Catalan nation has, for reasons of democratic legitimacy, the nature of political and legal sovereign subject" [and (The) process of the exercise of the right to decide will be strictly democratic and will especially guarantee plurality and respect to all options by deliberation and dialogue within the Catalan society, so that the pronouncement which will emerge as a result will be the majority expression of the popular will, which will be the essential guarantee of the right to decide. Spanish Constitution (specifically article 168).

[18] When a total revision of the Constitution is proposed, or a partial revision thereof, affecting the Preliminary Title, Chapter II, Section 1 of Title I, or Title II, the principle shall be approved by a two-thirds majority of the members of each Chamber, and the Parliament shall immediately be dissolved. 2. The Chambers elected must ratify the decision and proceed to examine the new Constitutional text, which must be approved by a two-thirds majority of the members of both Chambers. 3. Once the amendment has been passed by the Parliament, it shall be submitted to ratification by referendum. Spanish Constitution (article 92).

[19] Political decisions of special importance may be submitted for a consultative referendum of all the citizens. 2. The referendum shall be convoked by the King at the proposal of the President of the Government after previous authorization by the House of Representatives. 3. An organic law shall regulate the conditions and the procedure of the different kinds of referendums provided for in this Constitution.

[20] See www.legislation.gov.uk/uksi/2013/242/pdfs/uksi_20130242_en.pdf [visited: 15th of November 2014].

[21] BOE num. 172, from the 16th of July 2010: 1- 491.

[22] Shortly after this sentence, a massive demonstration took place, which went beyond the citizens' claim against the decision of the Constitutional Court, since its motto was «We are a Nation, We want to decide». Two years later, after the massive demonstration on September 11, 2012 (National Day of Catalonia) for the independence of Catalonia, and after the results of the Autonomic elections held on November 25, 2012, which granted a majority of pro-sovereignty and for the right to decide at the Parliament, there were different resolutions of the Catalan Chamber for the «right to decide» and for the celebration of a popular consultation within the legal framework regarding the political future of Catalonia and its relationship with Spain (742/IX, 5/X i 323/X).

[23] Information about the survey published by the Center of Opinion Studies of the Generalitat de Catalunya on March 18, 2014 <http://www.ara.cat/politica/ sondeig-CEO-independencia_0_1103889719.html> [visited on March 19, 2014].

[24] DOGC (Official Newspaper of the Generalitat de Catalunya) number 6715, 27th of September 2014: 1-19.

[25] Despite all the determining factors, the level of participation was similar, if slightly lower, to that of the 2014 European Parliamentary elections (http://elecciones.mir.es/resultados2014/99PE/DPE99999TO.htm) [visited on October, 10, 2017]. If nothing else, the vote recount offered a vision of the strong mobilization of the independent vote, with 80.76% of the answers in favour of an independent Catalan State (http://participa2014.cat/) [visited on October, 10, 2017].

[26] See Linde E. Estado *versus* nación. El fin de la era de los nacionalismos en Europa. Revista de Derecho de la Unión Europea 2013; 25(July-December): 29.

[27] A view on the tax effort in Catalonia from a pro-sovereignty point of view. http://www.elpuntavui.cat/ma/article/4-economia/18-economia/595749-lendeutament- espanyol-ens-fara-lliures.html.

[28] Article 50 ETU: «1. Any Member State may decide to withdraw from the Union in accordance with its own constitutional requirements; 2. A Member State which decides to withdraw shall notify the European Council of its intention. In the light of the guidelines provided by the European Council, the Union shall negotiate and conclude an agreement with that State, setting out the arrangements for its withdrawal, taking account of the framework for its future relationship with the Union. That agreement shall be negotiated in accordance with Article 218(3) of the Treaty on the Functioning of the European Union. It shall be concluded on behalf of the Union by the Council, acting by a qualified majority, after obtaining the consent of the European Parliament; [...]». http://www.lisbon-treaty.org/ wcm/the-lisbon-treaty/ treaty-on-european-union-and-comments/title-6-final-provisions/137-article-50.html [visited on October, 10, 2017].

[29] There have been speculations about the rejoining of Greenland to the European Union, as seen from the statements by the Greenland Prime Minister reported on the Danish Newspaper Jyllands-Posted on January 4, 2007.

[30] Prodi added: «[According to] article 49 of the European Union Treaty, any European State which respects the principles referred to in article 6 of the EU Treaty could apply for membership to the Union.» http://elecciones.mir.es/resultados2014/99PE/DPE99999TO.htm [visited on October, 10, 2017].

[31] Advisory Opinion of the International Court of Justice in accordance with the UDI regarding Kosovo from July 26, 2010. Available from http://www.un.org/es/comun/docs/?symbol=A/64/881 [visited on February 3, 2014].

[32] BBC program on the summit between Ukraine, Russia and the USA in Geneva on the East Ukraine conflict. http://www.bbc.com/news/world-europe-27072351.

[33] This clarification was done because several members of the procedure alleged that the principle of territorial integrity had recently been applied in several secessionist conflicts such as the ones in Georgia and Abkhazia and South Ossetia, Azerbaijan/Nagorno-Karabakh. Furthermore, the Security Council had passed several resolutions condemning some given declarations of independence: South

Rhodesia [216 (1965) [http://www.un.org/es/comun/docs/ ?symbol=S/RES/216%20(1965)] [visited on October, 10, 2017] and 217 (1965) [http://www.un.org/es/comun/docs/?symbol=S/ RES/202%20 (1965)] [visited on October, 10, 2017]; Septentrional Cyprus [541 (1983)] [http://www.un.org/es/ comun/docs/?symbol=S/RES/541% 20(1983)] [visited on October, 10, 2017]; and the Srpska Republic [787 (1992)] [http://www.un.org/es/comun/docs/?symbol=S/ RES/787%20(1992)] [visited on October, 10, 2017]. Indeed, the UN does not normally intervene in the authorization of the secession of groups that are not homogeneous nation-communities strictly speaking (e.g, the secession of the Bosnian-Serbians and the Croats from Bosnia).

[34] See note number 27.

[35] In several international agreements, prescriptions addressed to sub-state entities regarding the respect of territorial integrity [art.5 of the Convention for the Protection of National Minorities (CPNM); and art. 46 of the International Declaration of the rights of indigenous people] constitute a prohibition to sub-state entities to declare their independence. Respect for territorial integrity must not be understood separately from the object of these rules, addressed to subjects to which this regulation does not acknowledge legal personality (speakers of minority languages, national minorities or indigenous people).

[36] When the UDI was proclaimed, the legal framework of Kosovo was regulated by the Resolution of the Security Council of the UN 1244 (1999) which basically contemplated the authorization of the creation of international military presence (KFOR) to guarantee peace and demilitarization, as well as civil international presence (Interim Administration Mission called UNMIK). This is what established the frame for the administration of Kosovo, by using a provisional system of self-government and autonomy. http://www.un.org/es/comun/docs/?symbol=S/RES/1244%20(1999) [visited on October, 10, 2017].

[37] The ballot succeeded with the vote of 109 representatives out of 120, because Serbian representatives abandoned the session. https://elpais.com/internacional/2008/ 02/17/ actualidad/ 1203202809_ 850215.html [visited on October, 10, 2017].

[38] Throughout 2006 internal tensions in the governing party led to the resignation of Prime Minister Kosumi in March, his replacement by Agim Çeku and, finally, to the defeat of the Democratic League of Kosovo by the Democratic Party in the election of November 2007. The leader of this party, Hashim Thaçi, became prime minister of a coalition government with the League and it was under his management that the UDI was passed.

[39] The Resolution of the European Parliament, from March 29, 2012 on the process of integration of Kosovo in the European Union (2011/2885 (*RSP) (2013/C 257 I/05) acknowledges the satisfactory support and the recognition of Kosovo by many countries, and it also regrets the diplomatic pressure exercised by Serbia.

[40] It must be highlighted that the United States had military-strategic interests on the area, where they set Camp Bondsteel, the second biggest North-American base in the world. Source, Russia beyond (https://es.rbth.com/internacional/2013/06/18/una_base_militar_de_ee_uu_en_el_corazon_de_europa_ desafia_la_ge_28997) [[visited on October, 10, 2017].

[41] The resolution of the European Parliament from January 16, 2014, accepts, among other issues, to «Ask the Council to adopt the necessary decisions to allow Kosovo to be part of the programs of the EU as soon as possible». http://www.europarl.europa.eu/sides/ getDoc.do?pubRef=-//EP//TEXT+TA+P7-TA-2014- 0040+0+DOC+XML+V0//EN [Visited: 25th November 2014].

[42] On April 1st, 2014, there was a Meeting between the European Commissioner, Stefan Füle, and the government of Kosovo, to analyze the final stage of the annexation process to the EU. http://europa.eu/rapid/ press-release_STATEMENT-14-91_en.htm [Visited 25th of November 2014].

[43] Paradoxically, the process was interrupted when, in March 1991, a referendum was held exclusively regarding the preservation of the unit of the Republic within the USSR. It was won by the supporters of the «yes» (70.2%, with a turnout of 86.5%) who widely defeated the independence supporters. The difference in the results of the two referendums is explained with the loss of the Soviet supremacy, as

a result of the conspiracy carried out by members of the CPSU and the KGB, which contributed to the fall of president Gorbachov. https://es.wikipedia.org/ wiki/ Refer%C3%A9ndum_de_ independencia_de_Ucrania_de_1991 [[visited on October, 10, 2017].

[44] The Venice Commission, advisory body of the Parliamentary Assembly of the European Council, paid attention to the subject of the majority required to consider the referendum valid and issued a dictum under the petition of the Parliamentary Assembly and the High Representative of Foreign Affairs and Security Policy of the European Union. One of the set requirements was to establish the majority on a 55% of the issued votes for independence as a necessary result of the referendum, as well as a turnout of more than 50% of the electoral census. http://www.venice.coe. int/webforms/documents/CDL-AD (2005) 034.aspx [visited on February 1st, 2014].

CHAPTER 13

The Right to Access by Non-Dominant Linguistic Communities to the Mass Media

Iñigo Urrutia-Libarona*

Faculty of Economics and Business Studies, Department of Administrative Law, University of the Basque Country (UPV/EHU), Bilbao, Spain

Abstract: In this chapter, we address the relationship between the audiovisual sector and non-dominant linguistic communities. In Europe, the first coordinate is characterised by a progressive opening up of the sector to the free market through the free circulation of audiovisual media. The second coordinate of this study concerns non-dominant linguistic communities. This article deals with the legal possibilities for encouraging the use of the languages of the non-dominant linguistic communities in this field. We begin by analysing the linguistic characteristics of the human right to freedom of expression, examining the margins for developing linguistic policy for the media sector. Then, we shall refer to linguistic diversity as a limit for the audiovisual national linguistic policy. Finally, we analyse the different dimensions of the EU legal framework on this matter.

Keywords: Freedom of communication, Freedom of information, Language communities, Language policy, Linguistic law, Mass media, Minorities, Non-dominant groups, Regional languages.

1. INTRODUCTION

According to the 2003 UNESCO Report on Language Vitality and Endangerment, in most world regions, about 90% of the languages may be replaced by dominant languages by the end of the 21st century (p.2). There is a pressing need to build support for non-dominant language communities in their efforts to establish meaningful new roles for their endangered languages.

Raising awareness about language loss and language diversity will only be successful when meaningful contemporary roles for non-dominant languages can be established, for the requirements of modern life within the community as well as in national and international contexts. Meaningful contemporary roles include

* **Corresponding author Iñigo Urrutia-Libarona:** Faculty of Economics and Business Studies, Department of Administrative Law, University of the Basque Country (UPV/EHU), Bilbao, Spain; Tel. 0034 943 015956; Fax. 0034 943 018140; E-mail: i.urrutia@ehu.eus

J. Alberto del Real Alcalà (Ed.)

the use of these languages in everyday life, commerce, education, writing, the arts, and also the media.

Today no language can keep its influence unless it has access to the new forms of mass communications. However, new media, including broadcast media and the Internet, usually serve to expand the scope and power of the dominant language at the expense of endangered languages. The development of these new technologies throughout the world is leading to the weakening of the cultural influence of the non-dominant linguistic groups and their less widely spoken languages. The size of the audience is generally a decisive factor for media, and this does not fit well with the narrow and limited cultural markets of the non-dominant linguistic groups.

In order to ensure the access to the media of the non-dominant linguistic groups a public support is needed. This chapter deals with the legal possibilities for encouraging the use of the languages of the non-dominant linguistic communities in this field. In any event, the legal intervention on media shows specific characteristics such as the limited capacity of action by the public authorities by means of regulations, the varying degree of control over the media (according to whether or not the latter carry out a public service mission), the major role of the freedom of language in the field of the freedom of communication, or the specific characteristics of each type of media.

The theoretical framework of study lies at the point where the following two coordinates intersect: on the one hand, the audiovisual sector and non-dominant language groups or linguistic communities, on the other. In Europe, the first coordinate is characterised by a progressive opening up of the sector to the free market through the free circulation of audiovisual media. States have traditionally been concerned with this sector because broadcasting regulation has been used as a means to promote national identity. Television, radio (and also the cinema) have been used from their beginnings as instruments at the service of a collective identity, guaranteeing the cohesion of the country and counterbalancing social, cultural and linguistic differentiations [1]. National mass media systems emerged as instruments for creating public opinion and as a factor for the social, cultural and linguistic integration of the political community. The promotion and defence of national languages played a major role in the original regulation of the mass media.

In Europe, the situation changed due to the technological innovations of the 1980s, enabling broadcasts to cross frontiers and audiovisual services to circulate between States. The abolition of monopolies, the emergence of new players and rapid technological developments have fundamentally altered the media environment. Television broadcasting was traditionally a reserved activity. Since its inception, it has mostly been provided by public undertakings under a monopoly regime. The industry which, until relatively recently had been exclusively dependent on States, took on a supranational dimension that conditions States' ability to act, and also witnessed a process of internal deregulation.

Regulations issued by the Council of Europe and the European Union are the legal framework of reference in Europe. The European Convention on Transfrontier Television entered in force on 1 May 1993 after its ratification by seven States [2]. The Television without Frontiers Directive was adopted on 3 October 1989 by the Council of Ministers of the European Community [3]. It was amended several times [4] and finally it was codified as Directive 2010/13/EU of the European Parliament and of the Council of 10 March 2010 on the coordination of certain provisions laid down by law, regulation or administrative action in Member States concerning the provision of audiovisual media services (Audiovisual Media Services Directive) [5]. Despite the similarities between both instruments each one serves a different objective. The European Convention on Transfrontier Television is part of the Council of Europe's traditional cultural policy that seeks to promote the free flow of information [6]. The Audiovisual Media Services Directive has more of a free market orientation, aiming to guarantee the free movement of audiovisual services in the internal market. As we shall see, although the language of the broadcasting is not regulated by the Directive, the Directive does condition internal (domestic) regulations on media language insofar as they may affect the free movement of audiovisual services.

The situation can also be examined from the opposite perspective. An excessively economics-based, liberal view of the freedom of movement of audiovisual services can affect States' cultural competences and linguistic diversity [7]. Freedom of the market is not neutral from the linguistic perspective, favouring mass consumption cultural industries to the detriment of others; hence the proposal to guarantee the preservation of the values of identity and cultural and linguistic diversity within an increasingly globalised audiovisual environment. The preservation of cultural and linguistic diversity became increasingly important in the European Union and internationally, until it finally came of age with the UNESCO Convention on the protection and promotion of the diversity of cultural expressions [8], whose *raison d'être* has a lot to do with the tension that we have been discussing here. The EU is party to the UNESCO Convention on the Protection and Promotion of the Diversity of Cultural Expressions. As one way of protecting its own cultural diversity and promoting local productions, the EU has secured an exemption from the free-trade rules of the World Trade Organisation. Known as the 'cultural exception', this entitles its member countries to place limits on imports of cultural items like films [9]. In this work we attempt to identify the characteristics of this tension and highlight the parameters of balance.

The second coordinate of this study concerns non-dominant linguistic communities. This category has not been assumed or developed by the regulations but relates to the size of the linguistic community or their relative position vis--vis the dominant language(s). Regulating the use of language in television and the cinema through, in some cases, linguistic obligations in broadcasting and distribution, language quotas, requirements to produce programmes in national languages and financing for audiovisual works in national languages are commonly used instruments for defending non-dominant linguistic communities. One of the working hypotheses we develop is whether the basis for this type of legislative measures to protect languages can be found in the status of the languages, or rather in the specific contact relationships between languages. That is, in the globalised, interrelated cinema and audiovisual market, it seems that what drives protective legislation is not so much the formal legal status of languages as their characteristics (whether they have sufficient critical mass to develop a sufficiently dynamic market) and in particular, the relative position of languages in relation to the languages in their surrounding environment (international or state languages) that they are in contact or in conflict with. This perspective also raises issues for reflection. For example, issues concerned with guaranteeing internal linguistic pluralism, that is, the influence of the rights of members of linguistic minorities (and of regional and minority languages) as an integral part of the system of human rights protection.

We shall begin by analysing the linguistic characteristics of the human right to freedom of expression, examining the margins for developing linguistic policy for the media sector. Then we shall refer to linguistic diversity as a limit for the audiovisual national linguistic policy. Finally, we analyse the different dimensions of the EU legal framework on this matter.

2. INTERNATIONAL FRAMEWORK FOR DEVELOPING LINGUISTIC DETERMINATIONS IN THE AUDIOVISUAL SECTOR

2.1. Freedom of Information and Language Policy in Media

We shall begin by analysing the extent to which human rights determine linguistic policies for protecting non-dominant languages in the media sector. In the sphere of the Council of Europe, freedom of expression plays a central role as the basis and foundation for developing a democratic and participatory framework for citizens. The basic reference is Article 10 of the European Convention on the Protection of Human Rights and Fundamental Freedoms (ECHR), which guarantees freedom of expression and has been characterised by the European Court of Human Rights (ECtHR) as "[o]ne of the essential foundations of a democratic society and one of the basic conditions for its progress and for each individual's self-fulfilment [10]". This right shall include freedom to hold opinions and to receive and impart information and ideas without interference by public authority and regardless of frontiers.

The Convention configures freedom of expression as a public freedom that covers two perspectives, one active (freedom of opinion and to transmit information) and the other passive (to receive information), and emphasises the transfrontier scope of this freedom. In this latter respect, states are under an obligation to abstain or not hinder the freedom to receive and communicate information, as a positive obligation to act intended to ensure the free transfrontier flow of information [11]. The transfrontier perspective has been developed by the European Convention on Transfrontier Television [12].

Freedom of expression is configured broadly but it is a relative, rather than an absolute, right whose scope must be balanced so that this freedom can coexist with other values and rights that also deserve protection. Freedom of expression must be guaranteed by public powers, but that does not mean that it is an unlimited freedom or that any public intervention that might limit or condition "the freedom of language" is forbidden. Article 10 ECHR does not provide absolute protection for linguistic freedom, particularly in the public sphere [13].

Firstly, it must be remembered that the Convention itself contemplated the possibility of preliminary control over audiovisual broadcasting activities. Article 10(1) ECHR provides that freedom of expression shall not prevent States from requiring the licensing of broadcasting, television or cinema enterprises. As we shall see below, licensing schemes are often used to introduce linguistic requirements in the audiovisual sphere [14] and also in cinema. Furthermore, the second provision of article 10 states that the exercise of this freedom may be subject to formalities, conditions or restrictions if they are prescribed by law and necessary in a democratic society for the protection of one of a listed number of public interests [15]. The cultural or linguistic identity of States is not listened. However, linguistic rules and regulations/prescriptions are often found in national laws on broadcasting which, although they could be seen as limiting or determining the right to freedom of expression, can hardly be classified *per se* as being in breach of international human rights standards [16].

The ECtHR has not had the opportunity to directly decide whether linguistic obligations established by public powers are compatible with freedom of expression and to what extent. However, in the *Lentia* case (where the plaintiffs were demanding recognition of broadcasting rights in a minority language in the Austrian region of Carinthia) the Court affirmed States' wide margin of appreciation when establishing licensing regimes. The ECtHR established that, aside of technical aspects "[t]he grant or refusal of a licence may also be made conditional on other considerations, including such matters as the nature and objectives of a proposed station, its potential audience at national, regional or local level, the rights and needs of a specific audience and the obligations deriving from international legal instruments [17]". In conclusion "[t]his may lead to interferences whose aims will be legitimate under the third sentence of paragraph 1, even though they do not correspond to any of the aims set out in paragraph 2 [18]". The compatibility of such interferences with the Convention must nevertheless be assessed in the light of the other requirements of paragraph 2.

Following the ECtHR for restrictions or limitations to be understood as justified, they must be "necessary". This requirement is analysed on the basis of the existence of a "pressing social need" which scope is evaluated by the Contracting States with certain margin of appreciation in assessing whether such a need exists [19]. Justifications based on cultural and linguistic pluralism has been taken as a basis for restrictions on freedom of expression. The Commission has stated that "[t]he particular political circumstances in Switzerland ... necessitate the application of sensitive political criteria such as cultural and linguistic pluralism, balance between lowland and mountain regions and a balanced federal policy" [20]. On another occasion, also concerning Switzerland, the ECtHR analysed whether a measure that restricted the granting of licences because the television channel was exclusively devoted to automobiles matters was necessary or not. The Swiss government alleged the particular political and cultural structure of Switzerland and the ECtHR accepted the reasoning of the State based on cultural and linguistic justifications "[w]hich are of considerable importance for a federal State. Such factors, encouraging in particular pluralism in broadcasting, may legitimately be taken into account when authorizing radio and television broadcasts [21]".

Secondly, restrictions on the freedom of expression due to linguistic reasons must be proportionate. In this regard the European Commission of Human Rights in its decision on admissibility in the Case of *Verein Alternatives Lokalradio Bern* [22], citing the *Handyside* judgment, stated that a licensing system must respect the requirements of pluralism, tolerance and broadmindedness. The Commission explained that this includes the language of the broadcast, stating that the

> "[r]efusal to grant a broadcasting licence may raise a problem under Article 10, in conjunction with Article 14 of the Convention in specific circumstances. Such a problem would arise, for example, if the refusal to

> grant a licence resulted directly in a considerable proportion of the inhabitants of the area concerned being deprived of broadcasts in their mother tongue [23]."

In paragraph 32 of the *Lentia* Case, the Court enumerated the following considerations for appropriate licensing: "[t]he nature and objectives of a proposed station, its potential audience at national, regional or local level, the rights and needs of the specific audience and the obligations derived from international legal instruments". In other Judgment the Court found that the size of the target audience and their ease of access to alternative broadcasts (e.g., through cable television) are relevant factors in determining the proportionality of restrictions [24].

In the *Verein Alternatives* Case, the Commission specified that political circumstances – "such as cultural and linguistic pluralism…and a balanced federalist policy" – may also be taken into account when assessing proportionality of regulation.

In short, proportionality must be analysed on a case-by-case basis taking into account not only the language measure itself (*i.e.* language quota or broadcasting duties) but also the demographic and the situation of language contact upon which the language measure is established.

Restrictions on freedom of expression on the grounds of language and cultural identity of states could be justified by the application of article 10 of the Convention. Nevertheless, the ECtHR case-law has also highlighted the importance of pluralism in the audiovisual media as a basis of a democratic society [25]. The domestic law and practice must guarantee that the system provides a pluralistic service. The Court has focused on the material aspect of pluralism (opposing the concentration and control of audiovisual media) but has not referred specifically to the linguistic aspect.

In this regard, the Recommendation R(99) 1 of the Committee of Ministers of the Council of Europe to member states on measures to promote media pluralism [26] provides for the first time the definition of media pluralism, but the references on language are limited to the support schemas. Following the Recommendation, "[m]ember States could consider the possibility of introducing, with a view to enhancing media pluralism and diversity, direct or indirect financial support schemes for both the print and broadcast media, in particular at the regional and local levels. Subsidies for media entities printing or broadcasting in a minority language could also be considered". In the same line, the Recommendation (2007) 2 of the Committee of Ministers to member states on media pluralism and diversity of media content encourages the states to make space for other media, as well "[f]or example community, local, minority or social media". The Recommendation recognizes "[t]he crucial contribution of the media in fostering public debate, political pluralism and awareness of diverse opinions, notably by providing different groups in society – including cultural, linguistic, ethnic, religious or other minorities – with an opportunity to receive and impart information, to express themselves and to exchange ideas"; among the measures promoting content diversity, the Recommendation includes the following "[s]upport measures for media entities printing or broadcasting in a minority language should also be considered" (at II.4).

Furthermore, the Court has awarded greater scope to the right to receive information than to the right to broadcast through audiovisual media, insofar as only the latter can be subject to a licensing regime. Concerning the right to receive information in *Khurshid Mustafa* case the Court affirmed the particular importance of the right to receive (transfrontier) information for people (an immigrant family in that case) that "[w]ish to maintain contact with the culture and language of their country of origin [27]."

The case-law of the ECtHR shows that freedom of media is not only an individual manifestation of the right of freedom of expression; freedom of the media is also conceived as a means to promote the freedom of information. On that basis the Court has taken into account the social, cultural and political aspects of the media. From that social or collective perspective, States can establish requirements, limits and conditions with the aim of guaranteeing pluralism. Linguistic requirements are perfectly in keeping with that aim. Restrictions on the freedom of communication on grounds of the cultural and linguistic identity of the States could be justified by the application of article 10 ECHR, however, it must be compatible and proportionate to linguistic diversity itself, which will operate as a negative limit referred to below.

2.2. Linguistic Pluralism as a Limit for Language Policy

The principle of the free flow of information and the importance of the broadcasting for the development of culture and the free formation of opinions in conditions safeguarding pluralism and equality of opportunity among all democratic groups and political parties are two of the main principles of the European Convention on Transfrontier Television (ECTT) [28]. Article 10 of the ECTT is entitled "cultural objectives" but its content is limited to promoting and favouring the European works in the transmission time. Contracting states are under an obligation to "[e]nsure, where practicable and by appropriate means, that a broadcaster within its jurisdiction reserves for European works a majority proportion of its transmission time [29]." Broadcasters' cultural responsibilities are developed no further than the reference to a content quota.

What qualifies an audiovisual work as European work is neither based upon a particular expression of national or European identity nor does it require a reflection of cultural and linguistic diversity. The article does not refer to language, which is only mentioned in paragraph 3, affirming that the States

> "Undertake to look together for the most appropriate instruments and procedures to support, without discrimination between broadcasters, the activity and development of European production, particularly in countries with a low audiovisual production capacity or restricted language area [30]."

Promoting linguistic pluralism could form part of the content quota, but the regulation is really referring to the material (or substantial) aspect (European production) when it speaks of "cultural objectives". As we will see later on the Audiovisual Media Services Directive of the EU follows the same "substantial" criteria.

The two most important Council of Europe texts that help to focus operation of the principle of linguistic pluralism in audiovisual media are the Framework Convention for the Protection of national Minorities (FCNM) and the European Charter for Regional or Minority Languages (ECRML) [31]. Each one will be analysed separately.

2.2.1. The Framework Convention for the Protection of National Minorities

The Framework Convention for the Protection of national Minorities states in Article 6(1) that Parties shall "[p]romote mutual respect and understanding and co-operation" among persons, "[i]rrespective of linguistic identity", through, inter alia, the media. Article 9 is the operative provision. It reads as follows:

1. "The Parties undertake to recognise that the right to freedom of expression of every person belonging to a national minority includes freedom to hold opinions and to receive and impart information and ideas in the minority language, without interference by public authorities and regardless of frontiers. The Parties shall ensure, within the framework of their legal systems that persons belonging to a national minority are not discriminated against in their access to the media.
2. Paragraph 1 shall not prevent Parties from requiring the licensing, without discrimination and based on objective criteria, of sound radio and television broadcasting, or cinema enterprises.

3. The Parties shall not hinder the creation and the use of printed media by persons belonging to national minorities. In the legal framework of sound radio and television broadcasting, they shall ensure, as far as possible, and taking into account the provisions of paragraph 1, that persons belonging to national minorities are granted the possibility of creating and using their own media.
4. In the framework of their legal systems, the Parties shall adopt adequate measures in order to facilitate access to the media for persons belonging to national minorities and in order to promote tolerance and permit cultural pluralism."

This article focuses on the issue from the perspective of non-discrimination. As regards the scope of provision (provision from public authorities) it only confirms access to the media without discrimination; and with regard to the aspect of freedom of media, the article does not dispense with the need for licences, rather they must be granted according to the principle of equality. Similarly the duty to guarantee the possibility of creating and using their own media is subject to two limitations: States may provide that such use be undertaken within the legal framework of their broadcasting laws, and this opportunity must be ensured "as far as possible".

The main issues that have been considered in relation to the implementation of this article have centred on the adoption of legislation prescribing quotas for broadcasting time to promote the use of the State language in radio and television that have had an adverse effect on programmes in minority languages. In this regard the Advisory Committee on the Framework Convention has noted that

> "[l]anguage quotas to promote the use of the State language in radio and television broadcasting… raises issues of compatibility with the Framework Convention... The Advisory Committee takes the view that measures to promote the use of the state language should rather be principally pursued through incentive-based, voluntary methods since the imposition of rigid translation or dubbing requirements cause undue difficulties for persons belonging to national minorities [32]".

The key element here is to determine, in light of all relevant circumstances, the cut-off point at which a prescription favouring the use of one language begins to become a restriction on the use of others. In this regard "the Advisory Committee considers that, bearing in mind its implications for persons belonging to national minorities and the fact that excessive quotas may impair the implementation of the rights contained in Article 9 of Framework Convention, this practice needs to be implemented with caution. Furthermore, it would need to be rooted in a more precise legislative basis than what is contained in the above-quoted provision […] [33]".

The requirement to use a given language (to the exclusion of others) in licensing procedures has also proved problematic. In this regard the Advisory Committee in the Opinion on Russian federation of 2002 stated that "[W]hile recognising that the Russian Federation can legitimately demand broadcasting licensing of broadcasting enterprises and that the need to promote the state language can be one of the factors to be taken into account in that context, the said article appears to be overly restrictive as it implies an overall exclusion of the use of the languages of national minorities in federal radio and TV broadcasting. The Advisory Committee considers that such an a priori exclusion is not compatible with Article 9 of the Framework Convention, bearing in mind, inter alia, the size of the population concerned and the fact that a large number of persons belonging to national minorities are dispersed and reside within several subjects of the federation [34]".

The need for subtitling or dubbing audiovisual and cinematographic productions in minority languages into official national languages has also caused several problems. That is the case pointed out in the Opinion of Estonia of 2001, in which The Advisory Committee agrees that it is often advisable, and fully in the spirit of the Framework Convention, to accompany minority language broadcasting with sub-titles in the state language. However, the Advisory Committee considers that, as far as private broadcasting is concerned, this goal should be principally pursued through incentive-based, voluntary methods, and that the imposition of a rigid translation requirement mars the implementation of Article 9 of the Framework Convention by causing undue difficulties for persons belonging to a national minority in their efforts to create their own media [35].

2.2.2. The European Charter for Regional or Minority Languages

The European Charter for Regional or Minority Languages deals with media in article 11. The explanatory Report to the European Charter takes as a point of departure the following two factors: on the one hand it confirms the importance of the media for the future and the development of regional or minority languages stating that "[t]he time and space which regional or minority languages can secure in the media is vital for their safeguard" (Explanatory Report, paragraph 107) and on the other hand, it is based on the importance of the quantitative element in the audiovisual market, an aspect that does not favour regional or minority languages: "[t]he progress of technology is leading to the weakening of the cultural influence of less widely-spoken languages… for the major media, especially television, the size of the audience is generally the decisive factor [36]." The high cost of television production points to the crucial importance of creating economies of scale in order to put the industry on a stronger footing and increase opportunities for disseminating the language. From this point of view cross-border cooperation and the freedom to receive broadcasts from neighbour countries constitute essential factors for regional or minority languages [37]. The opening up of the audiovisual services market vis-à-vis the importance of the media for the future of regional and minority languages are basic arguments for encouraging the political and legal intervention in this field.

Article 11 of the ECRML focuses on regulation from three perspectives: public action to encourage use of regional or minority languages in media (paragraph 1), preventing restrictions on access to foreign media in a language identical or closely related to a regional or minority language (paragraph 2), and catering by media regulatory bodies for the interests of speakers of regional or minority languages (paragraph 3) [38]. Paragraph 1 establishes various obligations that States can choose from. This paragraph includes linguistic guarantees when radio and television carry out a public service mission, which may be performed by a public or private broadcasting body (1.a), and also linguistic obligations when radio and television are not attached to a public service mission (1.b y c). In this case, where broadcasting is conceived as a purely private-sector function, the state can do no more than encourage and/or facilitate. Where relevant, the undertaking given by the parties includes the allocation of the necessary frequencies to those broadcasting in regional or minority languages. Subparagraph d) of paragraph 1 refers to the obligation of the State to encourage and/or facilitate the production and distribution of audio and audiovisual works in the regional or minority language.

Paragraph 2 of article 11 deals with the reception of broadcasts in a cross-border context. In this regard the principle is that the State undertakes to guarantee freedom of direct reception of radio and television broadcasts from neighbouring countries in a language used in identical or similar form to a regional or minority language, and not to oppose the retransmission of radio and television broadcasts from neighbouring countries in such a language. This provision not only requires states to eliminate obstacles deliberately placed in the way of the freedom to receive communication media, but also the need for positive action by the authorities to make this possible. The Explanatory Report to the Charter expands the scope of the undertaking to guarantee freedom of reception relating not only to obstacles deliberately placed in the way of the reception of programmes broadcast from neighbouring countries but also to passive obstacles resulting from the failure of the competent authorities to take any action to make such reception possible [39]. The main aim of the provision is to increase the availability of radio and television programmes in regional or minority languages by making it possible for programmes in such languages to be received from other territories [40]. Such other territories or "neighbouring countries" include both states and regional authorities with powers relating to the media as subjects bound by these provisions [41].

The freedom to receive radio and television broadcasts in a cross-border context is also subject to limits. Article 11(2) concludes by providing that the exercise of the above-mentioned freedom, since it carries with it duties and responsibilities, may be subject to such formalities, conditions, restrictions or penalties as are prescribed by law and are necessary in a democratic society, in the interests of national security, territorial integrity or public safety, for the prevention of disorder or crime, for the protection of health or morals, for the protection of the reputation or rights of others, for preventing disclosure of information received in confidence, or for maintaining the authority and impartiality of the judiciary. The limitation is identical to that which applies in respect of the right to freedom of expression, set out in Article 10 of the European Convention on Human Rights. However, paragraph 112 of the Explanatory Report provides with respect to television, that for those states which are parties to the European Convention on Transfrontier Television, the circumstances and conditions under which the freedoms guaranteed by Article 11, paragraph 2, of the charter can be restricted will be determined by that Convention, in particular by the principle of non-restriction of the retransmission on their territories of programme services which comply with the terms of the Convention on Transfrontier Television. It has also to be taken into account that the free reception of transfrontier broadcasting is an aspect of the right of persons belonging to national minorities to establish and maintain free and peaceful contacts across frontiers particularly with those with whom they share an ethnic, cultural, linguistic or religious identity, or common cultural heritage, as stipulated in Article 17 of the Framework Convention.

In relation to the guarantee of transfrontier broadcasting the Committee of Experts of the European Charter for Regional or Minority Languages held that a decision adopted by the National Television and Radio Council according to which foreign programmes distributed in Ukraine *via* cable networks must have their programmes dubbed or translated into Ukrainian "[i]s not in conformity with the present undertaking" [42]. Dubbing or translating duties were considered obstacles unduly limiting the reception of regional or minority language programmes from neighbouring countries.

Another issue which the Committee of Experts has had to deal with is whether the legal requirement of use the state language in certain percentage could be considered compatible with the Charter language guarantees. Following the Committee of Experts "[a]n overall exclusion of the use of national minority languages in the nation-wide public service and private broadcasting sectors is not compatible with Article 11 of the Charter"[43]; and even "[t]he proportion of

[75% that was subsequently increased to 80, then to 85%] of programmes and broadcasts that must be in Ukrainian language was clearly inappropriate for minority language broadcasting, bearing in mind that the proportion of persons speaking regional or minority languages represent more than 50% of the population in several regions [44]." The Committee of Experts encouraged the authorities to revise the regulations on the broadcasting in regional or minority languages covered by the Charter, although the recommendations were not prescriptive as to how those regulations should be revised.

The Committee of Experts has also been critical of other forms of regulation to protect the position of the state language which disadvantages minority language broadcasters [45]. In its second report on Slovakia, the Committee of Experts noted a requirement that all private broadcasters which broadcast programmes in a regional or minority language must provide subtitles in Slovak, placing such broadcasters at a competitive disadvantage. They concluded that the Slovak undertaking was not fulfilled, [46] and in a box comment the Committee encouraged the authorities to remove the existing restrictive requirements for private broadcasters.

In the field of cinematography, the Committee of Experts has stressed that there is reason for concern that the requirement to dub, post-synchronise or sub-title every foreign film into Ukrainian may prove disproportionate for those films which are produced in Russian and in other minority languages, bearing in mind that the notion of "film distribution" not only covers the showing of films in special premises like cinemas, but also Television broadcasting channels.

3. THE EUROPEAN UNION

The law of the European Union affects the field of domestic language policies through three techniques which delimit member States' room for manoeuvre: firstly, the prescriptions in the EU legislation concerning audiovisual media services, mainly in the Audiovisual media Services Directive (positive integration); secondly, the impact on languages of the audiovisual market integration founded on the application of the free movement and the removal of national barriers (negative integration), and lastly the general prohibition of state aids under EU law and the alignment of the national economic assistance schemas for films and other audiovisual works with the competition rules.

3.1. Positive Integration: Audiovisual Media Services Directive and Languages (Between Economic Regulation and Cultural Policy)

The European Union has only recently intervened in the audiovisual sphere. On the basis of the cultural and constitutional role of the media this sector has been developed outside the market and the founding principles of the European Community. In the early 1980's the advent of cable and satellite technology led to a gradual internationalization of broadcasting services [47]. The proliferation of TV broadcasters and the exposition to competition of the traditional broadcasting public service monopolies of Member States marked the beginning of the Community's audiovisual media policy.

The European Court of Justice played an important role in expanding the scope of the Community action holding that the transmission of television and radio signals should be regarded as the provision of services [48]. The Court of Justice pointed out that there were frontiers in the Community audiovisual market although "[i]n the absence of any harmonization of the relevant rules" [49] such national restrictions fell within the residual power of each member state to regulate the television services. The Commission's audiovisual policy was in fact directed at establishing minimum bases in order to complete the internal market in an economically flourishing sector. The objective was to facilitate the provision of television services from one European country towards the others.

The Treaty of European Union, adopted in Maastricht in 1992, first introduced an explicit reference to the audiovisual sector within the new Title on "culture" of the TEC (see article 151.2 TEC – now 167.2 TFEU). The TFEU is also concerned with the audiovisual sector in article 207.4 requiring that the Council shall act unanimously for the negotiation and conclusion of agreements in the field, among others, "of trade in cultural and audiovisual services, where these agreements risk prejudicing the Union's cultural and linguistic diversity [50]." The Protocol on the System of Public Broadcasting annexed to the Treaty of Amsterdam (OJ [1997] C 340/109), confirmed the importance attached by the Member States to the role of public broadcasting, which is linked to the democratic, social and cultural needs of each society as well as to the need to safeguard plurality in the mass media

Despite the fact that the broadcasting was not one of the original regulatory domains of the Community, a Directive liberalizing transfrontier television was proposed, including some partial harmonisation which ensures the conditions necessary for the consolidation of the single market [51]. The Directive on television Without Frontiers was finally passed in 1989 [52] providing that no Member State can restrict reception or retransmission of a broadcast from another member State for reasons falling within the areas coordinated by the Directive. The TWF Directive was amended in 1997 [53] guaranteeing that events of major importance to society may not be broadcast in such a way as to deprive a substantial proportion of the public in that Member State of the possibility of following such events by live coverage or deferred coverage on free television [54]. A second amendment to the TWF Directive took place by the adoption of the Audiovisual Media Services Directive (AMSD), [55], extending the scope of the Directive to all content services, irrespective of the technology that delivers them. The new Directive defines the notion of "audiovisual media services" by making a distinction between television broadcast or linear services and on-demand or non-linear services. The former category covers "audiovisual media service provided by a media service provider for simultaneous viewing of programmes on the basis of a programme schedule" (art 1.e AMSD), whereas the later means an audiovisual media service "provided by a media service provider for the viewing of programmes at the moment chosen by the user and at his individual request on the basis of a catalogue of programmes selected by the media service provider" (art 1.g AMSD). Relating to the local content requirements non-linear services are subject to much lighter regime that the one applicable to the linear services even though Member States may establish harder rules [56]. We will see bellow that this is the case in some countries.

The development of the EU media policy shows that the primary rationale for this policy was economic, whereas the cultural dimension (cited in recitals 5, 6 and 7 of the AMSD) was first and foremost conceived as a protective measure. The content-oriented measures, as the "European-quota rules" intended to promote the distribution of European television programmes and independent productions were introduced as the result of a political bargaining [57]. It was inspired by the will to take legislative action at the Community level in order to counteract the dominance of American audio-visual productions in the European market.

Economic consideration was the primary rationale for this policy; nevertheless the attention given to the *cultural and linguistic diversity* by the EU shows a gradual greater recognition to this value [58]. After the Lisbon Treaty, the new Treaty on European Union states that the Union "[s]hall respect its rich cultural and linguistic diversity, and shall ensure that Europe's cultural heritage is safeguarded and enhanced [59]." The respect for the European cultural and linguistic diversity is affirmed among the objectives of the EU. The Union has also committed itself to respecting cultural and linguistic diversity in Article 22 of the Charter of Fundamental Rights of the European Union. Preservation of the European linguistic diversity is the main goal of Article 22 of the Charter for Fundamental Rights of the European Union, which states as follows "The Union shall respect cultural, religious and linguistic diversity". This article is considered as the "most flexible element of Equality Chapter" of the Charter of Fundamental Rights of the European Union [60]. The enforcement of the Treaty of Lisbon has modified the legal value of the Charter for Fundamental Rights, reaching the same legal value as the Treaties by virtue of the first subparagraph of Article 6(1) of the Treaty on European Union (as amended by the Lisbon Treaty).

Nevertheless, Article 22 is not drafted as an enforceable right, but rather as a principle for action. At the normative formulation, there are differences between "shall respect" and, for example, "guarantee" or "secure" [61]. No subjective right is configured. The respect for linguistic diversity requires that EU policies take into consideration any possible negative effect they may produce on linguistic pluralism, especially if they could produce homogenising effects. The respect for cultural diversity involves legal obligations for EU institutions and also for the Member States when they implement the EU policies [62].

The engagement of the Union in the flowering of the cultures of the Member States, while respecting their national and regional diversity and at the same time bringing the common cultural heritage to the fore is established in article 167(1) of the Treaty on the Functioning of the European Union. The article refers to the cultures of Member States and to the common cultural heritage, and promises to respect both national and regional diversity [63]. The ECJ has interpreted broadly the concept of common cultural heritage including the European languages [64].

Paragraph 4 of article 167 TFEU provides that "[T]he Union shall take cultural aspects into account in its action under other provisions of the Treaties, in particular in order to respect and to promote the diversity of its cultures". There are many ways in which EU law impact on languages and language policies of Member States (especially by legislation whose central aim is not cultural). This provision therefore requires that when dealing with purely economic or non-cultural areas the EU institutions and the Member States must act in compliance with the cultural and linguistic diversity value. Respect and promotion of the diversity of the cultures of the Member States, effectively comprises responsibilities that are incumbent across the whole activity of the European Union. The Lisbon Treaty has given a new impetus to this approach.

These Articles provide safeguards against homogenization of national or regional cultural and linguistic characteristics [65]. They do not set out to extend the competences of the EU but they comprise responsibilities, acting as a barrier for EU action. Their role appears to be more about setting boundaries that driving positive actions. From this point of view it is doubtful that article 167.4 TFEU could serves as the legal basis for the AMSD. The article could be considered problematic from the subsidiarity point of view but what is clear is that the Union has to model its action after the cultural concepts of its Member States [66]. In all events, whereas the protection of cultural diversity is proclaimed as a common European value, the definition of cultural policies is a matter for the Member State to decide and implement.

3.1.1. The Country of Origin Principle and the Procedure against Circumvention of Language Requirements

The country of origin principle is the core rule of the Audiovisual Media Services Directive. Member States are obliged to ensure freedom of reception and shall not restrict retransmissions on their territory of audiovisual media services from other Member States for reasons which fall within the fields coordinated by the Directive [67]. Media service providers are subject to the jurisdiction of their country of establishment, and the receiving state cannot exercise a secondary control if the broadcasts comply with the AMSD in the country where they originate. Article 2.3 AMSD provides practical criteria for determining when a media service provider shall be deemed to be established in a Member State. Only under exceptional circumstances governments can restrict the reception of foreign broadcasts of unsuitable content [68]. The country of origin principle goes beyond mutual recognition in that the grounds of general interest falling within the ambit of the directive which can be invoked by the state of destination are narrowly circumscribed [69].

The application of the country of origin principle is of a great significance for our analysis since the freedom of establishment and the freedom to provide services allow broadcasters to establish themselves in any Member State and to target other member states. Media service providers should in general be free to choose the Member States in which they establish themselves. The Court of Justice has also emphasized that 'the Treaty does not prohibit an undertaking from exercising the freedom to provide services if it does not offer services in the Member State in which it is established' [70]. That could be the case of the UK station 3+ that targets Latvia and Estonia without maintaining minimum percentages for original productions in these languages.

The language of the broadcasting is not one of the fields coordinated by the Directive. Being as so, it follows that the mechanisms for restricting the reception of foreign broadcasts provided for in the article 3 of the AMSD cannot be implemented based on the language criteria. In fact a language quota is arguably a more detailed rule compared to the Directive's quota.

Under Article 4 AMSD Member States are "[f]reed to require media service providers under their jurisdiction to comply with more detailed or stricter rules in the fields coordinated by this Directive" while ensuring that those rules are in compliance with Union law (Art 4.1 AMSD). At all events, the aforementioned reference at the end to the possibility of acting in the fields coordinated by this Directive, does not necessarily imply that said capacity to act should be restricted to the points governed there under but rather that the legal capacity of Member

States to act can also affect it. Specifically, Member States have legal competences to regulate issues within the terms set down in the Directive and must exercise that power while respecting the fundamental freedoms guaranteed under the Treaty. In other words, any (language related) legislation established by Member States must be compatible with other provisions of Community Law and particularly with the fundamental freedoms.

The original wording of Article 8 of the TWFD contained an explicit reference to the internal language policies making it possible to Member States to “lay down more detailed or stricter rules in particular on the basis of language criteria [71].” This explicit reference was removed from the articles of the Directive by Directive 97/36/EC of the European Parliament and of the Council of 30 June 1997 [72] but the main objective was addressed by recital 44 (now recital 78 of the AMSD) which provides as follows:

> “In order to allow for an active policy in favour of a specific language, Member States remain free to lay down more detailed or stricter rules in particular on the basis of language criteria, as long as those rules are in conformity with Union law, and in particular are not applicable to the retransmission of broadcasts originating in other Member States.”

The requirement to use the national languages is considered as a more detailed or stricter rule for the purpose of the AMSD. Member States remain free to apply them. Nevertheless, the Directive contains two explicit limits: the language rules should be in line with EU law, and there should not be applicable to retransmissions. As we will see bellow, such “more detailed or stricter rules” have to be “of general public interest”, a concept that has been developed by the Court of Justice in its case-law in relation to Articles 49 and 56 of the Treaty on the Functioning of the European Union (*ex* Articles 43 and 49 of the EC Treaty) and includes, inter alia, rules on cultural policy [73].

The second limit concerns the retransmissions. Unlike the European Convention on Transfrontier Television that defines retransmissions as “the fact of receiving and simultaneously transmitting, irrespective of the technical means employed, complete and unchanged television programme services, or important parts of such services, transmitted by broadcasters for reception by the general public [74]”. The AMSD does not contain any definition of this term. The problem of retransmission is whether the State being retransmitted from can control the retransmission or not (in addition to the control exercised by the State of origin). The European Court of Justice has stated that (cable) “retransmissions” fall within the scope of the Directive [75], that is to say, in the case of passive retransmissions the broadcasters have to comply only with the law of the country of establishment. The problem arises, however, when the foreign programmes are not retransmitted unchanged at the same time, but when cable distributors are empowered to interfere with their content.

From the point of view of the language requirements another interesting issue regards the possibility of circumvent the national language legislation by taking advance of the freedom of establishment. The circumvention of the internal language legislation may arise when a broadcaster establishes itself in a Member State with the intention of evading the linguistic policy of another Member State, to which it directs the most of their programmes.

The European Court of Justice examined the case of the Belgian legislation prohibiting cable operators from transmitting programmes originating from foreign broadcasting stations in the language or one of the languages of the Member State in which the station was established [76]. It was clearly an anti-circumvention measure but not so much an internal language policy measure insofar as its primary rationale was not to raise the use of the national language in the media but to restrict the reception of foreign broadcasts (also in Dutch language). The Court held that that legislation constitutes a barrier to the freedom to provide services, and also that the language barrier was discriminatory because it prevented stations established in a Member State other than the Netherlands from offering programmes in Duch to audiences in the Flemish Community.

The Court dismissed the argument of the Belgian Government according to which a person providing services cannot avoid the rules applicable to providers of services established in the Member State towards which his activity is directed. In this regard the Court held that while the State in which the service is provided may take measures to prevent a provider of services whose activity is entirely or principally directed towards its territory from exercising the freedom of establishment for the purpose of avoiding the rules which would be applicable to him if he were established within that State "it does not follow that it is permissible for a Member State to prohibit altogether the provision of certain services by operators established in other Member State, as that would be tantamount to abolish the freedom to provide services [77]."

The circumvention of linguistic legislation has not been analysed directly by the Court. In any case, the case-law [78] highlights a narrow construction of the circumvention principle:

- First, the activity must be entirely or principally directed towards the territory of the other state. Legal uncertainties on the interpretation of when a broadcast is "wholly or mostly" directed towards the territory of another Member State may arise. By way of clarification, recital 42 of the AMSD states that "[a] Member

State, when assessing on a case-by-case basis whether a broadcast by a media service provider established in another Member State is wholly or mostly directed towards its territory, may refer to indicators such as the origin of the television advertising and/or subscription revenues, the main language of the service or the existence of programmes or commercial communications targeted specifically at the public in the Member State where they are received." The main language of the service is therefore considered as a sign or evidence of circumvention, and also as an indicator of territorial competence.

-Secondly, the circumvention must actually be demonstrated by the Member State adopting the countervailing measure. Article 4.2 of the AMSD provides two possible successive procedures: a cooperation procedure between the Member States, and when the results achieved through this voluntary procedure are not satisfactory an executive procedure. The cooperative procedure consists of the following: the receiving member state can contact the Member State having jurisdiction with a view to achieving a mutually satisfactory solution to any problems posed. On receipt of a substantiated request by the first Member State, the Member State having jurisdiction shall request the broadcaster to comply with the rules of general public interest in question. The Member State having jurisdiction shall inform the first Member State of the results obtained following this request within 2 months [79].

If the results achieved through the application of said procedure are not satisfactory the receiving state may adopt appropriate measures against the broadcaster concerned, if the following requirements have been met: first, the broadcaster in question must have established itself in the Member State having jurisdiction in order to circumvent the stricter rules, in the fields coordinated by this Directive, which would be applicable to it if it were established in the first Member State, second, the receiving state must notify the Commission and the Member State in which the broadcaster is established of its intention to take such measures, and third, the Commission must have decided that the measures are compatible with Union law and in particular that assessments made by the Member State taking those measures are correctly founded [80]. If the three conditions set out are met the receiving state may adopt measures against the broadcaster concerned. In any case, such measures shall be objectively necessary, applied in a non- discriminatory manner and proportionate to the objectives which they pursue. As an overall assessment, it is worth highlighting the scepticism over the control system regulated by the Directive. It provides for a system of *ex post* control of doubtful theoretical and practical effectiveness [81]. A more effective solution could come from coordination between national regulatory authorities before granting a licence for broadcasting targeting a foreign State.

3.1.2. Cultural Content Quotas and Languages

Language use requirements (or language quotas) are usually included in the quota for European works or/and in the quota for independent works. Article 16 of the AMSD states that "[M]ember States shall ensure, where practicable and by appropriate means, that broadcasters reserve for European works a majority proportion of their transmission time, excluding the time allotted to news, sports events, games, advertising, teletext services and teleshopping [82]." Article 17 requires Member States to ensure that "[b]roadcasters reserve at least 10% of their transmission time, excluding the time allotted to news, sports events, games, advertising, teletext services and teleshopping, or alternately, at the discretion of the Member State, at least. Regarding on-demand services the quota is more flexible, asking Member States to ensure that providers "[u]nder their jurisdiction promote, where practicable and by appropriate means, the production of and access to European works [83]." The AMSD clarifies that "[s]uch promotion could relate, inter alia, to the financial contribution made by such services to the production and rights acquisition of European works or to the share and/or prominence of European works in the catalogue of programmes offered by the on-demand audiovisual media service [84]."

Some Member States have introduced language quotas with the aim of protection of their national language(s). This is the case in France, Italy, Portugal, Spain, Greece, the Netherlands, Poland, and Latvia among others. Member States have the power to adopt language quotas within the European quota, that are justified on the grounds of protection of national or regional languages, and that could fit without any difficulties with the more detailed or stricter rules in particular on the basis of language criteria in the sense of recitals 78 and 66 of the AMSD. Recital 66 of the AMSD refers to the importance of to seek appropriate instruments and procedures in accordance with Union law in order to promote the implementation of the objectives of this Directive with a view to adopting suitable measures to encourage the activity and development of European audiovisual production and distribution, particularly in countries with a low production capacity or a restricted language area.

The AMSD does not estipulate any fixed percentage reserved for television programmes made in European countries other than the country of establishment of the broadcaster, nor does it state a percentage of works made originally in European languages other the national language of the Member State. This allows to affirm that the European quota could be fulfilled by productions in the own language [85]. It is truth that national language quotas may act as a barrier to intra-Community trade but it is also true that the European quota does not really contribute to the free movement of European productions [86]. In fact the AMSD does not require Member States to report the proportion of transmission time devoted to non-national European works.

The European quota may have reinforced national objectives to protect and encourage the domestic content sector rather than fostering a truly European market in programming and encouraging the exchange and circulation of European TV programmes within Europe. There are many factors that influence the higher or lower circulation of European programmes and films, but the most important among them could be the linguistic affinity or the fact that they all share the same linguistic area. As Katsirea has highlight, that smaller Member States that share a language with a larger neighbouring Member State, such as Austria, Belgium and Ireland, have larger proportions of imported European works shown on television. Larger member States, such as France, Germany, Italy, Spain and the United Kingdom, have the smallest proportion. But small member States that do not share the same language with a larger State, such as Greece and Portugal, continue to broadcast only a small proportion of such works [87].

3.2. Negative Integration

The EU law certainly interfered with Member State's regulations in many fields despite recognising that such domains are included among the policy domains of Member States. Language policy is a clear example of that [88].

The emphasis of the economic integration process as a motor of EU's political integration is on a free operation of the market mechanisms under conditions ensuring effective and undistorted competition. This aim requires the removal of any kind of barriers which may obstruct this. From that point of view, any linguistic requirements that might be established at the State or sub-state level could be considered suspicious insofar they might affect the market freedoms [89].

As we know, Article 167.4 of the TFEU (*ex* art 151.4 TCE) demands that EU take cultural aspects into account in its action under other provisions of the Treaties, in particular in order to respect and to promote the diversity of its cultures. Nevertheless, the ECJ has avoided grappling with the implications of the cultural cross-sectional clause, and has moved in the opposite direction, shaping the linguistic configuration of the market freedoms, building its reasoning around principles with which it feels more comfortable such as the freedoms of movement and the non-discrimination clause [90]. Following to the case-law of the Court of Justice we can observe some language-based delimitation of EU freedoms (circulation, establishment) in areas relevant to the audiovisual services and film production.

The Court has consistently held that a measure that leads to a restriction on one of the fundamental freedoms guaranteed by the Treaty is warranted only if it pursues a legitimate objective compatible with the Treaty and is justified by overriding reasons of public interest [91]. If that is the case, the restriction must be suitable for securing the attainment of the objective which it pursues and not go beyond what is necessary in order to attain it [92]. In the *United Pan-Europe Communications* judgment [93] the Court dealt with the compatibility of the Belgian "must carry" regulation with the Treaties. The Court held that providers of services established in Member States other than the Kingdom of Belgium which are not designated under that legislation were charged with a burden which is not imposed on the providers of services designated by it. The Belgian Government argued that the aim of the measure was to preserve the pluralist and cultural range of programmes available on television distribution networks and to ensure that all television viewers had access to pluralism and to a wide range of programmes, particularly by guaranteeing to Belgian citizens of the bilingual region of Brussels-Capital that they will not be deprived of access to local and national news and to their culture. In this regard the European Court stated that "[I]t must be accepted that the national legislation at issue in the main proceedings pursues an aim in the general interest, since it seeks to preserve the pluralist nature of the range of television programmes available in the bilingual region of Brussels-Capital and thus forms part of a cultural policy the aim of which is to safeguard, in the audiovisual sector, the freedom of expression of the different social, cultural, religious, philosophical or linguistic components which exist in that region [94]".

The Court ruled that the purpose of this was indeed in the public interest and that it formed part of a general cultural policy [95]. However, the case-law show us that the principle of media pluralism that forms part of cultural policy is not interpreted in an expansive manner by the Court of Justice [96], but in a case-b--case basis in light of a strict proportionality and necessity test.

Regarding the proportionality of the language restrictions to the freedom to provide services the European Court stated in this ruling that "[h]aving regard to the bilingual nature of the Brussels-Capital region national legislation, such as that at issue in the main proceedings constitutes an appropriate means of achieving the cultural objective pursued, since it is capable of permitting, in that region, Dutch-speaking television viewers to have access, *via* the network of cable operators broadcasting in that area, to television programmes having a cultural and linguistic connection with the Flemish Community and French-speaking television viewers to have similar access to television programmes having a cultural and linguistic connection with the French Community. Such legislation thus guarantees to television viewers in that region that they will not be deprived of access, in their own language, to local and national news as well as to programmes which are representative of their culture [97]." Definitely guaranteeing the language diversity in the TV programming in a given bilingual region and in accordance with its cultural policy was considered an objective in the public interest.

The leading case on the consideration of language requirements as overriding reasons relating to the public interest is the *UTECA* case [98]. The ECJ was asked for a pronouncement on the compatibility with Articles 18 of the TFEU (*ex* art 12 TEC) and 107(1) (ex art. 87 TEC) of the requirement to reserve 60% of the compulsory investment for the pre-funding of European and Spanish cinematographic feature-length and short films and films made for television for the production of films of which the original language is one of the official languages of the Kingdom of Spain.

The European Court contextualized the language measure within the cultural field, namely "[t]he defence of Spanish multilingualism [99]." It should be said here that the Court, in this regard, does go farther than the approach proposed by the Advocate General in her Opinion, where she refers exclusively to promotion of multilingualism in European audiovisual productions [100]. This issue is important in that the European Court does not circumscribe its ruling to the audiovisual industry but rather takes it further to what might be termed the defence of multilingualism *in genere.*

Having thus acknowledged that language promotion is a common objective of the Union and of its member States, the European Court of Justice does confirm in no uncertain terms that "[t]he objective, pursued by a Member State, of defending and promoting one or several of its official languages constitutes an overriding reason in the public interest [101]." The Court had never, prior to this, quite so clearly expressed that the policy of defending and promoting one or several of the official languages within the Member State is deemed to be an overriding reason in the public interest which does to some extent legitimise certain degree of distortion to European Community freedoms. From that ruling onwards, there can be no doubt that measures aimed at defending and promoting any languages which, under the legal order of the European Union are considered official languages in part or in the whole of the national territory of any given Member State, do indeed amount to overriding requirements in the public interest.

Other interesting question relate to the borders between the cultural measures and the economic measures. In the *UTECA* case the Commission found the schema lacking in objective and verifiable criteria which might render it possible to ensure that the advanced financing scheme would only be applied to cinema and television products deemed to be "cultural products [102]." The European Court of Justice, however, did not agree with the opinion of the Commission and stated that… "[s]ince language and culture are intrinsically linked, ... the view cannot be taken that the objective pursued by a Member State of defending and promoting one or several of its official languages must of necessity be accompanied by other cultural criteria in order for it to justify a restriction on one of the fundamental freedoms guaranteed by the Treaty [103]." The European Court effectively sets down that measures for promoting languages, in order to be justified, may not refer to strictly cultural aspects (such as, for example, culture related companies or films which might be categorised as being "cultural products"). The criterion for weighing up is not the (cultural) nature of the object which the measure affects, but rather the linguistic instrument used to carry it out. The Court thus confirmed the autonomous nature of language criteria as an overriding reason in the public interest. It can furthermore not be denied that promoting languages in all areas, including the audiovisual industry, does appear cultural in nature, bearing in mind the importance of languages in defending and promoting cultural expression and the linguistic diversity itself [104].

The scheme was not considered as a protective measure, adopted on the basis of economic considerations and with the intention of benefitting production of the Member State and applied to the detriment of production in other Member States. The underlying motivation in this issue is not in fact a question of economic policy but rather a cultural/linguistic policy measure. The purpose is to defend and promote one or several official languages of the Member State and it is for that reason that the fact that production companies working in the languages comprising the object of the measure and standing to benefit the most from the measure is considered "inherent to the objective pursued [105]." In any event the Court does not say that language related measures are considered *per se* non-selective, but to de contrary only says that language measures are not *per se* selective. The selectivity of the measure will depend on its proportionality taking into account the linguistic objective and the contextual facts as the relative position of the language in the market.

4. CONCLUSION

The presence of non-dominant languages is mass media is often crucial to their survival. The weakness of non-dominant languages makes it difficult for them to gain access to the media outlets with most impact. The difficulties can be of different nature such as legal, economic, cultural or the facto linguistic monopolization of media resources.

Protection of non-dominant languages based on guarantees of freedom of expression or communication is only of limited value in ensuring that non-dominant languages have an equitable access to the media. A determined action on the domestic level and in the context of regional cooperation favouring the access to the media of non-dominant languages is needed.

In Europe we are witnessing the opening up of the media market through the free circulation of audiovisual media services. As it is well known, freedom of the market is not neutral from the linguistic perspective, favouring mass consumption cultural industries to the detriment of others. This effect makes it difficult to identify the dividing line between the dominant- and non-dominant languages in the audiovisual arena. In the European liberalized media environment the concept of non-dominant linguistic community is something relative rather than absolute. In any event the means available to the estate-languages for coping with this linguistic pressure are much more effective that the ones the regional or minority have at their disposal.

The content-oriented measures, as the European-quota rules intended to promote the distribution of European television programmes and independent productions was inspired by the will to take legislative action at the Community level in order to counteract the dominance of American audio-visual productions in the European market. The European quota may have reinforced national objectives to protect and encourage the domestic content sector rather than fostering a truly European market in programming and encouraging the exchange and circulation of European TV programmes within Europe. In any case, the attention given to the cultural and linguistic diversity by the EU shows a gradual greater recognition to this value, especially after the Treaty of Lisbon. Respect and promotion of the diversity of the cultures of the Member States, effectively comprises responsibilities that are incumbent across the whole activity of the European Union.

Linguistic obligations in broadcasting and distribution, language quotas, requirements to produce programmes in national languages and compulsory investment obligations for audiovisual works in national languages are commonly used instruments by the European States for defending and guaranteeing their languages in media. In some cases the objective is to ensure the development of the language in addressing the pressure exerted on them by international languages, and in other cases to guarantee the presence of languages of non-dominant linguistic communities face-to-face the State-languages.

The driver of the internal legislation to protect non-dominant languages depends on various internal and external factors. The policy of protecting the use of languages in the audiovisual sector is framed within two types of limits: supranational determinants established by international law for the protection of human rights and minorities (with a bottom-up effect); and by the European Union framework of liberalization and partial harmonisation of the audiovisual services market (with a top-down effect on national regulation). This latter regulation contains some foundations on which an internal policy for protecting non-dominant languages could be based on, but as we have seen it is not unlimited. The analyzed case-law shows that the principle of media pluralism that forms part of cultural policy is not interpreted in an expansive manner by the Court of Justice of the European Union, but in a case-by-case basis in light of a strict proportionality and necessity test.

Internal systems for guaranteeing the linguistic identity of linguistic communities and linguistic diversity also depend on various factors. Some of these factors are to do with the media landscape, the levels of media concentration, the public control or supervision over the media, the influence of the foreign language audiovisual services in the national market, the recognition of the internal language diversity (or language minorities)... In any case, linguistic policy in the audiovisual sector will be mainly determined by the specific relations of contact between the languages in each State.

CONFLICT OF INTEREST

The author declares no conflict of interest, financial or otherwise.

ACKNOWLEDGEMENTS

Declared none.

REFERENCES

[1] See Price ME. Television, the Public Sphere and National Identity. Oxford: Oxford University Press 1995, p. 5; see also Blumler J. and Hoffmann-Riem W. New Roles for Public Service Television. In Blumler JG, Ed. Television and the Public Interest: Vulnerable Values in West European Broadcasting. London: Sage 1992, p. 210.

[2] ETS No 132 amended according to the provisions of the Protocol (ETS No. 171) which entered into force, on 1 March 2002.

[3] The original title of the act was 'Council Directive 89/552/EEC of 3 October 1989 on the coordination of certain provisions laid down by law, regulation or administrative action in Member States concerning the pursuit of television broadcasting activities" (OJ L 298, 17.10.1989, p. 23–30).

[4] See Directive 97/36/EC of the European Parliament and of the Council, amending Council Directive 89/552/EEC (OJ L 202, 30.7.1997, p. 60); Directive 2007/65/EC of the European Parliament and of the Council (OJ L 332, 18.12.2007, p. 27).

[5] OJ L 95 15.4.2010, p. 1-24.

[6] See Karaca K. Guarding the watchdog: The Council of Europe and the Media. Strasbourg: Council of Europe Publishing 2003, p. 10 et seq.

[7] See Milian i Massana, A. Globalización y requisitos lingüísticos: una perspectiva jurídica. Supraestatalidad, libre circulación, inmigración y requisitos lingüísticos. Barcelona: Atelier 2008, 39 et seq.

[8] UNESCO Convention on the protection and promotion of the diversity of cultural expressions (20 October 2005, entered into force 18 March 2007).

[9] Nevertheless the scope of the Convention when interpreting trade obligations under the WTO is far from clear (see Graber CB. The New UNESCO Convention on Cultural Diversity: A counterbalance to the WTO" Journal of International Economic Law 2006; 9: 553).

[10] See ECtHR, *Arslan v. Turkey* judgment of 8 July 1999, para 44; *Zana v. Turkey* judgment of 25 November 1997, para 51.

[11] See Lazcano I. Art. 10. Libertad de Expresión. In Iñaki Lasagabaster Ed. Convenio Europeo de Derechos Humanos. Madrid: Thomson- Civitas 2010, p. 513; see also Sudre F. Droit européen et international des droits de l'homme. 9 ed Paris: PUF 2008, p. 530.

[12] European Treaty Series no 132, amended according to the provisions of the Protocol (ETS No. 171) which entered into force on 1 March 2002.

[13] See Ergec R. Protection européenne et international des droits de l'homme. 2 ed. Brusels: Bruylant 2006, p. 230; Urrutia I. Los requisitos lingüísticos en la actividad socioeconómica y en el mundo del audiovisual. In Milian A. Ed. Mundialització, lliure circulació i immigració, i l'exigència d'una llengua com a requisit. Barcelona: Institut d'Estudis Autonomics) 171 et seq.

[14] The licensing scheme is very widely used in Europe. That is the case of the following countries: France, Poland, Romania, Italy, Bulgaria, Austria, Georgia, Norway, Azerbaijan, Denmark, Czech Republic, Ireland, Macedonia, Switzerland and Estonia among others.

[15] See article 10(2) ECHR. State controls may be exercised only within certain formal and material limits, and in addition must be in accordance with other principles, such as the non-discrimination guaranteed by article 14 of the ECHR.

[16] Following de Witte B. the justification for rules aimed at protecting and guaranteeing the cultural identity should be sought in the notion of "rights of others" which is among the public interests mentioned in Article 10(2) ECHR. See de Witte B. The European Content Requirement in the EC Television Directive-Five Years After. Yearbook of Media and Entertainment Law 1995, p. 117.

[17] ECtHR, *Informationsverein Lentia and Others v. Austria* Para 32. The Court found in this case a violation of the right to freedom of expression as regards the applicants' complaints, in that they had been unable to set up radio and television stations due to the Austrian broadcasting monopoly, but declared it unnecessary to review the discrimination claim under Article 14.

[18] *Ibid.* The Court held that the Austrian broadcasting monopoly was not necessary to guarantee impartiality, balance and diversity in broadcasting.

[19] See inter alia *Handyside v. the United Kingdom*, 7 December 1976, Series A no. 24, p. 23, para. 49; *Lingens v. Austria*, 8 July 1986, Series A no. 103, p. 26, para. 41; and *Jersild v. Denmark*, 23 September 1994, Series A no. 298, p. 26, para. 37; *Hertel v. Switzerland*, judgment of 25 August 1998, *Reports* 1998-VI, pp. 2329-30, § 46; *Pedersen and Baadsgaard v. Denmark* [GC], no. 49017/99, §§ 68-71, ECtHR 2004-XI; *Steel and Morris v. the United Kingdom*, no. 68416/01, § 87, ECtHR 2005-II.

[20] See *Verein Alternatives Lokalradio v. Switzerland*, Application No. 10746/84, Decision of the European Commission of Human Rights of 16 October 1986, DR 49, at pp. 126-127.

[21] *Demuth v. Switzerland* no 38743/97, judgment of 5 November 2002, para 44.

[22] European Commission of Human Rights *Verein Alternatives Lokalradio Bern v. Switzerland*, App. No. 10746/84 (16 October 1986).

[23] *Ibid.*.

[24] ECtHR *Tele 1 Privatfernsehgesellschaft MBH v. Austria* judgment of 21 September 2000, App. No. 32240/96, paras. 39-40.

[25] ECtHR *Manole and others v. Moldova* Application no. 13936/02, 17 September 2009, paras 95-102.

[26] Recommendation R(99) 1 of the Committee of Ministers to member states on measures to promote media pluralism (Adopted by the Committee of Ministers on 19 January 1999, at the 656th meeting of the Ministers' Deputies).

[27] ECtHR *Khurshid Mustafa and Tarzibachi v. Sweden*, Application no. 23883/06, 16 December 2008, para 44.

[28] ETS no 132, amended by Protocol (ETS No. 171) which entered into force, on 1 March 2002 (hereinafter ECTT).

[29] Article 10(1) ECTT.

[30] Article 10(3) ECTT.

[31] The Council of Europe Framework Convention on the Value of Cultural Heritage for Society (Faro, 27.X.2005, ETS nº 1999) includes measures for promoting the protection of cultural heritage by the way, i.a. the information society. Article 14 requires State Parties to encourage initiatives which promote the quality of contents and endeavour to secure diversity of languages and cultures in the information society.

[32] Advisory Committee on the Framework Convention for the Protection of National Minorities. Second Opinion on Ukraine adopted on 30 May 2008. Strasbourg, 30 March 2011 ACFC/OP/II(2008)004, para 21.

[33] Advisory Committee, Opinion on Ukraine, 1 March 2002, para. 46.

[34] See Advisory Committee, Opinion on the Russian Federation, 13 September 2002, para. 76. See also the above mentioned second opinion on Ukraine, para 23.

[35] See Advisory Committee, Opinion on Estonia, adopted on 14 September 2001, para. 38. See McGonagle T. Commentary: Access of persons belonging to national minorities to the media. In Filling the frame: Five years of monitoring the Framework Convention for the Protection of National Minorities. Strasbourg: Council of Europe Publishing 2004, pp. 144-159.

[36] See the Explanatory Report of the European Charter for Regional or Minority Languages, para 107.

[37] See Pons-Parera E. Article 14. Transfrontier exchanges. In Nogueira A, Ruiz E, Urrutia I Eds. Shaping Language Rights. Commentary on the European Charter for Regional or Minority Languages in light of the Committee of Experts' evaluation. Strasbourg: Council of Europe Publishing 2012, 485-516.

[38] For an in deep analysis see Woehrling JM. The European Charter for Regional or Minority Languages: A critical Commentary. Strasbourh: Council of Europe Publishing 2005, 200-14.

[39] Explanatory Report to the European Charter for Regional or Minority Languages, para 111. In this Regard see Committee of Expert's Report on Application of the Charter in Denmark. 3rd monitoring cycle, 2 March 2011, para 75.

[40] See Dunbar R, Moring T. The European Charter for Regional and Minority Language and the Media. Strasbourg: Council of Europe Publishing 2008, 69-70.

[41] See Pons-Parera E. Article 14. Transfrontier exchanges. In Nogueira A, Ruiz E, Urrutia I Eds. Shaping Language Rights. Commentary on the European Charter for Regional or Minority Languages in light of the Committee of Experts' evaluation. Strasbourg: Council of Europe Publishing 2012, 495.

[42] Committee of Experts. Opinion on the Application of the Charter in Ukraine, 1st monitoring cycle, 7 July 2010, para. 562.

[43] *Op.* cit. *supra* note 42, at para. 448.

[44] *Op.* cit. *supra* note 42, at para. 451.

[45] The Committee of Experts' position coincides with principles tabled by the OSCE Guidelines on the use of Minority Languages in the Broadcast Media. OSCE, 2003.

[46] Committee of Experts, Opinion on the Application of the Charter in Slovakia. 2nd monitoring cycle 18 November 2009, paras, 130-1, 257-9, 379-81, 510-1, 646-7, and 807-8.

[47] See Negrine R, Papathanassopoulos S. The internationalization of Television. London: Pinter 1990; and Schwartz I. Broadcasting and the EEC Treaty. *European Law Review* 1986, 7, p. 10.

[48] Case 155/73 *Guiseppe Sacchi*, [1974] ECR 409. See also Case 62/79 *Coditel v. Ciné Vog Films* [1980] ECR 881, in which the Court held that the impediments to the cross-border transmission of television services could be justified by the general interest. See also Case 52/79 *Procureur du Roi v. Marc J V C Debauve and others* [1980] ECR 860,and case 262/81 *Coditel v. Ciné Vog Films* (Coditel II) [1982] ECR 3381.

[49] Case 52/79 *Procureur du Roi v. Marc J V C Debauve and others*, cit. supra note 48, para 15.

[50] A critical view on Article 167 TFEU (ex 151 CE) as the legal basis for the AMSD in Katsirea I. Public Broadcasting and European Law. The Netherlands: Kluwer 2008, 291 et seq.

[51] See Television Without Frontiers: Green Paper on the Establishment of the Common Market for Broadcasting, Especially by Cable and Satellite, COM(85)300; the next year the Commission presented the White Paper on Completing the Internal Market COM(85)310, proposing a directive liberalizing transfrontier television. See de Witte B. The European Content Requirement in the EC Television Directive-Five Years After. cit. *supra* note 14, 101-105; see Levy DAL. Europe's Digital revolution: Broadcasting and Regulation, the EU and the Nation State. London: Routledge 1999, 41 seq.

[52] Council Directive 89/552/EEC of 3 October 1989 cit. *supra* at note 3.

[53] Directive 97/36/EC of the European Parliament and the Council of 30 June 1997 amending Council Directive 89/552/EEC, cit. *supra* at note 4.

[54] See Case T-68/08 *FIFA v Commission* [2011].

[55] Directive 2007/65/EC of the European Parliament and of the Council of 11 December 2007 amending Council Directive 89/552/EEC on the coordination of certain provisions laid down by law, regulation or administrative action in Member States concerning the pursuit of television broadcasting activities (OJ L 332, 18.12.2007, p. 27–45). A codified version of the AMSD was adopted by the Council on 15 February 2010 and published in the Official Journal. This mainly changes the numbering of the Articles and provides a consolidated set of Recitals. See Directive 2010/13/EU of the European Parliament and of the Council of 10 March 2010 on the coordination of certain provisions laid down by law, regulation or administrative action in Member States concerning the provision of audiovisual media services (Audiovisual Media Services Directive) (OJ L 95, 15.4.2010).

[56] Article 13.1 of the Audiovisual Media Services Directive.

[57] See de Witte B. The European Content Requirement in the EC Television Directive-Five Years After. cit. *supra* note 14 at p. 104 reflecting on the consensus which took place between single-market supporters, who wanted the adoption of the Directive in order to liberalize the market for broadcasting, and cultural and industrial policy-makers, who made the quota a condition for agreeing to the text of the Directive, led to the inclusion of European television programme content requirements in the Directive which was eventually adopted in 1989.

[58] See de Witte B. The Value of Cultural Diversity in European Union Law. In Schneider H, Van den Bossche P Eds. Protection of Cultural Diversity from European and International Perspective. Antwerpen, Oxford, Portland: Intersentia-Maastricht Center for Human Rights 2008, at 222-225.

[59] Article 3.3 of the Treaty on the European Union.

[60] Bell M. The Right to Equality and Non-Discrimination. In Hervey TK, Kenner J Eds. Economic and social rights under the EU Charter of Fundamental Rights: A Legal Perspective. Portland: Hart Publishing 2003, at 107.

[61] McGonagle T. The Quota Quandary. In Ward D Ed. The European Union and the Culture Industries. Aldershot: Ashgate Publishing 2008 at. 204 highlighting that as such the wording involves a considerably lighter commitment for states.

[62] Urrutia I, Lasagabaster I. Language Rights and Community Law. European Integration online Papers (EIoP) 14, 2008, p. 8.

[63] Ross M. Cultural Protection a Matter for Union Citizenship or Human Rights?. In Neuwahl NA, Rosas A Eds. The European Union and Human Rights. The Hague: Martinus Nijhoff 1995, pp. 235-236.

[64] See Cae 42/97, *European Parliament v. Council of the European Union* [1999] ECR I-869.

[65] Craufurd SmithR. Community Intervention in the Cultural Field: Continuity or Change?. In Culture and European Union Law. Oxford: Oxford University Press 2004, p. 50.

[66] Katsirea I. Public Broadcasting and European Law cit. *supra* note 50, p. 175).

[67] Article 3 of the Audiovisual Media Services Directive.

[68] See Article 3.2 and 3.3 AMSD for TV broadcasts and 3.4 and 3.6 AMSD for on-demand content. See Humphreys PJ. Mass Media and Media Policy in Western Europe. Manchester University Press 1996) p. 270.

[69] Katsirea, I. Public Broadcasting… cit. *supra* note 50, p. 190.

[70] Case C-56/96 *VT4 Ltd v Vlaamse Gemeenschap* [1997] ECR I-3143, paragraph 22; Case C-212/97 *Centros v Erhvervs-og Selskabsstyrelsen* [1999] ECR I-1459; see also: Case C-11/95 *Commission v Belgium* [1996] ECR I-4115; and Case C-14/96 *Paul Denuit* [1997] ECR I-2785.

[71] The original wording of Article 8 Television Without Frontiers Directive (Council Directive 89/552/EEC of 3 October 1989) provided that "Where they consider it necessary for purposes of language policy, the Member States, whilst observing Community law, may as regards some or all programmes of television broadcasters under their jurisdiction, lay down more detailed or stricter rules in particular on the basis of language criteria".

[72] OJ L 202, 30.7.1997, p. 60–70.

[73] Urrutia I. Approach of the European Court of Justice on Accommodation of the European Language Diversity in the Internal Market: Overcoming Language Barriers or Fostering Linguistic Diversity? Columbia Journal of European Law, 18 (2) 2012, 243–276.

[74] Article 2(b) of the European Convention on Transfrontier Television (Reference ETS No.132).

[75] See Case C-11/95, *Commission v. Belgium* [1996] ECR I-4117.

[76] That prohibition was laid down in Articles 3 and 4 of the Decree of the Flemish Community of 28 January 1987 concerning the transmission of radio and television programmes on radio and cable television networks and the approval of non-public television broadcasting companies (*Moniteur Belge* of 19 March 1987, p. 4196).

[77] Case C-211/91 *Commission v. Kingdom of Belgium* [1992] ECR I-6757, para 12.

[78] Case C-212/97 *Centros v Erhvervs-og Selskabsstyrelsen*, cited *supra* note 71; Case 33/74 *Van Binsbergen v Bestuur van de Bedrijfsvereniging* [1974] ECR 1299; Case C-23/93 *TV 10 SA v Commissariaat voor de Media* [1994] ECR I-4795, paragraph 21.

[79] Article 4.2 of the Audiovisual Media Services Directive.

[80] Article 4.2 and 4.3 of the Audiovisual Media Services Directive.

[81] See Katsirea I. Public Broadcasting. cit. *supra* note 50, at p. 210.

[82] Article 16.1 AMSD. 10% of their programming budget, for European works created by producers who are independent of broadcasters.".

[83] Article 13.1 of the Audiovisual Media Services Directive.

[84] *Ibid.*

[85] De Witte B. The European Content Requirement… cit. *supra* note 14, p. 112.

[86] See European Commission. Issue Paper for the Liverpool Audiovisual Conference. Cultural Diversity and the promotion of European and Independent Audiovisual Production, July 2005.

[87] See Katsirea I. Public Broadcasting.. cit. *supra* note 50, at p. 294.

[88] Craufurd SmithR. Broadcasting Law and fundamental rights. Oxford: Oxford University Press 1997, at p. 186; De Witte B. Non-market values in internal market regulation. In Nic Shuibhne N Ed. Regulating the Internal Market Cheltenham: Edward Elgar Publishing 2006 at p. 61.

[89] Milian A. Globalización y requisitos lingüísticos: una perspectiva jurídica. Barcelona: Atelier 2008 at 41. *See also* De Witte B. Common Market freedoms *versus* linguistic requirements in the EU States. In Milian A. Ed. Mundialització, lliure circulació i immigració, i l'exigència d'una llengua com a requisito. Barcelona: Institut d'Estudis Autònomics 2008 at 119.

[90] Highlighting the little judicial consideration to the cultural cross-sectional clause Psychogiopoulou E. The integration of cultural considerations in EU law and policies. Leiden in Boston: Martinus Nijhoff 2008, at 145.

[91] See, *e.g.,* Case C-415/93 *Bosman* [1995] ECR I-4921, paragraph 104; Case C-367/98 *Commission / Portugal* [2002] ECR I-4731, paragraph 49; Joined Cases C-92/04 and C-202/04 *Cipolla and Others* [2006] ECR I-11421, paragraph 61; Case C-438/05 *International Transport Workers' Federation and Finnish Seamen's Union* [2007] ECR I-10779 ('*VikingLine*'), paragraph 75; and Case C-341/05 *Laval un Partneri* [2007] ECR I-11767, paragraph 101.

[92] See, *e.g.,* Case C-429/02 *Bacardi France* [2004] ECR I-6613, paragraph 33, and Joined Cases C-338/04, C-359/04 and C-360/04 *Placanica* [2007] ECR I-1891, paragraph 48.

[93] Case C-250/06, *United Pan-Europe Communications Belgium SA and others v Belgium* [2007] ECR I-11135.

[94] Case C-250/06, *United Pan-Europe Communications*, cit. *supra* note 93, paragraph 42.

[95] The ECJ has elaborated a consistent set of judgements regarding the application of the freedom of movement rules where the presence of national regulations that could result in impediments to trade can be justified, and thus upheld, because they aim to safeguard media pluralism. This approach stems from the reasoning that media pluralism forms part of cultural policy which may constitute an overriding requirement relating to the general interest thus justifying a restriction on the freedom to provide services. *See e.g.* Case 352/85, *Bond van Adverteerders and others / The Netherlands State*, [1988] ECR 2085; Case C-211/91, *Commission of the European Communities / Kingdom of Belgium*, [1992] ECR I-6757; Case C-288/89, *Stichting Collectieve Antennevoorziening Gouda and others / Commissariaat voor de Media ("Mediawet I")*, [1991] ECR I-04007; Case C-353/89, *Commission of the European Communities / Kingdom of the Netherlands*, [1991] ECR I-4069; Case C-148/91, *Vereniging Veronica Omroep Organisatie / Commissariaat voor de Media*, [1993] ECR I-00487.

[96] See Casarosa F. The case of the European Union and the Council of Europe. In Background information Report. Media Policies and Regulatory Practices in a Selected Set of European countries, the EU and the Council of Europe (available at http://www.mediadem.eliamep.gr/wp-content/uploads/2010/05/BIR.pdf) (last visited May 2015), p. 501.

[97] Case C-250/06, *United Pan-Europe Communications,*cit. *supra* note 93, paragraph 43.

[98] Case C-222/07 *Unión de Televisiones Comerciales Asociadas (UTECA)* [2009] ECR I-01407.

[99] Case C-222/07, *UTECA,* cit. *supra* note 98, paragraph 26.

[100] The Opinion of the Advocate General (case C-222/07, paragraph 90) referred "[t]o promote the production of European films the original language of which is one of the official languages recognised in Spain".

[101] Case C-222/07, *UTECA,* cit. *supra* note 98, paragraph 27.

[102] The Commission was guided, on this point, by the Case C-17/92 *Distribuidores Cinematográficos* [1993] ECR I-2239, paragraph 20. In that occasion the Court has rejected justification for Spanish legislation in the film promotion sector based inter alia on the argument that it promoted 'national films whatever their content or quality'. In the *UTECA* case, however, the reference point was not the Member State in which a film was produced but a linguistic criterion.

[103] Case C-222/07, *UTECA,* cit. *supra* note 98, paragraph 33.

[104] See Urrutia I. Libre competencia, prohibición de ayudas de Estado y fiscalidad lingüística. In Urrutia I *et al.*, Estudios Jurídicos sobre Fiscalidad Lingüística: Incentivos Fiscales como instrumento de Política Lingüística. Cizur Menor: Aranzadi – Thomson – Reuters 2010 at 67-80.

[105] Case C-222/07, *UTECA,* cit. *supra* note 98, paragraph 36.

SUBJECT INDEX

D

E

M

N

O

P

R

S

www.ingramcontent.com/pod-product-compliance
Lightning Source LLC
LaVergne TN
LVHW070933210926
848482LV00003B/233